Language, Power and Social Process   10

Editors

Monica Heller
Richard J. Watts

Mouton de Gruyter
Berlin · New York

At War with Words

Edited by
Mirjana N. Dedaić
Daniel N. Nelson

Mouton de Gruyter
Berlin · New York 2003

Mouton de Gruyter (formerly Mouton, The Hague)
is a Division of Walter de Gruyter GmbH & Co. KG, Berlin.

∞ Printed on acid-free paper which falls within the guidelines
of the ANSI to ensure permanence and durability.

ISBN 3 11 017649 1 Hb.
ISBN 3 11 017650 5 Pb.

Bibliographic information published by Die Deutsche Bibliothek

Die Deutsche Bibliothek lists this publication in the Deutsche
Nationalbibliografie; detailed bibliographic data is available in the
Internet at <http://dnb.ddb.de>.

War is sweet to those who have not experienced it.

Erasmus

Preface: Language as forms of death

Michael Billig

At the time of writing, it is commonplace to hear people say that the world has changed since September 11, 2001. After two hijacked planes destroyed the New York World Trade Center, with a loss of life that still has not been fully calculated, this thought has been expressed by pundits on the media and in countless ordinary conversations. It is not clear to speakers exactly how the world might have changed. The details are secondary to the conviction that something altered irreversibly as the world watched those pictures of the doomed planes, the collapsing buildings and the shocked faces on the streets of New York.

Clausewitz's famous maxim of war being just an extension of politics seemed inappropriate, for the horror of September 11, 2001 appeared to catch normal politics unaware. The regular words of party advantage had little significance in relation to those images of suffering and destruction. This was no time for spin-doctors and image consultants to be "playing politics", especially in the United States. Nor was party advantage to be sought when American planes, in response, were bombing Afghanistan from the skies and the elite troops were fighting on the ground. There was even a minor rhetorical miracle that illustrated the suspension of political routines. Previously when President Bush spoke, he would appear time and again helplessly lost in mid-sentence, having dispatched out his verbs before securing his end point. Suddenly this did not matter. The politician, elected by a minority of voters after some dodgy business in Florida, was transformed into a national leader, standing above differences of caucus and party.

There are, however, limits to miracles. The gift of fluency cannot be bestowed even to the leader of the "civilized" world. But now, when Bush's sentences hover at their mid-point, awaiting grammatical rescue, his audiences can see this as a sign that their President is sharing their own emotions.

Could any event have so dramatically signalled the limitations of a trend in social scientific thinking in the past twenty years? So many academics have been asserting the primacy of discourse, as if everything could be contained within texts, whose deeper meaning demand expert decoding. The textual thesis seems at home in a world of sound-bites, slogans and nightly verbal spins. Politicians and academics know that words are their business: they are never at a loss to construct phrases. Yet, with the suspension of party politics and the silent horror of the televised images, it seemed as if the old contrast between words and things had been brutally re-established. Words had become once more "mere words", incapable of expressing what was being felt. Reporters on the scene would say that words cannot do justice to the horror. Certainly words – "mere words" – could not right the destruction nor soothe the loss of the grieving. Something beyond words – the physicality of planes, velocity and bodies – had disrupted the familiar world. We can't just talk, it was said. Something must be done.

However the papers, which Mirjana Dedaić and Daniel Nelson have so judiciously gathered together in this timely volume, point in an opposite direction. They argue that it is too simple to contrast words and war, as if the facts of war stand at a deeper level of reality than the superficiality of rhetoric. As Daniel Nelson states so expressively in the concluding chapter, human conflict begins and ends with talk and text. In the period after the attack in New York and before the bombing of Afghanistan, there were words and more words. Behind the scenes, Bush was consulting with his military, political and diplomatic advisors. He was regularly phoning other leaders. The Prime Minister of the United Kingdom was boarding plane after plane to meet politicians across the world to build an alliance. When hands had been shaken and the photographs had been taken of those shaken hands, what did Blair and the leaders do? Doors were closed and they talked. And talked. This was necessary for the deals to be done, before the bombers could be dispatched (by more words – in this case the words of command and technical expertise). After the bombing started, then came the nightly rhetorical spinning: claims about civilian casualties had to be minimized, the evil of the enemy emphasised and the certainty of victory stressed. The public could not be trusted to interpret the images of the conflict unaided; they required rhetorical guidance. The grainy pictures of targets and bomb craters did not tell their own stories. The world had *not* completely changed.

To understand the relations between language and war, it is not sufficient merely to point to the use of words in warfare. As the contributors to this volume show so convincingly, there can be no war without communication. Warfare demands organization and mobilization, as well as the circulation of beliefs about the enemy and justifications for the need to kill and die. To explore these matters further, it is necessary to reformulate traditional psychological assumptions about human nature, particularly those relating to the links between language and emotion.

Historically, the contrast between war and language is a variant of an early psychological distinction between primitive instinct and higher thought. In late nineteenth and twentieth century psychologies such a distinction was commonplace. Reason was contrasted with emotion. It was generally thought that the human psyche was split between primitive, instinctual elements and higher conceptual ones. Warfare was seen as an expression of biological instinct while "civilization", or social order, depended upon the higher non-instinctual realm. For example, William McDougall, who wrote the first textbook in social psychology, expressed such views in his book *The Group Mind* (1920). Under normal circumstances, the demands of social life curtail basic, or "primitive", impulses. McDougall, who had definite ideas about a hierarchy of civilizations, believed that the most civilized nations demand the greatest control of impulses. However, under conditions of emotional intensity, the psychology of men (and McDougall was primarily writing about men) alters and the higher forces give way to the lower instincts. If the complexities of language belong to the higher rungs of civilization, then the chaos of war sees an unleashing of the lower wordless, formless instinctual impulses.

Freud was greatly attracted to this aspect of McDougall's ideas, quoting them in his book *Group Psychology and the Analysis of the Ego* (1985a). Like McDougall, Freud emphasised a contrast between civilization and instinct. In times of war, the control over the primitive instinctual forces is loosened. Freud discussed such themes in his famous letter on war to Einstein. Freud argued that it was too simple to attribute wars to conflicts of interests. Psychological forces, especially "a lust for aggression and destruction", must be at work (Freud 1985b: 357). Again the image is that war is an expression of primeval urges, although Freud was too sophisticated a thinker to suggest that only a simple instinct for aggression was involved. The protection against war, argued Freud, was through knowledge of the unconscious instinctual forces that drive human behaviour. The relevant knowledge was to be gained through language. As Freud stressed, nothing happens in the psychoanalytic situation except that people talk. Only by the reasoned talk of the ego would it be possible to understand and control the dangerous forces of the instincts.

In an important critique, the social psychologist Henri Tajfel referred to instinctual theories of warfare as "blood-and-guts theories" (Tajfel 1981; see Billig [in press] for an appreciation of Tajfel's critique of instinctual theories). At the time of writing during the 1960s, Tajfel was drawing attention to the popularity of quasi-biological, post-Freudian ideas in best-selling books such as those by the Nobel prize-winner biologist Konrad Lorenz, as well as those by popularising Freudians. As Tajfel so devastatingly argued, such biological theories suggest that humans have a constant need to aggress, and, as such, the instinctual theories cannot show why warfare waxes and wanes – why the so-called innate instinct sometimes expresses itself in war and sometimes does not. The seeming profundity of theories that cite inborn needs and impulses is helpless when confronted with the messy details of human history.

Tajfel, in criticising the blood-and-guts approaches, formulated a decisive shift in psychological thinking. However, his contribution to psychological thinking has been undeservedly neglected by social scientists beyond the particular specialism of social psychology. Tajfel argued that the seeming irrationality of phenomena such as prejudice and war have key cognitive, rather than emotional, roots. Warfare depends upon beliefs about one's own group and about the enemy. There must be a categorization of the world into "us" and "them". However, such categorization reflects wider processes of thought. As Tajfel argued, human knowledge generally depends on categorization, for categories provide meaning. Because humans are driven, above all, by the desire to understand their world, they cannot but use categories to impart sense. The very act of categorization, however, implies distinction and exaggeration. We tend to assume that instances of categories are more similar than they actually are and more different than instances of other categories. Tajfel suggested that social categories are no/ different from physical categories in this regard. Without social categories there could be no sense of social identity and the categories of "our" identity only make sense because there are categories that denote "others". Thus, social categories imply distinctions between social groups and the exaggerations of categorization provide the basis for stereotyping others. As the categories of ingroups and outgroups become salient and meaningful, so the distinctiveness between "us" and "them" is psychologically exaggerated.

If the role of categorization is recognized, argued Tajfel, it is unnecessary to postulate instinctual, blood-and-guts forces in order to understand the basis of prejudice and the psychological origins of warfare. Tajfel's insight leads to a psychological paradox. The apparent irrationality of war is not the product of irrational psychological drives, but is the outcome of the seemingly rational human propensity to make sense of the social world. Clausewitz is implicitly reinstated. When Bush and the majority of the American people advocated the bombing of Afghanistan after September 11 2001, they were not responding to a release of innate, instinctual urges. Their collective response was based upon understandings of the social world, which involved a heightened sense of "us" and "them". As Bush said a number of times in the days and weeks following the destruction of the World Trade Center, "if you're not with us in the war against terrorism, you're against us".

Perhaps one reason why Tajfel's approach has been comparatively neglected outside of social psychology is because of the way that he and many subsequent social psychological theorists understood the notion of categorization. All too often a perceptual model of categorization, rather than a rhetorical model, has been adopted (Billig 1985, 1996; Potter and Wetherell 1987). As Edwards has argued, categories are for talking: they are part of language (Edwards 1991). If factors such as social identity and stereotyping are based on categorization and if categorization is itself part of language-use, then the psychological factors underlying prejudice will themselves be rooted in language. After all, when Bush was declaring that "if you're not with us in the war against terrorism, you're against us" he was using language.

Recently, a number of social psychologists have been developing a discursive approach, that points to the key importance of language in human affairs (see, for instance, Antaki 1994; Billig 1996; Edwards 1997; Edwards and Potter 1992; Harré and Gillett 1994; Parker 1992; Potter 1996; Potter and Wetherell 1987). Discursive psychology claims that many of the phenomena that social psychologists have studied are constituted within language. For instance, social identities, prejudice, stereotyping depend upon utterances. That being so, psychological insight will not be gained by postulating internal cognitive or emotional processes that cannot be directly observed. Instead psychologists should be studying the rhetorical details and complexities of utterances that form the basis of social psychological phenomena. One of the key implications of this approach has been to question the conventional distinction between thought and emotion or between cognitive and affective processes. Emotions have their discursive basis: without talk we would be unable to display and recognize emotions such as jealousy, indignation, and embarrassment (Billig 1999; Edwards 1997; Harré and Parrott 1996; Lutz 1990). The talk is not an epiphenomenon, as if the emotions really exist wordlessly within the individual's body. Our emotions are part of our relations with others, our sense of morality and our understandings of how the social world should be. This is even true of unconscious repressed feelings (Billig 1999).

Recasting the psychology of emotions in terms of language has direct implications for understanding the intense emotions that accompany, and indeed lead to, warfare. An inner state, that remains locked within individuals, cannot be the impetus to war. But a discourse of indignation, threat and suffering, shared and communicated within a group, can become the basis for mobilization against an identified enemy. The horror and anger that followed the destruction of the World Trade Center was not worldless. From the outset, the anger was located within discourses that sought understanding and these discourses contained familiar themes of morality and nationhood.

The carnage of September 11 was unforeseen. In terms of scale the attack on New York was beyond comparison with previous terrorist actions. The effect – the killing of thousands of citizens – was disproportionate to the means. This was the sort of destruction that one would have associated with a heavy poundage of bombs and sophisticated technology. It seemed incredible that a small group of men equipped with household knives and a precise knowledge of airline timetables, could cause such devastation. How could the centre of capitalism be so vulnerable? There are no ready-made frames of reference for unexpected events of such magnitude. Yet, the reactions could not be left to wordless feeling nor wait for the construction of new vocabularies. Things had to be said straightaway.

Within hours of the destruction, television stations were interviewing American citizens, asking them about their feelings. A frequent response was given that the event was like Pearl Harbour. Here was an illustration of what the social psychologist Serge Moscovici has described as the anchoring of unfamiliar events in familiar social representations (Moscovici 1984). To understand something dangerously unfamiliar and seemingly incomprehensible, familiar categories of meaning have to be applied. Of course, in crucial respects Pearl Harbour differed from the destruction of the World Trade Center. The Japanese attack had been aimed at a military target and was carried out by the armed forces of a nation state which had formally been at war for some time. However, analogies are revealing. In describing the attack as resembling the attack on Pearl Harbour, the responses of television interviewees, and that of many other Americans, were equating the action with the event that brought the United States into warfare. In this way, the discursive understanding was a means of preparing for reaction. A similar understanding and preparation was shown as Bush was declaring "a war against terrorism".

Thus, the familiar discourse of "war" was being employed. This discourse contains a number of assumptions. In the contemporary age, warfare primarily involves nation-states. A national response, like the response to Pearl Harbour, was being expected. The flags, that were draped at the scene of the attack and that were being worn so generally by the citizenry of the United States, were a visible sign that the attack was being interpreted primarily as something national, rather than local or even international: New York or capitalism were not the prime victims, but America was. For this to occur so spontaneously in response to the extraordinary event, the assumptions and symbols of everyday nationalism have to be firmly established (Billig 1995). The national response together with the discourse of warfare suggested that there would be – indeed there would have to be – a military response. No amount of collectively shared feelings of anger, experienced purely wordlessly and individually, would produce a military response. The anger had to be formed within a series of understandings, uttered out aloud.

When a particular set of understandings is discursively uttered, then other possible understandings remain unsaid. In the days after the World Trade Center attack, it was rarely said, either by ordinary Americans on television or by their political leaders, that what had happened was primarily a criminal act which called for the mobilization of criminal justice systems nationally and inter-nationally. The words of criminality were subsumed by those of war.

The language of war was implicitly suggesting that this was not an event to be decided slowly and evenly by judges in courts of law: guns must be fired and bombs dropped rather than counsels for prosecution and defence appointed. The words of war, in this respect, are words of impatience.

The events of September 11, 2001 underlined factors that are stressed in this volume, whose contributions were prepared prior to that day. Those events provide yet another confirmation of the main theme of this volume: the words of war are central to the activity of war. Indeed one can ask whether there can be war without the very word "war".

Saying all this, does not, of course, mean that war is merely words. That would underestimate the nature and importance of words. As Wittgenstein wrote, "words are deeds" (1980: 46). Wittgenstein was making the important point that even words are not "mere" words. There is always more to words for they are not merely the verbal representation of a deeper reality but they are integrally part of our human reality. Words belong, as Wittgenstein stressed in *Philosophical Investigations*, to forms of life: "to imagine a language is to imagine a form of life" (1963: 8).

So, too, it is with the language of war. Such language belongs to particular forms of life. In our age these forms of life are primarily national forms. In a crucial respect, Wittgenstein's famous insight omits a crucial factor. These national forms of life are also forms of death.

References

Antaki, Charles
　1994　　*Explaining and Arguing.* London: Sage.

Billig, Michael
　1985　　Prejudice, categorization and particularization: from a perceptual to a rhetorical approach. *European Journal of Social Psychology* 15, 79–103.

1995   *Banal Nationalism*. London: Sage.

1996   *Arguing and Thinking*. Cambridge: Cambridge University Press.

1999   *Freudian Repression: Conversation Creating the Unconscious*. Cambridge: Cambridge University Press.

in press   Henri Tajfel's "Cognitive aspects of prejudice" and the psychology of bigotry. *British Journal of Social Psychology*.

Edwards, Derek
1991   Categories are for talking. *Theory and Psychology* 1, 515–542.

1997   *Discourse and Cognition*. London: Sage.

Edwards, Derek, and Jonathan Potter
1992   *Discursive Psychology*. London: Sage.

Freud, Sigmund
1985a   Group Psychology and the Analysis of the Ego. *Penguin Freud Library*, volume 12. Harmondsworth: Penguin. Original edition, 1921.

1985b   Why War? *Penguin Freud Library*, volume 12. Harmondsworth: Penguin. Original edition, 1933.

Harré, Rom, and Grant Gillett
1994   *The Discursive Mind*. London: Sage.

Harré, Rom, and W. Gerrod Parrott (eds.)
1996   *The Emotions: Social, Cultural and Biological Dimensions*. London/Thousand Oaks: Sage.

Lutz, Catherine A.
1990   Morality, domination, and understandings of "justifiable anger" among the Ifaluk. In Semin, Gün R., and K. J. Gergen (eds.), *Everyday Understandings*. London: Sage, 204–226.

McDougall, William
1920   *The Group Mind*. Cambridge: Cambridge University Press.

Moscovici, Serge
  1984   The phenomenon of social representations. In: Farr, Robert M., and
          Serge Moscovici (eds.), *Social Representations*. Cambridge:
          Cambridge University Press, 3–70.

Parker, Ian
  1992   *Discourse Dynamics: Critical Analysis for Social and Individual
          Psychology*. London: Routledge.

Potter, Jonathan
  1996   *Representing Reality*. London: Sage.

Potter, Jonathan, and Margaret Wetherell
  1987   *Discourse and Social Psychology*. London: Sage

Tajfel, Henri
  1981   *Human Groups and Social Categories*. Cambridge: Cambridge
          University Press.

Wittgenstein, Ludwig
  1963   *Philosophical Investigations*. Oxford: Blackwell.

  1980   *Culture and Value*. Oxford: Blackwell.

Contents

Notes on contributors

Getraud Benke, Department of Schools and Societal Learning, Institute for Interdisciplinary Research and Continuing Education (IFF), Vienna, Austria. Gertraud.Benke@univie.ac.at

Michael Billig, Department of Social Sciences, Loughborough University, Leicestershire, England. M.G.Billig@lboro.ac.uk

David Britain, Department of Language and Linguistics, Essex University, Colchester, England. DBritain@essex.ac.uk

Paul Chilton, The School of Language, Linguistics and Translation Studies, University of East Anglia, Norwich, UK. P.A.Chilton@uea.ac.uk

Mirjana N. Dedaić, Department of Linguistics, Georgetown University, Washington, D.C., USA. DedaicM@georgetown.edu

Renée Dickason, British and Irish History and Cultural Studies, Université de Caen, France. Renee.Dickason@wanadoo.fr

Marilena Karyolemou, Department of Byzantine and Modern Greek Studies, University of Cyprus, Nicosia, Cyprus. MaKar@ucy.ac.cy

Keith Langston, Germanic and Slavic Languages, University of Georgia, Athens, Georgia, USA. Langston@arches.uga.edu

Kazuko Matsumoto, Faculty of Contemporary Society, Musashino Women's University, Tokyo, Japan. KMatsu@musashino-wu.ac.jp

Daniel N. Nelson, College of Arts and Sciences, University of New Haven, West Haven, Connecticut, USA, and Editor-in-chief, *International Politics.* DNelson@newhaven.edu

Kweku Osam, Linguistics Department, University of Ghana, Legon, Ghana. KOsam@libr.ug.edu.gh

Mark Allen Peterson, Department of Sociology, Anthropology, Psychology and Egyptology, American University in Cairo, Egypt. Peterson@aucegypt.edu

Anita Peti-Stantić, Department of Slavic Linguistics and Literature, School of Philosophy, University of Zagreb, Croatia. Anita.Peti-Stantic@ffzg.hr

Alexander Pollak, Wittgenstein Research Center "Discourse, Politics, Identity", Austrian Academy of Sciences, Vienna, Austria. APollak-2000@yahoo.de

Theodore O. Prosise, Department of Communication, University of Washington, Seattle, Washington, USA. TProsise@aol.com

Kathryn Ruud, independent scholar, Middletown, Maryland, U.S.A. KRRuud@adelphia.net

Rumiko Shinzato, School of Modern Languages, Georgia Institute of Technology, Atlanta, Georgia, USA. Rumiko.Simonds@modlangs.gatech.edu

Suzanne Wong Scollon, Asian Sociocultural Research Project, Georgetown University, Washington, D.C., USA. SuzieScollon@earthlink.net

Robert E. Tucker, Department of Communication Studies, California State University, Long Beach, California, USA. Rob.Tucker@lrinet.com

Ruth Wodak, Wittgenstein Research Center "Discourse, Politics, Identity", Austrian Academy of Sciences, and Applied Linguistics, The University of Vienna, Austria. Ruth.Wodak@oeaw.ac.at

Introduction: A peace of word

Mirjana N. Dedaić

1. Language and war

Discourse and organized armed conflict are unique to humans. Despite the untold wealth and innumerable lives lost to mass or state organized violence, the genesis and prevention of armed conflict are poorly understood. Discourse, we believe, should be the first door opened as we try to explain and prevent state-or-group-organized killing of the other.

Political power cannot be divorced from the power of words. Apart from the technical difficulties of defining the linguistic concept of word, we understand that "words are loaded pistols," as Jean-Paul Sartre avowed. The power of words, indeed, lies in their ability to express the extremes of human feelings and intentions and to direct the spear towards "the other". The linguistic profile of political power reveals the message and the messenger, as well as the reception and response.

Indeed, every dispute starts with "othering". The phenomenon of making the distinction between Us and Them has received much attention from social psychology to critical linguistics. To explain why humans have a need to feel part of their group, and are quickly ready to fight with members of any other group, research has probed pre-conflict discourse.

Two protagonists start a war when they fail to negotiate interests, norms or identities. In such a case, any means is justified – all, of course, is fair in love and war. In an attempt to justify sending young people to death, the leadership will hide the truth of the event in a "deluge of dramatizations" (Ball 1991) creating social reality that calls for immediate retaliation. "*Otherization*" usually precedes justification, but these two paradigms might intersect and infuse each other from the initial stage of the conflict until its end.

Discriminating the society into Us and Others serves both *justification* for action and *propagation* of values and attitudes that call for protection of "conditions of liberty" (Gellner 1994). This task of pro-war discourse glorifies the legitimized (state) order and obliges us to fortify and defend.

Implicit to ingroup-outgroup differentiation is the language of stereotyping (Tajfel 1981). Such forms of violence are made tangible as states, organizations of states and principal interests deny resources and rights to minorities and "others". Pervasive insecurity and threatening discourse, when combined, evoke symbolic violence – an unmistakable message that maintains dominance, argues Antonio Gramsci (1957), even more effectively than brute force.

Foucault places significant emphasis upon a power struggle over the determination of discursive practices: "Discourse is not simply that which translates struggles or systems of domination, but is the thing for which and by which there is struggle; discourse is the power which is to be seized" (1984: 110). Thus, political scientists recognize the importance of dissemination of information, building up of nationalist images and images of animosity, nationalist propaganda, nationalist mythmaking, mobilization against alleged threats, but they fail to understand that all these actions are undertaken through language, essentially by the manipulation of the public discourse.[1] Within an expanding literature of discourse studies, however, only sporadic attention has been given to war discourse. Linguistic journals seem to offer such attention in the aftermath of particularly intense or intriguing conflicts such as those in the former Yugoslavia, Rwanda, or Chechnya. But, such articles are only seashells left by high tide, deprived of their origin and progeny.

Political linguistics has not treated the discourse related to the armed conflict liberally. Only in the late Eighties, with intensified emphasis on nuclear weapons, did linguists engage in structured analysis of the *discourse of the nuclear arms debate* (Chilton 1985; Connor-Linton 1988; Urban 1988; Wertsch 1987). Simultaneously, the longstanding question of *political power*, its origins and manifestations, has been tackled by linguists such as Fairclough (1989), Fowler (1985), Kedar (1987), van Dijk (1989), and Wodak (1989) among others.

It is worth noting that in the nineties, most analysis of war-related discourse found its home in the school that became known as Critical Discourse Analysis (CDA). Paul Chilton is among the leading figures; his methodology takes into account cognitive features such as metaphor and metonymy and, basing his linguistic investigation on philosophy and sociology, he focuses primarily on politician-generated discourse (speeches and written documents). His work is partly activism as well, in line with other CDA scholars who see a discourse analyst as an engaged and non-objective person – a scholar who is guilty of having opinions, and free to express them through fair and exhaustive scholarship.

In Vienna, Austria, another CDA scholar, Ruth Wodak, has developed a unique stream within this discipline. The so-called Discourse-Historical Approach has proven appropriate and fruitful for the study of texts that carry remembrance of the past wars and for dissection of guilt and empathy. As Wodak and others from the Vienna School of discourse analysis look into discursive reflections of the past to learn the future, linguists oriented towards language planning have for a long time studied the effects of nationalism and war on national language policies. The most respected among them, Joshua Fishman, discusses the national "othering" under the slogan "Language equals nationality and nationality equals language..."(1972: 48). He points out that "[m]odern societies have an endless need to define themselves as eternally unique and language is one of the few remaining mass symbols that answers this need without automatically implying one or another short-lived and non-distinctive institutional base" (1972: 50).

Language is often understood as property of the powerful, a symbolic entity that provides a tool for order, subjugation and demise. Symbolic violence starts with naming – a speech act imposed upon us by others. A name is given to us and it belongs to us as a sign after which others know and address us. Absent overt intimidation, the domination over the weak can be, and is, implemented through the most mundane of tasks – "official naming", says Bourdieu (1999: 239), whereby the holder of the monopoly of legitimate symbolic violence imposes, explicitly and publicly, a vision of the social world, exhibiting power over instituted taxonomies. Non-intimidating dominance, at once silent and insidious, constitutes to Bourdieu a kind of "secret code" (1999: 51) of the powerful seducing those who sometimes participate in their own domination.

The purpose of this book is to look into such epistemic, societal, discursive and political aspects of armed conflicts as they fall into two categories – war-language and language-war. War-language, in its varied discursive manifestations, is the focus of the first part of this volume; language wars around the globe are reflected in case studies that make up the second part.

2. Structure of the book

That language plays an important role in and after an armed conflict, and that national idioms are affected by wars are two underlying assumptions that unite this collection. Contributions in the first part of the book illustrate the essential and omnipresent tie between violence and its representation, between physical harm and symbolic injury. Discourse is seen as a conduit of power and as coveted goods for the powerful. Chapters in second part exemplify the fight over language as a symbol of national identity and power. In such studies, we see language itself as a victim of physical violence, suffering "purification" and "re-nationalization" while becoming capital over which groups, nations and states struggle. These perspectives provide bases for the structure of this volume – the first part examines power of discourse as it plays a critical part in war itself, and the second observes the manipulations of national language as a symbol of new, or retained, power. Although the contributions may in fact sway across or even away from their allotted domains, such a division soundly centers on the actual prevailing perspectives chosen by the authors themselves.

Our contributors crystallize three major roles of discourse related to armed conflict: mobilization, justification, and resolution. Further, three are positions a language undergoes vis-à-vis armed conflict: occupation, isolation, and control. Papers in this volume, then, provide a cultural context and temporal scope by joining the perspectives of discourse analysts with those of scholars interested in language policy. The analyses offer many angles from which to assess war and peace. As is appropriate for an emerging field, our contributors evoke no methodological orthodoxy and mine their data from a variety of sources (interviews, political documents, newspapers). Longitudinal and cross-cultural breadth incorporated into this collection through case studies span both time and space.

At War with Words begins by exploring ties between symbolic qua linguistic violence and the physical violence of large-scale conflict. To exemplify this, various social, political and linguistic contexts have been brought into focus, and multiple sources of data examined. The first section, War discourse, features seven contributions; war related discourse produced by media and politicians in America, China, Ghana and Austria is examined, providing a window to the broad spectrum of issues and methodologies to describe and explain behavior of a human warrior.

The theoretical question addressed by the first paper is: Is the physical violence associated with or precipitated by widespread symbolic violence in language and culture? Kathryn Ruud in *"Liberal parasites and other creepers: Rush Limbaugh, Ken Hamblin, and the discursive construction of group identities"* introduces the problem of discursive creation of polarized identities. The power of media in our era has been the subject of great interest for linguists and other scholars. Ruud goes one step further to exemplify how this power might be translated into physical violence. Ruud's study of the American right-wing talk radio language lends credence to Clausewitz's nineteenth century claim that war is omnipotent in Western civilization (1943), as she identifies the names and metaphors by which radio talk-show hosts denote liberals, disturbingly similar to the language of Hitler's genocidal machine. One has to distinguish between the *genocidal* state of mind of the Nazis and *"politicidal"* state of mind of the American extreme right which objects to liberals based on features far different than skull measurement or eye-color. Still, Ruud suggests that group differentiation – in the most extreme, creating warring political identities – uses linguistic means that are perilously similar to those used by heinous regimes. Ruud's auscultation of the language of American right-wing radio talk shows leads to dissection of the substrategies of polarization used by Rush Limbaugh (who sometimes refers to himself as "a talent on loan from God") and Ken Hamblin. Ruud warns that such a "misuse of language contains a terrible potential." This potential no doubt contributes to the "superempowered angry man" (Friedman 1999), who is single-handedly able to inflict massive destruction, such as bombing the Alfred P. Murrah Federal Building in Oklahoma City in April 1995. Whether a society in which political extremes are at "liberty" to engage in symbolic violence against others and create a vision of "enemies among us" can be truly at peace might be questioned.

Feeding animism is best done through hate speech. But to make the seed of hate speech grow, the land has to be ready for seeding. The vision, to be effective, must penetrate and be absorbed by bodies and minds of the faithful, who believe in nation and whose physical being and thoughts the nation considers its property. Once humans become government property, the state's power is extended. Whereas weapons once defined the state's reservoir of power to coerce and kill others, discourse offers another basis of power by which to se-duce, manipulate, and silence.

In *"Threat or business as usual? A multimodal, intertextual analysis of a political statement"* Suzanne Wong Scollon examines political discourse as it is selected, interpreted, and reinterpreted through media. The words reported by media are commonly warped according to the ideology of the media owner. Fairclough and Wodak (1997: 272) note the unresolved power imbalance between the media and politics, whether "mediatized political discourse is the domina-tion of the media over politicians, or the exploitation of the media by politicians". During a news conference held by Chinese Foreign Minister Qian Qichen on the eve of the 1996 Taiwanese elections, Scollon sees three simultaneous media "frames" – contemporary Chinese reformist media, the liberal western media, and the Taiwanese Nationalist Party media – all of which evince quite dis-tinct discourse. She dissects these respective ideologies as they each report on and mold one leader's comments at a single news confer-ence. From Scollon's multimodal, intertextual analysis it becomes clear that the interactions of media and governmental officials pro-duce varying messages from the same utterance, with threats and words of war emerging in some reports and not others. The fragility of peace and the precipice of war seem to hang, as it were, on words and how we say and hear them.

The paper by Paul Chilton *"Deixis and distance: President Clinton's justification of intervention in Kosovo"* is concerned with the discourse of justification to send members of the military to a war far away. His analysis of presidential rhetoric shows how crucial in political behavior it is to ensure that the populace shares "perceptions and misperceptions about political threats and issues" (Edelman 1971: 1). Belonging to a nation, understood as an "imagined community" (Renan 1882; Anderson 1983; Billig 1995), is itself an imagined membership. Consequently, its entailments, such as threats to national existence or well-being, are also imagined. Neighbors are, however, real, and so are territorial claims. Consequently, territorial contiguity is a potent variable predicting the onset of war.

But, what can be done when a nation conducts war far away from home? The territory in which the war is to be conducted must be made more contiguous and less distant, at least symbolically. This discursive construct helps people in imaging the threat and national importance. Discourse analysis untangles linguistic threads woven skillfully into speech text aimed at the reification of (imagined?) national feelings, love for a country, and remaining "the best in the world". These feelings are fueled most easily at the time of incipient war (Hobsbawm 1990).

By claiming that "justification of war is a form of political action that takes place most massively through language", Chilton applies cognitive discourse analysis to unravel the discursive complexities of Clinton's political oratory. Chilton finds vagueness and discursive manipulations as means to justify sending U.S. troops to participate in the Kosovo Force (KFOR) after Serb withdrawal in spring 1999.

Human nature – and human language – are both troubled by the unspeakability of extremes. Ultimate peace is suspected as merely a temporary pause (Clausewitz 1943), while the ultimate destruction is presented in biblical metaphors. Armageddon, Apocalypse, Dooms Day are still modern names for disasters humans inflict on other humans, while nuclear potentials are not yet matched by linguistic potentials. Robert E. Tucker and Theodore O. Prosise, in their paper entitled *"The language of atomic science and atomic conflict: Exploring the limits of symbolic representation"*, discuss that inability of language to match the destructive power of weaponry. Is nuclear power a weapon or not?

Tucker and Prosise analyze Second World War nuclear discourse employed to "domesticate" the nuclear experience. The ways in which atomic planners, scientists, civilian and military leaders named sub-atomic phenomena and atomic weaponry are significant for two key reasons. First, these names and naming strategies continue to play an active role in contemporary policymaking more than half a century later, concealing nuclear annihilation and making war less objectionable. The language of the first generation of atomic weaponeers molded and continues to shape our understanding of nuclear weapons and the role they should play in geopolitics. Second, by considering communication about nuclear weapons we can begin to understand the obstacles that exist between us and safer world.

Moving to African political discourse, Kweku Osam brings us a study of ideology's central role in the struggle for political dominance in Ghana. In his paper *"The politics of discontent: A discourse analysis of texts of the Reform Movement in Ghana"*, Osam claims that language is the key resource in gaining political supremacy. But, his study differs from others by highlighting the text and talk that *resist*, rather than create, dominance. Osam finds that, in the highly unstable political atmosphere of this West African country, the ideological constant is to challenge the status quo. He points out that words indicate when, after suppressing action, people stand up and act to improve their future in the metaphorical battlefield of Ghanaian politics in the late 1990s.

Having started this section with political discourse transmitted through media, we end the section with two papers that deal with Austrian media as they portray the guilt and contrition for past wars. Alexander Pollak in his paper *"When guilt becomes a foreign country: Guilt and responsibility in Austrian postwar media-representation of the Second World War"*, dissects 53 years (1945–1998) of Austrian print media as it concerns guilt covered by myths. In 1945, Austria proclaimed the *"Stunde Null"* – a new start from zero, tailored to rid Austria of the burden of the country's Nazi past. Thereafter it was possible to construct, via mass media, an image of the Second World War in which Austrian soldiers, who carried out the war of extermination and played an active part in the execution of the "Final Solution", were not perceived as perpetrators but rather as an ignorant and innocent collective. How could such images of history and "normal" soldiers be created without denying the existence of atrocities and heinous crimes sanctioned and implemented by the Nazi regime and carried out by its more or less willing executioners? To answer these questions, Pollak examines metaphors that serve as building blocks for establishing a historical image that allowed a positive Austrian self-construction.

The guilt and responsibility question is also the main thrust of the study *"Remembering and forgetting: The discursive construction of generational memories"* by Gertraud Benke and Ruth Wodak. They discern the linguistic expression of guilt and responsibility for the Nazi crimes committed by Austrian Wehrmacht soldiers through the prism of videotaped interviews with visitors to an exhibition of World War II documents. This exhibition, entitled "War of Annihilation", received exceptional coverage in the Austrian press characterized by vehement praise and criticism alike. Benke and Wodak distinguish three generations among visitors – direct war participants, their sons and grandsons. Analyzing the interviews, they detect elements of more distant or less distant guilt, and the level of the discursive actuation of the present versus the past.

Language in both cases serves as an indicator of the generational stances towards the crimes. It is also a matter of the philosophical reconciliation between the grandchildren of the offenders and the grandchildren of the offended, a process that South Africa hopes to have sped up via the Truth and Reconciliation Commission.[2]

The six contributions in Part II, Language wars, present anthropological studies of language issues in Croatia, Okinawa, Palau, Cyprus, Northern Ireland, and the United States. All focus on armed conflict as a consequence of an ideological clash in which language acts either as an attribute of ideology or as a conduit for ideological persuasion or dissemination. The Marxist philosopher Louis Althusser identified processes that help the powerful maintain power and reproduce existing power structure. The instruments in such processes are "ideological state apparatuses" such as the law, education, religion (church), but most of all so-called "repressive state apparatuses" consisting of armed forces and police. These apparatuses legitimize the existence and behavior of the ruling authorities by "bathing society in official discourse: laws, reports, parliamentary debates, sermons, text-books, lectures" (Fowler 1985: 68). In such official discourse the contributors to the second section of the book locate their data.

Coming full circle, the same official discourse subsequently reinforces the government, as Tocqueville (1945: 177) observes, especially at the times of "long and serious warfare". The vicious circle is hard to break, as seizing power means seizing discourse. Public discourse under the government control is then manipulated to mobilize masses to attack the "others". The saliency of identity is an existential requirement for growth of nationalism. Shotter (1993: 200–201) notes that nationalism is a way for people to argue about who and what they really are, or might be. War is seen by nationalists as "a test of collective fitness" (Hutchinson and Smith 1994: 9), and "a necessary dialectics in the evolution of nations" (Howard 1994: 254). And, so too is language.

Based on the research presented in this section, the impetus given by the work of Joshua Fishman and other scholars examining language planning has been invaluable for investigating influences world wars left on *sociolects* and *natiolects*. Fishman (1972, 1973) recapitulates numerous cases around the globe in which language is decidedly the key nationalist ideological underpinning and builds up the notion of language being "worthier than territory" (1972: 49). Work done on national language planning channels thinking into streams that lead towards two major causes for a nation's need for its "own" standard language: as a corollary to national freedom, and as contrastive self-identification:

"The frequency with which vernaculars have become part and parcel of the authenticity message of nationism (both directly and, again, indirectly, though their oral and written products) is certainly, in no small measure, due to the ease with which elites and masses alike could extrapolate from linguistic *differentiation* and literary *uniqueness* to sociocultural and political independence." Fishman (1972: 52)

Linguistics has a lot to say about territorial and linguistic congruencies. The old continent's linguistics was in its early stages deeply and widely concerned with studies of dialects – dividing neighbors and giving them identities; thus, linguistic *nationism* was born. As an upshot, many neighboring languages rushed apart in order to avoid assimilation with others. Having dissected descriptions and definitions throughout the language planning literature, Christian (1988) reveals the six key revolving features: intervention, explicitness, goal-orientation, systemacity, selection among alternatives, and institutionalization. Using these features, she defines language planning as "an explicit and systematic effort to resolve language problems and achieve related goals through institutionally organized intervention in the use and usage of languages" (p. 197). Noticeable is the military-metaphor-denoted feature – intervention. The war of words easily translates into a language war insofar as the powerful can intervene and change the normal course of events to influence future language use.

Both linguists and non-linguists understand the old adage that "language is a dialect with a navy and an army" to mean that a language is linked irrevocably to the formation of a nation-state. Borders of language are not only borders of identity, but also borders of power (see Hannan 1996). Nation-states often protect themselves by declaring a state language or eradicating regional variants; lately, Europe is far from being the only region of the world that sees an ethnic and linguistic revival (Wright 2000: 186), with accompanying lingopolitical turmoil.

The first paper in this part, Keith Langston's and Anita Peti-Stantić's *"Attitudes towards linguistic purism in Croatia: Evaluating efforts at language reform"* looks into the language purification efforts by the victorious nationalist party in Croatia after the 1991–1995 war. The corpus planning was undertaken to achieve two nationally important goals: to emphasize newly achieved national freedom, and to differentiate Croatians from the Serbs, with whom an official language was previously shared.[3] Croatian President Franjo Tudjman insisted on cleansing Croatian territories and the Croatian language of Serbian influence with the ambition of fortifying Croatian identity. To do so, he focused upon formal institutions (schools, government, religion) as means by which to impose the reproduction of linguistic authority. The epuration of language of what was perceived "Serbian" in origin or usage brought confusion among the speakers of Croatian. Even some linguists confessed to difficulties in speaking and writing. Despite official language policies, however, the "old" language has retained its authority through informal face-to-face relations. Langston and Peti-Stantić conducted a survey demonstrating that presenting oneself as speaking the "pure Croatian" may work in national institutions as a marker of national purity, but is seen and felt as strange and "too official" in everyday conversation. "Speaking properly" requires training so intense that it necessitates a passionate motivation. If such intensity is absent, the training is futile, and the survival rate of the previously imposed linguistic items is uncertain.

In Rumiko Shinzato's paper *"Wars, politics, and language: A case study of the Okinawan language"*, "a sudden tip" of Okinawan language is investigated in the light of domestic and international wars and accompanying changes in hegemony. After a series of conflicts and wars – within Japan and then the Sino-Japanese War and World War II – the indigenous language of the southern-most province of Japan was on a path towards extinction. When Okinawa was incorporated into the Japanese polity, Okinawan lost its status as a national language while Japanese spread, causing the language shift. Looking into the ways "language attitude translates into language policies", Shinzato shows how the stigmatization of Okinawan – an effect not unknown in other parts of the world – worked towards its extinction. But, she believes that Okinawan may have already seen the worst because the social mobilization patterns in Okinawa moved from "negative ethnicity" (i.e., the denial of Okinawan identity) to "positive ethnicity", and is stirring towards an "ethnic movement". In that, pragmatic issues are not negligible: in some business interactions, speaking Okinawan wins more trust, which translates into more business.

Resistance to symbolic violence is often quiet and persistent. The Pacific island of Palau, for example, has seen nearly a century of coercive institutional domination by colonizers who instilled English and Japanese into Palauan high culture. Kazuko Matsumoto and David Britain, in their *"Language choice and cultural hegemony: Linguistic symbols of domination and resistance in Palau"* investigate the fate of the Palauan, language only about 10 thousand speakers strong. They report on its historical ups and downs in terms of social importance and political power, characterizing colonial influences on Palauan as "mild violence" or *"violence douce"*. Cultural hegemony and symbolic domination have constituted and shaped language use in this trilingual nation-state that went through the political and linguistic hardship of seeking and achieving independence. And, while some other nation-states fight for their national monolingualism, Palauans have long had to choose which two of three languages to speak: Palauan, Japanese, or English. The authors demonstrate how this permanent diglossic choice facilitates hegemony – the colonial power can govern with the high variant, and the people comply because they can continue to live their daily routines in their native, low variant language. Paradoxically, both sides can then be portrayed as hegemonically satisfied. "Diglossia replaced diglossia", summarize Matsumoto and Britain regarding the long history of changing linguistic loyalties on Palau.

Some of the wars considered in this book are "spontaneous wars" of the past, while some are "wars in making". Most of today's armed conflicts, however, are of the kind that Billig (1995) calls "official wars" which are ended by "official peace", precisely dated for the history books. In her *"Advertising for peace as political communication"*, Renée Dickason explores one effort to generate peace amid the prolonged turmoil of Northern Ireland. She analyzes the experimental program of the British Conservative government (1988–1997) to mitigate violence through television advertisements, assessing such a campaign in terms of its form, purpose, and efficacy. Dickason finds that advertising for peace potentially offered new solutions to the problem of political communication.

Dickason's multimodal analysis of the "peace commercials" leads her to conclude that the government tried to persuade the public of the chance for a better life and a peaceful way. She identifies six themes: friendship, solidarity, humor, heritage, childhood innocence and sport, all features that encompass a simultaneous appeal to rational and emotional sympathies. Language was, therefore, integral to the attempt to create a sense of identity and a mood of complicity. This was, concludes Dickason, a "highly ambitious and perhaps excessively hopeful project" that lasted long enough to attain all the results it could have realized. An optimistic verdict would regard it as a stage in the gradual process of attitudinal transformation within Northern Ireland, which had a number of short-term and long-term benefits and may have contributed to ceasefires. After the advertising for peace campaign ended, Dickason is not sure that the war ended as well. But, when *does* war end?

Marilena Karyolemou's paper *" 'Keep your language and I'll keep mine': Politics, language, and the construction of identities in Cyprus"* discusses efforts to defuse the volatility of symbolic violence via language policy. Cyprus, divided by force since the mid 1970s, has experienced many kinds of polarization. The languages-of-instruction question at the University of Cyprus has been seen in many places as a central issue closely related to political climate, beyond the character of the University itself.

Through the language of education, the Greek Cypriot schools taught loyalty to the Hellenic world and Orthodoxy, while Turkish Cypriot schools conveyed loyalty to Turkey, the Turkish language, and Islam. These loyalties, perceived not only as distinct but also as completely incompatible, created and widened the gap between members of the two communities, leading to the formation of a strong ethno-nationalistic feeling. So, in 1986, ideologically opposite political parties – the communist left and the extreme right – united in a position that favored using *both* languages at the University of Cyprus. The main common arguments used to justify this option were the respect of the Constitutional provisions for the equal official status to both ethnic languages, and the respect of both communities' right to be instructed in their respective mother tongue. Some Cypriots hoped (and other feared) that peaceful coexistence and social prosperity would weaken ethnic barriers and divest ethnic languages of their identity values. According to Karyolemou, the alternative of a third language (English) for higher education institution has also been on the table, but thus far rejected.

Invisible borders of identity may have precluded Esperanto (or any other orphan language) to take root and to grow into a global *lingua franca*, if not a unifying force. The spread of English since World War II may have beaten the odds; courtesy of American military and economic power, every corner of the globe has become at least familiar with English for business and cultural exchange. This is especially true with the development of the Internet, which carries more and more information on human activities and is written predominantly (more than 80 percent [Fisher 1998/1999]) in English. However, English is welcome only as long as it does not represent a threat to national identity, and as long as speakers can choose which linguistic elements (words, phrases, syntax) they take from English and which they do not.[4] The symbolic feeling of linguistic identity is thus retained and English, although creeping into all languages through many different means, is not always greeted with an open door.

While the world learns English to enable more-than-mass communication, Americans seem to fear losing it. That question, and the question of linguistic vs. political identities, are focus of the last contribution in this volume – Mark Allen Peterson's *"American warriors speaking American: The metapragmatics of performance in the nation state"*. When a topic of war is joined with the English-only controversy in Congressional debate, like the one that took place in 1996 between several Democratic and Republican Congressmen, far more attention is attracted. Peterson seeks to resolve the enigma: "What are 'Americans' to think of people who speak no English yet are willing to risk their lives in wars the state says are necessary for the nation's survival?" The powerful American mythology of veterans' sacrifice is evoked as a criterion for credibility on the issue of a U.S. "national" language. Veterans are constructed in American popular mythology as persons who, at great personal cost, have "answered their country's call." From Congressional debate to the newsstand, this notion takes on wider meaning and is presented to a public audience. In return, this topic becomes multivoiced and is used to prove several initially unintended notions, most saliently the notion of "Americaness". Are those who speak English well more American than those who do not?

The "official English" bill, which generated the exchange analyzed by Peterson, passed in the House but never came to a vote in the Senate. This battle for control over the symbolic definition of an "American" was lost, but the war over who may or may not claim such an identity goes on.

3. Conclusion

The relationship between the violence of discourse and acts of war metamorphoses as war approaches, occurs and ebbs. Several contributors in this book are concerned by the initiation of large-scale human violence. This concern is not new. Cultural anthropologists have offered materialist, cultural and biological explanations (Haas 1990; Ferguson 1999). But, those who delve into classic literature find different inspiration. Kagan (1995), for example, argues that Thucydides' analysis of why wars begin (honor, fear, and interest) tells us the whole story of contemporary war and peace. Some authors think that humans are biologically aggressive and prone to fighting (Hebb and Thompson 1968; James 1968; McDougall 1968; see also Mead 1968 for an opposing account). No one regards language as the sole reason for violence, but everyone takes for granted that honor, fear, interest, and other possible *casus belli* are launched, justified, and spread via language (see, for example, Stoessinger 1993).

Scholars of nations and nationalism list the attributes of the nation-state as principal reasons for contemporary warfare. Billig (1995: 28) laconically summarizes this idea in the phrase "a nation state is itself a means of violence." The veracity of this statement is tested in cases where nations have no defined territory, such as the case with the Inuit and Roma, who do not wage wars. Individuals from such groups may fight amongst each other and engage in vendettas while some other groups may have prolonged feuds. Yet, the notion of widespread, costly, and long-term conflict namely "war" has been reserved for *states* until September 11, 2001, which involved a non-state *movement* as *actor*.

Identification of *state* as *actor* to start, maintain, and conclude war has been an important element in any approach to a state-generated discourse. Such attribution guides the analyst towards the examination of a collective as actor, rather than individuals whose intentions, means and ways have psychological grounding. Collective actors have collective dynamics, often erratic and rarely predictable. Most important, a collective actor uses language to communicate, inter-collectively as well as intra-collectively. Comparison between the two simultaneous planes of communication often yields interesting dichotomies that emphasize linguistic control over memberships and identities.

The power of discursively created warring identities is often shown as political, not ethnic, divides. Several studies in this collection lend credence to Clausewitz's nineteenth century claim that war is omnipotent in Western civilization (1943). Clausewitz regarded peace as but a pause between, or delay of, war.[5] In that respect, any public discourse can be taken as being within the domain of state's politics that might result in a war.

The authors included in this volume engage in what we call "linguistic war study" in contrast to existing lore about war that is usually described as "peace research" (see Schäffner and Wendon 1995). *Nomen est omen*, perhaps, and names can change the named. From this evolve questions such as: What is peace and what is war? Where is the delineation between the two?[6] That the American government's department housed in the Pentagon was renamed in 1947 from the Department of War to the Department of Defense[7], is one example that suggests the interlocked nature of these concepts. A year later, George Orwell informed us prudently that sometimes "peace is war, and war is peace".[8]

Today, war is where war rhetoric is. Analyzing the language of politics and the politics of language can bring important understanding of the role communication plays in establishing, maintaining, or destroying political relations. It follows that political scientists should not shy away from borrowing analytical tools from linguistics, while linguists can support their findings by understanding political relations. Global peace and prosperity will best be served if students of linguistics and politics pool their knowledge and methods to minimize conflict and maximize cooperative communications.

Notes

1. See, for instance, excellent papers on these topics in Brown et al. (1997).
2. The Truth and Reconciliation Commission suspended its work in mid 2001, when "all the amnesty hearings have been concluded and the final TRC Report has been released", as stated on the TRC web page www.truth.org.za.
3. The spoken variants of the official language in Serbia and Croatia differed in several features and the different variants were readily recognizable by the native speakers.
4. Some nations are trying to defy the spread of English by official means. Besides the well-known case of France, there have been anti-English movements in Spain, Germany, Mexico, Burma, India and several other countries (Wright 2000 passim).
5. The 17th century Dutch philosopher Baruch de Spinoza held a different view: "Peace is not constituted by the absence of war. Peace is a virtue, an attitude of mind, an inclination toward benevolence, trust and justice".
6. The delineation between peace and war, particularly in the contemporary world, is discussed in Nelson (1999).
7. Moreover, *secretaries of war* are around the world customarily titled *secretaries of defense*. A few states – Guatemala for instance – have a *secretary of peace*.
8. That this is not just a writer's construction has been well demonstrated in numerous clever analyses by Bugarski (1997, 2001) and others.

References

Althusser, L.
    1971   Ideology and ideological state apparatuses. In: *Lenin and Philosophy*, translated by B. Brewster. London: New Left Books.

Anderson, Benedict
1983   *Imagined Communities. Reflections on the Origin and Spread of Nationalism*. London: Verso Editions.

Ball, Moya Ann
1991   Revisiting the Gulf of Tonkin crisis: an analysis of the private communication of President Johnson and his advisers. *Discourse & Society* 2(3), 281–296.

Billig, Michael
1995   *Banal Nationalism*. London/Thousand Oaks/New Delhi: Sage.

Bourdieu, Pierre
1999   *Language and Symbolic Power*. Cambridge: Harvard University Press, fifth printing.

Brown, Michael E., Owen R. Coté, Jr., Sean M. Lynn-Jones, and Steven E. Miller (eds.)
1997   *Nationalism and Ethnic Conflict*. Cambridge: MIT Press.

Bugarski, Ranko
1997   *Jezik od mira do rata* [Language from Peace to War]. Belgrade: Čigoja Štampa/XX vek. First edition, 1995.

2001   *Lica jezika* [Faces of Language]. Belgrade: Čigoja Štampa/XX vek.

Chilton, Paul (ed.)
1985   *Language and the Nuclear Arms Debate: Nukespeak Today*. London: Pinter.

Christian, Donna
1988   Language planning: the view from linguistics. In: Newmeyer, Frederick J. (ed.), *Linguistics: The Cambridge Survey. Vol. IV, Language: The Socio-cultural Context*. Cambridge: Cambridge University Press, 193–209.

Clausewitz, Karl von
1943   *On War*. New York: Modern Library.

Connor-Linton, Jeff
1988   Author's style and world-view in nuclear discourse: A quantitative analysis. *Multilingua* 7(1/2), 95–132.

Edelman, Murray
    1971   *Politics as Symbolic Action: Mass Arousal and Quiescence*. Chicago: Markham.

Fairclough, Norman
    1989   *Language and Power*. London/New York: Longman.

Fairclough, Norman, and Ruth Wodak
    1997   Critical discourse analysis. In Teun van Dijk (ed.), *Discourse as social interaction*. London: Sage.

Ferguson, R. Brian
    1999   Materialist, cultural and biological theories on why Yanomami make war. *Anthropological Theory* 1(1), 99–116.

Fischer, Joshua
    1998/1999   The new linguistic order. *Foreign Policy* 113 (Winter 1998/1999), 26– 40.

Fishman, Joshua A.
    1972   *Language and Nationalism. Two Integrative Essays*. Rowley, Massachusetts: Newbury House.

    1973   Language modernization and planning in comparison with other types of national modernization and planning. *Language in Society* 2(1), 23–42.

Fowler, Roger
    1985   Power. In: van Dijk, Teun (ed.), *Handbook of Discourse Analysis, Vol. 4: Discourse Analysis in Society*. London: Academic Press, 61–82.

Friedman, Thomas
    1999   *The Lexus and the Olive Tree: Understanding Globalization*. New York: Farrar, Straus and Giroux.

Gellner, Ernest
    1994   *Conditions of Liberty. Civil Society and Its Rivals*. New York: Penguin Books.

Gramsci, Antonio
    1957   *The Modern Prince and Other Writings*. (Translated by Louis Marks.) New York: International Publishers.

Haas, Jonathan (ed.)
1990   *The Anthropology of War*. Cambridge: Cambridge University Press.

Hannan, Kevin
1996   Borders of language and identity in Teschen Silesia. *Berkeley Insights in Linguistics and Semiotics*, Vol. 28. New York: Peter Lang.

Hebb, D. O., and W. R. Thompson
1968   Emotion and society. In: Bramson, Leon, and George W. Goethals (eds.) *War: Studies from Psychology, Sociology, Anthropology*. Revised edition. New York/London: Basic Books, 45–64.

Hobsbawm, Eric J.
1990   *Nations and Nationalism Since 1780: Programme, Myths, Reality*. New York: Cambridge University Press.

Howard, Michael
1994   War and nations. In Hutcinson, John, and Anthony D. Smith (eds.) *Nationalism*. Oxford/New York: Oxford University Press, 254–257.

Hutchinson, John and Anthony D. Smith (eds.)
1994   *Nationalism*. Oxford/New York: Oxford University Press.

James, William
1968   The moral equivalent of war. In: Bramson, Leon, and George W. Goethals (eds.) *War: Studies from Psychology, Sociology, Anthropology*. Revised edition. New York/London: Basic Books, 21–32.

Kagan, Donald
1995   *On the Origins of War and the Preservation of Peace*. New York: Doubleday.

Kedar, Leah (ed.)
1987   *Power Through Discourse*. New Jersey: Ablex.

McDougall, William
1968   The instinct of pugnacity. In: Bramson, Leon, and George W. Goethals (eds.) *War: Studies from Psychology, Sociology, Anthropology*. Revised edition. New York/London: Basic Books, 33–44.

Mead, Margaret
  1968   Warfare is only an invention – not a biological necessity. In: Bramson, Leon, and George W. Goethals (eds.) *War: Studies from Psychology, Sociology, Anthropology*. Revised edition. New York/London: Basic Books, 269–274.

Nelson, Daniel N.
  1999   Stable peace or secure peace. *International: Die Zeitschrift für Internationale Politik* 5–6: 14–17.

Renan, Ernest
  1882   *Qu'est-ce qu'une nation? Conférence faite en Sorbonne, le 11 mars 1882*. Paris: Calmann Lévy.

Schäffner, Christina, and Anita L. Wenden (eds.)
  1995   *Language and Peace*. Amsterdam: Harwood Academic Publishers.

Shotter, John
  1993   *Cultural Politics of Everyday Life: Social Constructionism, Rhetoric and Knowing of the Third Kind*. Toronto: University of Toronto Press.

Stoessinger, John G.
  1993   *Why Nations Go to War*. Sixth edition. New York: St. Martin's Press.

Tajfel, Henri
  1981   Human Groups and Social Categories: Studies in Social Psychology. Cambridge: Cambridge University Press.

Tocqueville, Alexis de
  1945   *Democracy in America, Volume One*. New York: Vintage Books.

Urban, Greg
  1988   The pronominal pragmatics of nuclear war discourse. *Multilingua* 7(1/2), 67–93.

Van Dijk, Teun A.
  1989   Structures of Discourse and Structures of Power. In: Anderson, J. A. (ed.), *Communication Yearbook 12*. Newbury Park, CA: Sage, 18–59.

Wertsch, James V.
   1987   Modes of discourse in the nuclear arms debate. *Current Research on Peace and Violence* 10(2/3), 102–112.

Wodak, Ruth (ed.)
   1989   *Language, Power and Ideology: Studies in Political Discourse.* Philadelphia: John Benjamins.

Wright, Sue
   2000   *Community and Communication: The Role of Language in Nation State Building and European Integration.* Clevedon: Multilingual Matters LTD.

I. War discourse

Liberal parasites and other creepers: Rush Limbaugh, Ken Hamblin, and the discursive construction of group identities

Kathryn Ruud

1. Introduction

The April 1995 bombing of the Alfred P. Murrah Federal Building in Oklahoma City was an unprecedented act of domestic terrorism that killed 168 people. President Clinton 's criticism of "loud and angry" voices, reported widely in the media, implied that the speech of American political talk show hosts contributed to a climate that encouraged this terrorist act.

President Clinton's comment unleashed a public debate over the influence of political talk radio, and Rush Limbaugh and other conservative talk show hosts felt unjustly criticized. Limbaugh retorted on-air that "Talk radio didn't buy the fertilizer and fuel oil [used in the bombing]."[1]

A report on political talk radio was issued four months later by the University of Pennsylvania Annenberg Public Policy Center. The Annenberg Report found that many journalists had labeled conservative talk radio as "a discordant perhaps dangerous discourse that is intolerant and histrionic, unmindful of evidence, [and] classically propagandistic," and that it was "spreading the kind of hate and divisiveness that led to the bombing of the Federal Building in Oklahoma City" (Cappella et al 1996: 40, 42). A content analysis of several political talk radio programs (Conservative, Moderate and Liberal) led Annenberg researchers to conclude that the press had tended to exaggerate the effect of talk radio and inaccurately characterized such programs as "at best, routinely uncivil, and at worst downright dangerous" (Cappella et al 1996: 49).

The Annenberg Report contained this note of caution: "The analyses of the content of [political talk radio] ... concerns *what* is discussed on political talk radio and the mainstream news media, not *how* topics are discussed" (Cappella et al 1996: 22; emphasis added). Researchers did a quantitative analysis, but did not describe the style of language or linguistic structures or strategies hosts used to persuade listeners. To make these systematic factors evident, a critical analysis of qualitative elements at work in conservative political talk radio discourse is necessary.

In this article, I argue that from 1992 and to 1996, the discourse of Rush Limbaugh, Ken Hamblin and other conservative hosts went beyond a debate over programmatic differences between the right and the left to include the systematic construction of highly polarized group identities, in which "virtuous conservatives" are locked in battle with "vice-ridden liberals". A macro-level worldview, in which conservatives and liberals represent not only opposing political perspectives, but also oppositional social and cultural groups, was reproduced at the micro-level of discourse. This theme, communicated through a range of polarizing discourse strategies and structures, has also helped to construct ingroup and outgroup identities in racist, anti-Semitic, and communist party discourse.

Tactics of polarization used in the construction of group identity have long been an object of research in post-war Europe, particularly by German-speaking linguists. My approach draws upon this tradition as well as contemporary critical linguistics, particularly the socio-cognitive theory developed by Teun van Dijk and the discourse-historical theories and methodologies developed by the Vienna School of Discourse Analysis led by Ruth Wodak.

Was there a strategy of polarization evident in the discourse of Limbaugh and Hamblin from 1992–1996? And, if so, how might we describe that strategy via its structure?[2]

2. Propaganda, polarization, and group identities – approach and methods

2.1. Linguistic strategies of propaganda

Writing about the wartime propaganda of the Great Powers in the First World War, Brekle (1989: 83–85) points out that domestic propaganda was used far more successfully in England than in Germany, where the government limited its efforts to censoring of potentially damaging information. Brekle (1989: 85–86) cites Ponsonby[3] who found eight fundamental features used by the British press in war reports:

- Stereotypes ("bull-necked Prussian officer")
- Names with negative connotations ("huns")
- Selection and suppression of facts, often with palliative terms (retreats are called "straightening the front")
- Reports of cruelty ("Belgian nuns violated")
- Slogans ("a war to end all wars")
- One-sided reporting (small victories exaggerated, large defeats glossed over)
- Unmistakably negative characterization of the enemy ("German militarists")
- The so-called "bandwagon effect" ("every patriot joins up").

Brekle (1989: 87) noted that Adolf Hitler later lamented in his infamous *Mein Kampf* that the Germans had failed to appreciate the value of propaganda as a weapon, and he cited Eugen Hadomovsky, a deputy of Goebbels, who wrote that Nazi propagandists had much to learn from the English press propaganda of the First World War.

During World War II, propaganda was spread by the centralized and tightly controlled Ministry of Propaganda in the National Socialist Third Reich. It is well-documented, however, that Nazi propaganda took root in the democratic Weimar Republic several years before Adolf Hitler seized the reins of power. The source of this propaganda was "information" spread by the Nazi party through its rallies and publications.

Victor Klemperer, a German Jew and philologist teaching at a Dresden university during the democratic Weimar Republic, began to notice changes in the use of language by friends and acquaintances after the publication of Hitler's *Mein Kampf* in the mid-twenties. As the Nazi party grew, the use of altered words and phrases increased, and Klemperer began to take note of what he heard in a journal. In 1946 he wrote a book, *Lingua Tertii Imperii, Sprache des Dritten Reiches*, in the hope that it would contribute to a "final mass burial" of the linguistic tricks that brought the Nazis so much influence. Although his contribution is not a scientific analysis, LTI is an unparalleled eyewitness account of the evolution of language in that period.

German linguist Siegfried Bork (1970) analyzed the vocabulary used by Hitler in *Mein Kampf* and by contributors to the *Völkischer Beobachter*, the newspaper issued by the Nazi party. Bork defined language control (*Sprachregelung*) not as the official daily reports issued by the Reich's press, but rather as the common and latent use of terms that were repeatedly incorporated into the Nazi press by various writers. Bork sorted the vocabulary of Nazism into lexical fields, those that were aggressive, superlative, religious, dehumanizing, grandiose, etc. While Bork did not use terms such as "ingroup" and "outgroup", the polarization of groups through the use of contrasting descriptive language is clear. Metaphors, concepts and evaluative adjectives and adverbs used to describe Nazi party members and their supporters were positive; those used to describe opponents (Jews, socialists, communists and, later, the Allied Powers) were intensely negative.

In the 1980s, German linguist Nicoline Hortzitz analyzed written texts from the period of "early anti-Semitism" (1789–1872). As Wodak et al. (1990: 39–40) explains, Hortzitz sought to establish a connection between micro-level vocabulary and text, and the macro-level of argumentation. Hortzitz examined entire texts and highlighted predicates selected by authors that were designed to cast Jews in a negative light, such as "deceitful", "cunning" or "conspiratorial". Hortzitz evaluated structures in terms of their value as elements in argumentation. Her research on the macro-level of argumentation strategy (discrimination against Jews) and micro-levels of discourse structure (lexemes selected for their negative connotations) is a precursor to *"Wir-Diskurs"*.

One of the most significant studies on totalitarian language use in communist dictatorships, prior to the demise of European communism, was *La Langue de bois* by Françoise Thom (Paris 1987). In 1993, an international colloquium of scholars from Central and Eastern Europe convened in Vienna to discuss the post-communist evolution of languages in their respective countries. Contributions of several participants were later published in the book *Totalitäre Sprache-Langue de bois-Language of dictatorship* (Wodak and Kirsch 1995). One of the most interesting findings of this conference was the inherent flexibility of *langue de bois* to adapt to new circumstances (Wodak 1995). Participants found parallel and overlapping linguistic strategies in the language of Stalinist communism and anti-Semitic and nationalist discourse in post-communist Eastern Europe.

2.2. The added dimension: Critical discourse analysis

Quantitative content analysis of text and talk cannot tell the whole story, since it is used only to compare amounts or percentages of time spent discussing particular topics and to determine topical priorities in a particular text. As Fowler (1991: 231) points out, "critical linguistics [can] advance [content] analysis by demonstrating how the structure of language silently and continuously shapes" ideas presented by the speaker.

Bell and Garrett (1998: 6) note that critical discourse analysis "has produced the majority of the research into media discourse during the 1980s and 1990s, and has arguably become the standard framework for studying media texts within European linguistics and discourse studies". Critical discourse analysis draws on the study of classical rhetoric and more recent, discourse-oriented research in the social sciences, particularly anthropology, sociolinguistics, and cognitive and social psychology. Van Dijk's (1990, 1993, 1998) cross-disciplinary approach links micro-level properties of discourse with macro-level phenomena in the broader societal, cultural and political context and seeks to explain how these two levels influence one another.

Van Dijk (1990: 11) cites the need for a critical focus of research to address societal and political issues, particularly the abuse of power through "rhetoric, style of argumentation, or control of semantic content". The analyst takes the explicit position that the abuse of power has negative and corrosive effects on democratic values, such as fairness and equality. Manipulative discursive mechanisms are rarely self-evident. Consequently, systematic sociopolitical discourse analysis has focused on thematic content and specific structures or strategies used in a particular discourse genre. Through such techniques, critical discourse analysis can highlight and expose forms of power abuse, which directly or indirectly influence the mind, and ultimately our larger society, through text and talk.

2.3. Conservative political talk radio as a discourse genre

Rush Limbaugh's program is a hybrid-blending entertainment, a news medium, and a forum for political discussion. His program is heard on approximately 650 stations in the U.S. and, according to Limbaugh, his three-hour radio show reaches a weekly audience of 20 million. Like most talk radio hosts, Limbaugh is not a political figure himself and he frequently has declared that he has no interest in pursuing political office. His discourse, however, is not limited to political parody, satire and spoof. He openly seeks not only to inform, but also to instruct his listeners on political issues.

While liberals and moderates also listen to Limbaugh's program, the Annenberg report showed that regular listeners (those who listen at least two times per week) were conservatives (70%) and Republican (61.4%) (Capella et al 1996: 13). Although Annenberg researchers found the most extreme comments they heard were by Ken Hamblin, a black conservative whose show is syndicated on over 120 stations, they noted that coverage of Hamblin's program by the mainstream print media has been sparse.

Conservative talk radio is both a political and a social domain. Hosts offer political commentary and most of their listening audience is made up of individuals with similar interests. Taking these macro-level political and social functions into account, my analysis views language used on conservative talk radio as a genre of political and social discourse.

Data collected for this chapter are primarily from Rush Limbaugh (broadcasting from New York City), by far the most popular conservative host, and Ken Hamblin, whose program is one of the top ten (broadcast from Denver, Colorado). Twenty-three hours of Limbaugh's show and thirteen hours of Ken Hamblin's program were recorded (largely by the author) between March 1995 and October 1996. Additional tapes and cited excerpts were obtained from the author of *The Rush Watch*, Tom Frangicetto, who recorded most of Limbaugh's radio and television programs from 1992 until April 1997. Frangicetto's monthly newsletter was published from July 1995 to April 1997. Because materials written by Limbaugh and Hamblin contain features characteristic of spoken language (catchwords, short sentences, and various modal expressions including evaluative adverbs and adjectives), these sources can be considered an intertextual mode of the same political discourse genre. Materials include the books by Limbaugh (1993a, 1994a), and Hamblin (1996c). Additional sources are Limbaugh's official newsletter, the monthly *Limbaugh Letter* (Nov. 1992 to April 1995), and newspaper articles and interviews.[4]

2.4. Socio-cognitive theory

The strategy of polarization used by Limbaugh and Hamblin has the macrofunctional purpose of differentiating between two groups. On the one side is an ingroup of conservatives portrayed as possessing many positive attributes; on the other side is the outgroup of liberals, who are portrayed as having numerous negative traits. This macro-level strategy of polarization is manifested in a range of micro-level discursive mechanisms. These micro-level linguistic structures may, in turn, further produce and reproduce this polarized worldview in wider political and social dimensions. The foundation for this hypothesis is van Dijk's socio-cognitive theory (1993).

This theory is concerned with the connections between social structures and discourse structures. Van Dijk (1993: 37) explains that opinions shared with other members of a group are social representations (also called social cognitions). He understands social cognition to be

> the interplay of specific mental structures and processes; not only the cognitive representations shared by members of the group, ...but also the strategies that enable the effective uses of such representations in various social tasks, such as interpretations, inferences, categorization, comparisons, and evaluations, and even more fundamental processes such as those of storage and retrieval. In a broad sense, social representations embody all that people must know or believe in order to function as competent members of a group.

Analysis of conservative talk show discourse can identify social representations ("such as social knowledge, attitudes, norms, values and ideologies", van Dijk 1993: 38) used by hosts and highlight various linguistic structures and strategies they use in sharing these representations with their audiences. He has applied this theory to the problem of racism at the macro social and political level and the expression of racism at the micro-level of discourse. In the last decade in Europe, increasing xenophobia toward immigrant workers and a growth in the number and power of racist, right-wing political parties have been evident. Van Dijk (1993: 10) emphasizes that this racism is not always just a matter of general public resentment, but may be inspired by prejudiced anti-foreign arguments made by decision-makers and opinion leaders who are members of the white elite classes in these countries. Elite discourses are not blatantly racist or even primarily racial. Rather, such discourses are culturally based, emphasizing positive versus negative differences between the favored white in-group and minority out-groups (van Dijk 1993: 5–6).

Both Limbaugh and Hamblin would deny that they are racist, and my purpose is not to determine any personal bigotry on their part. Instead, this chapter is meant primarily to analyze the linguistic mechanisms they use on their talk radio programs in order to build negative and positive group identities. Central to this analysis are ideologies that influence these hosts as they produce discourse, and their selection of social representations derived from their individual mental models that reveal and promote a polarized worldview.

Van Dijk (1993: 38) makes an important distinction between personal opinions and shared social beliefs of groups. Mental models are personal and unique, based on our own experiences and understanding of events. These individual models link our personal knowledge with attitudes and values shared by various groups in society. Only when we communicate with others through text and talk do fragments of these models become evident. Further, he stresses that, particularly in public discourse, group members will use aspects of mental models that highlight the positive attributes of the perceived ingroup and the negative attributes of the perceived outgroup, while de-emphasizing information that is negative about the ingroup or positive about the outgroup (van Dijk 1998: 41). The fragments of our individual mental models selected to be shared with other members of a group will be those seen to have a functional purpose; that is, they are relevant to the interests and goals of the group (van Dijk 1993: 42). This is of particular significance for linguistic analysis of the discourses of powerful political or media figures (including talk radio hosts), whose commentary may have a strong impact on public opinion.

Most talk radio discourse is what van Dijk (1998: 26–30) calls "opinion discourse". He defines opinions as "beliefs that feature an evaluative aspect". When opinions are used to express conflicting interests between groups, they are ideological and social. Van Dijk distinguishes between factual beliefs, which differ from evaluative beliefs in that the former are based on "socially shared criteria of truth (e.g. observation, reliable communication, valid inference, scholarly research, etc.)". If truth is measured only by group norms, then a belief is evaluative and not factual.

When, for example, Limbaugh describes liberals (but not conservatives) as "whiners", he generalizes, categorizes, and assigns negative value to the behavior of outgroup members. There is no evidence available that has proven that liberals habitually whine or cry, even when expressing objections to conservative ideas or proposals. This social representation serves an ideological purpose in that it defines outgroup behavior by ingroup evaluation and opinion.

2.5. The *"discourses of difference"* and discourse-historical analysis

Ruth Wodak, who analyzed modern anti-Semitic discourse as well as xenophobic anti-immigrant discourse in Austria, says that "the point of departure of every form of prejudiced discourse is the constitution of groups". In "discourses of difference", discursive exclusion is based on ideologies which assume that differences in traits define groups (1996: 111–112, 117). Wodak (1996: 112–113) lists distin-guishing features between groups that may be used in prejudiced dis-course. Included are physical, spiritual or cultural traits, religion, eth-nicity, nationality, social traits, socioeconomic identity or political identification. In terms of social perception of the outgroup by in-group members, all of these traits may be fused to form a single group identity, or selected traits may be "clustered" to define the identity of a particular group.

Wodak (1996: 113) points out that the constellation of traits em-ployed in contemporary anti-Semitic discourse in Austria differ from those used in Nazi propaganda against Jews, which were largely ge-netic-racist and socio-cultural. Because of the Nazi past, references to supposed racial differences have become largely taboo, and in contemporary anti-Semitic discourse, ethnic, cultural, sociopolitical and religious differences are emphasized.

It is very important to underscore that the group traits selected by Limbaugh and Hamblin to define liberals and to construct group identity are not parallel to those used by the Nazis. The characteris-tics they attribute to liberals and other associated outgroups are based on perceived cultural and social, not genetic, differences. Much of the "discourse of difference" on conservative talk radio focuses on traits these hosts attribute to political identity.

I apply Wodak's discourse-analytical approach to the "discourses of difference" used on political talk radio. This methodology, as applied here to the construction of polarized group identities, consists of three components: an examination of thematic content (here, the theme of group differences), the identification and description of strategies used in the discursive construction of group identity, and a description of the linguistic realization of polarization in the structures of discourse.

Wodak does not measure content by the amount of time consumed by a topic. Instead, thematic elements used in the construction of common and "other" identities are identified. Themes that recur on conservative talk radio are those which define conservatives as being different from liberals, i.e. "How are our politics different from their politics?" "How is our culture different from their culture?" "How are our values different from their values?".

Strategy is defined by Wodak et al (1990: 31) as "a more or less accurate plan adopted to achieve [a] political, psychological, or other kind of objective". In her research on post-war anti-Semitism, Wodak includes an elaborated list of argumentation strategies used by ingroup members to delineate differences between groups and to distance themselves from the outgroup. Strategies identified by Wodak et al (1999: 31) relevant to the analysis of the polarizing language used on conservative political:talk radio include:

- Identifying the outgroup as an "enemy" and defining group members in terms of difference (black-and-white method), then ridiculing or criminalizing outgroup behavior;
- Using "we-discourse" ("*Wir-Diskurs*") to build a sense of solidarity among ingroup members by creating a dichotomy between the "good" moral qualities of the ingroup and the "bad" moral character of outgroup members;
- A positive self-presentation of ingroup members;
- Scapegoating;
- An exaggerated negative characterization of statements and behaviors of outgroup members.

The construction of ingroup and outgroup identities is realized in a range of linguistic forms. Some of these cited by Wodak are "personal pronouns [we/they], depersonalization (*Anonymisierung*), generalization and equation of incommensurable phenomena (*Gleichsetzung*), the use of vague characterizations, and the substantive definitions of groups" (Wodak 1996: 116).

A historical dimension addresses factors that distinguish the content and forms of prejudiced discourse in one country from those "discourses with similar functions in other countries" (Wodak et al 1999: 8). This approach provides historical background "in which discursive 'events' are embedded," and also allows researchers to investigate how a particular type of discourse may change over time.

3. Liberal-conservative polarization in American politics

3.1. The historical dimension

According to a history of the contemporary conservative movement written by Dan Balz and Ronald Brownstein, the trend toward confrontational partisanship between liberal Democrats and conservative Republicans is partially rooted in the cultural and political turmoil of the 1950's and 1960's civil rights movement (1996: 209–210). The civil rights movement and the dramatic increase in voter participation by African Americans after the 1965 Voting Rights Act led to a substantial shift of white voters to the Republican Party. Loss of power in the southern Democratic base was exacerbated by labor unions' demise in the more service-oriented economy as well as the growth of a Republican base in the expanding suburbs (Balz and Brownstein 1996: 210–211).

In the 1970s, conservative cultural and social forces began to coalesce around Ronald Reagan, and Republican strategists recognized that southern cultural conservatives, joined by a growing number of new business interests, would eagerly support Reagan's candidacy. He gave voice to their opposition to abortion, affirmative action, government regulations and government sponsored welfare (Berman 1998: 115–117).

Under the leadership of House member Newt Gingrich, conservative representatives sought to draw from Reagan's popularity, and in 1980 staged a campaign event on the Capitol steps, highlighting the agenda Reagan shared with Republican congressional candidates, such as spending and tax cuts, more funding for defense and increased private investment in job creation (Clift and Brazaitis 1997: 224).

Although Republicans carried the Senate in 1980, they failed to capture the House. Gingrich began to develop new strategies to elect a Republican majority to that chamber using media – particularly TV crews from C-Span then starting to convey speeches on the House floor – to reach a wider American audience (Clift and Brazaitis 1997: 223–228). By 1986, Gingrich had taken over GOPAC, a Republican political action committee, and began to instruct activists on how to create a new conservative majority in the House, including the application of divisive language to characterize Republicans and their Democratic opponents (Clift and Brazaitis 1997: 237–238).

The battle between the two parties was portrayed by Gingrich as a struggle between a "conservative opportunity" society and a "corrupt liberal welfare state" (Clift and Brazaitis 1997: 227). By juxtaposing positive attributes of his own party members against highly negative descriptions of Democrats ("pathetic", "sick", "corrupt", "bizarre", "traitors", Clift and Barzaitis 1997: 238), Gingrich used rhetoric to sharpen the divide between left and right.

Balz and Brownstein (1996) found that Republican antigovernment sentiment increased with the demise of communism in Eastern Europe. Don Fierce of the Republican National Committee said that "Washington has replaced communism as the glue for conservatives.... Washington is financially and morally bankrupt and because of that it is the glue that binds economic and social conservatives. These are people that love their country but hate their federal government. Where is the evil empire? The evil empire is in Washington" (Balz and Brownstein 1996: 15).

The potential of talk radio to channel anti-Washington sentiment first became apparent in 1988, when several stations devoted their programs to discussion of a congressional pay raise. So great was the expression of public outrage from both the left and the right, Congress abandoned its plans to guarantee an automatic increase in pay while a Republican committee developed a program called "Talk Right" in order to cultivate the interest of talk show hosts (Balz and Brownstein 1996: 166–167). A list of hundreds of talk show programs was compiled and the committee began to send issue briefs and lists of potential guests to conservative hosts.

Bill Clinton defeated Bush in fall 1992 by emphasizing economic issues and promising a "third way" between liberalism and conservatism. Although Clinton was elected as a centrist Democrat, his initial moves were to the left. His policy initiatives, including support for gays in the military, a proposed overhaul of the nation's health care system, and an endorsement of stricter gun laws were seen by many voters and conservative talk radio hosts as a radical agenda and more "big government" intrusion into the lives of citizens. Republican strategists used an increasingly confrontational approach to fight initiatives proposed by the President (Balz and Brownstein 1996: 182–184; Clift and Barzaitis 1997: 252–256). A tactic of outright opposition, rather than compromise, would be used to unite various groups against the Democrats' agenda. Conservative talk radio became an important means to energize and mobilize anti-Clinton, anti-Washington sentiment. By using the modern technology of fax machines, Republican leaders communicated on a nearly instantaneous basis with hundreds of talk show hosts. Chuck Greener, the Republican National Committee's communications director, said "[Talk radio listeners] became an audience that we simply had to talk to every day" (Balz and Brownstein 1996: 184). After forty years of Democratic Party control in Congress, Republicans captured both the Senate and the House in the 1994 elections. Ninety percent of the seventy-three Republican freshmen in the 104th Congress were elected by districts that had been represented by Democrats in the previous Congress (Fenno 1997: 23). Republican pollster Fred Steeper assessed the results as a success for the conservative vs. liberal strategy of polarization. "The voters perceived Republicans as representing a conservative direction and Democrats as representing a liberal direction and chose accordingly" (Balz and Brownstein 1996: 56). The contribution conservative talk radio had made in the construction of this perception was not lost on Republican freshmen, who hailed Rush Limbaugh as "the majority maker" (Balz and Brownstein 1996: 198).

3.2. Strategies and structures of polarization

The macro-strategy of polarization is only one in a range of different broad strategies of argumentation used by Limbaugh and Hamblin. I have selected this strategy and related substrategies as objects for research because these particular discourse features are integral to the macro function (theme) of constructing oppositional group identities. Van Dijk (1993) and Wodak et al (1999) have found that a strategy of polarization (positive self-presentation s. a negative presentation of "the other") is characteristic of and prominent in a variety of prejudiced discourse types.

The substrategies of polarization used by Limbaugh and Hamblin are a polarity in tone, the discrediting of other sources of information ("poisoning the well"), an emphasis on ideology over information, scapegoating, stereotyping, the manipulation of key moral concepts, and the use of dehumanizing imagery and enemy imagery.

3.2.1. Polarity in tone

Spoken language is processed much differently than written text. The reader can set the pace and choose the items in which s/he is most interested, and backtrack to reread a word or phrase to understand how it fits into the larger text. It is usually difficult, inconvenient or awkward to ask a speaker to repeat a word or phrase so that we can discern how it fits into the larger context. When we speak face to face, we are also picking up signals from the gestures and facial expressions used by our conversational partner. These cues provide information about the emotional state and intentions of the speaker.

Meaning in spoken text can also be conveyed by using prosodic features such as loudness, intonation, pitch and tone (Tannen 1986: 83). By shifting between two very different prosodic styles, using a negative, harsh and demeaning tone when talking about an outgroup, and a positive, enthusiastic and encouraging quality of voice when speaking about an ingroup, the speaker sends the message that these two groups are polar opposites. One deserves praise, while the other should be scorned. Tannen and Wallat (1993: 61) use the term "interactive frame" to describe the way in which we are able to interpret the intentions of speakers. If someone says "You're crazy!" in a hostile tone, it has a very different meaning than if this is said in a teasing or joking manner. Prosodic features act as paralinguistic cues which provide information about the intention of the speaker.

When Klemperer first listened to a broadcast of a speech by Hitler, he was struck by the intense polarity of Hitler's speech (Klemperer 1970: 63). When addressing his followers, Hitler's tone was rousing, ingratiating, and flattering. The community of Germans (*Volksgemeinschaft*) was destined for greatness (Bork 1970: 59). His "mission" (never just "task" or "obligation") was to save the true Germany from the forces of "decay" and cultural ruin (Bork 1970: 30, 81). As Hitler lashed out at those he called the "enemies of Germany" (never just "political opponents"), his delivery was sneering, scornful and sarcastic. He used language that belittled, disgraced and humiliated his opponents, calling them "thieves", "bloodsuckers", and a "pestilence" (Bork 1970: 29–32).

German linguist Johannes Volmert, who has used both text and film to study the rhetoric of National Socialism, has found that the use of paralinguistic cues by Nazi speakers at public gatherings was one of the distinguishing characteristics of these speech events (1995: 138). The use of tone, intonation, accentuation, pauses, etc. functioned to heighten the emotional intensity of these gatherings. According to Bork (1995: 29), the purpose of such emotionally charged propaganda is to set loose an unrestrained psychological attack on opponents through defamation, ridicule, and hate.

Limbaugh claims he is the "most polite talk show host in America" (1993a: 302) and a "harmless little fuzzball" (1993a: 22) who presents his views "with the utmost responsibility" (1993a: 63). Although he uses the screening process, the cut-off button and convenient commercial breaks to limit airtime given to callers, Limbaugh is generally polite when speaking directly with those who identify themselves as liberals. Nonetheless, in monologues and in conversations with conservatives his comments about liberals are derogatory, and he often employs a harsh and derisive tone. This strategy sends his audience an underlying message: "You can count on me to be polite until this liberal caller is off the air."

3.2.2. Poisoning the well

Ehlich (1995: 14–15) explains that fascist and other military dictatorships use violence to maintain power. Fascism is more complex, however, because it also seeks to cultivate support from the population to be dominated. The media play a critical role in spreading the ideology of fascism, which depends upon broad public participation (Ehlich 1995: 20). In order to inflate his own credibility in the minds of his listeners and to undermine information at odds with his viewpoint, the propagandist may ridicule other sources of information and link these to an "enemy". The propagandist uses derisive, anti-intellectual comments to subvert prominent critics and reinforce his position as a "man of the people".

In communist East Germany, radio programs and newspapers produced in the West were derided as tools of capitalism.[5] Lenin had taught that the primary role of the communist press was to guard against capitalism and to maintain rigid opposition to capitalist ideology.[6]

In his infamous Nazi manifesto *Mein Kampf*, Hitler called the respected *Frankfurter Zeitung* and *Berliner Tageblatt* the "intellectuals' press" or "Jewish press" and sneeringly referred to the readers of such papers as "so-called educated circles" (Bork 1970: 32). One Nazi slogan, that would eventually be displayed in classrooms, was *"Wenn der Jude ... schreibt, lügt er"* [Whenever the Jew writes, he lies] (Klemperer 1970: 37). When academics criticized him, Hitler dismissed their objections as the "miserable cowardice of our so-called intellectuals" (Bork 1970: 31).

On conservative talk show programs, the mainstream media are repeatedly characterized as "the liberal media". Limbaugh (1994f: 3) says that the mainstream media is a "superhighway of B.S." that has "spewed forth a morass of misspeak"[7] on a daily basis. He has written that American journalists "toe the liberal Democratic party line... under the guise of objectivity" and that America is "under assault "by liberals (1993d: 10) and "willing accomplices in the press" (1995c: 3). Limbaugh labeled prominent journalist William Schneider one of the "commie pinkos in the liberal media" (1996c) and said there is "literally no separation between liberal politics and the national press" (1995d).

Ken Hamblin has called *ABC News* part of the "left-wing liberal press" (1996c) and has claimed that "lies and deception [are] coordinated through every branch of the liberal media" (1996c). Both Limbaugh and Hamblin ridicule the *Atlanta Journal and Constitution* as the "Atlanta Urinal and Constipation" (Limbaugh undated; Hamblin 1996c). Limbaugh likens press scrutiny of conservatives to anal examinations[8] and "hit pieces" (1995f). He has mocked intellectuals as "fuzzy-headed academicians", "sandal-clad theoreticians" and "nearsighted pointy heads" (1994a: 147).

In contrast, Limbaugh lauds his own program as the "Turnpike of Truth" (1994k) and seeks to enhance his own credibility by repeatedly asserting that he is engaged in "the daily, relentless, unstoppable pursuit of the truth" (1995h). He is the "Doctor of Democracy" (1994a: 8) and "America's Truth Detector" (1995e).

The word combination exemplified above is not a new phenomenon. Linguist Willi Minnerup, who has studied changes in the language of the German press in 1933 after the Nazis took over power, cites examples from the newspaper *Germania* that reveal the growing influence of the dictatorship. The differentiation between shades on the political spectrum diminished, and writers would combine "liberal" and "socialist" in phrases such as "*liberal-sozialistischen Gedanken*" [liberal socialist thoughts] or "*liberal-sozialistischen Ungeist*" [liberal socialist demon] (Minnerup 1995: 221). Volmert, who found that the doubling of attributive adjectives ("Jewish marxist agitation") was a common feature in Nazi rhetoric, calls this linguistic structure "lexical fusion" (1995: 143).

By describing the mainstream media as the tool of an agenda that is simultaneously liberal, socialist, and communist, Limbaugh and

Hamblin categorize both liberals and the press as members of a radical, threatening outgroup.

3.2.3. Ideology over information

Romanian linguist Liviu Papadima, who has studied the features and structural traits of "Wooden Language", writes that as natural language evolves into totalitarian language, people "speak 'otherwise' than they used to. ...Totalitarian regimes tolerate only one type of political discourse, which is grounded in a uniquely accepted ideology [that] tends to rule out any counter-alternative..." (1995: 54).

Truth is defined through the language of opinion, based on the ideology and evaluative beliefs of the group (van Dijk 1998: 26–30). The propagandist will take a position of raw advocacy. The viewpoint of the opposition has no merit, period.

A propaganda organ concentrates all of its features on political education. The East German Ministry of Propaganda held that the citizenry of the state was *"erziehungsbedürftig"* [in need of patient instruction in ideology] (Richert et al 1958: 78). Language was seen as a tool to raise socialist consciousness. All coverage in the communist press, whether of current events, art, sports or science, pointedly highlighted the benefits of the party ideology.

Both Limbaugh and Hamblin stress that they welcome opposing opinions. By encouraging liberals to call in and by debating with them in a polite manner and tone, Limbaugh and Hamblin use the strategy of positive self-presentation ("we conservatives are polite"). During the post-call period intensely negative and derogatory characterizations of outgroup members may be used. This "we-discourse" reinforces ingroup identity and ideology and frames outgroup behavior and ideology as an unacceptable, or even repugnant, alternative.

Although Limbaugh has done a few spoofs on the excesses of the far right, both he and Hamblin use most components of their programs (interviews, monologues, call-in segments, and humorous pieces) to showcase conservative ideology or to attack liberalism. They argue that the liberal viewpoint has no merit, period.

3.2.4. Scapegoating

All groups are made up of complex individuals and competing factions. To give this diverse following a unifying goal, the propagandist offers a narrowed orientation and a common enemy, the scapegoat.

By presenting a scapegoat, the propagandist provides a focus and an outlet for frustrations and anger. What is whole is divided in half and society is polarized into opposing camps of "evil" and "good". Nazi propagandists called this the "black-white technique" of leadership.[9] The scapegoat is made to carry the burden for all social, economic, and cultural ills, even contradictory ones. In the Nazi era, Jews were blamed for being "capitalist" as well as "communist" (Bork 1970: 39).

On conservative talk radio the scapegoat of choice is "the liberal" or "liberal socialist" (Hamblin 1996a: 153) who is allegedly at fault for an array of social, cultural and economic ills. According to Limbaugh (1992), "there are Americans, and then there are liberals." This polarized worldview minimizes the possibility of genuine dialogue. The following exchange is typical of "moral vs. immoral" characterizations used by Limbaugh and his fans:

Mary in Nashville (9/21/95):	By the grace of God, I get to listen to you every day.. and I've had it with these Democrats, they just get on the air and lie and say whatever they want, they're just so completely disingenuous... and I've been taught you don't do these things.
Limbaugh:	That's the basic problem. You and I have morals, we have ethics, and we have honesty. (Limbaugh 1995g)

In this exchange, Limbaugh and Mary both participate in "we-discourse" and define and demarcate perceived differences between the ingroup (conservatives) and outgroup (Democrats/liberals). "They" are liars, out of control and lacking in good upbringing (negative personal and group attributes). "We" are moral, ethical and honest (positive personal and group attributes). To Limbaugh, this is "the basic problem". The world, according to Limbaugh, seems to be divided in two, and the good folks aren't Democrats.

The corollary to scapegoating is a promise made by the propagandist, which goes something like this: "If we rid society of the influence of "these people" (Jews/capitalists/liberals), we can replace our current state of disorder with a version of a better past or an idealized future." Ehlich (1995: 22–23) has found that this "promise of a simpler world" and a "verbally anticipated future" is characteristic of fascist speech.

3.2.5. Stereotyping

Another devastating tactic of negative propaganda is stereotyping, the use of impersonal and derisive images to narrow a concept. This tactic undermines the unique experience and personal judgment of the listener. Varied manifestations of humanity are made uniform. The Nazis sought to create a despicable but generic "Jew" in the minds of the Germans. Simplistic and generalized labels, the tools of stereotyping, enable the propagandist to define the outgroup.

In East Germany, capitalism was portrayed as a corrupt and morally bankrupt system. The capitalist personality was "inhumane" "greedy", "lawless", "barbaric" and "fascist" (Fleischer 1987: 254). The capitalist was the workers' *"Totengräber"* (grave digger).[10]

By repeatedly using evaluative adjectives and adverbs to label liberals as "arrogant"[11], "contemptuous" (1993b: 1), "hysterical" (1994e: 11), "dangerous" (1995c: 3), "lazy" (1995a: 13), "morally bankrupt" (1994c: 15), "namby-pamby" (1994l), "gutless" (1995i) or "whining"[12], Limbaugh has made the word "liberal" derogatory. The phrase "whining liberals" is standard for Limbaugh and Hamblin and some of those who call-in to their programs.

This and other descriptions such as liberal "crybabies" (Limbaugh 1994a: 282) may seem benign. However, they can have a powerful effect. The message is, "I am a mature person with legitimate concerns, but my opponent has an infantile, hapless and irritating personality and is limited to issuing complaints that have no merit."

Hitler understood the power of such characterizations and accused opponents of being "*Jammerlappen*" [whiners or sissies] and "*Schwätzer*" [babblers]. The parliament was a "babbler's club" (Bork 1970: 92).

Utz Maas, a German linguist who has written about language use during the period of Nazi consolidation of power (1933–1938), has documented that the adjective "*jämmerlich*" [implying a wretched, miserable, contemptible personality] was a "stereotypical attribute of devaluation" used by the Nazis during this period (1995: 185). This characterization was not only directed against individuals, but was also used to distance the Nazi party from mainstream political parties and representative bodies.

3.2.6. The manipulation of key moral concepts

A particularly insidious tactic of propaganda is to alter the moral value of key words (Bork 1970: 27). That which social norms had viewed as negative becomes positive, and vice versa. Nazis used words such as "brutal" and "fanatical" in context with virtues such as loyalty and courage ("brutal and courageous", "brutal loyalty", "fanatical loyalty"; Bork 1970: 25). The adjective "*fanatisch*" became very fashionable (Klemperer 1970: 66–71). Empathy and kindheartedness, especially toward any "enemy" (Jews, socialists, homosexuals, etc.), was a sign of weakness. Humane ideals became "*giftige Judenhumanität*" [poisonous Jewish humanitarianism][13] or "loathsome humanitarian morality" (Bork 1970: 24). Intolerance, particularly "fanatical intolerance", was a virtue (Bork 1970: 24). Hitler said the Nazi was "intolerant and pitiless" against those who would "destroy or disintegrate the body-politic (*Volkskörper*)" (Koenigsberg 1975: 23).

Within talk radio culture, there is a tendency in this direction with the use of words such as "tolerance" and "compassion". Those who are "tolerant" may be characterized as moral relativists who are unable to tell right from wrong. Limbaugh (1993a: 184) has written that liberals are "tolerant" of criminal activity. Likewise, the word "compassion" is associated with a "whining", "liberal" personality. Limbaugh (1993a: 183) equated "understanding" the reasons behind the L.A. riot with a liberal "compassion for rage". He has described liberals as "compassion fascists" (1993a: 79) and has accused the press of "liberal compassion-mongering" (1994a: 322). During the health care debate, liberals facilitated the "sobbing" or "whining of America" (1996a).

The devaluation of compassion also serves to undermine one of the foundations for assistance to the poor. If liberal programs are based on compassion, and if compassion is seen as negative and destructive, then there is no longer any moral reason to support these programs. It could seem, in fact, immoral to do so. This strategy allows conservatives to stay on high moral ground (as defined by ingroup opinion) while liberals are portrayed as captives of destructive motivations ("compassion fascists").

When the inherent positive or moral value of words is intentionally twisted, words are drained of their humanizing power. Manipulations of meaning release feelings of hostility and meanness previously held in check by true definitions (Bork 1970: 98–103).

3.2.7. Dehumanizing imagery

Research on contemporary racism and anti-Semitism in Europe demonstrates that dehumanizing imagery rarely is used in public or even semi-public discourse. This may be due to the fact that these social representations are strongly associated with Nazism in the public mind.

The propagandist uses the metaphor, a fundamental mechanism of language change (Miller 1981: 145), to build artificial, negative associations. Metaphors of disease, sickness or filth are used to activate gut-level feelings of revulsion toward the outgroup.

Hitler and Nazi publications said Germany suffered from the *"Verfaulungsprozess der Demokratie"* [decay of democracy] and a "plague of ethical, political, and moral infestation" (Bork 1970: 72). Jews were an "infection," a "pestilence" (Bork 1970: 73), "cancerous" (Blackburn 1985: 146), "poison" (Bork 1970: 72), "parasites" (Blackburn 1985: 140), "tumors" (Bork 1970: 72), "bacilli" (Bork

1970: 73), "vermin" (Bork 1970: 32), "leeches" (Bork 1970: 72), and "bacteria" (Bork 1970: 73). Marxism was a "racial tuberculosis" (Bork 1970: 71). Hitler used terms such as *"parliamentarische Raupen"* [parliamentary maggots] and likened Jews to "maggots" (Bork 1970: 49). The opposition was "infested" with bolshevism (Bork 1970: 72) and Jews were "worse than the black plague itself" (Klemperer 1970: 191). The body of the German people (*Volkskörper*) was being "poisoned" or "devoured" by "malignant ulcers" (Bork 1970: 72).

From these graphic images of disease and contamination, it was only a short linguistic step to proclaim the need to "cleanse" society and "exterminate" the "pest" (Bork 1970: 98). Bork (1970: 28) notes that the perversion of these terms by the Nazis and the frequency with which they were used was unprecedented in the history of the German language.

This is a misuse of language that contains a terrible potential. It is for this reason that "provocative talk" in vogue on talk radio should not be dismissed. While Limbaugh's use of this imagery is light-handed compared to others such as Hamblin, Limbaugh may have played a role in introducing and popularizing this strategy.

Limbaugh likens liberalism to a "disease" or "addiction" (1994a: 87) and has called liberals "maggot-infested, dope-smoking peace pansies" (1993a: 31), "maggot-infested... environmental wackos" and "maggot-infested FM types" (1993a: 161). He writes that "feminism [has] infested American life" (1993a: 143) and that liberals "exert a poisonous influence on American life" (1994b: 2). Liberals are "Utopian enemies" (1993a: 268) and "parasites"[14]; they have an "insidious nature" (1993a: 268) and "lethal" intent (1995c: 3).

In the *Limbaugh Letter*, he blames liberals for "cultural filth foisted on the public in the name of 'tolerance' and 'compassion'" and writes that society is wallowing in "ugly sewage" from liberal prescriptions (1994g: 13). Urban criminals are the "predator class" (Limbaugh 1993b: 1); their violent acts are "the swirling sewage of human degradation" (1993b: 1). America is caught in a "downward spiral of decay", and daytime TV is a "modern museum of decay" (1993b: 12).

Limbaugh has dropped some of these expressions and toned down his rhetoric over the years, which may be why some long-time listeners complain that he has lost his "passion". Ken Hamblin has stepped in to fill the void. Hamblin, who uses a far more intense and agitated style than Limbaugh, likens liberalism to cancer.[15] One of his standard phrases is "egg-sucking dog liberals" (1996a: 161). He has also said that, in reaction to a political controversy, Democrats "swarm like flies at a malfunctioning septic tank" (2002). Ghetto ("dark town", 1996a: 87) blacks breed "like rats" and "cockroaches" (1996b). "Liberal zookeepers" oversee welfare and recipients are "welfare pets" who are like "pampered beasts" or "bear[s] foraging … in a garbage dump" (2003). A truck carrying illegal immigrants is a "cockroach transport" (1996d). Liberals are like a "festering sore" (1996d) and a breaking story on a Housing and Urban Development scandal "is seeping out like pus from an infected wound" (Hamblin undated).

These descriptions seem to call out for defense against invasive, diseased elements (liberals, the black underclass, immigrants, and the government).

3.2.8. Our government, the "enemy"

One of the maxims of conservative ideology is that "big government" and liberalism go hand in hand. On conservative talk radio, the federal government is portrayed as a tool of liberals, and as a menacing force in its own right. Those who serve in government have been characterized as enthusiastic servants, or even prostitutes, of liberalism.

Limbaugh (1995d) says "the federal government has got their employees pimping their programs". Hamblin (1996a: 104) calls liberal congressional representatives from urban areas "poverty pimp government parasites". The portrayal of public servants as pimps and parasites serves to heighten the public's fear of exploitation by an unsavory government.

An additional image sure to conjure up fear of government is that of the Nazi. Limbaugh argues that he has used labels such as "feminazi" to simply "embellish" his language (*Playboy* Interview 1993: 69). The Nazi image is that of a cold, stiff, mechanical and robotic entity. It also represents one of the most inhumane and terrifying forces in history, and it is being used to portray the federal government as an enemy. By associating liberalism with fascism as well as communism, Limbaugh makes the outgroup ideology seem doubly threatening. In February 1995, Limbaugh labeled federal employees who regulate advertising the "high-fat Gestapo" and the "anti-smoking Gestapo" (1995b: 11). But he has also used government-as-Nazi imagery in a far more serious vein.

On his October 14, 1996 program, Limbaugh replayed a segment he had used twice during the government shutdown in November 1995. Using an ominous tone, lacking either humor or irony, he likens Democratic leaders and Clinton appointees to the Nazi propagandist Joseph Goebbels and accuses a "tidal wave of liberals, bureaucrats and the media" of spreading the "Big Lie" (Limbaugh (1995j).

3.3. Beyond conservative talk radio: Strategies of polarization in other public and semi-public realms

In their research on national identity, Wodak et al (1999) have found that strategies and topics used at the semi-public level of group discussion reflected those used at the public level (in their project, speeches by political representatives). Strategies used by individual in-group discussions resembled those used by the politicians they favored (Wodak et al 1999: 202). Whether a similar recontextualization of polarizing strategies is evident in American conservative political talk radio lies beyond the scope of this chapter. Yet, these strategies and their linguistic realizations *are* being used in other public and semi-public settings.

In 1996, Senator Frank Murkowski (R-Alaska) wrote a letter to the *Washington Post* in which he opposed federal tax abatement for "bloodsucking" D.C. citizens. In the 1996 presidential primary, Pat Buchanan complained of a "bloody assault" against the GOP in a fund-raising letter (Pat's peeves 1996). In two separate incidents in the 104th Congress, Democratic representatives attacked fellow members with labels such as "crybaby" and "fascist" (Gugliotta 1996). In 1998, Michigan Democratic gubernatorial candidate Geoff Fieger called his opponent "a bag of pus" and "a sniveling weasel" (Will 1998). Hispanic immigrants were called "parasites" by protesters at a public meeting in Arkansas (Romano 1998). In an 1998 editorial, conservative Gina Dalfonzo of the Family Research Council decried a "culture of tolerance" as one in which "there is no right or wrong" (Dalfonzo 1998). This would seem to imply that intolerance and morality go hand-in-hand.

The government-as-Nazi image entered the mainstream when it was picked up by the National Rifle Association, which described Bureau of Alcohol, Tobacco and Firearms agents as "jack-booted government thugs" in a fund-raising letter in 1995 (Edsall 1996). Later that year, former Rep. Bill Emerson said the National Biological Survey to protect endangered species would create a "militant eco-Gestapo force" (Matthews 1995) and Republican representative Tom DeLay likened the Environmental Protection Agency to a "Gestapo" (*Washington Post* Editorial 1995). Paul Roberts, a syndicated columnist, described parenthood as a "sitting duck" for an imminent "blitzkrieg" carried out by powerful social service bureaucracies endowed with "Gestapo-like" power (Roberts 1996). Senate Majority Leader Trent Lott recently sent out a fund-raising letter in which addressees were asked to "support the Republican National Committee in [its] campaign to, once and for all, end the IRS's [Internal Revenue Service's] 'reign of terror'" (*Washington Post* Editorial 2000).

4. Conclusion

Bork (1970: 98) warns that verbal abuse radicalizes the spiritual and political climate. This, in turn, can radicalize the ethical climate and break down psychological restraints on behavior. Propagandistic speech may harden the heart and unleash feelings of anger and aggression.

But when callers suggest that Limbaugh is a propagandist, his response to Ken from Great Falls, Montana (7/31/96) is typical:

Ken: I understand exactly what you do. You do propaganda.
Limbaugh: You don't want to talk to me about the issues, you want to talk to
                me about how I do what I do, and I'm not going to debate you on
                that... . (Limbaugh 1996b)

Limbaugh considers his manner of expression to be off limits. When
it comes to language, he wants to have it both ways. One of
Limbaugh's listed "undeniable truths" is that "words mean things"
(1994d: 16), and he has written that we should be responsible for the
consequences of our words (1994a: 238–239). When his words are
criticized, he takes refuge in the argument that he is just an enter-
tainer (*Playboy* Interview 1993: 69).

I have not sought to determine the degree to which either Limbaugh or Hamblin consciously has decided to use strategies of polarization for the construction of group identities. It is clear, however,
that the macrofunctional theme of socially and culturally based con-
servative-liberal group differences had become central to the political
strategy of the Republican Party in the early 1990s, and that the
party's leadership regularly contacted conservative talk radio hosts.
Limbaugh and Hamblin used polarizing strategies and structures on
their talk radio programs in the 1992–1996 time frame, and these
strategies contributed to the construction of a positive conservative
ingroup identity and a negative liberal outgroup identity. Some of the
polarizing discourse strategies and structures used by Limbaugh and
Hamblin have surfaced subsequently in other social and political domains[16].

Papadima (1995: 44) writes that

> what could be considered manifestations of "wooden language" in totalitar-
> ian regimes and what they would be in democratic ones... concern its forms
> and degree of institutionalization and penetration.... "Wooden language" is
> implied in the tendency to modify the forms of social and even inter-per-
> sonal interactions, and finally human thought and behavior.

As we enter an unprecedented age of information, some may dis-
miss propagandistic speech as nothing more than "provocative talk".
But the critical discourse analysis of this data suggests that the "ten-

dency to modify human thought and behavior" seems to be at work in the discourses of Limbaugh and Hamblin.

Notes

1. Rush Limbaugh, quoted in James Coates and Michael Dornin (1995) War of Words: Culprits, Technology and Talk? Internet Booms with Bias; Radio, Callers Deny Role. *Philadelphia Daily News*, 25 April 1995. Cited in Cappella et al (1996: 43).
2. While polarizing tactics have been used by the far left and far right in Europe, most of the extant research has focused on the use of these strategies by the extreme Right, particularly the Nazis. Most studies on the language of communism have focused on the vocabulary used by communist party officials. Since the demise of European communist regimes, scholars from Europe's eastern half have been able to examine the wider spectrum of public and semi-public propagandistic discourses by the Left; their findings are included as space and relevance allows. Unless otherwise noted, all translations here are my own.
3. Ponsonby, Arthur (1928), *Falsehood in War-Time: Containing an Assortment of Lies Circulated Throughout the Nations During the Great War.*
4. See the list of data sources for the dates and types of material.
5. *Unsere Presse- die schärfste Waffe der Partei. Referate und Diskussionsrede auf der Pressekonferenz der Parteivorstandes der SED vom 9.–10. Februar 1950 in Berlin.* Schriftenreihe für den Parteiarbeiter, Heft 3. Berlin: Dietz Verlag. Quoted in Richert et al (1958: 80).
6. W. I. Lenin, Die Organisierung des Wettbewerbs, in: Die nächsten Aufgaben der Sowjetmacht, in: *Lenin, Ausgewählte Werke* (Anm. I–118), II, 377. Cited in Richert et al (1958: 82).
7. Limbaugh (1995d) uses the phrase "morass of misspeak" in a commercial for one of his books.
8. Limbaugh (1994i: 7) used the expression "media anal".
9. Karl Kindt, Der Führer spricht. In *Die Neue Literatur 1934* (The Führer speaks. In *New Literature 1934*) Vol. 1, 4. Quoted in Bork (1970: 34–35).
10. Hans H. Reich (1968) *Sprache und Politik: Untersuchung zu Wortschatz und Wortwahl des offiziellen Sprachgebrauchs in der DDR.* Munich, 286. Quoted in Gudorf (1981: 27).
11. Limbaugh (1993b: 1) refers to liberals as a "militant bunch of arrogant elites".
12. Limbaugh (1994k) used the phrase "namby-pamby whining little left-wingers".
13. Klemperer (1970: 155) referring to the language of Rosenberg, Hitler and Goebbels.
14. Limbaugh (1993e) called liberals "parasites" three times within five minutes.

15. Hamblin (1996: 153) puts "liberalism first and cancer second when ranking the scourges that threaten humanity".
16. In the response to Bill Clinton's 2000 State of the Union Address, Republican Senator Bill Frist commented on president's health care proposals by repeating Rush Limbaugh's words heard on his radio-program the night before: "If David Letterman had lived in Canada, he'd still be waiting for his heart surgery". The direction of this channel is not important – the words fluctuate both ways. I am grateful to Mirjana Dedaić for alerting me to this instance.

Data source: Articles, newsletters and reports

Cappella, Joseph N., Joseph Turow, and Kathleen Hall Jamieson (directors)
    1996   *Call-inPolitical Talk Radio: Background, Content, Audiences, Por-trayal in Mainstream Media.* Annenberg Public Policy Center Re-port Series, n. 5. Philadelphia: Annenberg Public Policy Center.

Dalfonzo, Gina
    1998   Your kids are watching you. *Frederick (Md.) News-Post*, 13 August 1998.

WP Editorial
    1995   Riders from hell. *Washington Post*, 25 October 1995.

    2000   Reign of terror. *Washington Post,* 7 February 2000.

Edsall, Thomas B.
    1996   Democrats see future in "militant centrism". *Washington Post*, 4 No-vember 1996.

Frangicetto, Tom (ed.)
    1995–1997   *The Rush Watch.* Langhorne, PA: Frangicetto, Tom. Vol.1–3, 24 July 1995 – February 1997.

Gugliotta, Guy
    1996   Capital notebook: Taking decorum down. *Washington Post*, 2 Janu-ary 1996.

Hamblin, Ken
    1995   *Hamblin Radio Program.* Denver: American View, 20 December 1995. Broadcast on WFMD, Frederick, Md.

1996a   *Pick a Better Country: An Unassuming Colored Guy Speaks His Mind About America.* New York: Simon and Schuster.

1996b   *Hamblin Radio Program* (WFMD: 3 January 1996).

1996c   *Hamblin Radio Program.* Denver: American View, 4 February 1996). Broadcast on WFMD, Frederick, Md.

1996d   *Hamblin Radio Program* (WFMD: 26 May 1996).

2002   Reading a Lott into it. *The Denver Post*, 15 December 2002.

2003   "Don't feed the blacks", www.hamblin.com/articles/feed.html, 18 February 2003.

Undated   *Hamblin Radio Program* (WFMD).

Limbaugh, Rush
1992   *The Rush Limbaugh Radio Program* (WWDB: 17 May 1992).

1993a   *The Way Things Ought To Be.* New York: Pocket Books.

1993b   The left was wrong. *Limbaugh Letter* 1 (May 1993), 11–12.

1993c   The battle for American schools. *Limbaugh Letter* 1 (September 1993), 11–12.

1993d   According to me: Facts are "lies", lies are "facts". *Limbaugh Letter* (October 1993), 10.

1993e   *The Rush Limbaugh Radio Program* (WFMD: 14 June 1993).

1994a   *See, I Told You So.* New York: Pocket Books.
1994b   Rush Review: *Devaluing America*, by Bill Bennett. *Limbaugh Letter* (February 1994), 2.
1994c   The Clinton administration and sex. *Limbaugh Letter* 3–4 (March 1994), 15.

1994d   35 new undeniable truths. *Limbaugh Letter* (March 1994), 16.

1994e   Religious bigotry. *Limbaugh Letter* (Aug. 1994), 11.

1994f   The superhighway of B.S. *Limbaugh Letter* 3–4 (September 1994), 16.

1994g   Rush Review: The things that matter most, by Cal Thomas. *Limbaugh Letter* (September 1994), 13.

1994h   Are you surly? *Limbaugh Letter* (December 1994), 9.

1994i   In conversation with myself. *Limbaugh Letter* (December 1994), 6–8.

1994j   *Limbaugh TV Show* (July 14, 1994). Quoted in Frangicetto (1), 24 July 1995: 3.

1994k   *The Rush Limbaugh Radio Program* (WWDB: July 26, 1994).

1994l   Limbaugh, *Rush Limbaugh TV Show* (UPN 57/ "Philly 57", 14 July 1994). Quoted in Frangicetto (1), 24 July 1995: 3.

1995a   How to deal with a liberal teacher. *Limbaugh Letter* (February 1995): 13.

1995b   Food Gestapo, *Limbaugh Letter* (February 1995): 11.

1995c   Why liberals undermine the will of the people. *Limbaugh Letter* (March 1995): 3–4, 16.

1995d   *The Rush Limbaugh Radio Program* (New York: Jacor Broadcasting, 7 March 1995). Broadcast on WWDB Philadelphia.

1995e   *The Rush Limbaugh Radio Program*, (WWDB: 24 June 1995). Quoted in Frangicetto (1), 9 October 1995: 2.

1995f   *The Rush Limbaugh Radio Program* (WWDB: 9 August 1995). Quoted in Frangicetto (1), 28 August 1995: 1.

1995g   *The Rush Limbaugh Radio Program* (WWDB: 21 September 1995). Quoted in Frangicetto (2), 20 May 1996: 1.

1995h   *Limbaugh Radio Program* (WWDB: 11 October 1995). Quoted in Frangicetto (1), 9 October 1995: 1.

1995i   *Limbaugh Radio Program* (15 November 1995). Quoted in Frangicetto (2), March 1996: 5.

1995j   *The Rush Limbaugh Radio Program* (New York: Jacor Broadcasting, 21 November 1995). Broadcast on WWDB Philadelphia.

1996a   *The Rush Limbaugh Radio Program* (25 April 1996). Quoted in Frangicetto (2), 22 April 1996: 3.

1996b   *The Rush Limbaugh Radio Program* (WWDB: 31 July 1996). Quoted in Frangicetto (2), 5 and 12 August 1996: 3.

1996c   *The Rush Limbaugh Radio Program* (WWDB: 7 October 1996).

Undated   *The Rush Limbaugh Radio Program* (WFMD).

Matthews, Jessica
1995   Democracy without the facts. *Washington Post*, 16 May 1995.

Murkowski, Frank
1996   Monaco on the Potomac. *Washington Post*, 22 September 1996.

Pat's peeves
1996   Pat's peeves: Fund-raising letters reveal Buchanan's appeal to fears. *Frederick (Md.) News-Post*, 26 February 1996.

Playboy Interview
1993   Playboy interview: Rush Limbaugh. *Playboy* (December 1993), 59–84.

Roberts, Paul
1996   Another government assault on the family. *Frederick (Md.) News-Post*, 9 May 1996.

Romano, Lois
1998   A small town's transformation. *Washington Post*, 24 March 1998.

Will, George
1998   Michigan crude. *Washington Post*, 30 August 1998.

References

Balz, Dan, and Ronald Brownstein
1996   *Storming the Gates: Protest Politics and the Republican Revival.* Boston: Little, Brown and Company.

Bell, Allan, and Peter Garrett
1998   *Approaches to Media Discourse.* London/Malden: Blackwell.

60   *Kathryn Ruud*

Berman, William C.
1998   *America's Right Turn: From Nixon to Clinton.* Baltimore/London: The Johns Hopkins University Press.

Blackburn, Gilmer W.
1985   *Education in the Third Reich: Race and History in Nazi Textbooks.* Albany: State University of New York Press.

Bork, Siegfried
1970   *Missbrauch der Sprache: Tendenzen nationalsozialistischer Sprachregelung.* Bern/München: Francke Verlag.

Brekle, Herbert E.
1989   War with words. In: Wodak, Ruth (ed.), *Language, Power, and Ideology: Studies in Political Discourse.* Amsterdam/Philadelphia: John Benjamins, 81–91.

Clift, Eleanor, and Tom Brazaitis
1997   *War Without Bloodshed: The Art of Politics.* New York: Touchstone.

Ehlich, Konrad
1995   Über den Faschismus sprechen– Analyse und Diskurs. In: Ehlich, Konrad (ed.), *Sprache im Faschismus*, third edition. Frankfurt: Suhrkamp, 7–34.

Fenno, Richard F. Jr.
1997   *Learning to Govern: An Institutional View of the 104th Congress.* Washington D. C.: The Brookings Institution.

Fleischer, Wolfgang (ed.)
1987   *Wortschatz der deutschen Sprache in der DDR: Fragen seinesAufbaus und seiner Verwendungsweise.* Leipzig: Leipzig Bibliographisches Institut.

Fowler, Roger
1991   *Language in the News: Discourse and Ideology in the Press.* London/New York: Routledge.

Gudorf, Odilo
1981   *Sprache als Politik: Untersuchung zur Öffentlichen Sprache und Kommunikationsstruktur in der DDR.* Cologne: Wissenschaft und Politik.

Klemperer, Victor
1970   *LTI: Notizbuch eines Philologen.* Third edition. Darmstadt: Joseph Melzer Verlag.

Koenigsberg, Richard A.
1975   *Hitler's Ideology: A Study in Psychoanalytic Sociology.* New York: The Library of Social Science.

Maas, Utz
1995   Sprache im Nationalsozialismus. Analyse einer Rede eines Studentenfunktionärs. In: Ehlich, Konrad (ed.), *Sprache im Faschismus*, third edition. Frankfurt: Suhrkamp, 162–197.

Miller, George A.
1981   *Language and Speech.* San Francisco: W. H. Freeman and Co.

Minnerup, Willi
1995   Pressesprache und Machtergreifung am Beispiel der Berliner *Germania.* In: Ehlich, Konrad (ed.), *Sprache im Faschismus*, third edition. Frankfurt: Suhrkamp, 198–236.

Papadima, Liviu
1995   La langue de bois: An epistemological metaphor about past and future. In: Wodak, Ruth, and Fritz Peter Kirsch (eds.), *Totalitäre Sprache– Langue de bois– Language of Dictatorship.* Vienna: Passagen Verlag, 41–55.

Richert, Ernst, Carola Stern, and Peter Dietrich
1958   *Agitation und Propaganda: Das System der publizistischen Massenführung in der Sowjetzone.* Schriften des Instituts für politische Wissenschaft (Freie Universität u. Deutsche Hochschule für Politik) Band 10. Berlin: Verlag Franz Vahlen GmbH.

Tannen, Deborah
1986   *That's Not What I Meant!: How Conversational Style Makes or Breaks Relationships.* New York: Ballantine Books.

Tannen, Deborah, and Cynthia Wallat
1993   Interactive frames and knowledge schemas in interaction. In: Tannen, Deborah (ed.), *Framing in Discourse.* Oxford: Oxford University Press, 57–74.

van Dijk, Teun A.
1990   Discourse and Society: a new journal for a new research focus. *Discourse and Society* 1(1), 11.

1993   *Elite Discourse and Racism.* Newbury Park/London/New Delhi: Sage.

1998   Opinions and ideologies in the press. In: Bell, Allan, and Peter Garrett (eds.), *Approaches to Media Discourse.* London/Malden: Blackwell.

Volmert, Johannes
1995   Politische Rhetorik des Nationalsozialismus. In: Ehlich, Konrad (ed.), *Sprache im Faschismus*, third edition. Frankfurt: Suhrkamp, 137–161.

Wodak, Ruth
1995   Introduction. In: Wodak, Ruth, and Fritz Peter Kirsch (eds.), *Totalitäre Sprache– Langue de bois– Language of Dictatorship.* Vienna: Passagen Verlag.

1996   The genesis of racist discourse in Austria since 1989. In: Caldas-Coulthard, Carmen Rosa, and Malcolm Coulthard (eds.), *Texts and Practices: Readings in Critical Discourse Analysis.* London and New York: Routledge, 107–128.

Wodak, Ruth, Rudolf de Cillia, Martin Reisigl, and Karin Liebhart
1999   *The Discursive Construction of National Identity*, translated by Angelika Hirsch and Richard Mitten. Edinburgh: Edinburgh University Press.

Wodak, Ruth, and Fritz Peter Kirsch (eds.)
1995   *Totalitäre Sprache– Langue de bois– Language of Dictatorship.* Vienna: Passagen Verlag.

Wodak, Ruth, Peter Novak, Johanna Pelikan, Helmut Gruber, Rudolf De Cillia, and Richard Mitten
1990   *"Wir sind alle unschuldige Täter". Diskurs-historische Studie zum Nachkriegsantisemitismus.* Frankfurt am Main: Suhrkamp.

Threat or business as usual?
A multimodal, intertextual analysis of a political statement

Suzanne Wong Scollon

1. Introduction: Modernization, Cold War or China Threat

Fighting words do not start wars unless positioned in appropriate ways by authoritative figures, both political and journalistic. Missile firing can be framed as routine testing or attack depending on who has an interest in evoking the language of war. In covering military maneuvers, journalists adopt ideological stances toward the news stories they report through their choice of verbs of saying, their sequencing of questions and answers, and contextualization cues such as color, font and headline size. In coverage of one press conference during the Taiwan missile crisis that preceded the Taiwanese presidential elections of 1996 – at which Chinese Foreign Minister Qian Qichen spoke – journalists positioned themselves ideologically within three orders of discourse (Foucault 1976).

In this chapter I use intertextual and interdiscursive analysis (explicated in Fairclough 1992) to determine what was said by Foreign Minister Qian and examine how journalists framed their coverage within three distinct orders of discourse, producing ideological stances towards the news stories they report. I analyze verbs of saying which are used in quotation, the relationships among non-verbal contextualizations of a Chinese foreign minister, the framing of the news conference as a media event, and the subsequent editing and media production procedures through which window the original utterance is broadcast. Throughout, I extend Gumperz' (1982) notion of contextualization cues to encompass visual components of print and television reportage.

The problem I will address is how presuppositions underlying each order of discourse came to be embedded in the reporting of journalists covering the event. In particular, the ideology of what has been called the libertarian press (Siebert, Peterson and Schramm 1956) is rather opaque because it is shared by most citizens of Western or "modern democratic" states. Thus, most readers of this volume would probably agree that China was indeed threatening Taiwan when Qian Qichen uttered these words on March 11, 1996:

> It is commonplace that U.S. naval ships operate on the high seas. But it would be ridiculous for some people to call openly for the intervention by the Seventh Fleet of the United States on this issue. And they even go so far as to call for the defense of Taiwan. I think these people must have forgotten the fact that Taiwan is a part of Chinese territory; it's not a protectorate of the United States.

That China was, by threatening Taiwan, merely carrying out one of the four modernizations called for by Deng Xiaoping seems absurd. Yet, most observers of China would find it entirely believable that *Xinhua* – the New China Press Agency – would cast it in this vein, in accordance with China's official political ideology.

It may be difficult for many readers to perceive, then, that characterizing Foreign Minister Qian's statement as a warning or threat was shaped in any way by ideology. Such an interpretation seems, to a Western mind steeped in democratic culture, entirely reasonable. Aside from sharing the political ideology that China was threatening Taiwan, such reporters also hold the free press ideology that journalists ought to abide by standards of objectivity in reporting. But, there are at least two types of journalistic objectivity (Scollon and Scollon n.d.) operating here. One has to do with the choice of verbs of saying made by reporters to quote political leaders whether directly or indirectly. Another has to do with the number of times opposing sides are mentioned in a particular report. Because of these two forms of objectivity, an apparent paradox arises wherein representatives of the free press evince sympathy with the U.S. through their choice of verbs, while simultaneously maintaining impartiality by carefully giving equal coverage to China.

I suggest that this second type of objectivity arises from the history of broadcasting in the United States and elsewhere, although space permits no more than a bit of historical reflection to lend support to this hypothesis. I argue that the Western press paradoxically purports to be objective although it has pursued nationalistic, colonial, militaristic, commercial interests since the inception of the modern press during the Enlightenment (Scollon and Scollon n.d.).

Contrary to the liberal ideology of the free press, I demonstrate through a multimodal, intertextual analysis of the press conference statement cited above, that journalists with opposing political ideologies shared the journalistic ideology of neutral statement, while the liberal free press favored strongly evaluative reportage that positioned themselves ideologically while maintaining an impartial stance. That is, reporters from the PRC as well as Taiwan used the same style, reporting verbatim with little evaluation what the Chinese Foreign Minister said although they obviously differ in political ideology. The systemic ideological positioning by international media runs contrary to the assumptions and self-perceptions of the liberal free press. Whether a statement is perceived as threatening or ordinary depends on interpenetrating layers of framing by journalists and politicians.

Ideological framing of Foreign Minister Qian's statement can be viewed using Fairclough's notions of intertextuality and interdiscursivity (1992). His approach draws on Bakhtin, Foucault and Marx. I will also introduce Gumperz' notion of contextualization cues and extend it to include three levels of journalistic framing. In incorporating these two approaches, I work within the framework of mediated discourse analysis (R. Scollon 1998, 2001).

I then introduce the orders of discourse represented by the many journalists whose reports were carried in the Hong Kong media. I show how journalistic ideologies are embedded within national and global ideologies of utilitarian discourse (Scollon and Scollon 2001).

I present concrete data from newspaper and television reports to show how Qian's statement was contextualized by reporters from differing orders of discourse with their associated ideologies.

2. Political and journalistic ideologies

According to Luke (1991), "the term IDEOLOGY refers to systems of ideas, beliefs, practices and representations which operate in the interests of an identifiable social class or cultural group". He cautions that there is no agreement among social scientists about what ideology is, how it works in the modern state, or how it relates to language and discourse. Hawkes (1996) assumes a link between political and journalistic ideology, arguing that mass media legitimize the hegemony of the dominant group.

I take a modified Marxian view of ideology developed further by Voloshinov and Bakhtin who posit(s), besides the addressee, a *superaddressee* for every utterance, an ideal third party, "whose absolutely just responsive understanding is presumed, either in some metaphysical distance or in some distant historical time" (1986: 126). He asserts that this superaddressee assumes various ideological expressions depending on sociohistorical context, including "dispassionate human conscience, the people, the court of history, science, and so forth" (1986: 126). That is, the authority under which one pronounces depends on time, place and affiliation.

Bakhtin points out that, for Marx, only thought articulated in the word with the voice becomes a real thought for another person. Thus, there is a materialist basis for the dialogic relations set up by real utterance. In analyzing text, then, whether uttered in one's presence or derived from newspaper, radio, or television, the analyst needs to consider who had a hand or voice in its production, as well as the ideological context or order of discourse (Foucault 1976) within which an utterance was produced.

For Foucault, theory and practice become intertwined in discursive practices through which orders of discourse are constituted. Discursive practices do not simply produce discourse but are "embodied in technical processes, in institutions, in patterns for general behavior, in forms for transmission and diffusion, and in pedagogical forms which, at once, impose and maintain them. Finally, they possess specific modes of transformation" (Foucault 1977: 200). This transformation is linked to forms of production, social relationships, political institutions. Discursive practices are not only results but effective agents of choice and exclusion that are anonymous and polymorphous.

Critical discourse analysts such as Foucault, Wodak and Caldas-Coulthard are linguists who take discourse as social practice, showing how discourse constitutes social identities and relationships, treating social issues such as neoliberalism, racism and sexism as arising from historically constituted orders of discourse. They look at dialectical relationships in the three domains of media representation, interpersonal relations, and the construction of personal and social identities, taking a historical approach.

In this study I distinguish between political ideology and the liberal ideology of the free press. The former contrasts, for example, socialist with capitalist states. The latter relates to what we call the Utilitarian Discourse System, with its values of progress, individual freedom and equality, human beings being defined as rational, economic entities (Scollon and Scollon 2001). It is frequently assumed that economic progress depends on a capitalist economy with a democratic government. The last British Hong Kong Governor, Christopher Patten, can be seen to make this assumption in his public speeches, for example (Flowerdew 1998).

3. Mediated discourse analysis

My own approach to discourse analysis integrates critical discourse analysis and interactive sociolinguistic analysis in what R. Scollon calls mediated discourse analysis (R. Scollon 1998, 2001). I attempt to specify how ideologies which constitute orders of discourse play out in discursive practices including forms of discourse such as wordings and graphic elements. In this I develop an earlier concept of the discourse system (S. Scollon 1994; Scollon and Scollon 2001) including the Utilitarian Discourse System, which grew out of the Enlightenment and is the basis of libertarian as well as communist ideologies of the press.

In an earlier study of objectivity in television newscasts, I found a continuum along three broad styles of prosody and facial expression where wordings were predominantly neutral (S. Scollon 1995). The one I used to characterize Chinese presenters, whether speaking Putonghua in China or Cantonese in Hong Kong, we might call objective. In presenting the news, these readers used little facial expression or variety of intonation, speaking with steady volume in the same narrow pitch range. Presenters reading the news in English – whether Anglo, Chinese, or Indian – used an emphatic style, denoting important words and phrases with increased pitch or volume, head nods, and raised eyebrows. The third style, which I consider evaluative, was found in American newsreaders such as Connie Chung and other females probably educated in North America who spoke with American accents. In addition to emphasizing main points, these readers showed their attitude toward what they were reading by raising their eyebrows frequently, smiling and nodding or frowning and shaking their head to show approval or disapproval of the statements they were making.

There was a continuum among some 50 presenters whose delivery we analyzed, with American males falling between the emphatic British or Hong Kong style and the evaluative style of American female reporters. The difference between emphatic and evaluative delivery is that the former makes it easier for listeners to process the text being read so that they can interpret it themselves, while the latter makes visible and audible what the person reading feels about what she is reporting.

While all three styles could be said to uphold the standards of objectivity called for by the liberal free press, newscasters who use the evaluative style express their opinion or attitude toward the news they present as fact.

4. Theories of the press

The ideology of the liberal free press is exemplified by a set of essays that examine the changing relationship between the state (particularly the United States) and the press up to the mid-1950s. In their volume, *Four theories of the press: the authoritarian, libertarian, social responsibility and Soviet communist concepts of what the press should be and do,* Siebert, Peterson and Schramm

(1956) include the "new media" of mass communication – radio, movies and television. Their thesis is clear: "the press always takes on the form and coloration of the social and political structures within which it operates. Especially, it reflects the system of social control whereby the relations of individuals and institutions are adjusted" (1956: 1–2).

In the context of the Cold War, the authors pose two basic theories, better regarded as ideologies, developed since the beginning of mass communication in the Renaissance. The first, the Authoritarian, evolved into the Soviet Communist, and the Libertarian evolved into the Social Responsibility. The Authoritarian, a top down system that arose soon after the invention of printing, assumed the press was the servant of the state. It was undermined by the Enlightenment philosophical climate of political democracy, religious freedom, expansion of free trade and travel, and the acceptance of laissez-faire economics. The Libertarian, incipient in the 17th century, flowered in the 19th. It assumed that man was a rational being with the right to search for truth, an inalienable natural right. The press then became a partner in the search for truth by presenting evidence and argument that allowed the public to check on the activity of government.

After the Depression, mass communication required more and more expenditure of capital, making the role of the press as a free marketplace of ideas less tenable and giving rise to the articulation of Social Responsibility.

The basic differences between the Soviet and Anglo-American approaches, both Utilitarian, stem from the premises of Marx – that the way to improve man is to improve society – and Mill – that the way to improve society is to improve the individual man. Soviet mass communication was directed by a few for a preset result, while in the United States mass communication was assumed to enable voicing of social and public needs, interests, tastes, and ideas. Marxist philosophy assumed the public to be a malleable mass in need of leadership, while the libertarian philosophy of the Enlightenment with its assumptions of rationalism and natural rights saw the role of the press as a "free market place of ideas".

A "fifth theory" adds the role of development communication for the press in developing societies. That is, the press should create a favorable environment for the government's developmental agendas (Zhu 1991). Comparing the *People's Daily* of China and the *Central Daily News* of Taiwan, Zhu found that neither followed the development model, concluding that the traditional four theories better account for the actual function of these presses.

5. Three orders of discourse: Reform, liberal, Cold War

Fighting words are framed within broader national and international discourses. I will compare reportage within the reform discourse of contemporary China, the liberal western or international discourse, and the Cold War discourse of Taiwan's Guomindang (the long-ruling Nationalist Party).

Gu Yueguo (1996) contrasts discourse modes of revolution and reform in contemporary China. He argues that Chinese society under Mao was made to conform to the revolutionary discourse of the Party's leadership, while the late Deng Xiaoping introduced the discourse of reform to reflect the changes in the modern world impinging on China. These changes include the utilitarian values of economic growth and modernization, which entail greater intercourse with Western industrialized nations which share the ideology of the Utilitarian Discourse System (Scollon and Scollon 2001). At the same time, Deng strategized to maintain China's sovereignty by insisting on the "One China" principle in international relations and introducing the policy of peaceful reunification with Taiwan and the return of Hong Kong under the principle of "one country, two systems".

On March 11, 1996, the Chinese government announced their intention to conduct missile tests in the Taiwan Straits for two weeks. *Xinhua,* the official People's Republic of China New China News Agency, characterized the tests within the Reform discourse of Deng Xiaoping, positioning them as being nothing out of the ordinary and business-as-usual. The *Xinhua* announcement in the *China Daily* read, in part, "For the sake of safety, the Chinese Government requests the governments of relevant countries and the authorities of relevant regions to notify ships and aircraft of their countries and regions not to enter said sea area and air space during this period".

While the above notice in the *China Daily* was framed matter-of-factly by *Xinhua* reporters, journalists instantiating other ideologies reported the action of the Chinese government as a warning or even a threat. While journalists in the Western liberal tradition pride themselves on their objectivity in the coverage of news events, linguists have demonstrated that different journalists represent the speech of newsmakers filtered through their varying ideologies. Caldas-Coulthard writes, "In the stage of selecting and processing what to report, writers reveal their own stance towards what is represented. Through the comparison of different texts, we can say that no speech representation is objective or simply neutral" (1992: 68).

The liberal ideology of the free press presents the journalist as an impartial observer with the interests of the people in mind. As an advocate of the people, the press often takes a critical stance toward the government, reporting corruption and positioning lawmakers as less than fully honest and competent. Negativity as a news value underlies investigative reporting, as Bell has argued (1991). However, Zhu (1991) points out that government organs such as the *People's Daily* and the *China Daily* value news that reflects positively on national development and the character of its citizens. Mao Zedong directed reporters in China to report good news, saying nine fingers were good while only one was bad, according to Chen (1996). Fan (1996) also reported that the Chinese press tended to emphasize the positive and constructive, placing less emphasis on objectivity and balance than in the West. He further asserted that the Chinese press had been influenced by the West though it retained Chinese characteristics and was no longer a tool of politics, being subject to economic pressures.

Like the People's Republic of China, Taiwanese media were shaped by the politics of a single ruling party.[1] Although both have since opened to commercially operated media, they have had a long history of government control as the climate of the Cold War was a formative influence. Differences between these journalistic ideologies or orders of discourse are examined below as journalists from different newspapers, radio and television networks characterized the speech of Qian Qichen during the press conference held on March 11, 1996.

6. Intertextuality and interdiscursivity

Bakhtin and Voloshinov early in the last century were concerned with intertextuality or the way texts echo previous utterances, responding to prior texts. In speaking or writing, as Foucault pointed out (1976), we reflect the history of our social position within various orders of discourse. We also, as Bakhtin emphasized, anticipate response to our utterance. Journalists, in particular, work within a history of reporting practice and anticipate certain responses from their audience as they carefully choose their wording and other forms of representation.

Fairclough endeavors to integrate linguistic textual analysis with Foucaultian discourse analysis which focuses less on text but rather on how it is constituted and constitutes social relations within particular orders of discourse.[2] He investigates forms of what he terms discourse representation such as presupposition in which propositions embed assumptions by writers which shape the interpretation of the texts they write. These presuppositions are shared by members of sociohistorical orders of discourse. From Foucault comes an interest in the interview that is a genre which takes many forms besides the journalistic reporting on which I focus. The intertextuality of discourse representation is set within a broader framework of interdiscursivity in which broader cannons of "journalistic objectivity" are interpreted variably within liberal journalism and developmental journalism.

7. Data base

At City University of Hong Kong, we[3] developed a data base through comprehensive collection of newspapers, radio and television news broadcasts available in Hong Kong over a two-week period from

March 11 to March 23, 1996, the period ending with the Taiwanese presidential election and extending through the midst of the Taiwan missile crisis. The newspapers are both Chinese and English language papers and the broadcasts are in Cantonese, English and Putonghua.

The story selected for detailed study in this chapter centers around a statement made by Qian Qichen, who was quoted in newspaper headlines as "condemning" the U.S. for "ridiculous" actions. *The People's Daily* as well as *Wen Wei Po* carried full reports in question-and-answer format of the hour-long press conference in which the statement was read, and all printed and broadcast reports made reference to it in some form. I also analyze a few other statements made by Qian in the press conference that were widely quoted in newspaper coverage. Because of the nature of television news broadcasts, they tended to focus on one or two statements, while newspaper coverage was more varied. While the actual text covered by television was limited, we were able to analyze visual contextualization, from facial expression and body movement to the arrangement of speakers at the press conference and interior decoration. With the full text of the press conference in print as well as different voice recordings, we were able to compare each report against what was actually said.

7.1. Different accounts of a press conference: The focal statement

As part of the eighth National People's Congress, the press conference was held on March 11, 1996 in the Great Hall of the People in Beijing. Vice-Premier and Minister of Foreign Affairs Qian Qichen was asked to respond to Chinese and foreign reporters' questions about the international situation and China's foreign policy. Qian began by alluding to unanimous support for Premier Li Peng's report about the international situation and the reunification of the motherland expressed by Congress representatives. He opened the floor to questions relating to these matters. The first question from a *Xinhua* reporter had to do with the question of Taiwan's presidential election and independence. Next, an *NHK* reporter asked about

Qian's coming visit to Japan. The third questioner, a *People's Daily* reporter, asked about China's interpretation of what they called America's "China threat theory".

In the fourth question, a CNN reporter asked for China's view on the dispatch of the U.S. aircraft carrier "Independence" toward the Taiwan Straits. Qian's response to this question, as follows, is my focus here (original in Chinese)[4]:

> It is commonplace that U.S. naval ships operate on the high seas. But it would be ridiculous for some people to call in open for the intervention by the Seventh Fleet of the United States on this issue. And they even go so far as to call for the defense of Taiwan. I think these people must have forgotten the fact that Taiwan is a part of Chinese territory; it's not a protectorate of the United States.

This statement, edited in various ways to produce calculated effects, was at the core of all printed and broadcast news items. I will begin by looking at the linguistic framing of what some regarded as "fighting words" by Qian Qichen, and will then look in closer detail at visual and other extralinguistic framing.

7.2. Verbs of saying

In reporting on the speech of others, journalists and other authors use verbs to frame utterances.

Caldas-Coulthard (1987), in her study of the representation of speech in narrative, distinguished "neutral glossing verbs" such as "said" from "illocutionary glossing verbs" such as "warn" which attribute illocutionary intentions to the speaker. "Illocutionary" is a term used in speech act theory to indicate what a speaker is doing by speaking. For example, a threat or a promise are made with statements that may or may not include the words "threat" or "promise". "If you don't finish that pie I'll finish it for you" can be either a threat or a promise, depending on how badly the addressee wants to eat the pie. By writing "she threatened" or "he promised", an author assumes she or he knows not only what the speaker intends but how the hearer might respond. In journalism interpretation depends on presuppositions shared by journalists and audience who constitute orders of discourse.

In the same study, Caldas-Coulthard reports that popular papers tend to use neutral glossing verbs in a style for which Hemingway is noted. The lack of mediation between author and speaker gives more vivid text. The quality press, on the other hand, favors illocutionary glossing verbs and descriptive verbs such as "shout" and "giggle", making the writer's interpretation explicit. These introduce the author's position into the reportage. "Thus the vast majority of direct speech representation in factual reports are EVALUATIVE devices in Labov's (1972) sense" (1992: 32–33). By "evaluative" Labov means that a narrator evaluates the significance of the actions or events about which she or he reports. Uspensky, in his discussion of the different possible ways of reporting someone else's speech, writes of the "contaminations" of a speaker's text under the influence of authorial speech (1973: 32–33). He gives many examples of quasi-direct discourse, in which the author's text is influenced by the voice of the speaker being represented.

In a comparison of the same news story in radio, television and newspaper versions in Chinese and English, Li et al. (1993) found that the Chinese stories used comparatively neutral verbs to insert quotations into narrative text. *Ming Pao*, the Chinese paper used in Li's study, is usually considered to belong to the quality press, although it differs from the quality press in England studied by Caldas-Coulthard (1992). A further study of fourteen newspaper versions of a story reporting on President George H. Bush's meeting with Li Peng in Beijing in fall 1993 found the choice of verbs of saying to be one of the clearest distinctions between English and Chinese versions of Hong Kong newspapers (Scollon and Scollon 1997; Scollon et al. 2000). Only two of the ten Chinese language papers used evaluative verbs of saying in this story, while the English papers used illocutionary glossing verbs such as "criticized", "urged", "warned", and "lashed out".

Most of the newspapers in our sample limited their reporting to Qian's responses to six reporters, concentrating on his replies to four reporters from (1) *Xinhua* (New China News Agency), (2) *CNN* (Cable News Network), (3) Taiwan's *United News*, and (4)

Australian Broadcasting Corporation. Of the newspapers that printed a narrative report, *China Daily* gave the fullest coverage. The first statement was directly quoted in translation in full or in part by all three Hong Kong English dailies, and quoted directly or indirectly by all but two of the Chinese language dailies. *Wen Wei Po* was most faithful to the original, retaining the first person plural "we" (*women)* where others substitute "China" (*Zhong guo*) or "Communist China" (*Zhong gong*). One paraphrased it in the headline and another glossed it with "warned" (*jing gao*). A look at some of these versions will show how different newspapers position themselves, the newsmakers or government representatives, and their readers.

Before the press conference, Premier Li Peng had spoken on the international situation and Chinese reunification. Qian began the press conference by saying that representatives unanimously had supported Li and called for questions on related matters. The first questioner, a Xinhua reporter, mentioned the upcoming Taiwanese election and the military exercises and asked whether the Chinese government would use armed force to solve the Taiwan problem. Qian replied that Taiwan's leaders only have authority over a region of China, and that their reliance on foreign support to bring about independence and divide the motherland is futile and dangerous. He said,

> I want to emphatically point out, "Peaceful unification, one country two systems" has been our consistent stand. This stand has not changed today, and it will not change, but we have never undertaken to abandon the use of force. If foreign powers invade Taiwan or if Taiwanese "independence" appears, we cannot stand aside and do nothing.

This statement was reported in various ways by different newspapers and attributed to Jiang Zemin, Qian or Chinese leaders. As it had already been ratified unanimously by representatives to the National People's Congress, half of the newspapers used the word "reiterated" – the Chinese language dailies in a neutral manner but two English language dailies characterizing the statement as a warning:

"Chinese leaders yesterday <u>reiterated</u> China's warning that it would resort to force to prevent Taiwan from declaring independence." [*South China Morning Post*]

"In a stern warning to the United States, China <u>reiterated</u> that it will not 'sit back idly and remain indifferent' should the U.S. interfere with affairs between Taiwan and mainland China". [*Eastern Express*]

By using the verb "reiterate", journalists position themselves as being familiar with the proceedings of the National People's Congress. In this sense "reiterate" is being used as a verb that both structures the discourse and also evaluates in that it conveys the attitude that one has heard this message before, e.g. in the Taiwanese *China Times* subheadline with the oft-repeated two-part slogan coined by Deng Xiaoping:

Qian Qichen <u>reiterates</u> "peaceful reunification, one country two systems" policy . . . .
(*chong shen [he ping tong yi, yi guo liang zhi] zhu zhang*) [*China Times* subhead]

From their beginning in the nineteenth century, newspapers in Hong Kong, Chinese as well as English, have been associated with "foreign" news and interests, much like modern newspapers everywhere. Both the *South China Morning Post* and the *Eastern Express*, then, might be considered subscribers to the ideology of the liberal, free press. Nevertheless, their stance is hardly neutral, as they characterize Qian as delivering a warning, even a "stern" warning, while the *China Times*, a Taiwanese daily, as well as several Hong Kong Chinese language dailies used the verb "reiterate" more neutrally. The *Hong Kong Economic Daily* did not cite the passage but glossed it as "Qian 'warns' (*jing gao*) the U.S. not to interfere in Taiwan affairs".

7.3. "Blasting", "condemning", "warning" or "ridiculing"

Qian's response to the CNN reporter's question about the U.S. fleet was quoted directly or quasi-directly by all newspapers sampled except *Wen Wei Po*, which paraphrased it in a headline and printed the full text of the press conference. This statement was also the core of radio and television reports. Representatives of the commercial press used strongly evaluative verbs to report this statement, while the *Central Daily* (supported by the Taiwanese government) and the *Wen Wei Po* (sympathetic to China) printed a full text, not using "warning" (*jing gao*).

The *South China Morning Post* positions Qian as not taking American intervention seriously by reporting that he

> dismissed as "ridiculous" assumptions that Taiwan could be protected by the presence of a United States military fleet in the East China Sea.

This phrasing seems to question the capacity of the U.S. fleet to protect Taiwan rather than the presumptuousness of the U.S. government in dispatching the naval force, which seems to be Qian's intention. *Tin Tin* ran a headline in characters more than 3 cm. tall saying "Qian Qichen Angrily Condemns America Ridiculous" (*Qian Qichen Nu chi Meiguo Huang tang*) and used the same phrase in a caption accompanying a photograph with characters saying China and U.S. foreign ministers condemn each other from across the sea. With this strongly evaluative verb as well as placement of photograph and choice of font size, the editor responsible for headlines and layout positions the two foreign ministers as engaged in a serious battle, while the text uses the neutral verb "point out" (*ti chu*) and opens by quoting the passage quasi-directly in full. It continues, "He further said in warning (*Ta bing jinggao shuo*):

> 'The Taiwan problem is China's internal affair, foreigners should not make irresponsible remarks, and should be especially careful not to adopt any interfering action.' If foreign powers intervene, they will cause a chaotic situation in the straits."

Thus the newspaper positions the reader as wanting to be informed about affairs that may influence their lives, as many of their readers can be assumed to engage in trade in the region. It positions Qian as warning, implying that he has the power to retaliate.

The Taiwanese *China Times* positions Qian as engaged in a Cold War battle, warning the U.S. not to intervene in Taiwan affairs, as it is a part of China and not U.S. territory. It further positions Qian as retaliating against the U.S. for its support of Taiwan president Lee Denghui with its warning headlines:

Qian Qichen <u>Warns</u> the U.S.: Don't Try to Meddle in the Taiwan Problem
(*Qian Qichen* Jinggao *Meiguo: Wu Shitu Jieru Taiwan Wenti*)

<u>Reiterates</u> "Peaceful Reunification, One Country Two Systems" Policy;
<u>Points</u> Current Cross-Straits Relations Greatest Danger is People Relying on Foreign Power to Bring About Taiwan Independence (*Chongshen [Heping Tongyi, Yi Guo Liang Zhi] Zhuzhang;* Zhi *Muqian Liang An Guanxi Zui Weixian de shi Taiwan You Ren Yikao Wai Li Gao Tai Du*)

The lead of this story positions Qian as aiming his remarks at the upcoming Taiwanese presidential election. The paper thus positions itself as an interpreter of China's actions for the Taiwan people.

The *South China Morning Post* chose the word "blasted" to describe this response by Qian to a question put by a reporter from the Australian Broadcasting Corporation as to whether the U.S. deployment of warships was provocative:

I have had frequent contact with Secretary of State Christopher, it's also possible next month I will again have an opportunity to meet him. I will then ask him a little question, he criticized Chinese implementation of military exercises as a rash, reckless decision, even an erroneous decision. I want to ask him politely, was their decision not also rash and reckless? Moreover, I should say in the spring of '95 the cross-straits situation was very good, because of America's wrong decision, bringing about this sort of situation, they should think a bit, to try to correct this state of affairs.

"Blast" seems like rather strong language, even if it describes an intended effect, and Chinese language papers relish reporting on Qian's manner of delivering the bomb, using irony and a rhetorical question. Thus *Tin Tin* cites Qian saying he wants to "politely ask" *(wen yi wen)* Christopher whether their action was not rash and reckless. In order to read the intent one needs to be able to penetrate the ironic language. The *South China Morning Post* can count on its readers to accept their reading of the text.

8. Business as usual or strong warning

The above examples show how journalists, in framing political figures' utterances characterize them as neutral or hostile, casual or intimidating. Two characterizations of Qian's response to the *CNN* reporter are considered here – both the portrayal by *Xinhua* of Qian's matter-of-fact statement and the characterization by the liberal press of Qian's "warning".

Xinhua portrayed Qian conducting business as usual, answering reporters' questions about the international situation and China's policy of peaceful reunification as part of the annual National People's Congress. The missile tests, as we have seen, are framed as nothing more than modernization of the Army, necessary for the maintenance of sovereignty. The headline in the English language *China Daily* reports, "China resolved to safeguard sovereignty". From this point of view it is ridiculous for the United States to intervene in what is the normal conduct of China's internal affairs. One way the *China Daily* reporter framed this was to quote the statement, the first part indirectly and the last sentence directly, first by describing Qian as Vice Premier and after the quotation adding that Qian is also Foreign Minister.

> The military exercises by the People's Liberation Army will demonstrate that the Chinese Government has the resolve and ability to safeguard the country's sovereignty and territorial integrity, Vice-Premier Qian Qichen said yesterday in Beijing. ... He also told a press conference that it was ridiculous that some people in the United States declared that the aircraft carrier Independence of the Seventh Fleet should sail towards Taiwan from its base in Japan, for intervention and even for "defending Taiwan." "I think these people must have forgotten that Taiwan is a part of China's territory. It is not a protectorate of the United States," he said at the conference

organized by the press centre of the ongoing National People's Congress session.
Qian, who is also Foreign Minister, announced...

By separating Qian's roles as Vice Premier and Foreign Minister, the journalist frames the military exercises as internal, domestic affairs having to do with the protection of national sovereignty. Qian is positioned as a leader looking after his country's affairs and wondering how anyone could conceive of intervening in China's internal affairs.

The liberal press portrayed Qian as reacting to the U.S. decision to send warships toward Taiwan, and in particular to statements made by Secretary of State Warren Christopher in a television interview. For example, one Hong Kong television reporter, Jenny Lam of *TVB Pearl*, introduced the actuality by saying,

There is little new in China's warning against foreign interference in the Taiwan question but the wording is getting stronger and stronger.

She characterizes the statement not only as a warning, but a strong warning.

9. Extralinguistic framing: Casual or strong tone

Statements are framed not only with language but with photographs, headline size and layout. Now we will turn to what can be seen on the television screen as well, looking at the actual spoken utterance to see what contextualization cues such as manner, gesture, and tone of voice are available to aid in the analysis. Unlike ordinary conversation, Qian is addressing not individuals but journalists representing different ideologies of the press as well as different political stances. The journalists are filtering their interpretation through the lens of their ideological stance. While Qian can be seen reading out his statement with unmarked prosody and posture, through journalistic framing the statement can be broken up and his tone characterized first as casual and then as strong. For example, the *Oriental Daily News(C)* on March 12 ran a big headline proclaiming,

Qian Qichen: US Protect Taiwan Ridiculous.

The lead paragraph breaks up Qian's statement, characterizing his tone as "casual", then inserting text from Qian's reply to a later question "in a very strong tone". A photograph showing Qian speaking with his mouth open is captioned,

Qian Qichen censures U.S. protecting of Taiwan as a preposterous move.

While Qian in reading shows no change in tone, the reporter frames the first sentence as said "casually", while the rest is cast as being "in a very strong tone". The reporter takes the liberty of paraphrasing statements out of sequence, highlights the word "ridiculous" by preceding it with "utterly", uses laminating verbs like "remind", and uses the word "slogan" (*kou hao*), to characterize "protecting Taiwan". The editor puts the buzz words "protect Taiwan" and "ridiculous" in the headline, with a subhead threatening chaos, "great disorder under heaven" (*tian xia da luan*), and places the photograph of Qian side-by-side with one of Warren Christopher "explaining" the conditions for a one-China policy while Qian "censures" with the same buzz words. The second sentence of the lead states that China has never promised to renounce the use of force. The interpretation of the statement as warning and threatening lies not in Qian's delivery but in framing by the journalists according to their understanding of the sociopolitical context within their community of practicing journalists.

Qian's style positions him within the reform discourse of Deng Xiaoping, which preserves elements of Chinese hierarchical social relationships (Gu 1996) and rhetorical style (Pan 1995). His style departs from the Western Utilitarian ideal of rational, deductive, anti-rhetorical, creative individual statement, of public discourse as logical discussion among equal, autonomous individuals (Scollon and Scollon 2001). As Vice Premier and Foreign Minister, his statement reflects not his creative rational logic as an individual but the position of the Chinese government, of which *Xinhua* is a part. He reads from a text which might have been authored by any number of government officials, animating a message with the whole government of China as principal, including then still-living paramount leader Deng Xiaoping. His statement is structured with the main point left until the conclusion, leaving it open to restructuring by journalists. He uses the rhetorical strategy of understatement, which the *Oriental Daily News(C)* reporter interprets for his readers as a "strong tone".

Through multimodal analysis, by looking at the speaker to see how he delivers his message and listening to his tone of voice, as well as listening to the voice of the *Xinhua* translator, one might suggest that (aside from the content), the reading by English language reporters of a warning, threatening tone may have come from the English of the interpreter. His non-native stress patterns may have sounded threatening to reporters who could not understand Qian as he spoke in Chinese. Having access through various reports in three media to the actual wording in Chinese as well as the sequence and other aspects of the actual situation allows us to see how the various accounts shaped what was said according to particular points of view.

10. Multimodal framing in television

Framing in television newscasts is done by means of music, visuals, headlines, spatial arrangement of the news desk, visual sequencing as well as verbal and nonverbal cues in speaking. We see a three-way contrast among Chinese television broadcasts originating in Beijing, Taipei, and Hong Kong. The first presents the military exercises as well as the press conference as business as usual, showing the scene of the press conference as part of the National People's Congress, with the main concern being Chinese reunification under Deng's program of "one country, two systems". Notwithstanding the discussion of Hong Kong in connection with this agenda, the real issue is the "Taiwan problem" and the illusions of Taiwanese and their foreign supporters that their independence can be defended. The second presents Qian's statements at the press conference as an episode in the Cold War, a response to the military intervention of the United States. From this perspective, he is seen as being held to account by agents of the new world order, spewing propaganda in his defense. The third portrayal casts Taiwan as under military threat from China, showing battle clips and positioning Qian as condemning U.S. intervention. This ideological position is a carryover from the Cold War and tends to be held by U.S. political analysts as well as the liberal free press.

China Central TV's (C) telecast framed the press conference as an apparently unexceptional part of the meeting of the National People's Congress. As is typical in coverage of official functions, the report begins by showing the physical setting and the main participants (Scollon and Scollon 1997; Scollon et al. 2000).

The program begins with the anchorwoman announcing the main headline,

> Vice Premier and Foreign Minister Qian Qichen Answers Reporters' Questions.

We see the Great Hall of the People with a red banner over the table at which Qian and other officials sit behind pots of flowers. There is a cut to the anchorman's face as he introduces the press conference. We see cameras being focused, a Chinese reporter holding a microphone as the television reporter says,

> A reporter when asking about the Taiwan problem said, "Western public opinion has all manner of comment and conjecture about this set of military exercises. Will the government use the force of arms to solve the Taiwan problem?" Vice Premier Qian said, "Taiwan is an inseparable part of China. . . . we cannot stand aside and do nothing."

We see the faces of reporters. The television reporter continues,

> A reporter asked recently the U.S. government decided to let the US aircraft carrier "Independence" enter Taiwan waters, what is your view of this?

The form for "your" was the honorific *nin*[5]. We see a female Western reporter, then Qian as he starts to reply with the statement on which we are focusing. The camera cuts to a cameraman as Qian says and even goes so far as to raise the idea of "defending Taiwan",

then back to Qian, who removes his glasses, looks up from his sheaf of paper and finishes,

Perhaps they have forgotten that Taiwan is Chinese territory and not an American protectorate.

As he looks out at the audience he says, apparently by mistake, "protected territory" (*baohu tudi*), then corrects himself, "protectorate" (*baohu di*). The sound is turned down as he corrects himself.

We see nothing exceptional in this account of the press conference. The purpose of the event is framed by the *Xinhua* reporter, who is shown on the screen but not identified by the television reporter, asking whether the government will use armed force to solve the "Taiwan problem". The ostensible goal is to reassure those who do not understand that the military exercises are not a threat and certainly not a reason to deploy American warship to "defend Taiwan". Qian responds by reiterating the government's stance. Qian's tone and stance are extremely matter-of-fact as he reads his prepared text.

11. Business as usual, Cold War or China Threat?

Finally, we compare the stance of the Chinese government as presented by *Xinhua* and *CCTV* with two other broadcasts representative of distinct but related orders of discourse, one from Taiwan and the other from Hong Kong, both in Chinese.

Perhaps the greatest contrast is found in the coverage by Taiwan's *CTS* (C), which starts with the anchor relaying a report from the *Washington Post* that President Clinton had dispatched the Seventh Fleet from the Persian Gulf to sail towards the Taiwan Straits, to arrive before the Taiwanese presidential election. She then adds that Japan's *Fuji Broadcasting Corporation* had sent reporters aboard the Independence to cover the exercise situation. This orientation places the journalist on the side of the U.S. and Japan against China in the old framework of the Cold War.

We see how *China Television Service* frames the statement by Qian within the order of discourse of the Cold War. They construe the press conference as being not about the "Taiwan problem" or reunification of the motherland but about the threat to the people of Taiwan of China's military exercises. As such it is the latest episode in the Cold War, originating in Washington with a *Washington Post* reporter and "Meet the Press" covering an act of war by President Clinton, which is framed as a response to China's act of war in conducting military exercises. After more than three minutes, the shift from Washington to Beijing is signaled by a red map of China and a location indicator using the Guomindang name "Peiping" to avoid acknowledging Beijing as the capital. Along with these cues that they are contesting the name of the "Communist" capital, the anchor introduces Qian as Communist Chinese Foreign Minister, saying he called the press conference, aimed at the movement of the "Independence" toward the Taiwan Straits, and paraphrasing the statement, calling it *han hua*, "propaganda directed to the enemy at the front line". Qian is seen as leaving space for maneuvering in the face of intense questioning, surrounded by international reporters on an international battlefront.

The visual display on the television screen supports this political alignment. The *CTS* logo appears on the left top corner of the screen, identifying the station as the most conservative Taiwanese channel, operated not only by the government but by the old guard of the Guomindang. Washington is displayed in the complex characters used in Taiwan and Hong Kong[6], white on red, with Secretary of State Warren Christopher and a reporter, presumably from the *Washington Post*. The reporter is sitting across a table from Christopher, and we see alternate shots of each, with "*NBC* footage" on the left in complex characters and U.S. Secretary-of-State Christopher on the right, also in complex characters, both arranged vertically. The last two characters of Christopher's name are "much prosperity" (*duo fu*), in contrast to the "support or serve not or negative" (*tuo fu*) used by *PRC* and Hong Kong journalists. His remarks are translated into subtitles, shown in yellow Chinese characters at the bottom of the screen, as a voiceover translates the actuality into Mandarin. His name and title also appear in English on the screen. Writing from top to bottom is characteristic of old-fashioned Chinese writing and widespread in Taiwan but rare in China. The choice of characters to represent "Christopher" clearly convey the attitude of the Taiwanese military toward their supporter. The color yellow used in the subtitles translating Christopher's remarks align him with the color formerly reserved for the Chinese emperor.

The *CTS* reporter attributed the press conference to the air and sea missile exercises scheduled to start the next day, saying Qian's words were not only an index but a gauge by which they could fathom possible later developments. Unlike *Xinhua*, which framed the press conference as a routine part of the annual meeting of Congress held for the purpose of answering questions about the international situation and China's foreign policy, she portrayed the international media as active agents focusing on the movement of the Independence toward Taiwan and the escalating Taiwan crisis. She introduces the statement using an archaic phrase meaning to be entrapped, framing Qian as ensnared by the reporters' aggressive questions. The ostensible reason for the press conference, to respond to the approach of the US aircraft carrier "Independence", is construed as propaganda. The battle is framed as taking place during the press conference in the Great Hall of the People, with Qian under attack in his own territory, the enemy being the army of journalists.

Visual cues identify the station as aligned with the Guomindang. The colors red and yellow represent the Communist party on the one hand and the Guomindang on the other. The character set identifies the station as overseas rather than China proper, and the spelling "Peiping" is in keeping with the reactionary stance of the station.

Intermediate to the two broadcasts is that of *ATV Home*, the Cantonese channel of a Hong Kong station that also broadcasts in English. Their reportage adopts the stance of the liberal press that China is a military threat, presenting the story in two sections as part of the ongoing "Taiwan Missile Crisis". It also continues the language of the Cold War, showing the Taiwanese army preparing to fend off the Chinese missile attack with the support of U.S. warships.

The first section covers the U.S. action. The anchor announces in Cantonese,

> The U.S. sends fleet from the Gulf toward Taiwan; Qian Qichen warns U.S. not to interfere.

There is a clip of a naval vessel, then Qian, as music plays. A red logo shows characters indicating continuing coverage of the "Taiwan crisis". Blue characters say "missile exercises". This peels off to show a military style map with large arrows appearing with ships pointed toward Taiwan.

He says the Taiwan Guard is preparing for war. Then he says he'll first talk about the U.S. military, starting with the *Washington Post* report. They show a file clip of missiles firing, Lake and Christopher on "Meet the Press", a *CTS* clip of a plane taking off, a *CNN* clip of an aircraft carrier. The anchor says the dispatch of the aircraft carrier USS Nimitz constitutes a warning.

A second anchor describes the escalating tensions and the movement of the Nimitz, saying,

> Chinese Vice Premier and Foreign Minister Qian Qichen condemns U.S. military movement as "ridiculous".

Then a female reporter says the Chinese official *Xinhua* agency again published an article criticizing Lee Denghui for trying to establish a black gold government and false democracy.

> And Vice Premier and Foreign Minister Qian Qichen condemns the U.S. for dispatching the Seventh Fleet toward Taiwan and interfering in cross-straits affairs, and pretending that Taiwan is an American protectorate.

Qian's head appears on the screen as the reporter says this. Then he is seen walking to his place and being helped into his chair by a young woman. Five rows of seated reporters can be seen, and a row of cameras against the wall. Back to Qian as the reporter says, "he denies", then a female reporter writing, and Qian shuffling paper while we hear the Cantonese voiceover. More reporters' heads, then Qian calling the U.S. decision reckless and rash, and a warship. A file clip of a naval ship at sea, and a shot on board. Then Qian puts on his glasses and reads his response to the *CNN* reporter, who is not shown. Before he gets to "utterly ridiculous", he looks up and takes off his glasses. He corrects himself, then licks his lips when he finishes.

The clip of a warship introduces the idea of war into the routine proceedings of the press conference and Qian's low-key delivery of his message of "condemnation". Qian's calm manner and delivery are interspersed with images of war and punctuated with commentary that conveys a pugilistic stance, in an imagined "conversation" with Warren Christopher.

The focus of the crisis is Taiwanese war preparations. An actuality of Christopher is followed by Qian's rejoinder. This is introduced by a reporter in Beijing who summarizes Qian's remarks at the press conference without mentioning the conference itself, in the style of the Hong Kong liberal press as distinguished from *Xinhua* practice (Scollon and Scollon 1997; Scollon et al. 2000). She uses the Cantonese equivalents of the verbs "emphasized", "denied", "warned", and "impolitely condemned", in keeping with the practice of the Hong Kong English language press. Also in keeping with the liberal objective stance, she carefully presents both sides. The visual clips convey the sense of war, consonant with the portrayal of Qian giving a stern warning. The effect is to position the station within the order of discourse of the liberal western press, which considers China a military threat.

12. Conclusion

In the coverage of one press conference during the Taiwan missile crisis that preceded the first Taiwanese presidential elections, journalists positioned themselves ideologically by their use of neutral and evaluative verbs of saying to represent the speech of government leaders. Government organs with putatively opposed political ideologies share the same journalistic ideology which favors neutral statement, in contrast to the liberal free press ideology which favors the use of strongly evaluative verbs of saying and nominalizations of illocutionary acts that position newsmakers and audience as well as the journalist. Both journalistic ideologies present themselves as objective, but in addition the liberal press presents itself as impartial. Journalists position themselves and newsmakers not only by their use of evaluative verbs of saying but by the number of laminating verbs used. Thus *South China Morning Post*, for example, positions itself as impartial by using half of these verbs to report on China's leaders and the other half to report on U.S. and Taiwan leaders. However, the evaluative illocutionary verbs all position China as threatening, and the lead takes Washington's point of view.

The government organs and the *Wen Wei Po* have no need to hide their political bias, thus present coverage of both sides not in order to position themselves as impartial observers but to keep their readers informed as to what their political opponents are saying. By using neutral verbs of saying they position their readers as able to and responsible for reading between the lines, in contrast to liberal journalists who position their readers as needing help in interpreting political affairs.

The choice of verbs of saying is just one indicator of ideological bent, clustering with other features including choice of character set and font size and layout of photographs in newspapers and television as well as choice of color and selection of file clips from televised press conferences to naval vessels at sea and planes taking off from aircraft carriers. China Central television, in keeping with the *Xinhua* newspaper text, framed the press conference as business as usual, while the Guomindang station framed it as an episode in the Cold War, a defensive response to the U.S. military intervention. The Hong Kong station, like the foreign liberal press, presents China as a military threat to Taiwan, supported by the U.S.

Through a multimodal, intertextual analysis, not only words of war but acts of war are seen as constructed by intermeshing layers of interaction among journalists and government officials. Fighting words in the mouths of some justify sending warships or firing missiles. But, when reported by others, leaders' words become propaganda or threat.

Notes

1. Zhu (1991) provides a concise contrast of Chinese and Taiwanese press systems as of a decade ago.
2. See Fairclough (1992) for an extended treatment of intertextuality, interdiscursivity and discourse representation as a form of intertextuality prevalent in news and other discourse.
3. As part of a research project "Changing patterns of Genres and Identity in Hong Kong Public Discourse", this database relied on over a dozen researchers and assistants and was drawn on in other projects, including "Two Types of Journalistic Objectivity" and "Plagiarization as Social Practice". Kayin Wu and Donna M.S. Luk were instrumental in coding and analysis of verbs of saying, presented in Scollon, S., Wu and Luk (1996). Vicki Yung collaborated on analysis of discourse representation and intertextuality, c.f. Scollon, S. and Yung (1997). This chapter draws from both of these conference papers. I would like to thank these co-authors as well as Emma Rao and Rachel Scollon who assisted with translation.
4. Unless otherwise indicated, translations are those of the author.
5. As both Gu (1996) and Erbaugh (1994) point out, this use of the honorific second person pronoun adumbrates the discourse of reform.
6. Scollon and Scollon (1998) is an extended treatment of the significance of the different systems of writing Chinese in positioning texts within the reform or revolutionary discourse.

References

Bakhtin, Mikhail Mikhaïlovich
    1986   *Speech Genres and Other Late Essays*. Translated by V.W. McGee, edited by Caryl Emerson and Michael Holquist. Austin: University of Texas Press.

Bell, Allan
    1991   *The Language of the News Media*. Oxford: Basil Blackwell.

Caldas-Coulthard, Carmen Rosa
    1987   Reported speech in written narrative texts. In: *Discussing Discourse: Studies Presented to David Brazil on His Retirement*. Birmingham: English language research.

    1992   The representation of speech in factual and fictional narrative: Stylistic implications. *Occasional papers in systemic linguistics* 6, 61–70.

Chen, Chongshan
    1996   News values in China from an audience research perspective. Paper presented at the Chinese Values in Journalism Symposium, English Department and the Contemporary China Research Center, City University of Hong Kong, 3 May 1996.

Erbaugh, Mary
    1994   Western manners and Chinese childhood: The decline of the clan, the training of urban individuals. In: Wu, David Y-H, and Suzhen Xue (eds.), *Zhongguo ertong zhi shehuihua* [Chinese Childhood Socialization]. Shanghai: Sanlian chubanshe.

Fairclough, Norman
    1992   *Discourse and Social Change*. Cambridge: Polity Press.

Fan, Dongshen
    1996   The market economy influence on Chinese news media. Paper presented at the Chinese Values in Journalism Symposium, English Department and the Contermporary China Research Center, City University of Hong Kong, 3 May 1996.

Flowerdew, John
    1998   *The Final Years of British Hong Kong: The Discourse of Colonial Withdrawal*. London: Macmillan.

Foucault, Michel
    1976   *The Archeology of Knowledge*. New York: Harper and Row.

    1977   *Language, Countermemory, Practice: Selected Essays and Interviews*, edited by Donald F. Bouchard. Ithaca: Cornell University Press.

Gu, Yueguo
    1996   The changing modes of discourse in a changing China. Beijing Foreign Studies University, manuscript.

Hawkes, David
    1996   *Ideology*. London/New York: Routledge.

Labov, William
    1972   The transformation of experience in narrative syntax. In: *Language in the Inner City: Studies in the Black English Vernacular*. Philadelphia: University of Pennsylvania Press.

Li, Chor Shing David, Wanda Poon Lau Woon Yee, Pamela M Rogerson-Revell, Ron Scollon, Suzanne Scollon, Bartholomew Yu Shiu Kwong, and Kit Yee Vicki Yung
    1993   Contrastive discourse in English and Cantonese news stories: A preliminary analysis of newspaper, radio, and television versions of the Lan Kwai Fong news story. Department of English, City Polytechnic of Hong Kong, Research Report, No. 29.

Luke, Allan
    1991   Ideology. *Encyclopedia of Language and Linguistics.* Pergamon Press/Aberdeen University Press.

Marx, Karl
    1978   The German ideology. In: Tucker, Robert C. (ed.), *The Marx-Engels Reader, second edition.* New York/London: W.W. Norton and Company, 146–200.

Pan, Yuling
    1995   Power behind linguistic behavior: Analysis of politeness phenomena in Chinese official settings. *Journal of Language and Social Psychology,* 14(4), 462–481.

Scollon, Ron
    1998   *Mediated Discourse As Social Interaction: A Study of News Discourse.* New York: Longman.

    2001   *Mediated Discourse: The Nexus of Practice.* London: Routledge.

Scollon, Ron, and Suzanne Scollon
    n.d.   Two types of journalistic objectivity. Manuscript, City University of Hong Kong.

Scollon, Ron, and Suzanne Wong Scollon
    1997   Point of view and citation: Fourteen Chinese and English versions of the "same" news story. *Text* 17(1), 83–125.

    1998   Literate design in the discourses of revolution, reform, and transition: Hong Kong and China. *Written Language and Literacy* 1(1), 1–39.

    2001   *Intercultural Communication: A Discourse Approach, revised edition.* Oxford: Basil Blackwell.

Scollon, Ron, Suzanne Wong Scollon, and Andy Kirkpatrick
2000   *Contrastive Discourse in Chinese and English: A Critical Appraisal.*
        Beijing: Foreign Language Teaching and Research Press.

Scollon, Suzanne
1994   The utilitarian discourse system. In: Marsh, David, and Liisa Salo-
        Lee (eds.), *Europe on the Move: Fusion or Fission?* Proceedings
        1994 SIETAR Europa Symposium. Jyväskylä, Finland: SIETAR
        EUROPA and University of Jyväskylä, 126–131.

1995   The faces of World English: Nonverbal contextualization cues in TV
        news broadcasts. Paper presented at Second International Confer-
        ence on World Englishes, Nagoya, Japan, 25–28 May 1995.

Scollon, Suzanne, Kayin Wu, and Donna M. S. Luk
1996   Ideological positioning in verbs of reporting: A comparison of Eng-
        lish and Chinese newspapers. Paper presented at Sociolinguistics 11
        Conference, Cardiff, 5–7 September 1996.

Scollon, Suzanne, and Vicki Kit Yee Yung
1997   Framing, contextualization cues, and intertextuality in print and
        broadcast media: Discourse representation of one statement by Qian
        Qichen. Paper presented at the 6th International Conference on
        Cross-cultural Communication: East and West, Tempe, Arizona,
        March 1997.

Siebert, Fredrick S., Theodore Peterson, and Wilbur Schramm
1956   *Four Theories of the Press.* Urbana: University of Illinois Press.

Sutter, Robert G.
2000   *Chinese Policy Priorities and Their Implications for the United
        States.* Lanham, Maryland: Roman and Littlefield.

Uspensky, Boris
1973   *A Poetics of Composition.* Berkeley: University of California Press.

Zhao, Suisheng (ed.)
1999   *Across the Taiwan Strait: Mainland China, Taiwan, and the 1995–
        1996 Crisis.* New York/London: Routledge.

Zhu, Jianhua
1991   Between the prescriptive and descriptive roles: A comparison of
        international trade news in China and Taiwan. *Asian Journal of
        Communication* 2(1), 31–50.

Deixis and distance:
President Clinton's justification of intervention in Kosovo

Paul A. Chilton

"When I was coming up, it was a dangerous world, and you knew exactly who they were. It was us versus them, and it was clear who them was. Today, we are not so sure who the they are, but we know they're there."
(George W. Bush, 21 January 2000, at Iowa Western Community College)

1. Introduction

In March 1999 the human crisis in the Balkans led NATO to consider intervention. Within American political culture, European entanglements cause alarm bells to ring. The presidential address to the nation on March 24 1999 was, therefore, a complex and detailed speech event, designed to justify American involvement in a military action in a far-away place, among a far-away people, of whom the American electorate knew little.

Within the perspective of political philosophy the notion of justification might be related to legitimacy (usually taken to be legitimacy of regimes, forms of government) and, more specifically, to just war theory. Justification of war is a form of political action that takes place most massively through language.

From the standpoint of just war theory, codified by theologians and philosophers from medieval and early modern times (Augustine, Aquinas, Grotius, Pufendorf), and projected in later periods in the form of international law, discourse revolves around (1) the question whether it is right or just to go to war in the first place (*jus ad bellum*), and (2) what methods can be used in waging war (*jus in bello*). With respect to the *jus ad bellum*, traditional arguments hold that defensive wars are justified, as are wars to defend a third party.

With respect to *jus in bello*, there is appeal to the notion of "discrimination" (non-combatants should be immune from attack) and to "proportionality" (the harm inflicted on an enemy must not be disproportional to the harm received). A third concept in just war theory stipulates that there be a reasonable chance of success relative to the end.

In social psychology, ethnomethodology and Conversation Analysis, justification is seen as a type of "account", alongside excuses and apologies in ordinary conversation (cf. Austin 1961, Semin and Manstead 1983, and summaries in Potter and Wetherell 1992: 74–94). There have also been studies of justification in formal contexts, specifically legal proceedings (Atkinson and Drew 1979), but none of the formal context in which a president of the USA justifies going to war, or merely, as in the present case, having participated in military intervention. Justifications, unlike excuses, do not presuppose that a given action is wrong, and do not deny agency or responsibility. Rather they claim a given action is right, performed deliberately and for good purposes, or at least that it is permissible in the circumstances or with respect to certain values (Austin 1961). Various types, or components, of justifications include: denial or minimization of injury, claiming the victim deserved injury, making comparison with other actions allegedly not censured, appeal to higher authority, appeal to law and order, argument that benefits outweigh harm, appeal to political, moral or religious values, appeal to the need to maintain credibility or honor (Semin and Manstead 1983: 91–2).

Within a cognitive discourse-analytical perspective – that pursued in this chapter – justification can be regarded as a type of linguistic-social action, and more narrowly as a text-type. Texts can be understood as giving rise to cognitive-social processes, activated by the resources of a language system (English, in the present case) linked to cognitive structures and processes. Justification can be regarded as a text type, specifically a sub-type of "argumentation".

What form, then, do these justificatory text-types take? I adopt a dual-track approach to this question. First, it is possible to arrive at a description of the "arrangement" (or "disposition") of the text. The text's disposition is the sequence of units, sub-units defined in terms of propositions, and speech acts. This can be regarded as a macro-structure level for texts. Second, at the micro-structural level, I argue for the application of a theory of cognitive discourse processing: readers/hearers set up conceptual domains (ontological spaces), which carry a deictic "signature" for space, time and modality, and relationships among them. Analysis at both these levels gives some insight not only into text and discourse organization but also into the nature of justificatory text types, and more obviously into the nature of the particular text of Clinton's national address.

2. Textual arrangement

A starting point for this type of analysis is the decomposition of the text into units and sub-units. Sentences can be decomposed following various theoretical models. Yet, despite the work in text analysis, there is no explicit model for doing this with texts. A heuristic for discerning dispositional structure in a text of this type is to consider (1) propositional meanings, (2) speech acts, (3) discourse cohesion and coherence, and (4) discourse division markers. As for the "realities" set up through discourse, sometimes such "mental spaces" and subspaces, "text worlds" and sub-worlds will seem to constitute an entire dispositional unit or sub-unit. Very often, however, what I am calling ontological spaces here are complex interrelated systems at sub-sentential levels which do not enter directly into dispositional structure.

Figure 1 represents an initial step in deciding the dispositional structure of Clinton's speech.

These sections, which are derived from a reading of the text, are essentially discourse moves and speech acts. In general terms, the central section C has the predominant function of issuing an ultimatum to Milošević, although Milošević is not the direct ad-dressee. The flanking sections, B and D, are extremely complex structures: B has the overall function of establishing a conceptual frame for the Kosovo situation and thus the American response to it; D has the function of forestalling objections that American citizens are being exposed to risk, and incorporates a kind of moral accoun-

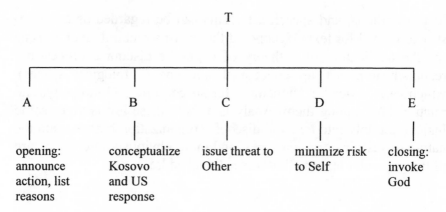

Figure 1

ting. A and E are required openings and closings. The closing for this genre conventionally requires a call for divine aid; the opening, which allows more latitude in content, here concentrates on the Self's (America's, and the President's) actions and motives (stated as purposes). Each of the major sections can be diagrammed for their inner disposition. In the following diagrams, as in Figure 1 above, the linear left-right sequence reflects the temporal sequence of constituent parts in the discourse disposition.

Since openings and closings probably have salience in discourse processing, it is worth noting that the opening words serve to establish common national ground and to mention the three central manifestations of Self represented throughout the discourse ontology of the speech – Americans, American Armed Forces, and NATO (a kind of extension of Self). The closing focuses on the same participants, without NATO.

The structure of the central (C) section labeled "issue threat" is more complex than A and E, but still much less so than B and D.

The units, based as they are on propositional and speech act considerations, not on sentence-syntactic divisions, intersect complex sentences (as in (53)). Some of the proposed units and labels are based on the assumption that hearers draw inferences, where there is no explicit formulation: for example, the "consequence" relation between (50–52) and (53). The structure seems to represent a classic

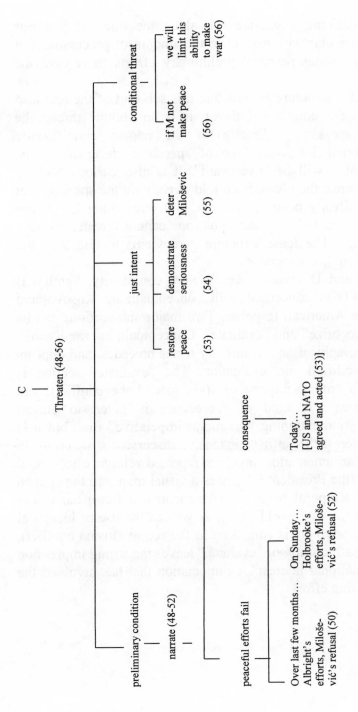

Figure 2

method for justifying a warlike act, along the lines of just war doctrine, in particular with respect to the amount of processing that goes into establishing peaceful preliminary efforts to resolve the conflict.

Curiously, this structure reveals that this sub-unit of the text also appears to issue a conditional threat. It is an oblique threat: the President is speaking indirectly to the person conditionally threatened. Nonetheless, this type of speech is designed in the expectation that it will be "overheard". It is also curious because hearers know, since they have been told already by the speaker, that an attack has already been carried out. But threatening has *future* action as one of its felicity conditions (one cannot threaten to have done something). The tense structure here seems to telescope the entire conditional threat sequence.

Sections B and D involve even greater complexity. Section B (sentences 7–47) is concerned with conceptualizing Kosovo and formulating the American response. Two major sub-sections can be discerned: "categorize" and "evaluate". Conceptualizing the Kosovo conflict in geographical and in military terms precedes, and appears to be a precondition for, evaluation. The "evaluate" section is subdivided into "moral imperative" (i.e. to end the conflict), and "national interest". A kind of precedence is given to ethical considerations by mentioning "the moral imperative" first, but it is the national interest that attracts extensive discursive structuring. In particular, the argumentation involves repeated reference to spatial configurations (the President integrates a visual map into the spoken discourse) and temporal sequence (American and European action and inaction in the two world wars), as well as the use of historical analogy (the Kosovo crisis compared to the recent Bosnia conflict). Analysis of the structuring of "evaluate" leaves the strong impression that it is the "national interest" argumentation that has involved the greatest processing effort.

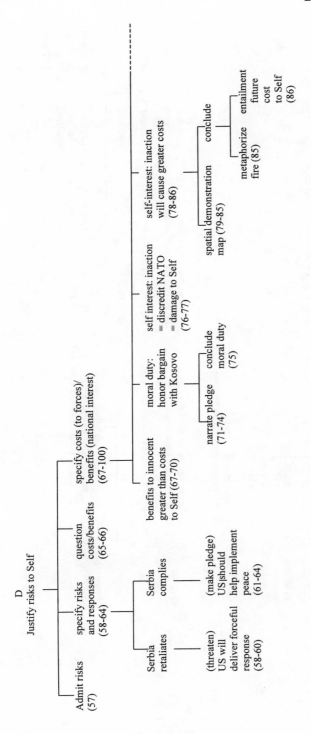

Figure 3a

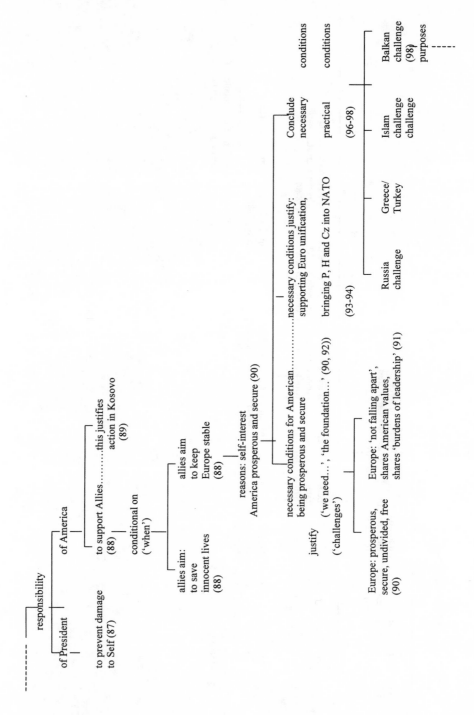

Figure 3b

Section D in our analysis of the dispositional structure coun-
terbalances section B, and is even more complex (Figures 3a and 3b).

The analysis in D, like the analyses of the other major text nodes,
is derived from a reader's interpretation primarily of propositions and
speech acts, and of the logical and other communicative links
holding between them. Sometimes there is vagueness or ambiguity.
For instance, consider:

(87) I have a responsibility as president to deal with problems such as this
before they do permanent harm to our national interests.
(88) America has a responsibility to stand with our allies when they are
trying to save innocent lives and preserve peace, freedom and stability in
Europe.
(89) That is what we are doing in Kosovo.

In (88) it is syntactically unclear whether the embedded sentence
"preserve peace, freedom and stability in Europe" is the complement
of "responsibility" or of "trying". And, in (89), the antecedent of
"That" is unclear. Does it refer only to (88) or to both (87) and (88)?
The diagram assumes the former.

Sentences (90) to (92) have a particularly dense propositional (and
syntactic) structure:

(90) If we've learned anything from the century drawing to a close, it is that
if America is going to be prosperous and secure, we need a Europe that is
prosperous, secure undivided and free.
(91) We need a Europe that is coming together, not falling apart; a Europe
that shares our values and shares the burdens of leadership.
(92) That is the foundation on which the security of our children will
depend.

The logical core seems to be the assertion that creating certain
conditions in Europe is a necessary (if not, presumably, sufficient)
condition for both American economic well-being and American
security – the latter concept being presented affectively by reference
to "our children" (92). The notion of necessary condition is textually
represented by "we need" and also by the metaphorical expression *X
is the foundation of Y*.

Although D seems primarily concerned with costs and benefits, part of it (sentences 58 to 64) comes close to enacting two speech acts – a threat to respond with force if Serbia retaliates and something approaching a pledge that The United States will join allies to implement a peace agreement:

(58) Serbia's air defenses are strong.
(59) It could decide to intensify its assault on Kosovo, or to seek to harm us or our allies elsewhere.
(60) If it does, we will deliver a forceful response.
(61) Hopefully, Mr. Milošević will realize his present course is self-destructive and unsustainable.
(62) If he decides to accept the peace agreement and demilitarize Kosovo, NATO has agreed to help to implement it with a peace-keeping force.
(63) If NATO is invited to do so, our troops should take part in that mission to keep the peace.

However, neither is clearly a performative for which the speaker could be held absolutely accountable. In the first case (60), it could be argued that a threat is not issued directly to the relevant recipient; the second sentence (63) further can be read as a careful qualification actually falling short of "implement it with a peace-keeping force", a proposition embedded in (62) and also therein hedged with "has agreed to help". Moreover, the real point is probably contained in (64), which denies the intention of committing troops:

(64) But I do not intend to put our troops in Kosovo to fight a war.

The syntax and the lexis of this sentence are interesting. Arguably, "I do not intend" is a hedge compared with (for example) "I will not". But more interesting, the scope of the negative operator is pragmatically ambiguous. The negative could be taken as having narrow scope over "intend". It could be taken as having scope over the entire complement "put our troops in Kosovo to fight a war", in which "not...put our troops in Kosovo" is more salient. Or, "not" might be taken to have scope over the purpose clause "to fight a war".

Another example of significantly complex embedding comes in (78–86). The use of para-linguistic means (a map) contributes to this impression, and more will be said below about the importance of spatial representations in this speech. In addition, the argumentation in the conclusion to this sub-unit crucially hinges on metaphorical entailment. The map shows "movement" both of refugees out of Kosovo and of troops out of Serbia into other parts of the rump Yugoslav federation. In terms of conceptual schemata, there is spill-over across containing boundaries, but this is not stated linguistically. Similarly, sentence (85) is inexplicit:

(85) Let a fire burn in this area and the flames will spread.

Co-operative discourse principles mean that (85) has to be related to (78–84). The inferences include: war is fire, fire spreads, therefore the war in this area will spread. Such argumentation is a conceptual short-cut, independent of empirical arguments.[1]

Reasons, purposes, self-interests and moral motivations are interwoven intricately in the sequential and syntactic structure of node D. The next point of complexity in the linear sequence – and it is the point of greatest complexity – is the President's explanation of the need for action in Kosovo. This is essentially a cost/benefit account, where the cost is expressed in terms of harm to American armed forces and benefit in terms of future security of the United States. In particular, the greatest detail seems to occur, not when there is an assertion of the moral duty to preserve the innocent (one may of course argue that this is a moral injunction not in need of elaboration), but when there is a need to account for giving support to allies.

This account, which involves much embedding, is announced by, and can be seen as embedded under, sentence (88) "America has a responsibility to stand with our allies...". This sentence has relevance only if commitment to allies is assumed to be problematic, i.e. in need of justification. Implicit in this is the American suspicion of European entanglements. Two conditions for commitment are mentioned, of which it is not the first – the purpose of protecting the innocent, but the second – the necessity of keeping Europe stable that is elaborated. The motivation for keeping Europe stable is presented as the preservation of American lives. This point appears to attract considerable detail, and the processing effort involved looks considerably greater than the effort involved in asserting moral arguments.

Perhaps it would be more precise to say that two moral arguments collide – an expressed altruistic concern for the innocent suffering of others and a self-oriented concern for American soldiers and citizens (the latter mentioned indirectly through reference to children). The convoluted arguments for intervention in terms of preserving European stability are particularly hard to capture, but one striking feature emerges – namely the final deeply discourse-embedded "purposes" section represented in (98), diagrammed in Figure 3c.

Figures 3a, 3b and 3c tell us a certain amount about Clinton's justification of American collaboration with NATO in the intervention in Kosovo in 1999, and probably also a certain amount about this text type in general. For example, it emerges that (an admittedly non-salient) speech act of threatening is "central" in the disposition – a result not anticipated before the analysis. It also emerges that the amount of linguistic material, especially in terms of discursive embedding, that goes into different thematic areas is variable – moral imperatives and national interests vie for space, and sometimes they merge or appear to be inconsistently linked. Most remarkable is section D, with its multiple sub-units clustering around the problem of justifying American support for European powers. The drift seems to be that there is a moral responsibility to keep Europe stable and a moral responsibility to protect the innocent. The latter is certainly mentioned explicitly (near the surface of the discourse disposition, as it were). But, the former is developed with great intricacy. Not only reasons but also requirements are given – that is to say, in addition to the giving of justificatory motivations and purposes, such as is found throughout the text, requirements (or, as the text has it "challenges") for the achievement of purposes are also given.

This kind of analysis does not tell us, however, about the detailed fashion in which deictic "signatures" are involved at the micro-level of discourse processing. This level cannot be ignored just because it is "micro", for it is only on the basis of the micro level that the gross dispositional structures described above can be derived. The following sections explore this dimension.

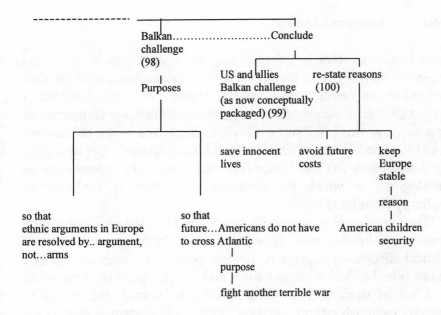

Figure 3c

3. Representations of reality

Texts enable hearers to generate cognitive structures in short and long-term memory, and they do it as it were, backstage, rather than up-front in the words themselves (cf. Turner 1991: 206, Fauconnier 1994: xxii–xxiii). Among these cognitive structures are complexes of "spaces", "worlds" or "sub-worlds", in the terminology of Fauconnier (1994) and Werth (1999), or "ontological spaces". Let us further say that speaker (S) and hearer (H) establish mental representations (ontologies), in which the existence of entities is explicitly or implicitly postulated.

These entities may be manifest to S and H in the physical setting of an interaction, but quite often they are not. In the particular case of political discourse, especially foreign policy, all relevant realities cannot possibly be co-present for S and H. The speaker, thus has to do a lot of discursive work to enable, or induce, the hearer to mentally establish a representation.[2] What is important is that such a representation "contains" entities which are literally *positioned* and *oriented* in relation to S and H. This process – the process of pointing to entities while simultaneously specifying their spatial, temporal and other kinds of relation to S and to H – is, of course, the process of deixis. The central point for present purposes is that geopolitical realities are mental representations of this type, conjured up by linguistic stimuli in texts.

What is the nature of this oriented positioning? How many dimensions are involved in the space where positioning occurs? These are theoretical questions that I shall not follow up here. We can, however, start with four dimensions: pronouns, time, location and modality. To simplify, we may assume that referents of pronouns are defined as a function of deictic positioning with respect to axes of space, time and modality. The deictic center (the Self, picked out by *I* or *we*) is the "origin" of the three dimensions. Other entities (arguments of predicates) "exist" relative to ontological spaces defined by their co-ordinates on the space (s), time (t) and modality (m) axes. This makes it possible to conceptualize the ongoing kaleidoscope of ontological configurations, activated by text, as a three-dimensional space. The "deictic center" is the common point of origin for three qualitatively scalar dimensions. Extreme points on all three axes can be characterized as types of "remoteness". The diagrams thus generated are representations of conceptual not linguistic organization. This is not the place for full theoretical justification, but the model works roughly as described below.

3.1. Space deixis

The *s* axis incorporates space deixis, including the pronominal system. The speaker (Self, which may be *I* or a *we*-group) is *here*. The entities indexed by second-person and third-person pronouns are situated along *s*. It is not being suggested that this can be done quantitatively; relative "distances" from Self are presumably represented by H as a function of discourse and background knowledge. Geographical places likewise are a function of long-term cognitive frames and current discourse cues – of mental maps, rather than of geographical measurement. At the remote end of *s* is Other. This scale, crucial to the interaction of language, conceptualization and social relationships, is of considerable relevance for political discourse, with its need to identify in-groups, allies, out-groups, potential enemies and actual enemies. In Clinton's speech, the "closeness" of troubled regions in Europe is of particular significance, as we shall see.

3.2. Time deixis

The origin on the *t* axis is the *time* of speaking surrounded, so to speak, by a pragmatically variable *now*. Of this model's three deictic dimensions, *t* is the only one that in some sense has negative and positive directionality (past and future). The role of directionality in the conceptualization (and linguistic expression) of time has been discussed by Lakoff and Johnson (1980) and Lakoff (1993). Both past and future can be "remote", but how remote is a function of discourse representation. In the Clinton speech, periods of time and historical events are quite precisely situated relative to one another.

Clinton also, however, brings relatively remote times in distant places into closer temporal focus by deliberate discursive effort. For political discourse, such changing representations are important; a nation's history, and which parts of that history, are "close" to the *we*-group is central to national ideologies and indeed to justifying present and future policy.

3.3. Modality as deixis

S (Self, *I* and some forms of *we*) is not only *here* and *now*, but also the origin of the epistemic *true* and the deontic *right*. Several points motivate such a view.

There are close connections between epistemic modality, deontic modality, and negation. The first two are commonly thought of as scales, and are closely linked. Sweetser (1990), modifying Talmy (1988), analyzes epistemic modals as metaphorically derived from root modals (deontic and dynamic), which she analyses as grounded in FORCE image schemata. A more unified approach to space, time and modality can be obtained by treating epistemic and deontic modalities as grounded in a proximity-remoteness scale, which is related to the CENTER-PERIPHERY image schema.[3]

The epistemic scale represents S's commitment to the truth of a proposition, ranging from confident prediction to near impossibility (for these terms and the scale, see Werth 1999: 314–5). Further, it can be argued that at each end the scale should be extended to include "true" (the modality of assertion), near to or co-located with Self, and "untrue" or, better, "falsity", at the remote end, that is, near to or co-located with Other. As many linguists have pointed out, negation is a function of discourse and takes its sense from its relation to propositions asserted elsewhere by S. Since we are modeling situated discourse, the end points are speech acts: assertion and negation. A consequence of this approach is that conditional sentences, which involve both counterfactuality and irreality, can also be accounted for in terms of the remote end of the modality scale.

The use of deontic modality, to cite Saeed (1997: 127), "is tied to social knowledge: the speaker's belief systems about morality and legality; as well as her estimations of power and authority." This nicely sums up the complex interconnection with social and political values. While the case is less clear than for epistemic modality, deontic modality can also be theorized as a scale ranging from obligation to permission. Can this too be regarded as a proximity-remoteness scale? Frawley (1992: 421–3) argues that deontic modality has this kind of structure, similar to that of epistemic modality. He also argues that deontic obligation and deontic permission are two separate categories and scales. However, I treat obligation and permission as a single scale (cf. examples in Werth 1999: 314). That which is morally or legally "wrong", or prohibited in a speech act, is distanced from Self. The scale is directional, oriented toward the Self's authoritative "position" with respect to Other. The end points are the speech acts command and prohibition. It is Self that issues "moral imperatives".

Both epistemic and deontic scales represent proximity and remoteness, with an asserted or known state of affairs located at Self, and a remote, uncertain, or imposed but not yet actual state of affairs located at a distance from Self. This is the *realis/irrealis* distinction integrated with a discourse-based account. The polysemy of "right" and "wrong" supports the idea that epistemic and deontic scales are closely related: what is right is both truth-conditionally "right" and legally or morally "right", and correspondingly for "wrong".[4] The scale *m* in the deictic space diagrams therefore stands for a composite scale, approximately as in the following schema, which shows only the English modal verbs, not other modal expressions:

RIGHT		WRONG
Self, near		remote, Other
realia	$\longrightarrow$	*irrealia*

deontic	will, must, should, ought, can/can, may, needn't,	
command	oughtn't, shouldn't, mustn't, won't, can't	**prohibition**

epistemic	will, must, should, ought, can, could, might,	
assertion	may, shouldn't, oughtn't, mustn't, won't, can't	**negation**

In the figures above, predications in the discourse analyzed are assumed to generate inter-linked ontological spaces with deictic co-ordinates. The co-ordinates are treated as points on a qualitative scale, established *in the discourse* as part of S's reality-space, the space that S expects H to know and accept. The co-ordinates are indexed in discourse by linguistic expressions ("space-builders" in Fauconnier's terminology, "world-builders" in Werth's) of various types: tense, prepositional phrases, pronouns, modal expressions, and so forth, in conjunction with extra-discourse frame-based knowledge. Predications may involve arguments (prototypically actors and patients) that have different deictic co-ordinates (actors may move in t and s, for instance), thus producing regions in three-dimensional space.

Further, there are links between the deictically indexed spaces. Anaphora (explicit and inferred), sequence and synchronicity are types of such relations. More interesting, however, are relations such as belief, hypothesis, purpose, intention, cause. Analogy and metonymy are also types of intra-discursive relations between spaces. These relations may be inferred rather than explicit, as may ontological spaces themselves: these are represented by broken lines in the space diagrams. I treat metaphors not as "worlds" (or ontological spaces) but rather as a special frame-based form of parallel inferencing. They are special because they map structure from one knowledge frame or image schema (the source domain) into a target domain, although these mappings often are grounded systematically in cognitive patterns.

3.4. Clinton's co-ordinates

The first two sentences of President Clinton's text set up some of the main parameters of the speech:

(1) My fellow Americans, today our Armed Forces joined our NATO allies in air strikes against Serbian forces responsible for the brutality in Kosovo.
(2) We have acted with resolve for several reasons.

Among other things, (1) and (2) establish the entities in the discourse reality, the relations between them, and their relation to the point of utterance. Sentence (1) sets up the participant entities *I (my), Americans, armed forces, NATO allies, Serbian forces, Kosovo.* Frame and script knowledge is also activated: warfare scripts, geographical frames, moral frames containing antithetical value orientations (*responsibility, brutality, resolve, reasons*). Geographical frames are particularly significant. Such frames might be poorly specified for some hearers, and specifying their content turns out to be an important feature of the speech. Geographical specification emerges not simply as objective geographical knowledge, but as deictically organized *geopolitical* knowledge. Sentence (2) induces a conflation of the *I* concept and the *our armed forces* concept into a *we* concept. Discourse expectations, based on frame knowledge of texts, induces the expectation that "reasons" will be stated in the succeeding portions of discourse. The deictic center is constructed (e.g. by "my fellow Americans") as a relation between speaker and hearers inside a common political entity.

A number of propositions are extractable from (1) by closely examining clauses, verbal nouns (*strikes*), and presupposition (*the*). Each one is deictically coordinated with respect to the deictic center. Thus:

i   joined (our armed forces, our NATO allies)
            deictic coordinates: *our, our, today, -ed*
            cognitive frames: America, armed forces, U.S. alliance structure
ii   air strikes (our armed forces and NATO, Serbian forces)
            deictic coordinates: *our, NATO, Serb, against,* by zero anaphors (the
            grammatical subject of *joined* is also the agent in *air strikes*)
            cognitive frames: warfare, U.S. alliance structure
iii   responsible (Serbian forces, brutality in Kosovo)
            deictic coordinates: *Serbian, in Kosovo*
            cognitive frames: ethical values, geography
iv   exists (brutality in Kosovo)
            deictic coordinates: *the, in Kosovo*
            cognitive frame: ethical values, geography.

Figure 4 represents the deictically specified reality spaces that are dependent upon those of the speaker, S. Bounded areas impressionistically represent spaces triggered by deictic expressions working together with cognitive frames. Within the spaces are entities called up by referring expressions or anaphoric expressions. The "locations" with respect to the three dimensions are assumed to be largely determined by knowledge-value frames: for example, in the frame assumed by S, *my fellow Americans* is closest to S, *NATO allies* are closer to S than *Kosovo,* and *Kosovo* is closer than *Serbian armed forces*. The positions indicated on the axes are relative.

In Figure 4 italicized *Kosovo* should not be taken to denote some real-world geographical place, but the concept *Kosovo* in some mutually expected frame. Entities are located with respect to their three co-ordinates, and indicated by "x". Straight arrows represent predicates impressionistically as processes in space and/or time. Arrowed arcs represent predicates that set up reality spaces. Links between spaces that exist if hearers make certain kinds of inference (using co-operative coherence principles and frames, for example) are indicated by broken arrowed arcs, without attempting to indicate the detailed nature of the inference.

In terms of *m*, the value is "proximate" – that is, actions referred to are asserted as true (and right) without modification. In terms of *t*, they are asserted to have taken place with the mutually understood vague time zone denoted by *today*.

For *s*, the situation is a little more complex. The propositions contained within the first sentence are syntactically linked (prepositions, zero anaphora), creating conceptual links. The deictic center is linked by pronominal anaphora. "[T]he brutality in Kosovo" may be interpreted as a separate ongoing space, if hearers have contextual knowledge. There are three spaces – one in which Self's forces join more distant but still relatively proximate allies, and one in which Self's forces and Self's allies attack distal entities. This second space is extended along the *s* dimension – an important feature of the entire text, and one of the key features that Clinton has to justify. The third space is a distant geopolitical area.

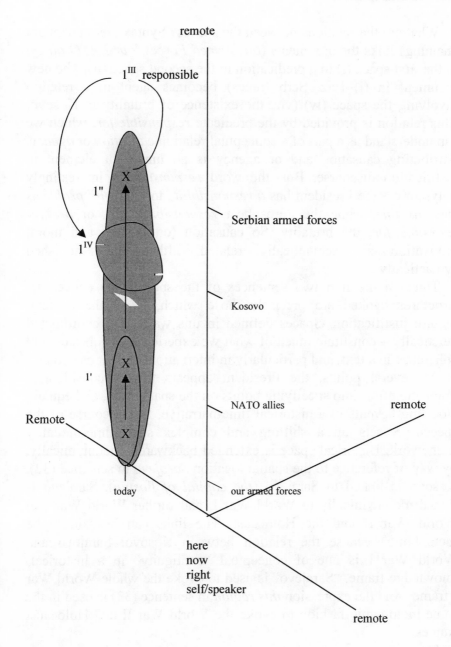

Figure 4

What are the relations between the spaces? Syntax (zero anaphora chaining) links the arguments (*our Armed Forces, our NATO allies*) in the first space (i) to a predication in the second space (ii). The new argument in (i) (viz. Serb forces) becomes agent in a relation involving the space (iv) (viz. the existence of brutality in Kosovo. This relation is provided by the predicate *responsible for*, which we can understand as a part of a conceptual relation *causation* or *agency*. Attributing causation and or agency is an important element in justification discourse. But, the word *responsible* is interestingly polysemic – the President has *a responsibility* to *deal with problems such as this*, while the Serbs bear *responsibility* for, or *are responsible for*, the brutality. So causation (or agency) and moral motivation are semantically related, although distinguished syntactically.

Thus, in the first two sentences of the speech, the conceptual structures evoked are precisely those which, given the context, require justification. Spaces defined in this way – i.e. coordinated deictically – constitute much of what we experience as cohesion and coherence in a text, and particularly in international relations texts.

At several points, the President appears to put considerable linguistic effort into specifying points on the spatial axis, and equally "locating" events in a historical time-narrative. In the course of the speech, S sets up a shifting and complex space-time-modality framework. Historical space is extended backwards, metonymically, by way of reference to the spatial location *Sarajevo* in sentence (32). Kosovo is linked to Sarajevo (*the capital of Bosnia*). Sarajevo is linked metonymically to World War I, and further World War I to World War II and the Holocaust. The links can be said to be metonymic because the relation between Kosovo, Sarajevo and World War I is one of conceptual "contiguity" in a historical-knowledge frame. "Sarajevo" is used to evoke the whole World War I frame. And the expression *this region* in sentence (33) is used in the same metonymic fashion to evoke the World War II and Holocaust frames.

Once in play in the emergent common ground of the discourse, these discursively linked frames are used as the basis for two sets of generalizations: sentence (31) relating to the geographical space conceptualized "around" Kosovo, and (34–35) relating to the flashback historical space conceptualized in connection with Sarajevo. These generalizations in turn – the chain of argumentation is surprisingly long and intricate – form the basis of (36) and its elaboration in (37–41). The chain is: Kosovo – Bosnia-Sarajevo – World War I – World War II – back to Bosnia – analogy between Bosnia (and by inference the other wars mentioned) with Kosovo. How does this work?

3.5. Metaphors and modalities

Both (31) and (85) involve metaphor. This is not coincidental. In both cases metaphor seems to be deployed strategically as part of an embedded piece of argumentation about the "closeness" of the danger and the urgency for America to act militarily. Both metaphors, moreover, use FIRE as their source domain and project this structured knowledge frame onto CONFLICT, yielding a number of entailments.

The linguistic cues that seem to require some form of metaphorical processing in (31) are the highlighted ones below:

> (31) All the ingredients for a major war are there: ancient grievances, struggling democracies, and (31') in the center of it all a dictator in Serbia (31'') who has done nothing since the Cold War ended but start new wars and pour gasoline on the flames of ethnic and religious division.

The word *ingredients* could be regarded as a conventionalized lexical item with associated meaning. Alternatively, it might be from a COOKING frame, and the sense of the discourse might be generated from a metaphorical inference based on a metaphor PRODUCING AN ARTIFACT IS COOKING, where the underlying concept is some form of causality.[5] The ingredients are *struggling democracies*, etc., and the unmentioned but entailed "cook" or causative agent is *a dictator*. This latter phrase is a definite description that H identifies, by inference, with the referent of *Milošević*. This particular way of maintaining the reference probably also enables H, by prompting frame knowledge of political concepts (prototypical dictators), to advance the argument that the Balkans are dangerous and bad. Text processors therefore may, at some level of cognition, infer that the dictator referred to is likely to cause a major war. This inference is partly triggered by the preposition *for*, and the space that this potentially sets up. As Figure 5 illustrates, such inferential space is modal and future (indicated by the indefinite article: *a war*). It is a space that is interpreted as some sort of modal possibility, in the unspecified although (the hearer may infer) not-too-remote future.

The prepositional phrase *in the center of it all* can be considered in two perspectives. On the one hand, it can be treated as a deictic "space builder" that sets up a geographical location for *a dictator*, where *it all* has (along with *there*) the locations mentioned in (28–30) as its antecedent. On the other hand, *in the center of it all* does mean a bit more than that. A text interpreter's discourse processes may access the CENTER-PERIPHERY schema – a ubiquitous image schema that underlies a number of lexically encoded concepts (Lakoff and Johnson 1980; Lakoff 1987; Johnson 1987), including the deictic coordinate system itself, as I suggested in section 3.3. In some contexts the center-periphery schema will be mapped onto Self and Other. However, in this context the center is related to Other's space. To speak of the Other's center is generally to indicate the Other's principal causal agency (cf. for example: "he was at the center of the conspiracy"). Further, this notion is linked in political discourse to the concept of containment. What is evoked is movement outward from the center of a contained space, threatening those (including Self) who are outside the space. In the text's overarching metaphorical structure, this notion is indeed linked to the fire metaphor, beginning with *pour gasoline on the flames*.

Metaphors are conceptual processes which use as their source domains basic image schemata (such as center-periphery, container) or basic social and cultural knowledge frames (cooking, fires). The metaphorical mapping from fire to violence and conflict is, of course, conventionalized. The point, however, is that metaphors are conceptually dynamic: in a mapping from fire to conflict, one's knowledge about the nature and behavior of fire also is entailed in the target domain, in this case conflict. Thus, if fire worsens when

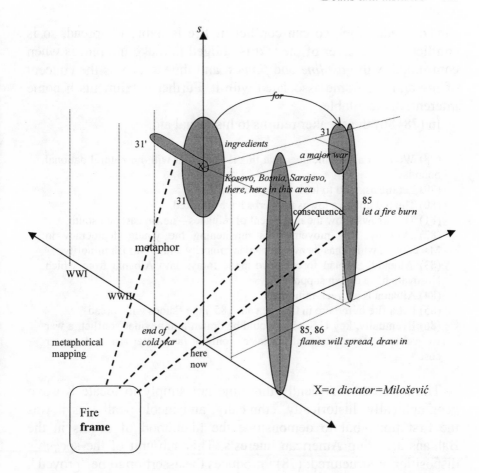

Figure 5

someone adds fuel, so can conflict; if fire is liable to spread, so is conflict. The receiver of the text is obliged to make inferences when confronted with *gasoline* and *flames*, and thus to access the concept of fire and the frame associated with it. Further entailments become inferentially available.

In (78–86) the speaker returns to his visual aid:

(78) We must also remember that this is a conflict with no natural national boundaries.
(79) Let me ask you to look again at a map.
(80) The red dots are towns the Serbs have attacked.
(81) The arrows show the movement of refugees – north, east and south.
(82) Already, this movement is threatening the young democracy in Macedonia, which has its own Albanian minority and a Turkish minority.
(83) Already, Serbian forces have made forays into Albania from which Kosovars have drawn support.
(84) Albania is a Greek minority.
(85) Let a fire burn here in this area and (85') the flames will spread.
(86) Eventually, key U.S. allies could be drawn into a wider conflict, a war we would be forced to confront later – only at far greater risk and greater cost.

The purpose is evidently this time not simply to locate Kosovo geographically, historically, ethnically, and ideologically, as it was the first time, but to demonstrate the likelihood of events in the Balkans affecting American interests. This sub-unit of the speech's disposition is structured: (78) introduces the assertion to be "proved", along with a concept of "natural" national boundaries that we will not dwell on here. Sentences (79–84) combined with the visual images rest on two basic image schemata: CONTAINER and PATH. The mental picture projected appears to one of contiguous bounded containing spaces with penetrations (*attacks* on *red dots*, *forays into*), evacuations and extractions (*arrows, movement of refugees, draw from*).

Thus far, the map and its accompanying verbal conceptualization serves presumably as a quasi-empirical demonstration that there are no "natural national boundaries". The cognitive frame for the nation-state (cf. Chilton 1996) is taken for granted, and further inference from frame based knowledge seems to be required **to make sense of** why refugee movement should *threaten ... young democracies* (83).

But, the claim that all these (represented) actors and activities influence American interests is not made until (86). The precise domestic, international and military events that could lead to America being involved in a war of World War I and II proportions are not spelled out. The argument is instead made by way of a meta-phorically-embedded enthymeme:

(a)   Fires are intensified by gasoline
      Fires spread
      Fires draw combustible material into them
      Fires damage or destroy the things they burn

(b)   The conflict is a fire

(c)   The conflict can be intensified by certain actions
      The conflict can extend
      The conflict could cause America to be involved
      The conflict could damage America.

Figure 5 shows some of the co-ordinate shifts, and some of the inferencing involved in (31) and (85). The referents in (31) have co-ordinates in the recent past on t and at somewhat remote points on s. They are presented assertorically by S and hence appear at the positive end of m. However, linguistic elements in (31) imply a causal relation between events as described above and a hypothetical "major war" in the unspecified (but presumably not too far distant) future. There is a complementary structure in (85) which, as we have noted, serves a comparable role in the sequential disposition of the speech. In (85) *here in this area* locates the ontological space in play at the same point as in (31). The non-finite *let* is the conditional part of a conditional sentence, whose consequent is in the future tense (*the flames will spread*). Conditional sentences are linked closely to causal meanings: if such-and-such a condition is met, then such-and-such will inevitably follow, and behind this is a *post hoc ergo propter hoc* reasoning schema. The link, however, is inferable rather than explicitly coded. In (86) *eventually* indexes a more remote t in the conditional m space.

There are several complementary tendencies in the complex manipulation of ontological spaces that we have no more than begun to analyze. The first is the mobilization of conceptual schemata to represent remote effects as spatially close, temporally new and modally probable encroachments on the space of the Self. The second is the linking of historical episodes and the drawing of conclusions by analogy. Third, there is the linking of temporally remote spaces with the space of the present speaker and hearers. Fourth, inference that inaction causes undesirable effects are made available.

4. Concluding thoughts

Analysis of the disposition of President Clinton's speech indicates propositions and speech acts that correspond to some, but not all, of the categories of just war discourse. Clinton's text primarily addresses *jus ad bellum* themes, in two forms. On the one hand, just purposes and intents are listed explicitly and with discursive prominence. Atrocities perpetrated by the enemy are listed. The moral duty of the Self to intervene is made occasionally explicit, although more often it appears to be expressed by implication. Efforts to achieve a peaceful resolution are also listed, both as part of the justification and as the preparatory phase of the issuance of a threat. On the other hand, there is lengthy appeal to the need for self-preservation and to the moral duty of the leader to safeguard the nation. In this process, because the Balkan region is so remote psychologically in the world-representations of most Americans, major discursive effort apparently is necessary.

Strikingly absent, in comparison with just war doctrine, is the absence of any consideration of discrimination and proportionality. The kind and quantity of forces deployed, their strategy and goals, are not discussed, except in so far as they involve co-operation with allies and risk to the Self's own armed forces. Proportionality enters the discourse only in the form of a cost-benefits calculation, where costs are (only) American lives, and the claim to benefits rests essentially on the argument that a seemingly remote threat is "closer" than one might imagine. The *jus in bello* themes regarding harm to civilians and the sufficiency of force seem have been replaced by extensive discursive justification of the risk to Self.

Analysis of the text's disposition also reveals propositions and speech acts that are not traditionally part of just war discourse, but which are detected in the social-psychological and ethnomethodological theory of accounts. Of Semin and Manstead's categories we find: appeal to political, moral and religious values, a rather implicit appeal to law and order, appeal to the need to maintain credibility and honor, the claim that the victim (here Milošević) deserves injury – at least in the sense that Milošević's behavior is to be "deterred", and the argument that the benefits (both to the Kosovars and to America) outweigh the costs. But, none of these fit the justification-of-war text very well without careful modification. Dispositional analysis shows where effort and complexity are focused. The greatest discourse complexity, and thus presumably effort, seems to occur with respect to the representation of the location of Kosovo in geopolitical space, the representation of potential dangers to Self (the United States), and the representation of morally outrageous acts perpetrated by the enemy.

However, neither dispositional analysis, nor the comparisons with just war discourse nor the theory of accounts reveals the extent of the deictic centering on the collective Self. Such centering is fundamental to discourse processing. The center-periphery schema seems to be at the heart of the close-remote system. It is inherently bound up with political behavior. Taking the particular case of Clinton's text, there is a striking linkage and integration of remote and near spaces, both spatial and temporal. Military action cannot be justified in Clinton's context unless linkage is established – the remote is made threateningly near. However, Clinton does not emphasize an evil Other (or a *them* whose whereabouts *we* do not know though *we* know *they* are *there*), in contrast to previous presidents. This, perhaps, is characteristic of the post-Cold War environment. Or, perhaps, Milošević, who had no nuclear weapons, was not a particularly convincing threat. A parallel feature also seems to be that Clinton brings victims closer to home. Clearly, however, human rights violations, international law, and moral values are not in themselves sufficient (or deemed sufficient for hearers) to justify action.

Clinton's speech is marked by extremely frequent shifts in deictic co-ordination – scene-shifts in space, flashbacks in time and "flash-sideways" in modality. Great cognitive complexity appears to be involved in the representation of the Kosovo conflict by means of deictically coordinated spatial, temporal and modal spaces. The spatial spaces represent Kosovo as "close"; the temporal and spatial spaces together represent Kosovo as "central" to a historical process that could eventuate in some major threat to the USA; the modal spaces of potential, predictive, and causal argumentation are shored up, in two key passages, by metaphorical argumentation.

The deictic "origin", which is crucial for hearers to make sense of the speech, is the "position" of the USA with respect to the rest of the world, the current "distance" between the US and Europe, and the "distance" between regions such as the "Balkans" and "Europe" – where "distance" is not measured in geographical kilometers or miles but in terms of cognitive remoteness of future events. The rightness or the wrongness of intervention *qua* intervention in Kosovo in 1999 is not at issue here. The point of the analyses that I have outlined is to show the extremely detailed linguistic work that goes into constructing a conceptual framework to persuade an American audience of the rightness of intervention.

Nonetheless, one of the striking features of the speech's construction is worth highlighting. Substantial processing effort apparently goes into a specific argument – namely, the argument that World War I and World War II were caused, or at least not stopped, by the tardiness of Europe and America. Yet Americans, as well as Europeans (who, it might be argued bore the greater responsibility), had already delayed intervening to stop the war in the Balkans at the time of Clinton's speech. A critical discourse analyst might find this ironic, and possibly even the explanation for why the argumentation is so weighty.

Notes

1. To make this point, incidentally, is not to indicate a commitment one way or the other, as far as the rightness of intervention was concerned in this historical context. I am concerned here with how discourse is structured and processed.
2. The process by which H has to assume the existence of an entity or state of affairs is called "accommodation" by Werth (1999: 253–7, 280–7).
3. Cf. On CENTER-PERIPHERY see Johnson (1987), Lakoff (1987). This approach is supported by evidence from polysemy: *not remotely possible, close to the truth, getting close to the truth,* and so forth.
4. Similarly, *true* and *false* have epistemic and deontic meanings.
5. Evidence for some such metaphor in English: *raw facts, cook up a new theory, half-baked ideas.*

References

Atkinson, J. Maxwell, and Paul Drew
  1979   *Order in Court: The Organization of Verbal Interaction in Judicial Settings.* London: Macmillan.

Austin, John L.
  1961   A plea for excuses. In: Urmson, James O., and Geoffrey J. Warnock (eds.), *Philosophical Papers.* Oxford: Clarendon Press.

Chilton, Paul A.
  1996   *Security Metaphors: Cold War Discourse from Containment to Common House.* New York: Lang.

Fauconnier, Gilles
  1994   *Mental Spaces.* Cambridge: Cambridge University Press.

Frawley, William
  1992   *Linguistic Semantics.* Hillsdale, NJ: Erlbaum.

Johnson, Mark
  1987   *The Body in the Mind: The Bodily Basis of Meaning, Imagination, and Reason.* Chicago: Chicago University Press.

Lakoff, George
  1987   *Women, Fire and Dangerous Things: What Categories Reveal about the Mind.* Chicago: Chicago University Press.

1993   The contemporary theory of metaphor. In: Ortony, Andrew (ed.), *Metaphor and Thought*. Cambridge: Cambridge University Press.

Lakoff, George, and Mark Johnson
1980   *Metaphors We Live By*. Chicago: Chicago University Press.

Potter, John, and Margaret Wetherell
1992   *Discourse and Social Psychology: Beyond Attitudes and Behaviour*. London: Sage.

Saeed, John I.
1997   *Semantics*. Oxford: Blackwell.

Semin, Gün R., and Antony S. R. Manstead
1983   *The Accountablity of Conduct: A Social Psychological Analysis*. London: Academic Press.

Sweetser, Eve
1990   *From Etymology to Pragmatics: Metaphorical and Cultural Aspects of Semantic Structure*. Cambridge: Cambridge University Press.

Talmy, Leonard
1988   Force dynamics in language and cognition. *Cognitive Science* 2, 49–100.

Turner, Mark
1991   *Reading Minds*. Princeton: Princeton University Press.

Werth, Paul
1999   *Text Worlds: Representing Conceptual Space in Discourse*. London: Longman.

The language of atomic science and atomic conflict: Exploring the limits of symbolic representation

Robert E. Tucker and Theodore O. Prosise

1. Introduction

Our language evolved in a particular environment to accomplish particular tasks. The breathtaking flexibility of the linguistic system helps to hide this central truth. Enamored with the rich array of things that we *can* say, we pay less attention to the ways in which our language is limited – to the things that we are unable to say. Nowhere is this oversight more glaring than in our analysis of the language of war. When it comes to what Oliver Wendell Holmes called "the incommunicable experience of war," we have yet to examine the exact ways in which language falls short.

This essay is an initial foray into this gap. Specifically, we try to chart a particular kind of failure in language – the inability of ordinary language to represent matters and issues of a scale beyond that with which we are familiar. To accomplish our task, we begin with an analysis of language used to describe nuclear and quantum phenomena – particularly the view of language held by the Danish physicist Niels Bohr. Though such a discussion might initially seem far afield, our contention is that the ways in which Bohr sought to invent a new language for describing sub-atomic and quantum phenomena offers important lessons about the limits of language in general. We contend that the scientific discovery of quantum phenomena was an early example of the discovery of a phenomenal realm beyond that in which language developed.

After noting Bohr's recognition of this linguistic dilemma and his making unique conclusions regarding the role of language in describing phenomena at the frontiers of human experience, we turn to an analysis of nuclear discourse during the Second World War. We contend that the rhetorical situation faced by the first generation of atomic weaponeers – that is, the situation in which suasive and persuasive devices were created and deployed to justify the development and use of atomic weapons – was similar to that faced by the first generation of quantum scientists. In particular, scientists and policy-makers entered and attempted to orient themselves in a context far removed from that in which their ordinary language developed. We will examine the specific responses scientists and policy-makers made to this rhetorical crisis. Finally, we conclude by describing the political risks of rhetorical means used to "domesticate" the nuclear experience. We refer to these collected rhetorical means as the strategy of "naming" – first, naming the experience of sub-atomic phenomena and, second, naming the experience of atomic weapons and war.

The ways in which atomic planners, scientists, civilian and military leaders named sub-atomic phenomena and atomic weaponry is significant for two key reasons. First, these names and naming strategies continue to play an active role in contemporary policy making. The language of Bohr and the first generation of atomic weaponeers molded and continues to shape our understanding of nuclear weapons and the role they should play in geopolitics (Boyer 1994, 1998). Second, by considering communication about nuclear weapons we can begin to understand the obstacles that exist between us and a safer world. Brummett (1989: 85) has observed that "no subject is as critical politically as the rhetoric of nuclear war". Brummett (1989: 93) continued: "what people are motivated to do with weapons is directly related to what they say about them". In short, how people talk about nuclear weapons influences how people think about nuclear weapons and nuclear war. We turn now to an analysis of the ways in which difficulties in the description of atomic phenomena were first noticed and theorized about – the period during which the Copenhagen Interpretation of quantum mechanics emerged and stabilized.

2. The discovery of the unspeakable – the first generation of quantum mechanics

The emergence of quantum mechanics in 1925 and 1926 was a scientific triumph comparable to Galileo's demonstration of the heliocentric solar system and Darwin's description of evolution. During these two brief years, two distinct mathematical formalisms, the wave mechanics of Erwin Schrödinger and the matrix mechanics of Werner Heisenberg, allowed unprecedented understanding of the structure and behavior of sub-atomic phenomena. These formalisms, mathematically equivalent and reducible to one another, came to represent the core of the human understanding of quantum mechanics.

The development of quantum mechanics, however, entailed a significant and unprecedented rhetorical dilemma. While the mathematical formalisms of Heisenberg and Schrödinger proved tremendously successful in predicting new and previously unexplained atomic phenomena, the physical meaning of their equations remained obscure. The nature of the electron was particularly confusing, and all efforts to provide a visualizable description of its behavior met with intractable difficulties. As Niels Bohr (1949: 204) described the situation, "the quantitative comprehension of a vast amount of empirical evidence could leave no doubt as to the fertility and adequacy of the quantum-mechanical formalism, but its abstract character gave rise to a widespread feeling of uneasiness". Much of this uneasiness stemmed from the near total renunciation of visualization required by the new quantum theory.

As it became clear that descriptions of electrons "orbiting" the nucleus were fundamentally inaccurate, and that such terms as momentum, velocity, and position were in some ways ambiguous when applied to electrons, the previous image of the atom as a miniature solar system was abandoned. New pictorial representations invented to take the place of the Copernican image were demonstrably inadequate. By April 1928, the editors of *Nature* lamented:

> It must be confessed that the new quantum mechanics is far from satisfying the requirements of the layman who seeks to clothe his conceptions in figurative language. Indeed, its originators probably hold that such symbolic

representation is inherently impossible. It is earnestly to be hoped that this is not their last word on the subject, and that they may yet be successful in expressing the quantum postulate in picturesque form.[1]

Between 1925 and 1928, Niels Bohr formulated, among other things, a new doctrine of scientific communication. He regarded this communicative doctrine as more significant and of more lasting value than his 1913 masterpieces on the quantum structure of the atom.[2] It was Bohr's contention that the nature of sub-atomic phenomena demanded a radical revision in the communicative practices of atomic scientists. He regarded the communicative lessons of quantum mechanics as *generalizable* to other fields of human study – particularly other fields in which human beings discovered and began to operate in contexts far beyond the realm of ordinary physical experience.

As mental images failed in the quantum domain, particularly the classical images of particle and wave, Bohr was led to an ever-widening analysis of the limits of scientific language and communication.

Niels Bohr noted a particular rhetorical dilemma. He noticed that the words we use to describe the physical world are adapted to the physical phenomena we routinely encounter. Crucially, he noted that our everyday language is adapted to a particular *scale* of phenomena. Bohr grappled with the ultra-small and the fantastically brief, a realm in which our words and phrases begin to fall flat. This flatness, or what Bohr called ambiguity, is the result of an application of language beyond the sphere in which it developed.

Just as language can be maladapted to the very small and the very brief, so too it can fall flat in the description of phenomena more vast than any context to which we are accustomed. We turn now to an analysis of the communicative situation faced by developers of atomic weapons in the United States. The linguistic maladaptation that bedeviled efforts to portray the very small was evident for the vast as well, with substantial and significant political consequences.

3. Communication about the development and use of the bomb

On July 16, 1945 in a remote region of the New Mexico desert the Manhattan Project's first atomic bomb was detonated. Code named "Trinity," the blast exceeded expectations and provoked joy, wonder, awe, and concern among those who witnessed it. Several weeks later, on August 6, 1945, the United States Army Air Force dropped a single atomic weapon on the city of Hiroshima, Japan. The "Little Boy bomb" exploded with a force equivalent to twelve-thousand five hundred tons of TNT, leveling the city of Hiroshima (Schell 1982). Captain Van Kirk, navigator of the *Enola Gay* said of the sight: "if you want to describe it as something you are familiar with" the city was "a pot of boiling black oil" (Rhodes 1986: 711). The destruction of Hiroshima on August 6th, and Nagasaki three days later, was a human tragedy. Referring to Hiroshima, Rhodes (1986: 734) states that

> recent estimates place the number of deaths up to the end of 1945 at 140,000. The dying continued; five-year deaths related to the bombing reached 200,000. The death rate for deaths up to the end of 1945 was 54 percent, an extraordinary density of killing; by contrast the death rate for the March 9 firebombing of Tokyo, 100,000 deaths among 1 million casualties, was only 10 percent.

Such atomic destruction represents a rhetorical dilemma with significant similarities to the situation described by Bohr. Specifically, just as quantum phenomena were difficult if not impossible to describe because of the parochialness of language and its maladaptation to the quantum context, so too did language's adaptation to the relatively small scale of human existence make it maladapted for discussing the enormous power of nuclear weapons. The scale of atomic destruction was simply too great to be adequately represented by ordinary language. The inadequacies of the language about nuclear physics at the micro-level thus found analogous expression in the inadequate language employed by those involved in the United States atomic weapons effort during World War II. More than metaphorically, atomic destruction is as *unspeakable* as quantum phenomena.

Exploring the relationship between the "unspeakable" and constrained perceptions about nuclear weapons provides a valuable lesson about the limits and dangers of nuclear rhetoric. In this section, we first explore the language about nuclear technology as scientists and civilian and military leaders discussed the atomic bomb from 1939–1945. Evidence exists that such leaders recognized the "unspeakability" of atomic destruction. We then describe reactions to this communicative crisis. Faced with the inadequacy of ordinary language, scientists and policy makers adopted a linguistic strategy of *domestication* – attempting to recycle and reuse previous words and concepts to the new context of atomic warfare. Significantly, these scientists "mined" those areas of language richest in their expressive connotations – particularly their expressive abilities regarding size, grandeur, and an incomprehensible scale. Thus, when faced with the reality of nuclear weapons and the inadequacy of language to describe the effect of such weapons, even the most skeptical of scientists was thrown back into theological and mythological vocabulary. We will detail the metaphors and "god-terms" used in these planners' sense-making process. Next we consider the narrativizing of the atomic bomb and evaluate the adequacy of this rhetoric. Finally, we comment on the seeming paralysis of public understanding and the limits to public agitation over nuclear weapons.

3.1. Naming the atomic bomb – an explosive, a race, discovery or birth?

Scientists and civilian and military leaders accounted for the bomb with a number of linguistic resources. Metaphors, "god-terms," and narratives help us understand unfamiliar or difficult concepts in terms that can be more easily grasped.[3] Those discussing the advent of the atomic age understood the development of the bomb as (1) conventional explosive; (2) a race; and (3) discovery and birth. They also named the development of the bomb in celebratory terms. But these wartime planners viewed nuclear fission as altogether unprecedented and exceptional. Their rhetoric is an example of how something is described in familiar terms, but also described as revolutionary and unprecedented. The basic rhetorical pattern involves a threshold crossed with the development and use of the bomb. The bomb's significance was narrativized. Its development and use symbolized a qualitative and revolutionary advance, fundamentally changing America and human civilization.

The possibility of developing a nuclear weapon came to the attention of U.S. leaders most prominently with the Einstein/Szilard letter to Present Roosevelt in the summer of 1939. The letter reads: "the element uranium may be turned into a new and important source of energy" (Stoff, 1991: 18). Through "a nuclear chain reaction... extremely powerful bombs of a new type may be... exploded". Vannevar Bush, the Director of the Office of Scientific Research and Development, who oversaw aspects of the Manhattan Project, referred (1942) to the new technology as a "super-explosive". The Truman Statement of August 6, 1945, announcing the Hiroshima Bombing, says (p. 4) that one bomb, having "more power than 20,000 tons of TNT," was "dropped on Hiroshima, an important army base".

This comparison to conventional explosive no doubt came from the wartime planners' efforts to understand the scope of a controlled nuclear chain reaction as a weapon of war. In the meeting notes of the Interim Committee, the body set up to advise President Truman about the development and use of the bomb, Robert Oppenheimer, director of the Los Alamos weapons laboratory, spoke of the various stages of atomic development through references to conventional explosives. The first stage "was estimated to have the explosive force of 2,000–20,000 tons of TNT". The "second stage [of] the explosive force was estimated to be equal to 50,000–100,000 tons of TNT". And it was "possible that a bomb developed from the third stage might produce an explosive force equal to 10,000,000–100,000,000 tons of TNT" (Notes of the Interim Committee Meeting 1945).

Although we have come to "know" a type of nuclear chain reaction as a "bomb," we should question if this comparison to conventional explosives is adequate. First of all, there is considerable estimation evidenced by the vast range between the minimum and maximum TNT equivalents in each stage. Second, can one adequately conceive of or describe an explosive that has the equivalent of 100,000 tons of TNT? The difficulty with conceptualizing the macro-level of nuclear physics seems as difficult as conceptualizing the micro-level. Third, even if we could fathom such an explosion, this word fails to invoke important details that would make a nuclear detonation much different from "simply" detonating 100,000 tons of TNT.

Much of the communication about the atomic bomb situates it within larger symbolic structures. One means by which scientists framed an understanding of the bomb's development to policy-makers was with a race metaphor. For Arthur Compton, a nuclear physicist and an integral player in the Manhattan Project leadership, "[t]he quest" to produce the bomb started "as a race to win a precious prize" (1956: 11). Vannevar Bush explained to Roosevelt that it would soon be possible to develop a "super-explosive of overwhelming military might". But, he cautioned, the U.S. needed to move quickly; the U.S. was in a "race" against Germany, which may have been "ahead of us" (Bush to Roosevelt 1942). This orientational metaphor simplifies the development and use of the bomb as a contest directed at an end state – the production and use of a powerful weapon.

Many of those involved in the Manhattan Project also sought to explain the controlled nuclear chain reaction *qua* weapon with discovery and birth metaphors. For example, after hearing of Enrico Fermi's successful controlled chain reaction in a University of Chicago squash court-turned-secret laboratory, Arthur Compton called James Conant, Bush's assistant, Chairman of the National Defense Research Committee, and president of Harvard. "'Jim' I said, 'you'll be interested to know that the Italian navigator [Fermi] has just landed in the new world.'" Accounting for the early success of the experiment, he continued: "the earth was not as large as he had estimated, and he arrived at the new world sooner than he had expected" (Compton 1956: 144).

Others defined the detonation through birth metaphors. General Thomas Farrell wrote a section of Leslie Groves' report on the Trinity test. Farrell wrote that the bomb "was almost full grown at birth" (Stoff 1991: 191). Further, Farrell opined:

All seemed to feel that they had been present at the birth of a new age – the age of atomic energy – and felt their profound responsibility to help in guiding into right channels the tremendous forces which had been unlocked for the first time in history.[4]

George Harrison, Secretary of War Henry Stimson's assistant, sent a "coded" message to Stimson:

Doctor has just returned most enthusiastic and confident that the little boy is as husky as his big brother. The light in his eyes discernible from here to Highhold and I could hear his screams from here to my farm. (Hewlett and Anderson 1962: 386)

Metaphors, tropes and "god-terms," both enable and constrain our understanding. The language used to describe the bomb featured not the physical characteristics of a nuclear chain reaction as a weapon, and what that would do to a heavily populated city, but rather featured the weapon as part of a larger process. Why are these linguistic resources chosen? One answer lies in the recognized inability to speak about atomic detonations.

3.2. Recognizing the "unspeakability"

It is interesting to compare the language of "explosions" and a "race" with the reaction of several of those witnessing the Trinity blast, the first test of a plutonium implosion device. Those who witnessed the first nuclear chain reaction recognized the difficulty expressing the event symbolically. For General Farrell, the bombing was sublime, inadequately captured by words: "The effects could well be called unprecedented, magnificent, beautiful, stupendous and terrifying." There was no way to capture the experience. "It was," Farrell opined, "that beauty the great poets dream about but describe most poorly and inadequately." Indeed, "words are inadequate tools for the job of aquatinting those not present with the physical, mental and psychological effects. It had to be witnessed to be realized".[5]

Additional evidence of the recognized difficulty the bomb presented to our "old ways of thinking" found expression in a document titled "The Disposition of the Atomic Bomb." The document reads:

> Or does the bomb, instead, constitute merely a first step in a new control by
> man over the forces of nature too revolutionary and dangerous to fit into the
> old pattern? In that event, on the new uncharted sea boldness in seeking our
> new objective and "damn the torpedoes" may be our only reasonable chance
> of avoiding the wreck of the future human existence. In determining our
> course in such a novel situation, there is a danger of our being insensibly
> bound by accustomed ways of thinking suitable enough to the old pattern
> but not suited to the new situation.

Upon witnessing the Trinity test, Oppenheimer, drawing his famous
words from the Hindu *Bhagavad Gita*, said: "Now I have become
death, the destroyer of worlds" (Stoff 1991: 5).

The descriptions of the Hiroshima blast suggest further the "unspeakability" of the event. James H. Foard notes of the Hiroshima
blast:

> even the most basic descriptions have presented problems. Witnesses to the
> atomic bomb have seen another world, full of weird, unspeakable sights:
> people walking with skin falling off, unrecognizable even to relatives, the
> natural world gone mad with black rain and birds exploding in the air, and
> one's own self able to pick casually through human bones. The most com-
> mon image used by survivors is that of the Buddhist hells with all their
> stench and smoke. In general, the claim from testimonial writings is that
> those who did not experience it cannot know it. (Foard 1991: 13)

At first it may seem a stretch to equate the difficulties faced by
Bohr with those faced by the survivors of Hiroshima and Nagasaki.
But, their *rhetorical* situation was similar: Speaking about quantum
phenomena is difficult because the behavior of such phenomena is
unlike anything else in human experience. Speaking about the horror
of nuclear conflict is difficult because its destructive *scale* would be
unlike anything else in human experience. As Foard's comment
above demonstrates, there is a fundamental inability on the part of
those who have experienced an atomic attack to communicate that
experience.

3.3. Framing the bomb

Many of the wartime planners named the bomb in ways symbolizing innovation, change, and progress. Comparisons of the development of the bomb with the Sun, and with the power of the universe, and to the great scientific discoveries of human history are tropical devices to explain profound innovations, ground-breaking changes, and the crossing of a threshold between material and metaphysical. For example, Farrell wrote: "No man-made phenomenon of such tremendous power had ever occurred before." The "awesome roar...warned of doomsday and made us feel that we puny things were blasphemous to dare tamper with the force heretofore reserved to The Almighty".[6] Ernest O. Lawrence, a Nobel-prize winning physicist and a member of the Scientific Advisory Panel to the Interim Committee, described the blast rising from the earth to the heavens:

> Just as I put my foot on the ground I was enveloped with a warm brilliant yellow white light – from darkness to brilliant sunshine in an instant and as I remember I momentarily was stunned by the surprise...and then through my dark sunglasses there was a gigantic ball of fire rising rapidly from the earth – at first as brilliant as the sun, growing less brilliant as it grew boiling and swirling into the heavens.[7]

Secretary of War Henry Stimson, according to Interim Committee meeting notes,

> expressed the view, a view shared by General Marshall, that this project should not be considered simply in terms of military weapons, but as a new relationship of man to the universe. This discovery might be compared to the discoveries of the Copernican theory and of the laws of gravity, but far more important than these in its effects on the lives of men.[8]

For these and other important figures in the Manhattan Project, the bomb marked a turning point and a transition between ages. Compton (1956: 219) recalls Stimson as saying: "Gentlemen, it is our responsibility to recommend action that may turn the course of civilization. In our hands we expect soon to have a weapon of wholly unprecedented destructive power." Lawrence said of the Trinity blast:

> The grand, indeed almost cataclysmic proportion of the explosion produced
> a kind of solemnity in everyone's behavior immediately afterwards. There
> was restrained applause, but more a hushed murmuring bordering on rever-
> ence in manner as the event was commented upon by Dr. Charles Thomas
> (Monsanto) spoke to me of this being the greatest single event in the history
> of mankind, etc. etc. [sic]
> As far as all of us are concerned although we knew the fundamentals were
> sound and that the explosion could be produced, we share a feeling that we
> have this day crossed a great milestone in human progress.[9]

These strategies allowed individuals to understand nuclear weapons in more accessible and familiar terms, but also as a most profound development in the history of human affairs. In addition, wartime planners framed the bomb within a story of American exceptionalism.

3.4. The bomb and America

The myriad symbolic devices employed suggest that these planners
were grasping to understand and make sense of the atomic bomb.
The naming of nuclear physics with the familiar, through metaphors,
and as something profoundly new and different, in a sense "ungraspable," suggests the initial inadequacies in peoples' ability to speak
about the bomb. The seeming tension in the naming of nuclear
physics in terms of the familiar as well as novel and altogether unprecedented was accomplished through narrativizing the significance
of the bomb. The bomb's significance was compared to cosmological
and grand events in human history, and it was also narrativized as an
event within a grand scope of human and American development.

The development of nuclear weapons was named in familiar and
profound terms. Although it was an "explosive" and the "prize" at
the end of the "race," for wartime planners it was much more than
just a weapon to be used in World War II. It was an agency of profound and unprecedented import. The bomb represented America's
control of a new revolutionary power and America's ascendance in
the post-war world. The bomb, as agency, was significant because of
what it represented to American *power*.

Truman read the report on Alamogordo in its entirety, according to Stimson.[10] Truman recalled: "As I read the message from Stimson, I realized that the [Trinity] test not only met the most optimistic expectations of the scientists but that the United States had in its possession an explosive force of unparalleled power." This was, in short, a "revolutionary development" (Truman 1995: 415). The success was attributed to providence and America's exceptional characteristics. Truman in his August 6, 1945 statement thanks "Providence" for the bomb. It was a unique product of American innovation and character. The statement also asserts that America has harnessed "the basic power of the universe," and that this "force from which the sun draws its powers has been loosed against those who brought war to the Far East." Truman concluded the statement proclaiming that nuclear energy [and an American monopoly of atomic energy] would be a "forceful influence on world peace".[11] Henry Stimson, the Secretary of War, wrote in his diary on May 31, 1945:

> I told [the Interim Committee] that we did not regard it as a new weapon merely but as a revolutionary change in the relations of man to the universe and that we wanted to take advantage of this; that the project might even mean the doom of civilization or it might mean the perfection of civilization; that it might be a project "by which the peace of the world would be helped in becoming secure". (Stoff 1991: 121)

By emplotting the bomb, the narrative elements are featured as a whole, of which, ironically, the bomb is a part of something much larger. This enabled one understanding of the bomb and constrains other ways in which the bomb may be conceived. Furthermore, White (1980: 5–27) maintains that, with narrativizing, comes moralizing. And, indeed, the bomb was framed within a moral order – a celebration of American superiority and exceptionalism.

The development of the atomic bomb was an event within human and American progress – an event punctuating a qualitative change in human and American civilization. The story involves a collective agent, America, in a quest to unlock the basic force of the universe, to develop and use the power of the Sun on its enemies. The development was an achievement like no other, ushering in a new era of world peace, marked by the ascendance of America in the post-war world.

Conceptualizing the devastation wrought by nuclear weapons is most difficult, especially for those who have never witnessed such phenomena. The metaphorical naming and the domestication of the bomb made it easier to make sense of the bomb by framing it within familiar or more accessible terms. But, this narrativizing frames the bomb in a particular way, placing a premium on the process of human advancement and American supremacy. Thereby, it deflects detailed understanding of what nuclear fission does to material entities as well as to individual and collective psyches.

While we should be concerned about the inability of those who have witnessed a nuclear detonation to speak of that experience, there is an equivalent, and more dangerous, problem encountered when those who have *not* experienced such an event attempt to mobilize political support for or against it. As Jonathan Schell (1982: 4) reflected:

> In spite of the immeasurable importance of nuclear weapons, the world has declined, on the whole, to think about them very much. We have thus far failed to fashion, or to discover within ourselves, an emotional or intellectual or political response to them. This peculiar failure of response... has itself been such a striking phenomenon that it has to be regarded as an extremely important part of the nuclear predicament as this has existed so far.

While Schell groped towards a connection between "the uncanny quality of modern physics violation of common sense" and "the seemingly ungraspable, and therefore "unreal" power of nuclear weapons," he ignored the commonalties between these two contexts to emphasize the societal repression of nuclear risk (Schell 1982: 10). While such repression is, no doubt, a significant component of the problem, it seems likely that another significant component is Bohr's dynamic: our modes of description are adapted to the context of ordinary physical phenomena. Humankind lacks an effective grammar and vocabulary to describe nuclear war. Words like "conflict," "war," and "bomb" cannot convey the scale of destruction made possible by the invention of atomic weapons. And, those in positions to make decisions about the use of nuclear weapons are several steps removed from an understanding of what nuclear weapons do.

At one point, in the effort to symbolically and linguistically grapple with such destructive force, humans have attempted to fit it into the theological framework of "doomsday" or "Armageddon".[12] It is arguable whether such words were effective. But Foard (1991: 3) observes, the religious image of Armageddon helped to incorporate the immense destructive power of nuclear weapons into human structures of meaning. Unfortunately, as Foard concludes:

> With the end of the Cold War... apocalyptic imagery itself appears doomed, as our geo-political situation no longer sustains its plausibility. Our images of the nuclear threat are now as obsolete as our strategies. Without such imagery, though, we are left with little to think with in contemplating the meaning of these weapons, a situation that could well prove dangerous. (1991: 3)

It may be that the images and language stemming from the Hiroshima and Nagasaki attacks are our best hope to adequately conceptualize the threat that nuclear weapons pose. Perhaps this explains the power of John Hersey's *Hiroshima* (1989), a short book about the experience of six people at Hiroshima, to evoke compassion and concern. Perhaps Foard (1991: 2–3) is correct when he argues that "since nuclear weapons now appear to threaten cities more than the human species as a whole, we might do well to return to Hiroshima to discover" ways of representing more adequately nuclear weapons "into structures of meaning".

4. Implications and conclusions

Previous scholars have examined the language of domestication and bureaucratization regarding nuclear weapons (Bjork 1988: 181–192; Brummett 1989: 85–95; Farrell and Goodnight 1981: 271–300; Kane 1988: 143–154; Kauffman 1989: 273–285; Manoff 1989: 59–84; Prosise 1998; Rubin and Cummings 1989: 39–58; Rushing 1986: 415–433; Schiappa 1989: 253–272; Taylor 1993: 367–394). These scholars have sought to explore the reasons behind debased public deliberation over atomic weapons and the odd paralysis that seems to attend the nuclear debate.

While these previous studies are informative, this essay has offered a previously unnoticed aspect of the communicative situation facing the nuclear advocate. The "unspeakability" or difficulty in conceptualizing the scale of nuclear conflict helps to explain difficulties encountered in our efforts to, quite literally, "come to terms" with nuclear weapons. Nuclear destruction is of such a scale that it is difficult, if not impossible, to name adequately. We find ourselves in a deadly paradox. The language that we have come to use to describe atomic warfare is inadequate to convey the true horror of such an event. No matter how one phrases nuclear advocacy, an inexorable tie remains to a symbolic structure best suited for the representation of vastly more mundane events. There is a way in which any attempt to describe atomic bombs has the first and necessary consequence of taming the nightmarish surreal quality of such warfare.

We must rely on words to name situations and events (Burke 1984). Is our language adequate to express or capture the experience of a nuclear explosion? We think not. Instead, we "mis-use" symbols, fooling ourselves into thinking that our vocabularies appropriately name the significance of nuclear weapons (see Burke 1966: 6).

We must consider this line of question further. It is plausible that the "unspeakability" of nuclear phenomena at the micro and macro levels helps to explain public paralysis in the face of such grave threats to material and spiritual well-being. We regard it as probable that this "unspeakability" accounts, at least in part, for the failures of anti-nuclear rhetoric, and the ability for politicians and nuclear experts to diffuse anti-nuclear agitation through mythic and simplistic metaphorical appeals.[13] While beyond the scope of the current essay, we regard the resort to such over-simplifications as comparatively more persuasive than much anti-nuclear rhetoric not on the merits of its claims but because of the comparative familiarity of its narrative scope.

Is a new language of nuclear conflict possible? Much like the challenge faced by those who would speak about the Holocaust, we face the challenge of speaking about the possibility of nuclear conflict in such a way that the visceral reality of the consequences of such conflict are conveyed to the audience. The only way to produce more adequate language about nuclear weapons is to first recognize our symbolic limitations. The effective communication of knowledge of phenomena at the boundaries of ordinary experience may depend on the fruitful cooperation between the scientists, military elites, and policy-makers and rhetoricians. As Wrage (1947: 453) concludes,

> At this juncture a special kind of skill becomes useful, for the problem now relates directly to the craftsmanship of the rhetorician. The student who is sensitized to rhetoric, who is schooled in its principles and techniques, brings an interest, insight, discernment, and essential skill which are assets for scholarship in the history of ideas.

A task of the scholar who would analyze the language of war is to understand such expressive difficulties with the intent of alleviating them.

We should consider Wittgenstein's (1961: 74) comment: "in language… the limit can be drawn, and what lies on the other side of the limit will simply be nonsense." Wittgenstein advocated silence under such circumstances, but such an alternative is not tenable here. Bohr's analysis of the rhetorical situation of atomic science, and its subsequent elaboration here, has shown that the maladaptation of language is a phenomenon with important consequences for our daily lives. As Bohr once said when told that words don't fit, "They have to fit, they're all we have". We must try to find a vocabulary that will allow us to grasp as best as possible the risks and dangers that nuclear weapons pose.

Notes

1. *Nature*, Suppl. No. 3050, April 14, 1928. Reprinted in Collected Works, Volume 6: 52.
2. See Pais (1986: 211), where Pais argued, "from my own experiences in talking with him, I would say that to Bohr himself his struggles with complementarity were ultimately of greater importance than his work on the hydrogen atom, on the old quantum theory."
3. For a simple and informative discussion of common human experience and the use of metaphor, see Lakoff and Johnson (1980). For a discussion of "god-

terms," see Brummet (1989). For a discussion of narrative and human rationality, see Fisher (1987).

4. Grove's Memo to Stimson, July 18, 1945, Stoff (1991: 191).
5. Grove's Memo to Stimson, July 18, 1945, Stoff (1991: 191).
6. Grove's Memo to Stimson, July 18, 1945, Stoff (1991: 191).
7. "Thoughts by E. O. Lawrence", *Harrison-Bundy Files Relating to the Development of the Atomic Bomb 1942–1946*.
8. Notes of the Interim Committee Meeting, 1945.
9. "Thoughts by E. O. Lawrence," *Harrison-Bundy Files Relating to the Development of the Atomic Bomb 1942–1946*, National Archives, Washington, D.C., Record Group 77, File no. 49.
10. Stimson Diary Entry, July 21 and 22, 1945, Stoff (1991: 203).
11. Truman Statement; for evidence of the "monopoly" strategy and comments about the role of the bomb to enforce world peace, see Prosise (2000: 93–97).
12. For the definitive examination of the rhetoric of the apocalypse see O'Leary (1991).
13. For a discussion of mythic and metaphoric responses to anti-nuclear activism, see Rushing (1986) and Bjork (1988), respectively.

References

Bjork, Rebecca S.
   1988   Reagan and the nuclear freeze: "Star Wars" as a rhetorical strategy. *Journal of the American Forensic Association* 24, 181–192.

Bohr, Niels
   1934   *Atomic Theory and the Description of Nature.* Cambridge: Cambridge University Press. Reprinted in 1961 and again in 1987 as *The Philosophical Writings of Niels Bohr, Vol. I.* Woodbridge: Ox Bow Press.

   1949   Discussion with Einstein on epistemological problems in atomic physics. In: Schilpp, Paul Arthur (ed.), *Albert Einstein: Philosopher-Scientist.* New York: Tudor, 201–241.

   1958   *Atomic Physics and Human Knowledge.* New York: Wiley. Reprint in 1987 as *The Philosophical Writings of Niels Bohr, Vol. II, Essays 1932–1957 on Atomic Physics and Human Knowledge,* Woodbridge: Ox Bow Press.

   1985   *Niels Bohr Collected Works, Vol. 6. Foundations of Quantum Physics I (1926–1932).* Edited by Jorgen Kalckar. Amsterdam: North Holland.

Boyer, Paul
1994   *By the Bomb's Early Light: American Thought and Culture at the Dawn of the Atomic Age.* Chapel Hill, NC: University of North Carolina Press.

1998   *Fallout: A Historian Reflects on America's Half-Century Encounter with Nuclear Weapons.* Columbus, Ohio: Ohio State University Press.

Brummett, Barry
1989   Perfection and the bomb: Nuclear weapons, teleology, and motives. *Journal of Communication* 39(1), 85.

Burke, Kenneth
1966   *Language as Symbolic Action: Essays on Life, Literature, and Method.* Berkeley, CA: University of California Press.

1984   *Permanence and Change: An Anatomy of Change,* 3rd ed. Berkeley, CA: University of California Press.

Bush to Roosevelt
December 16, 1942 Correspondences ("Top Secret") of the Manhattan Engineer District 1942–1946. National Archives, Washington, D.C., Record Group 77, File no. 25.

Bush, Vannevar
1990   *Science – The Endless Frontier A Report to the President on a Program of Postwar Scientific Research.* Washington: National Science Foundation.

Compton, Arthur
1956   *Atomic Quest: A Personal Narrative.* New York: Oxford University Press.

Einstein, Albert
1924   Letter to H.A. Lorentz, December 16, 1924, as reprinted in: Pais, Abraham (1991) *Niels Bohr's Times, in Physics, Philosophy, and Polity.* Oxford: Clarendon Press.

Farrell, Thomas B., and G. Thomas Goodnight
1981   Accidental rhetoric: The root metaphors of Three Mile Island. *Communication Monographs* 48, 271–300.

Foard, James H.
    1991   Imagining nuclear weapons: Hiroshima, Armageddon and the
            annihilation of the students of Ichijo school. *Journal of the American
            Academy of Religion* 65, 1–18.

Freeman, A.
    1982   *College Physics*, second edition. New York: Addison Wesley.
            Heisenberg, Werner

    1971   *Physics and Beyond; Encounters and Conversations.* Translated
            from the German by Arnold J. Pomerans. New York: Harper & Row.

Hersey, John
    1989   *Hiroshima.* New York: Vintage Books.

Hewlett, Richard G., and Oscar E. Anderson, Jr.
    1962   *The New World, 1939/1946: Volume 1: A History of the United
            States Atomic Energy Commission.* University Park, PA: Pennsyl-
            vania University Press.

Kane, Thomas
    1988   Rhetorical histories and arms negotiations. *Journal of the American
            Forensic Association* 24, 143–154.

Kauffman, Charles
    1989   Names and Weapons. *Communication Monographs* 56, 273–285.

Lakoff, George, and Mark Johnson
    1980   *Metaphors We Live By.* Chicago: University of Chicago Press.

Manoff, Robert Karl
    1989   Modes of war and modes of social address: The text of SDI. *Journal
            of Communication* 39(1), 59–84.

Nature
    1985   Suppl. No. 3050, April 14, 1928. Reprinted in Niels Bohr 1985.
            Notes of the Interim Committee Meeting

O'Leary, Stephen J.
    1991   *Arguing the Apocalypse.* Oxford: Oxford University Press.

Pais, Abraham
    1982   *Subtle is the Lord: The Science and Life of Albert Einstein.* Oxford:
            Oxford University Press.

1986   *Inward Bound: Of Matter and Forces in the Physical World*. New York: Oxford University Press.

1991   *Niels Bohr's Times, in Physics, Philosophy, and Polity*. Oxford: Clarendon Press.

Planck, Max
1950   *Scientific Autobiography and Other Papers*. Translated by F. Gaynor. London: William and Norgate.

Prosise, Theodore O.
1998   The collective memory of the atomic bombings misrecognized as objective history: The case of the public opposition to the National Air and Space Museum's atom bomb exhibit. *Western Journal of Communication* 62, 316–347.

2000   "Rotten with perfection": Myth and transcendence in the decision to bomb Hiroshima. Ph.D. dissertation, University of Southern California.

Rhodes, Richard
1986   *The Making of the Atomic Bomb*. New York: Simon & Schuster.

Rubin, David M., and Constance Cummings
1989   Nuclear war and its consequences on television news. *Journal of Communication* 39(1), 39–58.

Rushing, Janice Hocker
1986   Ronald Reagan's "Star Wars" address: Mythic containment of technical reasoning. *Quarterly Journal of Speech* 72, 415–433.

Schell, Jonathan
1982   *The Fate of the Earth*. New York: Alfred A. Knopf.

Schiappa, Edward
1989   The rhetoric of nukespeak. *Communication Monographs* 56, 253–272.

Stoff, Michael B.
1991   *The Manhattan Project: A Documentary Introduction to the Atomic Age*. New York: McGraw-Hill Companies.

Taylor, Bryan C.
    1993   Fat Man and Little Boy: The cinematic representation of interests in
                the nuclear weapons organization. *Critical Studies in Mass Commu-
                nication* 10, 367–394.

Toulmin, Stephen, and June Goodfield
    1962   *The Architecture of Matter*. New York: Harper and Row.

Truman, Harry
    1995   *Memoirs: 1945: Year of Decisions*. New York: Smithmark.

White, Hayden
    1980   The value of narrativity in the representation of reality. *Critical In-
                quiry* 7, 5–27.

Wittgenstein, Ludwig
    1961   *Tractatus Logico-Philosophicus*. Translated by D.F. Pears and B.F.
                McGuinness. London: Routledge & K. Paul; New York: Humanities
                Press International.

Wrage, Ernest
    1947   Public address: A study in social and intellectual history. *Quarterly
                Journal of Speech* 33, 453–457.

The politics of discontent:
A discourse analysis of texts of the Reform Movement in Ghana

Kweku Osam

1. Introduction

While political texts in Western political systems frequently have
been examined, the same cannot be said about African political discourse.[1]

Political systems on the continent seem to be in constant flux –
swinging from de facto single party systems, through military regimes, to some form of multiple party systems. Within the patchwork
of African political systems, there is a massive corpus of political
text and talk that requires the attention of discourse analysts. This
paper attempts to examine power relations, especially the fight for
ideological "high ground", in the newly plural context of Ghana. I
use discourse analytic methods to identify the ideology of the
Reform Movement in Ghana. Such an ideology – emphasizing
popular participation – is constrained by the Movement with several
strategies. Central to a contest for political power, ideology
rationalizes a party's or leader's dominance. Language is the key
resource in gaining such a political rationale – and this is my focus
below.

2. Theoretical framework

This study is situated within the approach to discourse analysis that
has come to be known as Critical Discourse Analysis (CDA). Over
the last two decades, this approach has been very influential in the
study of various discourses. The focus of CDA is on the relationship

between social interaction and discourse structures. Specifically, CDA is concerned with "the way social power abuse, dominance and inequality are enacted, reproduced and resisted by text and talk in the social and political context" (van Dijk 2002). In other words, CDA studies the link between socio-political power abuse and resistance to such abuse and how discourse structures and strategies and other features of text and talk are used to represent such power relationship (van Dijk 1987, 1993, 1995, 1996, 1997, 2002; Chilton and Schäffner 1997; Fairclough 1989, 1995; Fairclough and Wodak 1997).

Although there are varied strands of CDA, they all developed from the school of Critical Linguistics as it developed in the United Kingdom and Australia.[2] Philosophically, both CDA and its predecessor, Critical Linguistics, derive their intellectual strength from the Marxist and Neo-Marxist thoughts, the Frankfurt School and Gramsci.

A principal concern of CDA is the reflection of power abuse in discourse, and the inequality and injustice that arise out of such abuse (van Dijk 1993: 252–254). This concern is derived from the critical discourse analyst's interest in socio-political issues.

Within CDA, power and dominance are central concepts to discourse analysis. The kind of power relevant here is social power found in relations between social groups – specifically, how one group or institution exercises control over another. This implies that in CDA, power is viewed as control – the control a group or institution has over another. Social control in an inter-group relationship would manifest itself in the control of the mind and actions of the dominated group. As a result of such control, the dominant group can restrict the freedom of the dominated group and influence their knowledge and attitudes. Domination of a group through manipulating minds can be so intense and prolonged that group members come to accept their domination as natural. This condition is referred to as hegemony (van Dijk 1993, 1998a, 2002).

Although within the CDA framework, where the demonstration of power, dominance, or power abuse is most critical, dominance is not always absolute (van Dijk, 1993, 1996, 2002). Dominance can be contested, challenged or resisted. "As is the case with power, dominance is seldom total. It may be restricted to specific domains, and it may be contested by various modes of challenge, that is, counter-power" (van Dijk, 1993: 255).

CDA treats power and dominance as discursively mediated. Power and dominance arising out of an inter-group relationship is achieved through the manipulation of various discourse structures and patterns of text and talk. As pointed out by Fairclough and Wodak (1997: 272), "CDA highlights the substantively linguistic and discursive nature of social relations power in contemporary societies. This is partly a matter of how power relations are exercised and negotiated in discourse."

Another crucial notion in CDA is access to and control over public discourse. Usually, dominant groups and elites – politicians and journalists, for example – have greater access to various forms of public discourse. In a dictatorship where there is control over the press, only those with political views aligned with those of the dictator can be published. Access to discourse also involves control over discourse type, topics and style. For example, only editors have access to the editorial as a discourse type. Control over access to discourse is also demonstrated through topic control. Again citing media examples, television viewers have no control over topics covered in news broadcasts.

The framework of CDA provides the backdrop for this study. Most work within CDA has examined the discursive construction and legitimation of dominance. However, as argued by Morrison and Love (1996), and by Sotillo and Starace-Nastasi (1999), not enough attention has been paid to text and talk that challenge and resist dominance. This is especially so when we consider the African political context. The continent has experienced, and continues to encounter, political dictatorship through the imposition of military or quasi-military rule and nondemocratic forms of political systems intolerant of pluralistic opinions. In the midst of political repression, masses of people have engaged in resistance oriented text and talk. The case of Nigeria during the military regime of General Abacha and his predecessors is a good example. These oppressive governments in Nigeria generated a substantial body of dissident text and talk that sought to resist undemocratic rule. While similar examples can be recounted across the continent, little analytical attention has been paid to such discourse.

The application of CDA consistently has shown that dominant groups use various discourse strategies to legitimate their dominance. The idea, however, has been suggested that these same strategies can be used by any resistance movement to counter the power of the dominant class: "Many of the discourse strategies used by the power-ful for coercion may be counter-deployed by those who regard them-selves as opposing power" (Chilton and Schäffner 1997: 212). This perspective informs my analysis. CDA practitioners will continue to examine and expose the discursive enactment of the reproduction of domination. Yet, the discursive resistance of the dominated needs to be documented, recognised and validated – tasks to which CDA is amply suited.

3. Political discourse

Although numerous studies have examined the relationship between politics and discourse, defining political discourse has not been an easy intellectual undertaking.[3] I cannot settle this definitional prob-lem. Instead, I take van Dijk's view (1998b: 16–17) – that political discourse is the text and talk arising out of the "activities and prac-tices" of politicians and citizens that affect the political process. Such text and talk would have something to do with political systems, val-ues, ideologies, institutions, organizations, groups, actors, political relations, political processes, and political actions.

With this background, it is clear that the Reform Movement texts are political. The texts emanate from people who intend to contest political power, and want to implement policies and programs in-formed by a particular ideological orientation.

4. Political context

Ghana's political history and events that led to the Reform Movement require a brief description to situate texts under consideration in a proper historico-political context. Since many publications have been written on Ghana's political history, I offer here a distilled form of a highly complex narrative.[4]

The Gold Coast, a British colony, became independent Ghana in 1957. In 1966, the civilian government was overthrown in one of the first military coups in independent Africa. The military government returned the country to a constitutional government in 1969. This government was also overthrown in a second military coup in 1972. The coup leader, Lt. Col. I. K. Acheampong, became the head of state and ruled through the National Redemption Council (NRC) which consisted mostly of military officers. In 1978, a palace coup occurred during which the head of state was removed and replaced by Lt. Gen. Akuffo.

In 1979, the military government started implementing plans to return the country to an elected civilian administration. On May 15, 1979, there was an attempted coup lead by Flt. Lt. J. J. Rawlings to overthrow the military government.

On June 4, 1979, while the abortive coup leaders were still on trial before a Court Martial, there was a mutiny in the army. The result was that the military government was overthrown and Flt. Lt. J. J. Rawlings was released from military detention to head the Armed Forces Revolutionary Council (AFRC). In terms of Ghana's political history, one of the most significant events during this period was the execution of eight senior military officers on grounds of corruption. These included three former heads of state: General Acheampong, General Akuffo, and General Afrifa who, for a brief period in 1969, headed the National Liberation Council, the first military government of Ghana.

Despite the military uprising of June 4, 1979, plans to return the country to civilian rule continued, and elections were held in June of the same year, after which the AFRC handed power over to the People's National Party headed by Hilla Limann.

However, on December 31, 1981, Flt. Lt. Rawlings, who had headed the AFRC government, overthrew the new civilian administration and set up the Provisional National Defence Council (PNDC). Rawlings headed the council as the Chairman and the head of state. There were also four military and three civilian members on the PNDC. From the beginning, there were indications that the government of the PNDC was "leftist"; it attracted many leftist intellectuals into the national politics and there were efforts to bring the masses into active roles in the nation's political life. Consequently, various structures oriented towards mass participation were established. However, through purges and resignations, such a leftist leaning became more rhetorical than real.

By the second half of the 1980s, pressure had mounted from various political constituencies and organisations for the PNDC government to hand power to an elected civilian government. The decade of the 1990s, therefore, saw moves by the PNDC headed by Flt. Lt. Rawlings to return the country to constitutional rule. As Nugent (1995: 207) puts it:

> By the end of 1991, the "31st December Revolution" was definitely a thing of the past. Egalitarian and economic self-reliance were the first tracts of the revolutionary canon to be set aside. The participatory vision had lasted longer, but in the end the PNDC accepted that most Ghanaians did regard elections as fundamental to democracy . . .

In the course of 1992, firm arrangements were made to have multiparty elections as a means to return the country to an elected civilian government. The military government of Rawlings, the PNDC, transformed itself into a political party, the National Democratic Congress (NDC). Led by Rawlings, the NDC won the elections and he became the first president of the fourth Republic of Ghana. In 1996, he again led the NDC to their second electoral victory.

Until 1998, the NDC as a political party, on the surface, looked internally cohesive. However, in July 1998, a group within the NDC calling itself the NDC Reform Movement issued an open letter to the National Executive Committee of the NDC. This letter appeared in three national newspapers.

The letter's contents covered what the Reform Movement considered to be the weaknesses within the NDC as a democratic party and ways to redress these. The excerpts below from their letter constituted their main criticisms:

• We [NDC] have failed to lead a political programme to sustain activism in the branches. This has all but killed the branches and undermined the Party's democratic foundation.
• Without active branches the annual Constituency and Regional Party Conferences we hold are meaningless events that formally satisfy the letter of the party constitution but that do not give a say on substantive issues.
• The "Annual" National Delegates Congress itself is increasingly staged just as a media event...Delegates are given just few hours to adopt reports and policy positions presented by the NEC [National Executive Committee of the party]
• The party's mass organs – its youth and women's wings are moribund.
• There is increasing evidence that the NEC itself merely administers agendas developed externally by various powerful individuals and groups who constitute the real "powers behind the throne" – an oligarchy that manages both Party and State as if they were one entity and to the detriment of both .(Reform Movement 1998: 2)

In their demands, they asked the National Executive Committee of the party to provide an agenda for rebuilding the party, to be allowed to compete for NEC positions and to review the party's own guidelines for intra-party elections.

To deal with the issues raised by the Reform Movement, the National Executive Committee of the NDC set up a negotiation team that met with a contact group from the Reform Movement. The two teams met on four occasions from September to October, 1998. Since there was no agreement, negotiations were suspended indefinitely and each side went on with their respective programmes. This marked the formal break of the NDC Reform Group from the main party. In early 1999, the Reform Movement was registered as a political party in Ghana under the name the National Reform Party.

Texts analysed in this study were produced in such a socio-political milieu. Having been part of the political status quo (as part of the political establishment under the military rule of the PNDC and the NDC), the decision of the Reform Movement to break away and challenge ruling political forces for political power means that textual comprehension and their intellectual analysis cannot be meaningfully accomplished without due cognizance of the historico-political context.

The competition for political power is also situated within the domain of an ideological struggle within which the RM justifies its breakaway from the NDC.

5. Ideology

The diversity and depth of literature about ideology precludes thorough review here. Still, the term has varied interpretations. One sense, according to Thompson (1987), is "...a neutral conception of ideology...It is in this sense that one speaks, for example, of the "ideology" of a political party, referring to the basic ideas or beliefs which are traditionally associated with the party and which are drawn upon by the party leaders in the formulation of policies and manifestos." Thompson (1987: 518) also identifies a second sense of the term: "In the writings of some authors, ideology is essentially linked to the process of sustaining asymmetrical relations of power – that is, to the process of maintaining domination. The use of the term expresses what may be called a critical conception of ideology." This second sense is that of Critical Discourse Analysis in work on discourse strategies in the construction of dominance and power.

However, as van Dijk has often and strongly indicated, ideology *includes* opposition or resistance to domination:

> Contrary to traditional critical approaches, however, this does not mean that the definition of ideology is limited to a concept that sees ideology only as an instrument of domination. There are good theoretical and empirical reasons to assume that there are also ideologies of opposition or resistance or ideologies of competition between equally powerful groups, or ideologies that promote the internal cohesion of a group, or ideologies about the survival of humankind. This implies that, as such, ideologies in my approach are not inherently negative, nor limited to social structures of domination. (van Dijk 1998a: 11) [5]

I subscribe to this broad view of ideology. In the context of this study, the secession of Reform Movement (RM) from the ruling

party and the texts resulting from that schism constitute political resistance and a challenge to political domination. Thus, this is a study
of the discourse strategies of political resistance and competition.

6. Discourse structures

In the production of political discourse, various discourse structures
are used. Below, I examine discourse features of the RM texts along
several parameters: topics/thematic organisation; local semantics;
style – lexical choice and syntactic style; and rhetorical features.
Three of the RM's statements have been selected for scrutiny
because they provide what I consider to be the core ideological
outlook of the Movement.

The first is *The Genesis of the Reform Movement* issued in 1998,
referred to as "Text I". This 2025 word text, written for public distribution, was issued after negotiations with the NDC broke down and
sets out the origins and political orientation of the Reform Movement. The second text (2190 words), *Reform Movement: Press
Statement* (referred to here as Text II), was a statement read to the
press on January 25, 1999. Versions of the statement were later published by private newspapers in Ghana.

After the movement broke away from the ruling National Democratic Congress in October 1998, there was a long silence and presumed inactivity from the RM. In December 1998, the ruling party
held its annual congress and there was a general anticipation that the
Reform Movement would follow with their own congress. When
nothing was forthcoming, substantial media speculation ensued. This
was the condition under which Text II was issued. It recounts the
failed negotiations with the NDC, establishes the Movement's political philosophy, and maps out the RM's future.

Text III (1566 words), entitled *The 21st Century*, was the address
read by the Co-ordinator of the Reform Movement at their congress
held at the University of Ghana on February 4, 1999. The congress
was attended by delegates of the Movement from all parts of the
country. The audience also included representatives from organisations the Movement considers "progressive" and "democratic". The

text covers what the Movement leaders thought to be failures of the political status quo and provides some insights into the political character of the Reform Movement.

6.1. Thematic structures

The topic of discourse or the global content of a text refers to "its overall topics or themes, that is, the most important information expressed by a text" (van Dijk 1987: 169). Political discourse can be about anything political: "political discourse will be primarily about politics...That is, we may typically expect overall meanings related to political systems, ideologies, institutions, the political process, political actors, and political events. In other words much political discourse is reflexive" (van Dijk 1998b: 25).

A consistent and dominant theme that runs through the RM texts is the ideology of popular participation. The texts express the view that the mass of the people must empower themselves to participate actively in governance and policy development.

(1)
a. The purpose of the Reform Movement is to initiate profound and meaningful reforms in our national political life that will enable the people of this country to take the lead in positively affecting the course of their lives. (Text I)

b. Our aim is the self-empowerment of ordinary Ghanaians through open and democratic political goals and activities. (Text I)

c. We abide by the principle of popular participation. (Text I)

d. The Reform Movement believes in a culture of politics that systematically and actively involves the regular, even daily, participation of increasing numbers of ordinary people. The most secure and legitimate democratic traditions can only be developed on the basis of millions of Ghanaians freely developing ideas and openly engaging in activities aimed at understanding and resolving the problems of our society and the challenges of development. (Text I)

Closely related to the theme of popular participation is that of the struggle for power. The texts assert that the mass of the people need to struggle for the power to enable them participate in national decisions:

(2)

a. We have to continue to fight for the power to defend our conditions of life and to improve them. This power is never given to us freely as we learnt in our struggle for Independence from our colonial masters in 1957 or in our countless struggles, big and small, for democratic reforms, better wages or better services since then. Without power, the majority will remain hostage to the whims and narrow interests of a tiny minority. There is only one way to gain power – it has to be won. (Text I)

b. Indeed the Reform constituency extends beyond the political establishment and includes all those involved in the broader struggle for democratic participation and good governance that is building up in our society... This struggle is evident in the growing assertiveness of civil society as it confronts the state and the traditional administrative arrogance of officialdom. It is evident also in struggles taking place within all our national civil institutions. Ghanaians are demanding greater democracy in our trades unions and other professional associations. Struggles for democratic reform are shaping our churches and rocking our educational establishments. (Text I)

The texts also talk about the failure of the ruling NDC to encourage popular participation within the party.

(3)

a. The NDC is made up of millions of well-intentioned Ghanaians. These form the rank and file of the party whose tireless and selfless work has brought the NDC two successive election victories. These ordinary members are not part of the undemocratic decision making of party and government leaders or of the subjection of the party to the government and state. In fact, the undemocratic tendency fatally deprives ordinary members of meaningful and popular participation. (Text I)

Another significant theme is that of a nation in crisis, as illustrated by the excerpt in (4a). The texts make it clear that the cause of this crisis is the failure of leadership (4b) – a theme that intersects and links up with the theme of the failure of the NDC to promote popular participation.

(4)

a. Just six years ago, Ghana entered the fourth Republic on a high note. Everything was in place for a take-off. Ghanaians were energised by the prospect of sustained economic development under stable constitutional rule. Confidence and the will to succeed were high. The 21st century was an inviting prospect. Today much of this confidence has dissipated. With a few significant exceptions, we have under-performed in almost every sector... Hope is disappearing. Social tensions are bubbling leading to increasing frequent outbreaks of community violence. That much of this has been directed at the police signals a public perception that the state is somehow responsible for the crisis. In addition to the perceived drift in policy, scandal after scandal has rocked state institutions. These scandals have lowered morale and the willingness of ordinary Ghanaians to sacrifice for national goals. (Text III)

b. Ladies and Gentlemen: Simply Ghana's crisis is a crisis of social leadership. (Text III)

Predictably, the texts present RM as the agent that will ensure popular participation.

(5)

a. RM is a non-partisan political movement...A broad-based movement is necessary to mobilise ordinary Ghanaians into the political struggle to reform our national leadership and political culture...we will advocate good governance at all levels. We will demand that leadership becomes and remains responsive to the needs of ordinary people. For example, RM cells will mobilise communities to protect their interests in issues that affect them. Through such struggle, our communities will develop the confidence and skills to keep officialdom on its toes. (Text II)

b. Another important function RM will perform will be to draw ordinary Ghanaians into the process of national policy formation. We must move away from a bureaucratic approach that sees development exclusively as a technical matter for experts. We must make development policy more of a democratic political issue for the citizens. (Text II)

This positive presentation of the Reform Movement and the negative presentation of the NDC fit into what van Dijk calls the Ideological Square. More will be said about the reflection of the Ideological Square in the RM texts in the section on style.

6.2. Local semantics

6.2.1. Implication

One feature of local semantics is implication. The notion of implication adopted here is very much related to that of implicatures as treated in pragmatics.[6] Van Dijk (1995: 268) has indicated that "It is a well-known feature of sentence and discourse semantics that meanings are not always explicitly expressed, but somehow semantically implied, or entailed by other, explicit expressions and their meanings." He also points out that "Most information is personally or socially shared and cognitively represented by the language users and, therefore, may remain implicit in the text and presupposed by the speaker" (2002: 63).

That implicativity can be used to convey ideology is accepted: "Implications may have important ideological functions if the meanings more or less strongly implied by asserted propositions are being derived on the basis of attitudes and ideologies" (van Dijk 1995: 269). In other words, by examining explicitly stated propositions, it is possible to arrive at implied meanings that arise out of a certain ideological orientation. This phenomenon can be detected in Reform Movement texts.

On the whole, the RM adopts a direct and critical perspective about their political opposition. However, such criticism is also achieved through implicativity – as the Reform Movement presents its agenda, it implies what the ruling elites should have done but did not. The excerpts in Example 6 taken from Text I clearly illustrate this observation:

(6)
a. Our specific aim is to help <u>create a new type of democratic and accountable political party</u> . . .

b. We will demand that <u>leadership becomes and remains responsive to the needs of ordinary people.</u>

c. Another important function RM will perform will be to <u>draw ordinary Ghanaians into the process of national policy formation.</u>

d. We must move away from a bureaucratic approach that sees development exclusively as a technical matter for experts. We must demystify policy management.

In (6a), if the RM aims to *"create a new type of democratic and accountable political party"*, it implies that the ruling party is neither *"democratic"* nor *"accountable"*. In (6b) the implication is that *"leadership"* in the prevailing political establishment is not *"responsive to the needs of ordinary people"*; (6c) implies that the NDC has excluded *"ordinary Ghanaians"* from the *"process of national policy formation"*. There are a number of implications in (6d): (i) that the ruling class is *"bureaucratic"* in its approach to development since it *"sees development exclusively as a technical matter for experts"*; (ii) that the *"experts"* are in charge to the exclusion of the mass of the people; (iii) that the ruling class has *"mystified"* policy management.

These implications reinforce RM's ideology of popular participation – that leadership needs to be accountable to the people, thereby subjecting leadership to the citizens' control and that technocracy should be abandoned for popular rule.

Implicativity is also displayed when RM talks about its qualities. By implication, these qualities are missing from the NDC. The excerpts in Example 7 are all from Text II and illustrate this point:

(7)
a. RM will be inclusive. We face a new century and we bring to it no prejudices about anyone.

b. RM will be transparent. Leadership will be accountable to its members and indeed to the public. A national political movement cannot be run on principles of secrecy. We will live in the public eye. We will be open about our finances. Our internal differences will be a matter of open debate. RM and this country cannot afford to be afraid of ideas or discussion. It costs too much.

c. RM will be democratic. We are building a movement that "belongs" to its members. "Ownership" is important for us...There will be no place for the politics of patronage in RM. The culture of patronage has been one of the most destructive forces in our politics through the years. Patronage comes with systematic corruption.

d. <u>RM will be tolerant</u>.

By identifying themselves with these qualities, members of the Reform Movement intend to set up a contrast between themselves and the ruling political elites.

6.2.2. Perspective

Throughout the texts, RM assumes two viewpoints; both, however, are in relation to their central ideology of popular participation constructed through the discourse. In some places, the perspective represents RM as a political organisation. In the excerpts in Example 8, we see the views of the political organisation.

(8)

a. On July 6 this year [1998], our organisation, the Reform Movement (RM) issued a full page "Open Letter to the National Executive Committee of the NDC"…(Text I)

b. Our aim is the self-empowerment of ordinary Ghanaians through open and democratic political goals and activities. (Text I)

c. We had high and well founded hopes of creating a new democratic party that belonged to a new calibre of ordinary members who could not easily [be] dominated or cast aside by "big men" without merit. We sought to mobilise ordinary people whose political experience and readiness to sacrifice was far from ordinary. We were sure that if we were successful we would inspire millions of Ghanaians across the country to new heights. (Text I)

At other times, the texts assume the "voice of the people". This is where RM speaks as if it represents the views of the nation as a whole. The excerpt in (2a) illustrates this. It also comes out in *"Ghanaians are demanding greater democracy in <u>our</u> trades unions and other professional associations. Struggles for democratic reform are shaping <u>our</u> churches and rocking <u>our</u> educational establishments."*
There are many instances where the pronouns *we* and *our* are used where the referents are the people of Ghana. Sometimes the transition from *we/our* (as RM) to *we/our* (populace) is so effectively done that it is difficult to tell the referents of those pronominal forms.

When RM assumes the "voice of the people", it emphasises the ideology of popular participation and positions itself, discursively, to compete with the ruling elite for political power.

Obviously, the "vox populi" strategy adopted by RM shows that it is more than "a well-known populist ploy in Conservative rhetoric" (van Dijk 1993: 276). It is a strategy used by all politicians, regardless of ideology (Chilton and Schäffner 1997: 217–219).

6.3. Style

6.3.1. Lexical style

The theme and sub-themes associated with RM's ideology of popular participation are reflected very much in the choice of lexical items. The lexical choices confirm the notion of Ideological Square put forward by van Dijk (1998b). The Ideological Square is the partisan representation of SELF and OTHER – while using positive terms to describe ourselves, our opponents are presented in negative terms.

In choosing verbs, the Reform Movement presents itself as a political entity ready for action. This comes out in the verbs that are associated with the RM: *initiate, create, continue to fight, defend, develop, sustain, help, battle, resist, debate, reclaim, strengthen, achieving* (Text I); *call for, reform, argue, improve, confront, demand, overhaul, democratise, demystify, influence, contribute, contest, invigorate* (Text II).

RM describes itself in other complimentary terms: it considers itself a *broad-based movement, inclusive, transparent, democratic, tolerant, serious*; it will provide *appropriate leadership*; RM will *create opportunities for people*; it can *make substantial contributions*.

On the other hand, the political OTHER, in this case the ruling NDC, are presented in less laudatory terms. They are a *tiny minority* holding the majority *hostage* to their *whims* and *narrow interests*. The ruling elites practice *political patronage*; to them politics is *the big man's game*; They have *monopoly of power* which can become *suffocating*, provoking *crises* and resulting in *national political turmoil*. The minority *excludes* the majority from power and *subjects* them to *slavish standards of life commensurate with slave wages*. So the majority are *slaves* and the *tiny minority* consists of slave masters. Again, the political establishment is becoming an *oligarchy*, turning politics into *an industry* and *keeping the rest of us out*.

The precursor of the NDC, the PNDC, is seen as part of the political elite which prevented popular participation from taking root in the 1980s. The government of the PNDC *viciously stamped out* the people's attempt at democracy. The PNDC had a *militarist tendency*, *sidelining* popular participation. The NDC is *fascistic* and *suppressed* a popular protest against the introduction of a Value Added Tax in 1995. The hierarchy of the NDC has an *undemocratic tendency* which *fatally deprives ordinary members [of the party] meaningful and popular participation*. The ruling elite is an *entrenched minority of despots in the NDC* and to *co-exist* with them in the same party *is to betray the aspirations of millions of Ghanaians for the sake of a rotten and dishonest compromise*.

The political OTHER is also presented as being exclusionary in its perspective. They adopt a *bureaucratic approach* to the process of national policy formulation. For them, development is *exclusively...a technical matter* that only *experts* can handle. The elites have *mystified* the process of policy management and allowed *technocrats to experiment* with different development models. When it comes to political debate, the political elites engage in *vague generalisations*.

The RM also holds the political OTHER responsible for the corruption in the country because they practice the *politics of patronage* which leads to the *culture of patronage* because they believe in politics as the *big man's game*.

The OTHER is described as being *arbitrary, vindictive, intimidatory*, and *repressive*: *The arbitrariness, vindictiveness, intimidation and repression that has characterised politics in Ghana is outdated* (Text II).

In contrast to the enormous amount of space dedicated to negative characteristics of their political opposition, their own weaknesses are conveyed in one brief sentence: *We have made many mistakes...* Nowhere in the texts do they recount in any detail what these *many mistakes* are – a clear case of mitigation (van Dijk 1987: 195–196).

The ideology of popular participation expounded by RM is reflected in the plethora of lexical references to *ordinary Ghanaians*.

Variously, they are *ordinary Ghanaians, ordinary people, the masses, the rest of the population, the ordinary majority, many other Ghanaians, all Ghanaians, all our people, our generation, the citizens, people, this country, the Ghanaian people, the broadest number of the Ghanaian people.*

The choice of lexical items reflects the contestation for power that underlies the ideology of popular participation. The idea of *fighting* for power is clearly stated in Text I: *We have to continue to fight for the power to defend our conditions of life and to improve them.* Lexical items that emphasise this – for example, the word *struggle* (as a verb or noun) occurs 19 times in the three texts. Other relevant items are *take control, defend, gain power, sparks, turmoil, control* (as a verb).

6.3.2. Syntactic style

While the syntactic style of selected texts varies, a pervasive feature is the subjectivisation of noun phrases that refer to RM and its constituency. The effect is to topicalize RM and place it in a position of prominence (see the discussion in section 6.4.1 on the use of *we*). Another prevalent structural pattern is the co-ordination of phrases. Again, such a pattern emphasises ideas communicated by the conjoined phrase: *profound and meaningful; a new type of democratic and accountable party; our core principles and our demands; to deepen and broaden democratic views and culture; whose tireless and selfless work; a reawakened sense of clarity and sense of struggle; a defence of free expression and a free media; a rotten and dishonest compromise* (emphasis added).

6.4. Rhetorical features

As is typical of political discourse generally, these texts make use of various rhetorical structures – repetition, metaphors, numbers game, and modality – to enhance persuasion.

6.4.1. Repetition

There is lexical as well as structural repetition. In van Dijk's (2002: 35) view, repetition is "one of the major strategies to draw attention to preferred meanings and to enhance construction of such meanings in mental models and their memorisation in ongoing persuasion attempts or later recall."

Various lexical items are used repetitively in the texts. The most frequently occurring items are the pronouns *we* and *our*. As mentioned earlier (6.2.2), referents of *we* and *our* switch between the Reform Movement as a political entity and the citizens of the country. The preponderance of *we* illustrates that the conflation of RM and Ghanaians frequently occurs in subject position and, thus, ensures discourse prominence. Similarly, the frequent use of *our* is a strategy that allows RM to solidarize with the masses regarding values for which RM stands. This is a design in solidarity formation in shared values. There are other frequently repeated lexical items, as presented in Table 1. This table is not meant to compare the frequency of these items across texts. The main idea is to show how the Reform Movement uses the discourse strategy of lexical repetition in *all* the texts (totals), not relative frequency.

Table 1. Frequency of certain lexical items in Reform Movement texts

Words	Text I	Text II	Text III	Total
We	25	61	42	128
Our	27	50	41	118
People	13	13	2	28
Ghanaians	19	9	7	26
Struggle	5	12	2	19
Democratic	11	6	2	18

Sometimes a repeated item occurs in sentences very close to each other, as illustrated by the presence of *we* and *our* in Example 9. By making RM (*we*) the subject of all the sentences, it helps to bring RM into prominence in the mental model of the reader.

(9)   <u>We</u> recognise that this has in part been due to <u>our</u> silence. <u>We</u> appreciate the media's effort to keep the reform agenda alive and in the public focus. <u>We</u> also appreciate the public interest in the future of RM. <u>We</u> assure you that <u>our</u> silence has not been the result of inactivity. Rather <u>we</u> have been busy doing the groundwork that can propel <u>our</u> agenda into its next phase. Today <u>we</u> are at last ready to out-door <u>our</u> programme for the next phase and even point to <u>our</u> future direction. <u>We</u> hope by this short presentation and in the question and answer session that follows to address all the issues that have exercised the minds of <u>our</u> many supporters. (Text II)

Structural repetition or parallelism abounds in the texts. The repetition of rhythm and pattern ensures ease of mental processing and storage. Consider the following example:

(10)   <u>That is why we helped</u> form the NDC in 1992. <u>That is why</u> from then until now <u>we have battled</u> to resist the remnant of the PNDC style within the party. <u>That is why we expressed</u> our unreserved public outrage against the "fascistic" attempt to suppress the democratic right of ordinary people and the Alliance for Change to protest against the VAT in 1995. (Text II)

In Text II, there are four successive paragraphs that open with the same structural pattern.

(11)   RM will be inclusive...
        RM will be transparent...
        RM will be democratic...
        RM will be tolerant...

Similarly, in Text III, one finds a paragraph in which sentences in the second half start with the same structural pattern:

(12)   The good news is that our national crisis has sparked off a new wave of political activism. This is currently contained within specific institutions or communities. The energies that we see building up all around us in these limited democratic struggles is precisely what we need to overhaul and democratise our national political culture and thereby get our economy moving again. <u>The challenge is to harness</u> this energy. <u>The challenge is to chan-</u>

nel it towards the generation of well thought out solutions and away from frustration and despondency and ad hoc eruptions. The challenge is to enhance its consciousness of its national context. Then the challenge is to unleash it as a force for constructive change! This is the task **REFORM** has set itself. (Text III)

In the paragraph immediately following Example 12, the theme of the RM's task is taken up, and there is parallel structuring:

(13)   **REFORM** is about breaking the barriers to participation in leadership at all levels. It is about enabling all Ghanaians to contribute to national development and direction at all levels including in particular an ability to hold leadership to account. **REFORM** is about making our political culture one of tolerant debate over issues and programmes, free from intimidation and violence. **REFORM** is about making leadership competition a matter of vision and perceived competence. **REFORM** is about making democracy work for development in Ghana! (Text III)

As this segment illustrates, lexical repetition is also present involving *reform*. The capitalisation and bolding of this word is in the original and the strategy is to reinforce the mental location of the name.

6.4.2. Numbers game

The selective use of figures, the numbers game, is one characteristic of political discourse. In the texts, this strategy is used by RM to portray themselves as having *millions* of Ghanaians on their side of the political divide. This is an effective strategy in the competition for political power. In Text I, for example, the lexical item *millions* is used seven times. There are also forms like *tens of thousands of ordinary people, unprecedented numbers of representation from the masses, many Ghanaians, majority of Ghanaians*. These phrases are used in the context of conveying positive values in the process of SELF representation.

6.4.3. Metaphor

Another rhetorical feature is the use of metaphor. A number of studies on political discourse have established that metaphors play critical function in the communication of political ideas. For example, Straehle et al. (1999) analysing discourse from the EU, show that the problem of unemployment is constructed through the metaphor of "struggle". In his study of worldviews of conservatives and liberals in American politics, Lakoff (1996) observes that a predominant metaphor used in the moral system of both conservatives and liberals is to see government as parent, though in contrasting terms.[7] The term metaphor adopted here should be understood in terms of conceptual metaphors as treated in studies in cognitive linguistics: "A conceptual metaphor is a conventional way of conceptualising one domain of experience in terms of another, often unconsciously" (Lakoff 1996: 4).

In the texts of the Reform Movement, political competition is structured by the concept of war. This is reflected in the many lexical items and related forms that derive from the semantic field of war: *fight, struggle, contest, defend, reclaim, crises, disorder, power, turmoil, take control, resistance, defeat, militarist tendency, mobilise, sparked off, fearlessly, confront, battled, suppress, hostage.*

For example, in Text I, we read *We have to continue to fight for the power to defend our conditions of life and to improve them.* In normal wars, parties may fight over issues like land, resources, group freedom or for other reasons. In the competition for political supremacy conceptualised by the Reform Movement in terms of war, the fight is over political resource: power – the power to fully control one's destiny. It is recognised that this resource would not be handed over freely by those who hold it, in this case the NDC; just as in a war one side does not freely give up its hold over the resource that is at the center of the war. This clearly comes through in the statement: *"This power is never given to us freely as we learnt in our struggle for Independence from our colonial masters in 1957 or in our countless struggles, big and small, for democratic reforms, better wages or better services since then."* (Text I)

Wars are normally fought in physical locations – the battlefield. Similarly, the texts conjure up the battlefield of this metaphorical war through references such as: *"Ordinary people have only burst onto the national political stage . . . millions of ordinary people entered the political arena."*

In a war, there are soldiers. On the side of the RM, the soldiers are the *millions of ordinary people*; *millions of Ghanaians*; *millions of Defence Committee activists*; *unprecedented numbers*. These *millions of ordinary Ghanaians* are pitched against *a tiny minority, the powerful, the big men, the natural leaders,* those with *limited political vision*. Without doubt, the RM, from their perspective, have an overwhelming numbers of foot soldiers in the political war.

The war metaphor is complemented by the metaphor of slavery which is recurrent in Text I. This is a powerful metaphor since the concept of slavery is very familiar to the people of Ghana.

As part of the conceptual structure of slavery, there are slave masters/owners and slaves. The members of the status quo – *the tiny minority* – are the slave masters, just as in real slavery the slave owners/masters are always a minority. As expected, the slaves are *the majority, the millions of ordinary people*. The *tiny minority* of slave masters subject the *millions of ordinary people* to *slavish standards of life* by giving them *slave wages rather than living wages*. With their *monopoly of power*, the hold of the *tiny minority* over *the millions of ordinary people* becomes *so suffocating as to provoke crises*. This is the beginning of the *struggle*, the *fight*, the *battle*.

Definitely, the slave metaphor generates a number of negative images – including control, abuse, disrespect for basic human values, subjection of others to inhuman conditions – about those in authority. Obviously, such a rhetorical strategy stands the potential of aligning the reader with the viewpoint of the text creators.

The slave metaphor is reinforced by the metaphor of "big men" – the patrons who the rest of the people have to depend on for their survival. The concept of "big men" has been explored in many treatise on the African political practice. It has also been the thematic engagement of a number of political novels.[8] In commenting on the phenomenon of "big men" in Ghanaian politics, Nugent (1995: 5) states that because money has always been a vital ingredient of electoral success, the rich have always enjoyed a material advantage. The men of means...have conventionally sought to win over potential voters by insinuating that some of this wealth would rub off on them – either directly (through patronage) or indirectly (because of the application of their business acumen to national affairs).

In Text I, the notion of "big men" is variously represented. National politics is seen as the game played only by the "big men" – those with wealth and influence who can buy their way into political power and having dubiously gained such power subject the rest of the population to all forms of abuse: *Politics in Ghana has remained a "big man's game"*. Since the "big men" have preferred access to various state resources, they can use that access to hold *the millions of ordinary people hostage* to their *whims and narrow interests*, just like the slave masters.

6.4.4. Modality

Political discourse is usually future-oriented (van Dijk 1998b: 27). Especially for those in political opposition, references to conditions of the present are always negative, whereas those of the future are positive. The responsible agents of the present conditions are the current political rulers; but, for the future, it is those currently in opposition. Evidence from the RM texts confirms this view. Various examples cited throughout the paper show the negative way in which RM describes the present conditions of the country. The following excerpts from Text III as well as what has been stated in Example 4 capture the negative representation of the present.

(14)   Excellencies, ladies and gentlemen, our political establishment (and I refer to both majority and minority parties) is a ready accomplice in the development of this negative culture. The political establishment discourages popular participation in national policy making processes. Politics is again becoming an "industry". We are developing an oligarchy with a vested interest in keeping the rest of us out – except as rally fodder and docile voters. Political discussion is once again moving away from the questions of national direction to character assassination, appeals to nostalgia, and trivia.

The contrast to the negative present is the positive future with RM as the political actors – the actors of change. This is captured in the excerpt in Example 13. The futuristic nature of the programme of RM is also demonstrated in the plenitude of the modal will in these texts. The excerpts in (5a), (5b) and (7) illustrate this. So does Example (11).

7. Conclusion

Our knowledge of the relationship between political ideology and language use is expanded via looking at such texts. Within such texts, interesting patterns were found in the thematic structure, local semantics, style and rhetorical features of the texts. Thematically, the dominant issue in the texts is the ideology of popular participation. The Reform Movement is committed to ensuring that ordinary Ghanaians play an active role in the management of the nation through their participation in matters which are critical to the socio-political development of the country. Another significant theme is the perceived undemocratic nature of the NDC. Since the Reform Movement believes in the mass participation of people in things that affect them, it makes sense why they would separate from a party they see as stifling popular participation.

The presentation of these themes is achieved through the manipulation of various stylistic strategies. For example, in their choice of lexical items, the Reform Movement portrays the NDC in very negative light; at the same time, they present themselves in positive terms, reflecting what has been called the ideological square. The texts also use rhetorical strategies like repetition, the numbers game, and metaphor in the process of contesting political power.

In the struggle for political power, political groupings of varying ideological orientation explore the resources of language to enhance their standing. The results of the analysis of the RM texts clearly confirm what other research has established. As Lu (1999: 490) rightly points out, "While ideology often divides peoples and nations, it is interesting to note that whatever ideology a society values and promotes, the role, function, and effect of political language is similar..." The manipulation of discourse strategies tends to fall along the same lines whether we are dealing with the (re)production and maintenance of dominance or the challenge of dominance.

Notes

1. But see: Akioye (1994); Blommaert (1990); Morrison and Love (1996); Obeng (1997).
2. The following are representative works of the Critical Linguistics tradition: Fowler (1996); Fowler et al. (1979); Hodge and Kress (1988, 1993).
3. See the discussion in van Dijk (1998b), and Chilton and Schäffner (1997).
4. See, for example, Chazan (1983); Jones (1976); Nugent (1995); Oquaye (1980); Price (1974); Shillington (1992); and Yeebo (1991).
5. Compare, also, van Dijk (1995: 245): "Thus we assume that not only dominant groups, but also dominated groups have ideologies that control their self-identification, goals and actions." And, van Dijk (1998c: 24): "Contrary to the conventional view, however, we do not limit ideologies to their role in the reproduction and legitimation of class domination...dominated groups also need ideologies, for example as a basis for resistance."
6. See, for example, Levinson (1983), and Mey (1993).
7. For more discussions on conceptual metaphors, see also Lakoff (1987); Lakoff and Johnson (1980).
8. Two novels that are classic regarding the theme of political corruption through the patronage of "big men" are: Achebe (1966); Armah (1968).

References

Achebe, Chinua
    1966   *A Man of the People*. London: Heinemann.

Akioye, A. A.
    1994   The rhetorical construction of radical Africanism at the United Nations: Metaphoric cluster as strategy. *Discourse and Society* (5)11, 7–31.

Armah, Ayi Kwei
    1968   *The Beautyful Ones Are Not Yet Born*. London: Heinemann.

Blommaert, Jan
    1990   Modern African political style: Strategies and genre in Swahili political discourse. *Discourse and Society* (1)2, 115–131.

Chazan, Naomi
1983 *An Anatomy of Ghanaian Politics: Managing Political Recession, 1969–1982.* Boulder: Westview.

Chilton, Paul, and Christina Schäffner
1997 Discourse and politics. In: van Dijk, Teun A. (ed.), *Discourse as Social Interaction,* Vol. 2. London: Sage, 206–230.

Fairclough, Norman
1989 *Language and Power.* London: Longman.

1995 *Critical Discourse Analysis.* London: Longman.

Fairclough, Norman, and Ruth Wodak
1997 Critical discourse analysis. In: van Dijk, Teun A. (ed.), *Discourse as Social Interaction,* Vol. 1. London: Sage, 258–284.

Fowler, Roger
1996 *Linguistic Criticism.* Second Edition. Oxford: Oxford University Press.

Fowler, Roger, Robert Hodge, Gunther Kress, and Tony Trew
1979 *Language and Control.* London: Routledge and Kegan Paul.

Hodge, Robert, and Gunther Kress
1988 *Social Semiotics.* London: Polity Press.

1993 *Language as Ideology.* London: Routledge.

Jones, Trevor
1976 *Ghana's First Republic: The Pursuit of the Political Kingdom.* London: Methuen.

Lakoff, George
1987 *Women, Fire, and Dangerous Things: What Categories Reveal about the Mind.* Chicago: University of Chicago Press.

1996 *Moral Politics.* Chicago: University of Chicago Press.

Lakoff, George, and Mark Johnson
1980 *Metaphors We Live By.* Chicago: University of Chicago Press.

Levinson, Stephen C.
1983 *Pragmatics* Cambridge: Cambridge University Press.

Lu, Xing
    1999   An ideological cultural analysis of political slogans in communist
             China. *Discourse and Society* 10(4), 487–508.

Mey, Jacob L.
    1993   *Pragmatics: An Introduction.* Oxford: Blackwell.

Morrison, Andrew, and Alison Love
    1996   A discourse of disillusionment: Letters to the editor in two Zimbab-
             wean magazines 10 years after independence. *Discourse and Society*
             7(1), 39–75.

Nugent, Paul
    1995   *Big Men, Small Boys and Politics in Ghana.* Ghana Edition. Accra:
             Asempa Publishers.

Obeng, Samuel G.
    1997   Language and politics: Indirectness in political discourse. *Discourse
             and Society* 8(1), 49–83.

Oquaye, Mike
    1980   *Politics in Ghana, 1972–1979.* Accra: Tornado Publications.

Price, Robert
    1974   Politics and culture in contemporary Ghana: The big-man small-boy
             syndrome. *Journal of African Studies* 1(2), 173–204.

Reform Movement
    1998   Open letter to the national executive committee of the NDC vision
             2000: A party of the people. *Public AGENDA,* July 6–12.

Shillington, Kevin
    1992   *Ghana and the Rawlings Factor.* London: Macmillan.

Sotillo, Susana M., and Dana Stace-Nastasi
    1999   Political discourse of a working-class town. *Discourse and Society*
             10(3), 411–438.

Straehle, Carolyn, Gilbert Weiss, Ruth Wodak, Peter Muntigl, and Maria Sedlak
    1999   Struggle as metaphor in European Union discourses on unemploy-
             ment. *Discourse and Society* 10(1), 67–199.

Thompson, John B.
1987   Language and ideology: A framework for analysis. *Sociological Review* 35, 516–536.

van Dijk, Teun A.
1987   *News Analysis*. Hillsdale, NJ: Lawrence Erlbaum Associates.

1993   Principles of critical discourse analysis. *Discourse and Society* 4(2), 249–283.

1995   Discourse semantics and ideology. *Discourse and Society* 5(2), 243–289.

1996   Discourse, power and access. In: Caldas-Coulthard, Carmen Rosa and Malcolm Coulthard (eds.), *Texts and Practices: Readings in Critical Discourse Analysis*. London: Routledge, 84–104.

1997   Discourse as interaction in society. In: van Dijk, Teun A. (ed.), *Discourse as Social Interaction*, Vol. 2. London: Sage, 1–37.

1998ab *Ideology*. Sage: London.

1998bc What is political discourse analysis? In: Blommaert, Jan (ed.), *Political Linguistics*. Amsterdam: John Benjamins, 11–52.

1998cd Opinions and ideologies in the press. In: Bell, Allan, and Peter Garrett (eds.), *Approaches to Media Discourse*. Oxford: Blackwell, 21–63.

2002   Critical discourse analysis. In: Schiffrin, Deborah, Heidi Hamilton, and Deborah Tannen (eds.), *Handbook of Discourse Analysis*. Oxford: Blackwell.

Yeebo, Zaya
1991   *Ghana: The Struggle for Popular Power. Rawlings: Saviour or Demagogue*. London: New Beacon.

When guilt becomes a foreign country: Guilt and responsibility in Austrian postwar media representations of the Second World War

Alexander Pollak

1. Introduction

1.1. Three founding myths

The establishment of the so-called Second Austrian Republic in 1945 was accompanied by two central founding myths: The myth of Austria as the first victim of Nazi Germany and the myth of the *"Stunde Null"* (zero hour). In the Moscow declaration of 1943, in a strategic move intended to stimulate resistance against the National Socialist leadership in Austria, the Allies had deemed Austria the "first victim" of the Nazi aggression (Bunzl 1987: 4, as quoted in Bunzl 1996: 10–12). This formulation was not only mirrored in Austria's declaration of independence, signed on April 27, 1945, but became the reference point for the official Austrian perspective on the years 1938 to 1945 (Pelinka 1987: 145, as quoted in Bunzl 1996: 10–12). Both the denial of Austria's immense support for Hitler (by 1942 the National Socialists had almost 700,000 members in Austria) and the denial of the participation of many Austrians (a significant number of whom were in high positions) in war crimes and crimes against humanity became a dominant view that lasted more than forty years (Botz 1987a: 148).

Narrowly connected with the myth of Austria as the first victim of Nazi Germany was the view that a completely new Austria had been born with the declaration of independence, an Austria that had nothing in common with the "Ostmark" of the years 1938–45. The aim of

the so called "Stunde Null" (zero hour) myth was to deny all continuities between the Third Reich and the Second Republic and to create an Austria that had overnight rid itself of its past.

In fact, however, the people who had supported the Nazi movement had not disappeared from one day to the next. After a short period of "denazification" – where ex-National Socialists were removed from the state apparatus and denied voting rights, and so called
"highly incriminated" Nazis had to face legal actions – former Nazis
were quickly restored to positions of power and became, partly because of the regained right to vote in the 1949 elections, an important
political factor in Austria (Bunzl 1996: 10–12). Both the victimization of Austria and the myth of the "Stunde Null" were part of
a reluctance to acknowledge responsibility and guilt for deeds of the
past.

Still, it would not have been possible to remain silent about Austria's Nazi past had there not been a third legend, interrelated with
the two other myths. This legend was firmly grounded in local and
private social levels, and was rooted in family narratives and in the
commemorative rituals and war memorials of local communities.
Only this third legend enabled the Austrian society to gain a positive
self-identity after the Second World War. This legend was that of the
"saubere Wehrmacht" (the good/clean German Army).

Whereas the myths[1] of Austria as the first victim and of the
"Stunde Null" were state-produced myths which served mainly political aims (Uhl 1997: 183–202), the legend of the "saubere
Wehrmacht" pervaded the whole society and was (and to some
extent still is) a belief shared by large parts of the population.

It was possible, after 1945, to construct via mass media an image
of the Second World War in which soldiers who carried out the war
of extermination and played an active part in the execution of the
"Final Solution" were not perceived as perpetrators but rather as an
ignorant and innocent collective. How were they seen as victims of
circumstances and brutal enemies and as tragic heroes who did *"their
duty"* (Köck 1988) for their home country? How could such an image of history, such an image of the "normal" soldiers, be created
without denying the very existence of the atrocities and dreadful

crimes sanctioned and implemented by the Nazi Regime and carried out by its more or less willing executioners?

To answer these questions, I examine Austrian newspaper articles published between 1945 and 1998, and investigate their contribution to the establishment of an image of history – an image of the Second World War – that allowed a positive Austrian self-construction to evolve after 1945 and that contributed to the refusal to admit guilt and accept responsibility for the deeds committed during the war.

2. Method and theory of media-constructed history

When mass media refer to the past – describing, analyzing, and interpreting past events – this takes place in the form of images of history. Each of these images consists of certain configurations of actions and events and represents a particular chronological and causal ordering of these events. Through this ordering, a general image of the historical event is created.

In this context, I investigate the purpose of specific images of history being employed by the mass media. What is the function of certain images of the past in certain contexts in the present? Dealing with the past and employing certain conceptions of the past is no end in itself. The past becomes of interest in contexts where it can be linked to the present. Hence, images of history – by means of producing and reproducing collective memories – serve the aim of constructing the present. Since individuals and groups have different – and often contradictory – perspectives on how the present (and the future) should be constructed, and since the enforcement of these perspectives is connected with the possibility of influencing present and/or future developments, there is a permanent struggle both for the accepted/dominant perspective on the past and the valid connection of the past with the present. Images of history become powerful in that, as they are established, points of identification are being created. These serve the constitution of new, or the modification of existing identity constructions. Summing up, specific conceptions of history are aimed at supporting and transporting specific present-day values and identity concepts, in order to preserve or change existing views and power relations.

Concerning the development of a theory of media constructed historical accounts, my starting assumption is that there exist what I call "discourse spaces" (Diskursräume). These spaces of discourse "frame" historical events – that is, they contain all possible forms of constructions and recontextualizations[2] of these events. Therefore, if we talk about the space of "Second World War" discourse, we mean all possible accounts of the Second World War.

Since the space of "Second World War" discourse contains a countless number of topics connected with the event under discussion, the first step in constructing a specific account would be to focus on one or a small number of the potential topics. Possible topics connected with the Second World War can for instance be prisoners of war, concentration camps, the execution of the "Final Solution", bombing of cities, battles in certain geographical areas, reconciliation, war crimes of the Allies, war crimes of the Wehrmacht, and so on. Media usually pick out one of these topics, which then becomes the frame, i.e., the leading topic, which again consists of many interconnected subtopics.

The next step in the process of construction, after focusing on a specific headline topic, is the selection of the perspective – that is, the angle from which the represented topic is highlighted. With whom does the author identify? Which "facts" or sub-events are being mentioned and which are omitted? For example, if the war between Pan-Germany and the Soviet Union is selected as a topic, it is possible to write about the crimes of the German Army (against civilians, Jews, prisoners of war, etc.) or to highlight sub-events, such as the battle of Stalingrad, in which German soldiers are victimized. It is possible to identify with inmates of concentration camps – for many of whom the Soviet advance after 1942–43 meant liberation – or to identify with the German population in the East[3] who had to either escape or suffer during the Soviet advance?

After choosing the perspective from which the selected event is being shown, the final step in constructing images of history is the argumentative and rhetorical elaboration of this perspective. This includes choosing and applying the linguistic means and strategies estimated as most suitable for reaching the aspired discursive aims.[4] My approach is analytical, which (concerning the succession of the individual steps in the process of construction) does not necessarily reflect the mental processes of subjects writing newspaper articles about historical events. Nevertheless, all these steps – maybe in a different order, maybe all at the same time – are part of the process of constructing images of history and represent a useful analytical framework.

Images of history is my focus, within which the topics of guilt and responsibility are most central. How are particular images of World War II connected to the establishment of certain views on guilt and responsibility?

Six major discursive strategies guide the following analysis[5]. These strategies enable the perception and assignment of guilt and responsibility. All six strategies have one characteristic in common: they function as filters to the past, giving the events of the Second World War a certain color and shape. Viewing the past through these "filters" results in the transformation and, even more important, elimination of certain aspects of the past: namely guilt and responsibility. The six strategies are: (1) Self-Presentation as Victims, (2) Transforming the Chain of Causalities, (3) Relativizing and Justifying the Past, (4) Focusing Guilt, (5) Selecting Events that Symbolize the Past, and (6) Individualizing the Past.

The strategy of "Self-Presentation as Victims" establishes certain premises concerning the assessment of Austrian involvement in the war. These premises then form the context for the perception – for an "Austrian-specific" perception – of the whole space of "Second World War" discourse. Both the strategy of "Transforming the Chain of Causalities" and "Relativizing and Justifying the Past"[6] can be seen as meta-strategies – strategic frames that determine the topics and events selected, the perspective chosen, and the argumentative and rhetorical elaboration applied. Therefore, these strategies cannot be linked only to one level of the analytical framework; rather, they transgress levels. "Focusing Guilt" perspectivizes particular events of World War II – events in which there is a confrontation with criminal deeds of (members of) the Third Reich – by focusing on specific (groups of) actors in the elaboration of these events.

The strategy of "Selecting Events that Symbolize the Past" operates by equalizing a certain event of the war with a certain perspective on the war. That means that the event selected is established as a symbol for a certain perspective on, and thus a certain perception of, the war.

Finally, "Individualizing the Past" is a strategy applied on the elaborative level of accounts dealing with topics and events that are concerned with certain aspects of World War II, thus influencing the perception of these topics and events.

Since thousands of articles have appeared on the topics related with World War II in Austrian newspapers since 1945, I concentrate on three major Austrian newspapers[7] – the conservative broadsheet *Die Presse*[8], the most popular Austrian tabloid *Neue Kronenzeitung*[9] and the *Kurier*[10]. From these sources, I select only articles that contribute to both the construction of an image of German/Austrian soldiers in the war and to the question of denying or accepting guilt and responsibility for crimes committed by the members of the Pan-German Army during wartime.

My analytical approach is interpretative. Guiding following interpretations are findings of discourse-analytical research on prejudiced language usage[11], and qualitative methods of textual analysis (content analysis, rhetorical analysis). Further inspiration is derived from historical constructivism[12] and the discourse-historical approach of the Vienna School[13]. Findings reported below do not equally represent *all* Austrian newspapers or *all* newspaper articles, particularly since none of the articles were free of ambivalence or ambiguity. Nevertheless, the portrait I am drawing of Austrian media's dealings with the past is not arbitrary and a comprehensive image emerges from sampled newspaper articles.

3. Self-presentation as victims

Austrian accounts about World War II differ from German postwar accounts because of an unquestioned premise – that Austria and the Austrians were *victims* of Nazi Germany. This premise had a specific discursive function, namely to filter the past. From an Austrian perspective, this filtering was applied systematically to give events of the Second World War a different color and shape. Viewing the past through this filter transformed and, more important, eliminated guilt and responsibility for the past.

The reasoning behind establishing and reproducing the victim thesis as a filter to the past was as simple as it was convincing: A country that had been assaulted by a hostile foreign power and had been extinguished from the political map could not be made responsible for the deeds of the assaulting power. According to this argumentation, the population of the "Ostmark" had lived under foreign law and had served in a foreign army with foreign tasks. One central image in this context is that of the Austrian soldiers[14] *"who were pressed into the German Wehrmacht ... [and] forced to wear German uniforms"*[15]. Thus, the crimes of "the Nazis" were not "their" (the Austrians) crimes and the years from 1938 to 1945 could be presented as *"a catastrophe to the Austrian people"* rather than a catastrophe co-caused by many Austrians. The myth of Austria as the first victim of the Nazi aggression is rounded off by the image of the Austrians *"waking up from a nightmare"* in 1945 and showing the world – after the *"zero hour"* – that they are *"a mature people"*.

In addition to the accounts asserting the victim status and the innocence of the Austrian people, two further narratives were employed as "Austrian" filters to the past. First, particularly in the first fifteen years after the war, strong emphasis – or rather, overemphasis – was given to the Austrian resistance movement, thereby trying to prove that large parts of the population were Austrian patriots rather than supporters of the Third Reich. In the "resistance" narratives Austria becomes *"the first country that resisted gallantly and at the beginning successfully against the Third Reich"*. Only after *"being abandoned by Mussolini and the Western Powers and after being put under massive pressure by the German Wehrmacht Austria became a part of the National Socialist Pan-German Reich."* Other resistance accounts do not deal with the resistance before the coming to power of National Socialists in Austria, but rather with resistance activities taking place at a time when the defeat of the Third Reich was already foreseeable. In the latter case the *"many thousands of Austrian patriots who risked their lives to save their people and their home country"* and *"who fought with arms in their hands against the troops of Hitler"* become the central figures of the historical accounts.

A second argumentative strategy is applied in narratives that deal less with Austrian patriotism but rather with accentuating alleged differences between the character of Austrians and Germans. Establishing stereotypical beliefs about the *"more human"* Austrians, these narratives try to draw a clear line between the German "Nazis" and Austrian soldiers.

4. Transforming the causal chain

When analyzing or explaining past events like the Second World War, media accounts tend to build up a causal chain. Starting from somewhere in the past, certain actions or events are said to have caused subsequent actions or events, thus constructing a particular explanatory path through history. Hence, one powerful way to change the perception of past events is by altering or reassessing a major link of the chain, thereby transforming the entire causal chain.

4.1. The question of the responsibility for triggering war in 1939

One major causal link constructed in media accounts is the responsibility for unleashing World War II. Many German and Austrian historical revisionists have "specialized" on this topic. They see a possibility to mitigate German/Austrian guilt by either asserting that war was inescapable or emphasizing that the Allies – particularly Great Britain and the Soviet Union – were also responsible for the outbreak of the war (or at least for the war becoming a world war).

That war was inescapable is an assertion usually connected with the post-World War I global order. In this context, special emphasis is given to the *"disgraceful"* Treaty of Versailles[16] which is not only presented *"as a foundation for new conflicts"* but serves also as a vantage point for asserting the legitimacy of territorial demands directed against Poland by the German leadership.

Yet, the criticism of the so called "Westmächte" (the western powers France and Britain) is not limited to the Treaty of Versailles. It refers also to their appeasement policy that was reluctant to stop Hitler at an earlier stage and to Great Britain's responsibility for allowing "the limited war" between Germany and Poland to become a world war through Great Britain's declaration of war on Germany after its attack on Poland. This somewhat contradictory argumentation implies that the western powers took the wrong actions at the wrong time and thus bear responsibility for sparking war.

While the criticism of the "Westmächte" is often presented subtly, the Soviet Union is far more openly made responsible for war's outbreak. In this context, central importance is ascribed to the Stalin-Hitler Pact (otherwise known as the Molotov-Ribbentrop Pact), i.e., a non-aggression treaty that also allotted conquered territories in Eastern Europe. Some of the accounts dealing with this accord and the outbreak of the war attribute a passive role to the Soviet Union, that is, the pact between the Soviet Union and the Pan-German Reich is seen as rear cover for Hitler's plans of conquest. Other accounts assess Stalin as holding all cards in his hand, and as culpable for the decisive impulse for the war's outbreak. Such assessments see Stalin as *"having abused Hitler as a ram against the capitalist democracies of the West"*. In these constructions of history, Stalin becomes *"the only winner of the war in September 1939"* and *"the new referee of Europe"*. Consequently, the German attack on Poland becomes, *"in its depth"* a strategic move of the Soviet Union.

4.2. Assessing the German attack on the Soviet Union in 1941

With the German attack on the Soviet Union in June 1941 an un-precedented war of extermination had begun. According to German historian Gerd Überschär:

> From German side this war [the war against the Soviet Union] had been car-ried on, from the very beginning, as a political-ideologically and racially motivated [....] war of extermination. The political aim of the war was a very concrete one: it was a matter of conquering, ruling/dominating/controlling and exploiting the European part of the Soviet Union for the German "members of the master race" (Herrenmenschen) (Überschär and Wette 1999: 7). The special quality of this war, the total dif-ference in comparison to the "normal wars" in Western and Northern Europe is not only revealed in Hitler's declaration concerning the intended strategy of war which aimed at the total "destruction" and "shattering of Russia" as a nation, but is also expressed in the subsequently in great detail traced out instruments and mechanisms of control for the "living space" (Lebensraum) to be conquered in the East. (Überschär 1999: 40)

Millions of civilians and prisoners of war, and the industrial kill-ing of millions of Jews by Pan-German units in the course of the so-called "Final Solution", were parts of the war in the east. The ques-tion of guilt and responsibility is directly connected with activities of German soldiers and members of *"Sondereinheiten"* ("special units") during the war in the East. Hence, one strategy by which to deny or relativize guilt is to transfer responsibility from the perpetrator to the victim, from the attacker to the attacked. The *"Präventivkriegsthese"* ("preventive war thesis")[17] thus attempts to transfer responsibility for German attacks on the Soviet Union to the Soviet Union by asserting that Germans had only anticipated, and thereby prevented, an already planned Soviet attack. To use the words of a newspaper commentary aimed at supporting this thesis: *"The Soviet dictator had provoked his German colleague [Hitler] to attack his country, to be later able to show himself in public as 'the victim of a malicious fascist assault' and to present his plans to conquer Germany as a reaction to the previous assault'..."*

To underscore the "preventive war thesis", four interconnected ar-gumentative lines are presented:

(1) The rationality and inevitability of war between the German Reich and the Soviet Union: *"The perception of insurmountable political, strategic and ideological contrasts ... leads to the perception of a subjective inevitability of a military conflict...."*

(2) The long-term consequences of not attacking the Soviet Union: *"The mere defense of the so far gained would have meant the defeat in a long-term perspective."*; *"The consequences of the Hitler-Stalin-Pact in August 1939 brought, in a long-term perspective, more advantages for the Soviet Union than for Germany."*; *"The Third Reich ... was threatened to become fatally dependent on its new partner, the USSR."*

(3) The alleged military threat of the Soviet Union to the Third Reich: *"The fact that the German attack on the Soviet Union was also aimed to prevent a too powerful military threat ..., can, after the latest investigations on this subject, no longer be played down as a 'rhetoric of justification'."*

(4) "The fact" that the Soviet Union was about to attack Germany: *"The German Wehrmacht anticipated a Soviet attack by a few weeks."*; *"Even Soviet historians state that Stalin deliberately sought war."*

In such accounts, an image is drawn of the situation prior to the German attack that aims to justify and naturalize such a decision. Indeed, the German attack on the Soviet Union is presented as a natural reaction of a nation that felt threatened by *"the military potential of the Soviet Union"*. In contrast to such media accounts, Überschär opines that:

> There is no doubt about it: The 22 June 1941 stands for the classical case/instance of an offensive war, executed/carried out by the Army (Wehrmacht) of the German Reich by order of their "Fuehrer" and supreme commander Adolf Hitler (Überschär and Wette 1999: 8). The arguments presented, are moreover based on the long since secured knowledge that Hitler, with the contract-breaching assault in summer 1941, had not executed a "preventive strike" and that he therefore had not wanted to anticipate with the German attack an allegedly forthcoming Soviet offensive. (Überschär 1999: 14)

5. Relativizing and justifying the past

Relativizing the past means detaching past events from their uniqueness and putting them into a context in which they are assessed according to their relation to other events. As a strategy, relativizing the past reduces the weight of certain actions or events in order to avoid dealing with them or with questions of guilt and responsibility.

Thus, three questions must be considered: (1) Which events are chosen to be relativized? (2) With which other – presumably comparable – events are these events juxtaposed? (3) What argumentative function does this juxtaposition fulfill?

To the first question, it is clear that relativizable or justifiable events of the Second World War are those related to guilt and responsibility, where active participants did things considered to be morally reprehensible.

Few newspaper articles directly juxtapose a World War II action or event with a more innocent comparison. Instead, most historical accounts refer only to actions of others or events elsewhere, rather than linking directly to German actions for which they are meant to lessen guilt or diffuse responsibility. Analysis of these accounts is, thus, difficult since it is not always possible to say with certainty whether an account serves a relativizing function or not. Still, some recurrent efforts to relativize stand out.

5.1. Comparison with the deeds of the Allies

Deeds of the Allies serve as the most common relativizers for the Pan-German crimes. The logic behind this is very simple: since the Allied countries had been – during the Nuremberg Trials – the judges of the German crimes, the tables are now being turned on the Allies, because it is now being argued that they were in no way morally superior to the Germans/Austrians. The strategic motives for seeking Allied relativizers is twofold. First, this approach allows the possibility to set off one's crimes against the crimes of the former enemy while providing a chance to "normalize" pan-German deeds by either stating that they are not specific to one side only or by asserting that behaviors of both are part of "normal" war.

Comparing German deeds with those of the Allies involved three media-employed relativizing strategies:

- Emphasizing factual or putative war crimes of the Allies;
- Presenting Allied war crimes in a far more drastic way than those committed by Germans/Austrians;
- Presenting German crimes merely as a reaction to the brutal warfare of the enemy.

5.1.1. Emphasizing factual or putative war crimes of the allies

"The death of Dresden" and the bombing of Austrian cities, is an event often mentioned and discussed in Austrian newspapers. The commemoration year 1995 – fifty years had passed since the end of the war – was used especially for making the destruction of German and Austrian cities from the air and the deliberate killing of thousands *of people a major topic. These* "senseless" *bombings are regarded as evidence that the Allies, too, did not shrink back from committing war crimes. Particularly the role of Great Britain as the driving force behind "Operation Thunderstorm" – the carpet bombings of German cities – is critically emphasized.*

Newspaper coverage of Allied bombings marginalizes the simultaneous destruction of cities by the Pan-German military. Neither the bombing of Warsaw, Belgrade, Coventry, Stalingrad nor that of other European cities receives nearly as much attention as the bombings by the Allied forces. Emphasizing the destruction of Dresden serves specific identity-related functions – functions which, apparently, could be achieved only by keeping in the background the devastation wrought by the German Army.

Another strongly accentuated issue is the expulsion and persecution of the so-called "Ethnic Germans" (*Volksdeutsche*) in Middle and Eastern Europe at the end of and after the war. Two ways of dealing with this topic can be distinguished. Some of the articles indeed put the crimes against the "Ethnic Germans" as equal to Nazi crimes but, nevertheless, see "Ethnic Germans" more as victims of Hitler and his policies than victims of the victorious powers. For example:

> The systematic, industrial bestiality of the Nazis was responded to with, one might say, spontaneous bestiality. Again, the Sudeten-Germans [Germans living on Czech territory], whose expulsion was accompanied by massive atrocities by the Czechs, were the main victims. Of course, in their official publications the Sudeten-Germans see themselves still as victims of the victorious powers and not as victims of Hitler, thereby mistaking the [true] historical causalities. (Rauscher 1985)

Other accounts refuse to develop a differentiated view and see the "Ethnic Germans" solely as victims *"of barbaric acts of revenge"* and *"the biggest expulsion in history"*. These accounts, by stating that they intend *"to remove the mask of humanity from the victorious powers"* and demonstrate *"the hypocrisy of Roosevelt and Churchill"*, are clearly aimed at offsetting German crimes by pointing out the treatment of the "Ethnic Germans" after the war. In the words of one writer: *"Hitler started it in the course of the war, but the victors continued modern slavery even after the war had ended…"*.

The massacre of Katyn, a place in Poland where thousands of Polish officers were killed by Soviet units, is another event given the role of an important relativizer. For a period of more than forty years, the Soviet Union had denied responsibility for this crime and asserted that German units had killed Polish officers. In Austrian media accounts, Katyn became *"a symbol for falsification of history and unpunished crimes"*, and provided an opportunity to state or imply that the Soviets must come to terms with their past. Moreover, by emphasizing *"dark chapters"* in the history of one major ally, it was again possible to contextualize German deeds within a generally criminal period of history. To lessen guilt and diffuse responsibility, it is clear that some media made ample use of Katyn.

Additional efforts to relativize pan-German deeds are too numerous to detail here. Still, one should note the story of the *"tragedy"* of the Cossacks who, after fighting for the Pan-German Army during the war, were handed over to the Soviets by the British Army. Many Cossacks were subsequently executed, which then is described as *"a blemish in the book of British History"*. Similarly, the execution of presumed collaborators by the Yugoslavian

Partisans in Slovenia after the war was described in a major Austrian newspaper as the *"Super-Katyn of Slovenia"*.

5.1.2. Exaggerating Allied war crimes

Allied war crimes are emphasized not only by the frequency of their appearance but also by the argumentation strategies applied. Most striking about these accounts is the linguistic and semiotic manner in which they are presented. The language used and the pictures selected to describe, analyze, and comment on Allied crimes differ significantly from the way German/Austrian crimes are presented. This leads to a potentially much stronger and emotional perception of the Allied crimes and, again, to the backgrounding and marginalizing of German/Austrian crimes.

As seen in some of the texts above, the language used to present crimes of the Allies is often harsh, direct and loaded with emotions. Moreover, the deeds are described in much greater detail, actors/agents named much more often, and active constructions used with a significantly higher frequency than when describing German/Austrian crimes. The desire to emotionalize can be detected easily in cases where the naming of the actors is accompanied by amplifying/intensifying attributes, as in *"the bloodthirsty Partisans"*. Or, to give further examples for the language employed: *"... the whole Third Battalion was butchered [by the Partisans]."*; and *"With their spades the Bolsheviks crushed the skulls of the wounded [German soldiers]."*

In contrast to these examples, "bloodlust" is never attributed to the "normal" German/Austrian soldiers, and their deeds are never described with verbs like "butcher". Moreover, most sentence constructions that talk about German crimes are passive ones that do not mention the actor. Such passive constructions are exemplified by the following: *"At that time some persons were shot."* ; and *"The Jews from Hungary, who survived working under inhuman conditions, were driven in death marches to the West. Persons, who were not able to march any more, were shot or beaten to death by the wayside."* In most of these cases, the reader of the article can only guess who committed the crimes. Sometimes, totally abstract constructions are used: *"Millions were killed, went missing, were driven away, wounded, millions were killed in the gas chambers with the aid of a merciless machinery."* The only thing that can be inferred directly from the last example is that there was a machinery that helped in the killing. Neither is it clear of what the machinery consisted nor by whom the machinery was operated or directed to kill.

Exceptions to this kind of presentation are crimes committed by members of the SS, where a completely different language is applied. In connection with the SS, agents are not always hidden. Here is an example of an active construction: *"One year beforehand, the Police Battalion 306 [...] had shot several thousands of Soviet POW's in the camp Terespol"* (see also "Focusing guilt"). Further, the use of superlatives is noteworthy in connection with Allied crimes. To give an example: *"The worst example of barbarism is the picture of the burning Dresden, which, apart from the dropping of the nuclear bomb on Hiroshima and Nagasaki, is one of the darkest chapters of human destructiveness"* The aim of employing superlatives for crimes of the Allies is clear: mitigating Pan-German crimes and, consequently, questioning the necessity of dealing with these crimes.

Accounts dealing with Allied crimes are also remarkable for the strong presence of victims. They are devoted a great deal of attention in event coverage plus space for interviews and biographical accounts. In this way, emphatic feelings for the victims are produced. Attention accorded victims results in general descriptions of their fate and their suffering and in specific and detailed descriptions of their mistreatment. Examples for the former are to be found in connection with the bombing of Dresden, in which some accounts give a list of how many and what groups of civilians were in Dresden during the air attack and a description of the consequences of the bombings.

Detailed descriptions of mistreatments of people are provided in the context of both the expulsion and persecution of the "Ethnic Germans" and in connection with the entry of Soviet troops into Austria. Concerning the fate of the "Ethnic Germans" there are descriptions of *"young women whose kids' eyes were put out"* and *"young women who were burned in public"*. Concerning the Soviet troops it was said that they *"were plundering and assaulting women"* and that they had caused *"dark postwar years"* for the Austrian population.

While only very few photographs are presented to accompany accounts about Pan-German crimes, crimes of the Allies are much more often illustrated with very graphic pictures. Pictures of destroyed German cities are shown as well as images of corpses, illustrating the brutality of the expulsions and persecutions of the "Ethnic Germans". In the latter context there is, for example, a picture presented showing a man pulling a wooden cart with an old woman and a lot of luggage on it. The caption writes: *"Together with his old mother this man also takes a piece of home with him"*. Another picture shows two hanged men, with the following caption: *"When hate, terror, rape and mass murder became bloody routine: no pole without a German hanging on it."* To give a different example: In the context of accounts about Soviet excesses a picture shows dead bodies lying in one row on the ground, with the caption saying: *"Numerous victims of Soviet outrages"*.

A different strategy to relativize Pan-German crimes is to present them as a mere reaction to preceding crimes or brutalities of the enemy. This strategy is applied when mentioning *"the brutalities committed by Poland on 'Ethnic Germans' in the last weeks of August"* in the course of discussing the German reasons for attacking Poland in September 1939. This argumentative strategy comes fully into play when talking about – or rather, justifying – German/ Austrian action against Partisans in Greece and Yugoslavia. An example of such is: *"Especially in Yugoslavia, but also in Greece, a merciless partisan warfare, several years lasting, was initiated by [the partisan leader] Josip Broz Tito who after the war became the head of state of Yugoslavia. Actions of Tito's Partisans against the German occupants provoked their cruel reactions, ... "* Again the aim of such accounts is to relativize and mitigate German/Austrian crimes by characterizing Partisans' "merciless warfare" while presenting German cruelties as mere reactions.

5.2. Comparison with other wars / crimes against humanity

In some of Austrian newspaper articles, Pan-German crimes are set off not against other crimes of the Second World War but rather vis-à-vis crimes in different contexts. A borderline case is the dropping of nuclear bombs on Hiroshima and Nagasaki, which happened during the Second World War but not in direct confrontation with the Third Reich. The nuclear attacks on Japan are presented as the absolute "super-crime" that equals or even exceeds the German "super-crime", the Holocaust. In the course of comparing the Holocaust with other crimes, the uniqueness of the former is in the following example reduced to its mere technical perfection:

> The genocide committed on the Jews indeed was the technically most perfect organized mass murder, but it was not the only genocide in history ....
> To give only two examples: The extinction of the North American Indians was beyond all doubt a genocide as well as the partial annihilation of the Armenians through the Ottoman Empire. In both cases [...] nobody has demanded that the Turks or the White Americans of today should do mourning work. Therefore there is no reason for doing mourning work in connection with the Holocaust. (Barazon 1987)

5.3. Reconciliation with former enemies

A completely different strategy of relativizing the crimes of the past emphasizes the readiness of former enemies to reconcile. The act of reconciliation is in this context seen as *"drawing a symbolic final stroke beneath our historic conflict"*. Thus, *"while some try to defame our soldiers of the Second World War as criminals, the enemies of the past can now meet in [an atmosphere] of respect"*. The latter quotation gives a clear sense of the aim of emphasizing reconciliation: It is used as a strategy to delegitimize critical discussions about the participation of soldiers in crimes during the Second World War.

6. Focusing guilt

We are still confronted with the situation that German/Austrian crimes themselves although often relativized, mitigated and kept in the background are not denied in newspaper accounts. Someone must have committed the crimes. If the collectively victimized Austrians did not do it, who else did it? Finding themselves compelled to search for "the guilty party", authors of media articles about World War II apply different approaches to come to terms with and finally answer this question.

6.1. Personalizing guilt – Hitler did it

Focusing on one person, namely Adolf Hitler, is one possible answer to the question of guilt and responsibility. Consequently the war becomes – *"the undertaking of one man"* – *"Hitler's war"* and Hitler, *"this abysmal psycho with ingenious traits"*, becomes *"the biggest mass murderer in history"*.

But what about the German/Austrian people? How is the role of the populace described and evaluated in the Hitler-centered approach? *"The attack on Poland [...] did not meet with any enthusiasm, rather 'dark presentiments' were wakened."* In narratives focused on Hitler, it seems that nobody but him had the will to go to war, and that he was making war against the will of his people. Still unanswered, however, is how Hitler could implement all his plans? Hitler's ability to proceed with his plans is said to derive from his "hypnotic impact" on the German/Austrian people, that is on *"the blind adoration of the "Führer" by so many Germans and (former) Austrians."* The relation of Hitler with the masses is described as an *"almost mystic communication, a holy delusion"*. Hence, Hitler had the Germans/Austrians *"firmly under his control"*. The view of Hitler as the only one responsible and the German/Austrian people as his hostages is made explicit in a commentary that claims *"that the German People have atoned for the sins of Hitler ... more than any other nation in history"*.

6.2. Marginalizing guilt – the SS did it

Who is to be blamed for the crimes committed during the Second World War also leads some writers to focus on a small group of people. This group of people, these "real Nazis", are then defined and described in such a way that they could be perceived as a separate unit, detached from the rest of the population.

Two steps were necessary to reach this aim of detachment. First, the "normal" population had to be presented as a mass of innocent people for whom *"even today [in 1957] only a few know about the vicious crimes they [the SS] were capable of committing"*. On the other hand, the (small) group of "capable" persons had to be presented as some kind of dehumanized monsters: The typical member of the SS is therefore described as *"[A man] who calmly smokes a cigarette at the site of mass graves and who bumps off thousands of human beings in cold blood."* Or it is said that *"wherever the SS appeared, they left behind traces of death. [...] Not only Jews or 'subhumans from the east' were liquidated, but also parents and children from Germans, who had to sacrifice their life on the battlefields ..."*

6.3. Presenting "normal" soldiers as (tragic) victims of their own regime

There was, however, not only a firm line drawn between the SS units and the populace as such, but particularly between the "special units" of the SS and the "normal" or "fighting" military units of the Wehrmacht. Whereas the crimes committed "in the hinterland" were attributed to the former, the latter were presented as frontline soldiers participating in a "regular" war. Moreover, whereas the SS was seen as executing Hitler's racist policy, the soldiers of the Wehrmacht became victims of the National Socialist regime:

> It is not admissible to contrast the dead German soldiers to the other [sic] victims and present them as perpetrators, as has unfortunately been done. The soldiers were not the "perpetrators", but the perpetrators were those whose political power initiated crises and wars ... (Dregger 1986)

To give some further examples on this view:

> "The soldiers of the Wehrmacht were as a rule no volunteers but obliged to
> do war service; in contrary to the member of the black-uniformed "SS",
> death's head units or NS-special units, who served a criminal power-
> ideology." (Seinitz 1995); "All of us, who had to do war service at that
> time, were abused by a criminal regime." (Lorber 1996); "Devoutness, spirit
> of sacrifice, readiness for action [of the Wehrmacht-soldiers] were abused
> for Hitler's power-policy." (Strohal 1969)

As these examples suggest, a very clear picture was drawn in
media accounts between who is to be blamed for war crimes and who
not. In all cases, the "abused" are the mass of soldiers and the abu-
sers a small group of inhuman people, namely the leadership and
their executive forces.

7. Selecting events that symbolize the past

As noted in initial remarks about methods, media accounts examined
here rarely try to cover the whole Second World War. Instead, they
select certain aspects or sub-events of the war for presentation and
discussion. Yet, this process of selection is not arbitrary. It is part of
an ongoing attempt to place emphasis on specific historical perspectives and, thereby, to create dominant views of history. In this context, a very powerful strategy is using sub-events as symbols of the
whole event, thus establishing and transporting a particular historical
perspective as the valid one.

The Second World War and questions of guilt and responsibility
linked to this event require identifying which sub-event was chosen
by media for symbolic attribution. One event with potentially high
symbolic power was the Holocaust, but it remained very abstract,
employed only occasionally in the Austrian media, and one that
seemingly absorbed rather than triggered discussions of guilt and responsibility. Hence, such discussions of guilt and responsibility regarding the Holocaust were either totally avoided or they were focused on the "madman" Hitler or the SS "monsters", as described

above. In any case, Austrian mass media chose a different event of the war to invest with symbolism – the battle of Stalingrad.

7.1. Focusing on "Stalingrad"

In summer 1942, the Sixth German Army tried to capture/conquer the city of Stalingrad. During the advance of the German Army, large parts of Stalingrad were destroyed. Even though the German troops – among them many former Austrians – were able to capture most of Stalingrad by the fall of 1942, all attempts to conquer the whole city failed. In addition, the Soviet Army became more and more capable of forcing the German troops into a defensive position. At the end of November, the Soviet Army succeeded in encircling the Sixth German Army and, after a two month long siege, the remaining German troops were forced to capitulate. In the course of the battle of Stalingrad, more than one 1.1 million Russian soldiers and up to 800,000 soldiers of the Pan-German Army were killed. The Soviet Army captured about 100,000 soldiers of the Wehrmacht. Most of them died during captivity as an aftereffect of malnourishment and illnesses suffered during the siege. About 6,000 prisoners of war – among them about 1,000 Austrians – returned to their home countries (Kumpfmüller 1995).

In media accounts, "Stalingrad" became a symbol for the whole war in the East and particularly a symbol for the fate of the "normal" German/Austrian soldiers. The event of "Stalingrad" served as an identity-founding construct – that is, as a point of reference for showing the cruelty of the war and as evidence supporting the collective victimization of Wehrmacht soldiers. The war was put into the literary form of a tragedy, a tragedy for the soldiers who participated, and a tragedy for the German/Austrian people as a whole.

In order to attribute to the battle of Stalingrad the functions mentioned above, it was necessary to construct a specific "Stalingrad". The context of the war of extermination, Stalingrad's destruction by the German Army and more than one million dead Soviet soldiers all were air-brushed out of the picture. Suffering was reserved for the German Army. Moreover, in the "Stalingrad" constructed there were no perpetrators. The perpetrators – Hitler and his generals – were sitting far away in Germany.

This image of the battle of Stalingrad was challenged only in the 1980s and 1990s when at least some parts of the media established a more differentiated view. Nevertheless, in the 1990s, "Stalingrad" was still seen as a focus for remembrance, detached from, but symbolic of the war. A committee[18], supported by almost all major Austrian political parties[19], was founded in 1992 to erect a monument in Stalingrad for commemorating the soldiers who died in the battle. After some years of controversial discussion, the monument was erected in 1996.

"Stalingrad" as tragedy presents German/Austrian soldiers as either solely victims or with the additional trait of tragic heroes who fought in good faith for their home country. In media accounts, the soldiers of the Sixth Army who advanced to capture Stalingrad were described as *"innocents, who were transported [by train] to Russia"* in order to *"fight in the cold hell of the Second World War"*. They were seen as *"poor devils"*, *"unfortunates"* or as *"suffering creatures"*. What counted in this *"cold hell"* was *"merely surviving"*; *"The soldiers were freezing, starving, sick with fever, and living between dream and hope in the half-open foxholes [...], from which they moved into battle and to die."*

Many accounts refer to the content of letters composed by German/Austrian soldiers. The letters written *"during the battle [of Stalingrad]"* were seen as *"shaking documents of momentousness and cruelty"*. *"These letters were filled with desires and dreams, determined by hunger and fear ..."*. When *"the cruel end"* of the Sixth German Army came closer, the faces of the soldiers were described as *"faces of the catastrophe"*. *"Ill, injured, full of lice, exhausted, tortured by coldness and hunger, [the] captured soldiers of the Sixth Army [were] on their way into the Russian camps"*. And, finally: *"The last days of humanity – for ten of thousands – took place in Stalingrad"*.

That the Sixth German Army – on their long way to Stalingrad – had killed civilians and POW's and had strongly cooperated with and supported SS units killing Jews[20] was, until 1995[21], entirely absent in Austrian media. Nevertheless, the question of guilt and responsibility was raised, but in a different way. Points of discussion were the responsibility for the military defeat in Stalingrad and the question of who was to be blamed for the hundreds of thousands Austrian/ German soldiers who died.

Concerning these issues, there was a clear consensus in the media about the *"true enemy"* of the soldiers. *"Hitler's absurd order to hold out to the end"* was said to have caused the end of the Sixth Army. In the words of another writer: *"Hitler bears all the responsibility for this, probably, biggest crime in the history of modern war."* But Hitler was not the only one portrayed as responsible in the Austrian press. The discouragement of Field Marshal Paulus[22] was also made responsible for the fate of the soldiers. Hence, the generals and Hitler were said to have *"sent the troops to the slaughter"* and they were seen, in this context, as traitors to their own people.

Reducing the questions of guilt and responsibility to the fate of the German/Austrian soldiers and, thereby, avoiding a discussion of war crimes committed by the Sixth Army during its advance leads to the creation of peculiar media accounts. Most accounts consisted of three very different parts: First, the advance of the Wehrmacht, described solely from a sober, unemotional, military-strategic perspective. Second, after the encirclement of the German Army, military-strategic remarks alternate with emotionalized portrayals of the situation of the soldiers during the battle. And, finally, come highly emotionalized and dramatic descriptions of *"the end"* of the Sixth Army and the *"long and dreadful road"* into captivity.

Only a few newspaper articles deal with the Soviet perspective on "Stalingrad". In 1983, an article was published in the newspaper *Die Presse* which was completely out of the ordinary. It talked about *"the heroic struggle and the self-sacrificing victory"* of the Soviet people and stated that *"this battle, like no other, is still inexhaustible, concerning examples of individual courage and great patriotic feats [of the Soviet people]"*. The context of this article was the forty-year celebration in Moscow of the defeat of the German Army in Stalingrad.

All other articles located that dealt with the Soviet view on "Stalingrad" were published in relation to the erection of an Austrian monument in Stalingrad (noted above). These articles contain mainly three elements: (1) the equalization of the sacrifices of the German/Austrian and the Russian soldiers, (2) the necessity of the monument to be erected and (3) the reaction of Russian politicians and population concerning the erection of such a monument. Equalizing the sacrifices of Wehrmacht soldiers with those of the "Red Army" served the aim to diminish the role of the battle in Stalingrad in the Pan-German Army's assault on the Soviet Union. Moreover, this equalization was meant to support the argument that the monument should be in the interest of both Austrians and Russians.

Russian reactions to Austrian attempts to erect a monument were, in major parts of the media[23], assessed according to the reacting persons being "communists" or "non-communists". The opponents of the monument were said to be former communists, unwilling to reconcile. Russians accepting the monument were described as being non-communist and progressive.

That the monument finally was approved by the city government of Stalingrad was described as a victory for the will to reconcile, thereby neglecting the economic reasons for the approval, namely the Austrian financial and medical allocations and promises made in the course of the negotiations.

8. Individualizing the past

Viewing accounts of the Second World War from a more technical perspective – at the way they are elaborated – one becomes aware that many are based on biographical narratives that recount individual experiences. The usage of biographical accounts has a twofold impact on the creation of images of history. On the one hand, the war is brought to a more concrete and understandable level so that readers can identify with the concretized individuals. On the other hand, the danger arises that the overall context of actions and events is lost and that, through the selection of the biographies, a non-comprehensive and distorted image of the past is presented. This issue was highly discussed in connection with the emergence of so called *"Alltagsgeschichte"* (everyday history) as a form of representing the Second World War.

8.1. Biographical accounts – experiences of individuals

Four kinds of biographical accounts can be distinguished: (1) authors writing about their past in newspapers, (2) accounts that give individuals space for articulation (either in the form of interviews or by means of quotation), (3) obituaries, and (4) accounts about experiences of individuals that appear in a descriptive form. Of these, the latter has been discussed above, while the other three deserve some amplification here.

Some of the accounts about World War II have an auto-biographical and/or anecdotal character. The authors make themselves and their experiences part of their story. This self-involvement is used as a means to strengthen the truth claim of their account since; after all, they had been there. A different function of these anecdotes is opening up of the possibility that the larger context of events can be set aside, with a focus instead on the everyday life and everyday problems of specific persons. At a time of global war and industrial death camps, the world is reduced to the micro world of persons, actions and events surrounding the author. Hans Dibold, for example, focuses in his article *"Christmas, thirty years ago in Stalingrad"* solely on the suffering of the German/Austrian soldiers, thereby excluding any other possible perspective and all contextual factors of the battle of Stalingrad. At the end of his article he uses his narrow perspective to conclude: *"this generation [the soldiers] was from childhood on burdened with disaster (unheilbeladen). What is left to them is a star – the one that leads the way for people searching for peace."* Thus, in Dibold's account, given authority by his personal experience, the soldiers are reduced to a suffering collective, burdened with disaster and searching only for peace.

Many authors refer to experiences of other people to form accounts about events of the Second World War. These references appear as quotations from letters, inquiries or interviews, or as life

stories of persons using quotes to illustrate these persons' experiences. Not surprisingly, accounts about "Stalingrad" contain, by a
wide margin and with the highest frequency of use, all these types of
biographical references. In relation to "Stalingrad" there are field-
post letters – *"letters in the face of death"* – quoted, autobiographical
books – *"I was eyewitness in Stalingrad"* – reviewed, inquiries –
"What does Stalingrad mean to you?" – carried out, and there are
accounts about survivors – *"The man who escaped through two
frontiers"* – supported by quotes.

A strong use of biographical experiences is evident in accounts
dealing with crimes of the Allies. The bombing of Dresden – *"If you
see such a thing as a kid, you will never forget it again."* – is
described through the eyes of witnesses as well as the deeds – *"from
this moment on we killed the prisoners"* – of the Partisan troops in
Yugoslavia.

Obituaries are a special form of descriptive accounts, dealing with
biographies of deceased persons to whom certain relevance is
ascribed. In our case, most of these obituaries deal with high generals
of the Wehrmacht. What is interesting about these accounts is the
stereotypical beliefs about generals, which they produce and reproduce. The generals are, in a way, taken out of the context of a war of
extermination and described only from a perspective dealing with
their military careers. Thus, they are ascribed attributes like *"plucky
(schneidig)"* or *"tough (beinhart)"* and named as *"old war-horses"*
or as *"desert foxes (Wüstenfüchse)"*. Finally, all these generals are
described as having been unlucky and as not having received the
honor they would have deserved.

9. Struggling for the valid past – the 1980s and the emergence of a critical historical approach

Thus far, I have concentrated on accounts aimed at superseding guilt
and responsibility in connection with the deeds of "normal" Ger-
mans/Austrians. Yet, there were of course counter-accounts trying to
establish a different, more critical view, on the events of the past.
Already in the 1960s, isolated accounts or comments appeared that

mentioned that *"members of the Wehrmacht had been involved in the extinction of the Jews"*. Nevertheless, the consensus about central images of history got its first significant tears only in the 1970s with the emergence of the critical newsmagazine *Profil* and with the Kreisky-Peter-Wiesenthal affair. The latter dealt with the past of Friedrich Peter, who was chairman of the Austrian Freedom Party[24] at that time and was regarded – concerning the elections in 1975 – as a potential coalition partner for the social democratic Austrian Chancellor Bruno Kreisky. After the election, triggered by the newsmagazine *Profil* and by Simon Wiesenthal, who revealed that Peter had been a member of an SS brigade[25], a short discussion about the role of the SS ensued, but without causing lasting changes in the perception of the war.

Another ten years had to pass until, beginning in 1986, in the course of the Waldheim Affair, a longer-lasting and deeper debate about the way the Austrian society had dealt with its past was unleashed. Kurt Waldheim, a post-war Austrian diplomat, became Austria's President after serving as U.N. Secretary General from 1972–1981. During World War Two, he had been a Wehrmacht officer stationed in Yugoslavia and working with the Croatian fascist government. When this past, and his role in facilitating the Holocaust, became known and documentation revealed, Austria's Nazi-era history began to be openly discussed.

In 1987 an article written by the historian Gerhard Botz appeared in the Austrian newspaper *Kurier* in which he stated that "it was not only the SS (and Waffen-SS), but also the Wehrmacht that carried out the fight against the Partisans, ordered by the "Führer", with the most brutal means already in 1942" (Botz 1987b). Still, this view of the past was a rather controversial one and did not express a consensual reassessment of the role of the "normal" Wehrmacht soldiers. The real achievements of the Waldheim debate were, on the one hand, that the thesis of Austria as the first victim of Nazi Germany was publicly and strongly questioned, and, on the other hand, that the term *"Pflichterfüllung"* [doing one's duty] in connection with the participation of the soldiers in the Second World War was reassessed and endowed with a more negative connotation.

In 1987 there was also a major change in the Austrian newspaper landscape, namely the emergence of the liberal quality newspaper *Der Standard*, which took a critical stance towards the role of Austria during World War II. At the beginning of the 1990s there were some articles dealing with Austrian war monuments and the hero-worship of the fallen soldiers, critically investigating the social functions of these monuments.

In 1995, another "milestone" was set by an exhibition dealing with the crimes of the Wehrmacht during World War II[26], which caused a controversial debate in the mass media about the role of the Wehrmacht and the "normal" soldiers in the war of extermination. Parts of the media at that time still defended the view that the soldiers were to be seen solely as innocent and as tragic victims, while other media outlets started to reassess their position at least insofar as they gave both the preservative and the critical view, space for articulation. Yet, the debate did not end and, although the traumatic effects of the participation in World War II have lost strength over the decades, they still have a strong impact on the perception of that time in the Austrian media.

10. Conclusion

This article endeavored to gain an insight into the way the Austrian society – represented by the mass media – dealt with the traumatizing event "Second World War". Two basic assumptions, strongly backed by the material I investigated, were the starting point of my analysis:

(1) Austrian mass media has not denied war crimes and crimes against humanity committed by German/Austrian units.
(2) The newspapers produced and reproduced, over a period of fifty years, a more or less unchallenged and positive image of "normal" Austrian soldiers.

Derived from these assumptions the main question that arose was how the media managed to construct and transport a positive image of the "normal" Austrian soldier while, at the same time, recognizing the dreadful crimes of the war.

To answer this question, I want to come back to the analytical framework set up at the beginning of this article. I claimed the existence of three main steps in the construction of images of history in the media:

1. The selection of certain topics/events for discussion
2. The perspectivization of these topics/events
3. The elaboration of the chosen perspective

This investigation has revealed dominant topics, perspectives, and forms of elaboration in connection with images of World War II and the question of guilt and responsibility. Two dominant topics are those that show German/Austrian soldiers as victims and have the potential to produce empathy for the soldiers (Stalingrad, POW's, the defensive battle of the Wehrmacht, the fate of certain divisions...), and those that deal with crimes of the Allies (the murders of Katyn, the bombing of Dresden, the expulsion of the "Ethnic Germans"...). It is not, however, the dominance of certain items on different levels of the analytical framework that is most important. Rather, the interplay between such themes across analytical levels is vital. Considering the interdependencies among topic, perspective, and elaboration, certain powerful configurations of these three factors can be identified, constituting dominant representations of the past.

These dominant representations of the past manifest themselves, for example, in stereotypical beliefs about the roles of certain groups of World War II participants. One of these homogenized and collectivized groups, to whom are ascribed stereotypical beliefs, are the "normal" soldiers. The interplay of topic, perspective, and elaboration constitutes them as victims, as a suffering collective. Even when an event was chosen for discussion in which crimes of the German/Austrian side were central, the question of guilt was answered on the level of perspectivizing by focusing principally on either Hitler/SS or by showing that German/Austrian crimes were merely reactions to brutalities committed by enemies. At the elaborative stage, moreover, a language of mitigation described these crimes. Therefore, even when media accounts dealt with German/Austrian crimes, such accounts contributed little to a change in the perception of Wehrmacht soldiers. This indeed explains why there still exists a widespread – yet, not any more unchallenged – positive image of the "frontline soldiers".

Notes

1. According to Roland Barthes (1964: 92 and thereafter), myths can be seen as a secondary semiotic system. After being linguistically encoded, things are again coded with meaning. This secondary coding is established in a discursive process. Thereby, one established meaning excludes all other possible meanings. In our case, however, Austrian myths are not only myths in the Barthian sense. Although they are symbols endowed with a collective meaning that shapes collective identities, these myths are also deliberately constructed against well-documented and (more or less) well-known "facts". In this sense, the myths to which I am referring do not represent discursively constructed reality, but rather a distorted reality.
2. In accordance with van Leeuwen (1993), I define recontextualization as a linguistic activity "that makes social practices pass through the filter of the practice in which they are inserted. [...] Recontextualization is recursive – it can happen over and over again."
3. In his controversial book "Zweierlei Untergang" (*Twofold Fall*) the German historian Andreas Hillgruber viewed the last year of the war, 1944–45, from the perspective of the German population in the East and the German soldiers fighting at the Eastern front.
4. For a detailed listing of rhetorical and argumentative strategies, see Reisigl and Wodak (2000).
5. In accordance with Mautner (1997: 104–105), I define strategies as general plans of acting. Thus, strategic acting consists of the selection, structuring and placing of contents to reach a persuasive goal.
6. A detailed list of different sub-strategies that are related to the macro-strategies "relativizing" and "justifying" can be found in Wodak et al. (1999b).
7. The three newspapers I chose represent the mainstream in the landscape of Austrian daily newspapers. For decades the *Neue Kronenzeitung* and the *Kurier* have been the most popular newspapers in Austria. The *Presse* is the only Austrian quality newspaper that has existed from 1945 until today.
8. The conservative broadsheet *Die Presse* was founded in 1848. After the Second World War, it was at first published on a weekly and, after 1948, on a daily ba-

sis. According to the latest media analysis in 1999, about 343,000 Austrians read *Die Presse* every day.

9. The *Neue Kronenzeitung* is famous as "the newspaper read by a larger percentage of its country's population than any other newspaper in the world" (van Leeuwen and Wodak 1999: 112). According to the latest media analysis in 1999, about 800,000 Austrians read the *Neue Kronenzeitung* every day. Founded in 1900, the *Neue Kronenzeitung* re-emerged 14 years after the end of World War II in 1959. It is not only seen as the politically most influential newspaper in Austria, but also highly criticized for its partly antisemitic and xenophobic articles.

10. From 1945 to 1954 – the time of the Allied presence in Austria – the *Vienna Kurier* was the paper of the American Information Service in Austria. Since 1954, the paper has been an independent middle-class newspaper. According to the latest media analysis in 1999, about 800,000 Austrians read the *Kurier* every day.

11. Concerning research on prejudicial language use, findings on argumentative strategies and on the representation of social actors (actors-analysis) are of particular importance for this paper.

12. One of my main premises in this paper is that human beings are neither exposed to nor able to create or transport unmediated reality. Hence, the reality transported by mass media is a constructed reality. Nevertheless, contrary to radical constructivist theories, I assume that there exists a reference-reality to which different constructions of reality can be related and thereby evaluated. Without this assumption, it would be impossible to judge constructions of reality on its correspondence with the events they describe.

13. The "Discourse-Historical Approach" takes into account the historical context of linguistic realizations (see Wodak et al. 1990, 1999a, 1999b, and Benke and Wodak 2000 for details). Three dimensions are central to the discourse-historical method: the content of the data, the discursive strategies employed, and the linguistic realisation of these contents and strategies.

14. About 1.2 million Austrian soldiers served in the German Wehrmacht.

15. The purpose of this quotation and the following ones is to illustrate the argumentative strategies employed by the newspapers under investigation. Most of the quotations stem from the newspapers *Die Presse, Kurier* and *Kronenzeitung*. Unfortunately, due to a lack of space, I cannot give full reference for all quotations referred to within this paper.

16. The decisive Treaty for Austria, after World War I, was the Treaty of St. Germain, which is blamed for triggering Pan-German thoughts in Austria.

17. The *"Präventivkriegsthese"* (preventive war thesis) was one of the major subjects of the German *"Historikerstreit"* (historians' debate) in the 1980s.

18. The "Stalingrad Project" (*Aktion Stalingrad*) was founded in 1992 by Walter Seledec, a journalist of the National Austrian Broadcasting Company (*ORF*). The aim of this project was to establish a dignified memorial for the 40,000 Austrians who died in the battle of Stalingrad. Subsequently the committee *"50*

years Stalingrad'' was founded, which was supported by nearly all Austrian politicians and financed by the state and by private contributions.

19. In fact, only the Green Party did not support this committee.
20. Hamburger Institut für Sozialforschung, Exhibition Catalogue, *Vernichtungskrieg. Verbrechen der Wehrmacht 1941 bis 1944.* Hamburg: Hamburger Edition, May 1999.
21. The exhibition *"Vernichtungskrieg. Verbrechen der Wehrmacht 1941 bis 1944."* ("War of extermination. Crimes of the Wehrmacht from 1941 to 1944") changed the perception of the Sixth Army at least in some newspapers.
22. Field marshal Paulus had been the head of the Sixth Army during the time of the German attack on Stalingrad.
23. The discussion of the erection of the monument was a very controversial one in Austria. Nevertheless, a major part of the media, particularly the *Neue Kronenzeitung* and the *Presse*, strongly supported the monument. The *Kurier* had a far more differentiated few on this issue, trying to mirror the arguments of both, the opponents and the ones in favor of the monument.
24. The Freedom Party was founded in 1955 as the successor of the Union of the Independents, which had been a reservoir for former Austrian Nazis. In the 1970s, the Freedom Party had a liberal and a so-called German nationalist wing. Until the mid 1980s, the leadership of the *Freedom Party* tried to strengthen the liberal wing of the party by moving towards a more centrist policy. In 1986, however, the nationalist Jörg Haider was elected as the new party leader and, with him, came a turnaround in policy, which became nationalistic and populist with strong emphases on xenophobic and racist resentments.
25. Friedrich Peter had served in the First SS Infantry Brigade, "a notorious unit that was responsible for terrible crimes in the hinterland of the eastern front" (Böhler 1995: 502–503).
26. The exhibition *"Vernichtungskrieg: Verbrechen der Wehrmacht 1941–1944"* was for the first time shown in 1995 in Hamburg. Subsequently, it was shown in other German and Austrian cities and initiated controversial discussions about the role of the "normal" soldiers during the war. In 1999, the exhibition was stopped because it had been alleged that some of the photos shown had incorrect captions. A commission was set up by the Hamburg Institute for Social Research to investigate the accuracy of the photos and the captions. At the time of this article, no decision had been made yet about the continuation or revision of the exhibition. See the next chapter in this volume, authored by Benke and Wodak, for a detailed discussion.

References

Barazon, Heinz
    1987   Hass, Trauma, Schuld – Wider Radikale allerorten. *Die Presse,* October 24, 1987.

Barthes, Roland
1964   *Mythen des Alltags*. Frankfurt am Main: Suhrkamp Verlag.

Benke, Gertraud, and Ruth Wodak
2000   *Neutralität als ideologisches Konzept. Die diskursive Konstruktion der österreichischen Neutralität von 1955–1997*. Wien: Böhlau.

Böhler, Ingrid
1995   "Wenn die Juden ein Volk sind, so ist es ein mieses Volk" – Die Kreisky-Peter-Wiesenthal-Affäre 1975. In: Gehler, Michale and Hubert Sickinger (eds.), *Politische Affären und Skandale in Österreich*. Vienna/Munich: Thaur Verlag.

Botz, Gerhard
1987a   Österreich und die NS-Vergangenheit. In: Diner, Dan (ed.), *Ist der Nationalsozialismus Geschichte?* Frankfurt am Main: Fischer-Verlag, 141–152.

1987b   Pflichterfüllung (I). *Kurier,* May 13.

Bunzl, John
1987   Austrian identity and antisemitism. *Patterns of Prejudice,* 21.

Bunzl, Matti
1996   On the politics and semantics of Austrian memory: Vienna's monument against war and fascism. *History and Memory* 7(2), 7–40.

Dregger, Alfred
1986   Grosse Ehrfurcht vor allen Kriegsopfern. *Die Presse,* November 20, 1986.

Hamburger Institut für Sozialforschung (ed.)
1999a   *Eine Ausstellung und ihre Folgen*. Hamburg: Hamburger Edition.

1999b   *Ausstellungskatalog: Vernichtungskrieg. Verbrechen der Wehrmacht 1941 bis 1944*, 4th ed. Hamburg: Hamburger Edition.

Köck, Heribert Franz
1988   Der Fall Waldheim und das Völkerrecht. *Die Presse,* January 25.

Kumpfmüller, Michael
1995   *Die Schlacht von Stalingrad*. München: Wilhelm Fink Verlag.

Lorber, Siegfried
1996   Pauschalverurteilung unserer Frontsoldaten. *Neue Kronenzeitung,* September 6.

Mautner, Gerlinde
1997   *Der britische Europa-Diskurs: Reflexion und Gestaltung in der Tagespresse.* Thesis submitted for the certificate of habilitation, University of Vienna.

Pelinka, Anton
1987   Der verdraengte Bürgerkrieg. In: Pelinka, Anton and Erika Weinzierl (eds.), *Das große Tabu: Österreichs Umgang mit seiner Vergangenheit.* Vienna: Verlag der österreichischen Staatsdruckerei, 143–153.

Rauscher, Hans
1985   Die Vertriebenen – die Volksdeutschen und ihr Schicksal. *Kurier,* May 8, 1985.

Reisigl, Martin, and Ruth Wodak
2000   *Discourse and Discrimination.* London: Routledge.

Seinitz, Kurt
1995   "...der werfe den ersten Stein". *Neue Kronenzeitung,* November 4.

Strohal, Eberhard
1969   Startschuss ins Chaos. *Kurier,* September 1.

Überschär, Gerd R.
1999   Hitlers Entschluß zum "Lebensraum"-Krieg im Osten. In: Überschär, Gerd R., and Wolfram Wette (eds.), *Der deutsche Überfall auf die Sowjetunion.* Frankfurt: Fischer Taschenbuch-Verlag.

Überschär, Gerd R. and Wolfram Wette (eds.)
1999   *Der deutsche Überfall auf die Sowjetunion.* Frankfurt: Fischer Taschenbuch-Verlag.

Uhl, Heidemarie
1997   The politics of memory: Austria's perception of the Second World War and the National Socialist period. In: Bischof, Günter and Anton Pelinka (eds.), *Austrian Historical Memory and National Identity.* Contemporary Austrian Studies. New Brunswick, NJ/ London: Transaction Publishers.

van Leeuwen, Theo
  1993   The Recontextualization of Social Practice. Unpublished paper, University of Wales Cardiff.

van Leeuwen, Theo, and Ruth Wodak
  1999   Legitimizing immigration control: A discourse-historical analysis. *Discourse Studies* 10(1), 83–118.

Wodak, Ruth, Johanna Pelikan, Peter Nowak, Helmut Gruber, Rudolf De Cillia, and Richard Mitten
  1990   *„Wie sind alle unschuldige Täter" – Diskurshistorische Studien zum Nachkriegsantisemitismus.* Frankfurt: Suhrkamp.

Wodak, Ruth, Florian Menz, Richard Mitten, and Frank Stern
  1994   *Die Sprachen der Vergangenheiten.* Frankfurt: Suhrkamp.

Wodak, Ruth, Gertraud Benke, Karin Liebhart, Claudia Palt, Susanne Kirchner, and Fritz Hausjell
  1999a   *Neutralität und Identität.* Final Project-Report, April 1999, Vienna, Austria: Wittgenstein Research Center for Discourse, Politics and Identity.

Wodak, Ruth, Rudolf de Cilia, Martin Reisigl, and Karin Liebhart
  1999b   *The Discursive Construction of National Identity.* Edinburgh: Edinburgh University Press.

Remembering and forgetting:
The discursive construction of generational memories

Gertraud Benke and Ruth Wodak

1. Introduction

Austrian soldiers were part of the German Wehrmacht in World War II because Austria was incorporated into the German Reich on March 12th, 1938 (see Binder 1966). Thereafter, the male population was forced to be part of the German army and it was very difficult to resist conscription. Some, of course, were also volunteers. The Wehrmacht enlisted 18 million people throughout WWII, among whom were about 1.2 million Austrians.

The Eastern Front – the *Angriffskrieg* (war of aggression) against the former Soviet Union – led to the deaths of millions of Wehrmacht and Russian soldiers, plus tens of millions of civilians. This war was fought under the slogan *Vernichtungskrieg* (war of annihilation). A Wehrmacht general named Reichenau issued an infamous order on October 10, 1941, in which he asked for the

> erbarmungslose Ausrottung artfremder Heimtücke und Grausamkeit und damit die Sicherung des Lebens der deutschen Wehrmacht in Rußland. Nur so werden wir unserer geschichtlichen Aufgabe gerecht, das deutsche Volk von der asiatisch-jüdischen Gefahr ein für allemal zu befreien.
> [merciless extermination of maliciousness and cruelty of beings who are not of the (German) people, thus [for] the preservation of the life of the German Wehrmacht in Russia. Only this way, will we stand up to our historical obligation, to free the German people from the Asian-Jewish threat once and for all times.]

In this chapter[1], we are interested in examining how members of different generations who learned about the war atrocities first-hand, from their family histories, or primarily from history books, react to the blunt presentation of past heinous acts. We interviewed former Austrian soldiers and their families during an exhibition of war documents in which they were confronted with the war crimes of the German Wehrmacht. Our interviews were made with visitors, among whom some were former soldiers.[2] The exhibition "Vernichtsungskrieg: Verbrechen der Wehrmacht 1941 bis 1944" [War of Annihilation: Crimes of the Wehrmacht 1941–1944] was the first public display of war crimes committed by the Wehrmacht – as opposed to other military and paramilitary Nazi formations such as the SS and SA.

The exhibition caused numerous scandals in many German and Austrian cities because it destroyed the postwar myth of the "*saubere Wehrmacht*" (the "clean" Wehrmacht). The thousands of documents (films, photographs and letters) showed that the Wehrmacht and many of its agents were intimately involved in the machinery of extermination; for example, tens of thousands Jews on the Eastern Front were deported or killed with the help of the Wehrmacht soldiers. In Austria, a larger myth was created, which allowed Austria and Austrians to deny participation in any of the crimes under the Nazi system and thereby to deny any guilt. Referring to the Moscow Declaration from 1943 (Siegler 1959), Austria claimed to be the "first victim" and, with respect to the Wehrmacht, Austria and Austrians stressed that its men were *forced* into the Wehrmacht.

Not surprisingly, then, Austrian Wehrmacht soldiers visiting the exhibition claimed that they were forced to commit crimes or that they had neither seen nor known anything (see Manoschek 1993; Wodak et al. 1994; Beckermann 1998; Naumann 1998; Heer 1999). Thus, "Who knew what, saw what, did what" became central issues in the debates. Numerous justifications, rationalizations, balancing and squaring strategies and denials were the consequence.

The moral problem of Austria's guilt and responsibility because of the participation of its people in the National-Socialist state has not been adequately debated or resolved (Jaspers 1979; Brainin, Ligeti and Teicher 1993; Mitten 2000). A reflection process commenced with the so-called "Waldheim Affair" in 1996 (see Wodak et al. 1990; Mitten 1992; Pollak, this volume) and, thereafter, such questions became part of Austrian scholarly debates and political discussions (see Botz and Sprengnagel 1994). Waldheim always defended himself by claiming that he had only done his duty. The denial of responsibility for its part in Nazi crimes and the preemptive claim to be the "first victim" are major characteristics of Austrian political culture. Moreover, the topos of "just doing one's duty" is present in schoolbooks, speeches of presidents and media (see Gruber 1991).

We focus on individuals' processes of handling guilt and responsibility. In three case studies, selected from a much larger corpus, we analyze one individual from each of three generations of spectators: those actively involved in the Wehrmacht, the sons of the Wehrmacht generation, and finally the generation of the soldiers' grandchildren.

The selection of cases depended on the authors' reaction to the screening of the whole corpus (i.e., all of the filmed interviews). The interviews we selected struck us as interesting because of their elaborate accounts. In addition, analyzed cases parallel other case studies on narratives about the Nazi past (see Wodak et al. 1990; Rosenthal 1999). As critical discourse analysts, we see the value of such analyses less in their representativity (which we have not empirically established), but rather in the reflection of the norms under which the conversation operates. Most of the interviews we reviewed had "overhearers" standing at the side. Seldom, however, did someone step in and attack the speaker or show disagreement. The speakers seemed comfortable in saying what they were saying, believing their attitudes, stories and arguments to be acceptable and normal for Austrian discourse, which the overhearers confirmed.

What differences and continuities are evident in stories about the past told by the different generations (Erdheim 1992)? And, how do individuals position themselves when they are asked about these memories or their knowledge about Wehrmacht crimes in the exhibition context? While this pilot study can illuminate only a subset of all possible ways of elaborating, constructing and denying the past, strategies chosen by our three case studies may be typical for the larger sample.

The central question – how do countries, nation states and societies deal with sensitive issues of the past like the Nazi past – marks the critical focus of this paper. We do not suggest that only one way exists to cope with the past. Neither do we evaluate the way people, groups or societies have dealt with taboos. Our aim is to make explicit some of the reasons why Austrians face the Nazi past in certain ways and what kind of generational differences might exist. This, of course, is not only an Austrian problem, but – as mentioned above – a problem which concerns all nation states.

2. Theoretical considerations

Life stories are self constructions – usually told to present the teller as an integrated and socially valued individual, thus drawing on suitable experiences which fit this narrative (see Wodak and van Dijk 2000; van Dijk 1984).

We see interviews in the exhibition as partial life stories that confront documented crimes displayed on exhibition room walls that suggest a different narrative than the one usually told about the past. People tell personal experiences and draw on occurrences in lives of family members, integrating both into their own story, which presents a very personal reaction to this context. These stories are naturally very different from stories of either Holocaust survivors or perpetrators, recorded under different conditions (see Schiffrin 2000; Rosenthal 1997).

In these interviews, the confrontation with the "other" narrative does not take place in a sheltered room. Rather, it takes place in public or at least semi-public arenas. Norms of public discussion about the National Socialist past and the Shoa are present and, with that, discourse intermingles description and exposition with evaluation (Neidhardt and Bischof 2000) and personal appraisal. Thus, the question of personal and collective guilt is frequently explicit and implicit. Such a topic is all the more present because the exhibition stresses that the "Wehrmacht" as an institutional was co-responsible for the Holocaust, the killing of millions of Russian POWs, and other war crimes. Exhibition visitors, of course, are unlikely to distinguish between an institution as structure and its agents therein, and would therefore see themselves or their loved ones personally accused with horrific crimes well documented in the exhibit.

Everyone has an experiential reservoir from which one can develop a story of the self and/or their experiences. There are innumerable stories to be told, all of which are "true" in the sense that they reflect truthfully the subjective memory and interpretation of that which has been (which does not mean that there are no contradictions in these stories; see Billig et al. 1988). However, "truth" is not the only evaluative criterion. In our opinion, stories to be valued should also be "complete" and appropriate for the occasion, as will be discussed in more detail below.

In our interactions, we usually require from someone telling a story in which something happens to him or her, that s/he provides a sufficient causal chain to explain how things came to be that way, i.e. completeness (see Quasthoff 1989; Sacks 1995; Ehlich 1980). For example, if A tells B that C hit him, B may ask "why". If it turns out that A has teased C before, and A omitted this detail, B may consider A's story as a misrepresentation or as incomplete. At the same time, B will not ask for the whole history of the relationship between A and C.

Even in a court proceeding, defendants are expected to provide a credible story (see Leodolter 1975) which will allow the judge to render a quick and valid decision (see Lendl 1999). Thus, even in a judicial process, most people know that something acceptable as an account, not "truth" per se, prevails. Especially in everyday life, most people follow such a strategy. Hence, under circumstances of "dealing with the Nazi past and the myth of the *saubere* Wehrmacht", such discursive construction will be decisive. Applying such observations, when we heard former Wehrmacht soldiers "appeal" by suggesting they were forced into that role by "the state", we asked how such a state was created and how they contributed to its development. Likewise, stories of wartime bombings and other experiences are incomplete without an account of how and why there came to be war, what kind of war (war of annihilation) and other deeper explanations.

We believe that many stories of the Austrian-soldier-victims and similar victim-narratives will be put into perspective,[3] if they are framed by that person's agency (responsibility) in bringing about conditions that later had painful consequences for the individual. By contrast, those victimized by Nazi racial doctrine will have no agentive earlier story-line.

The second issue is a story's appropriateness for a given context. Not every story should be told in every context. For example, let us consider stories of soldiers in POW camps, stories of civilians whose homes were bombed, stories of soldiers killed at some war site in Russia, stories of racially persecuted people in concentration camps, stories of politically persecuted (e.g. socialists) in concentration camps, stories of soldiers as perpetrators in combat, stories of soldiers aiding Nazi special forces in concentration camps, and soldiers shooting innocent Jewish children in Ukrainian villages (Friedländer 1999). When talking to former soldiers of the Red Army at a joint commemorative event, for example, a story about how soldiers of the Wehrmacht were "victims" – given the Wehrmacht's ideologically charged war of aggression against the Soviet Union – would certainly be morally unjustified. Similarly, when talking to Holocaust survivors or commemorating the Shoa, it is not the place to talk about the suffering of the perpetrators because this necessarily relativizes the unspeakable suffering and injustice and is used to relativize or deny participation in such crimes (Stern 1991).

On the other hand, public remembrance of suffering among Austrians and Germans – those in the army or civilians who endured Allied bombing – ought always be: (a) complete in the sense of showing that there was a willful contribution (and still a view of "it" just "happening") and (b) accompanied by the story of victims who were persecuted, i.e. by a public memory of those who suffered and were killed without a chance to "arrange" themselves within the system or to contribute to it.

In our opinion, it is primarily in the private sphere, where stories of personal tragedies are to be told. But, as Rosenthal (1997) illustrates, these stories are either not told or, if they *are* told, usually they are not accompanied by experiences of crime and/or consciousness of having committed crimes. Silence and guilt are the result – emotions about which there is no talk but which are transferred in families and often lead to big psychological crises in subsequent generations. Myths are carried on – suffering absent the contribution of perpetrators – leading to the shock, sickness and guilt of children and grandchildren, with which they cannot cope. Thus, deconstruction of silence and taboos has a cathartic effect if done in a way that leads to more reflection, understanding and moral evaluation.

Rosenthal and her co-researchers (1999) showed that younger generations rebel against the silence, denial and one-sidedness. Such rebellion is seen as political activism, neurotic and psychosomatic symptoms, and rationalizations or defense mechanisms (see analysis of young men below). Societies cope differently with collective responsibility and crimes. We have no recipe of how this should be done in a fruitful and therapeutic manner – and, perhaps, it is not feasible at all. Certain attempts have been made (e.g. Truth and Reconciliation Commission in South Africa). Why have German and Austrian societies not been able to provide space and discourses that allow for a relevant debate of guilt, shame and responsibility – discourses that provide space for all accounts and for the evaluation of these accounts? Our paper may be a first attempt to meet such a need.

In talking about this part of the past, however, the discursive space looks quite different than societal reality. Fairclough's theory of interdiscursivity and intertextuality (Fairclough 1995) leads us to call this public discourse, in which soldiers and civilians replace past societal reality in whole or part by their "victim discourse" (Wodak 2000b), a colonialization and monopolization. A context-sensitive treatment of the past should have ensured that both the context of suffering is not hidden and that sensitivity to victims' feelings about perpetrators is revealed. Instead, however, we see an almost uniform discourse in which the context is ignored and, absent differentiation, everyone is lumped together in a single "victim" category. Wehrmacht soldiers and Austrian/German civilians are the prototypical victims (see Wodak 2000a). A single story – the story of the suf-

fering soldier and civilian, which in our ideal picture is marginalized
– becomes **the** story which forms the picture of **the** Austrian Nazi
past.

One additional factor accounts for colonialization and monopolization of the discourse on the Nazi past: Contexts are not "just there"
but are rather themselves constructed. Public occasions for talking
about the past do not "pop up", but are planned and orchestrated.
People are invited and others are not invited (e.g. Heinz Galinski,
then president of the national organization of Jews in Germany,
"Zentralrat der Juden in Deutschland", was not invited to the com-
memoratory meeting of the German national assembly on the 50th
anniversary of the *Kristallnacht*; see Wodak et al. 1994). Through
this and similar means contexts are preformed, setting the stage for
one narrative and for one story to be appropriated more than the
other. The elites and the powerful decide (Mitten 1992). Thus, while
the soldier-as-victim-story might be marginal in our picture presented above, the context in which it can be stated is much more frequent than for instance a context in which the concentration camps
are publicly commemorated.

Colonialization thus happens, first, by telling a story in a context
appropriate for another story. Second, colonialization occurs by "ap-
propriating" these contexts to the story, i.e. by habitualization and
through slight changes in the contextual "setup", thereby creating a
link between the "new story" and the context, so that one starts to
expect the "new story" in this context.

Linguistically we can study this colonialization as a misfit between discourse, discourse topics, topoi and its context and functions, and as an invasion by concepts of one discursive sphere into
another.

For this generation of soldiers – but even more for the other generations – we may thus expect that "knowledge", beliefs, and opinions of the past are fragmented, and that two or more systems of belief and understanding are co-present. On one hand, a soldier's remembrance of the past is drawn from an individual perspective, with
his/her personal experiences and exculpations; on the other hand, the
past is portrayed with images from the "grand narrative" taught in
school or in scientific literature, which finds its way into public me-

dia and offers an explanation beyond the individual's grasp. Ideological dilemmas are to be expected (Billig et al. 1988). (This "grand
narrative" can have multiple forms, e.g. a functionalistic or inten-
tionalistic explanation of the SS-state, as well as Nazi party narratives and other sources.)

3. Research questions

As discussed above, different generations (of men) dealt in varied
ways with the exhibition, the "other" narrative, and the projected
notion of "guilt", associated with this narrative. Such observations
led us to focus attention on two principal themes within which we
see multiple subsidiary issues:

1. Different generations have different access to the past. Knowing
   and not knowing is intimately associated with afforded or re-
   quested actions and guilt. The discourse of knowing and not
   knowing is thus also telling others of the individual's perception
   about acts for which one should, or should not, feel guilty. In the
   context of our research, such discourse indirectly reveals their
   present understanding of what constitutes a war crime and/or
   morally repulsive act. Thus, we consider:
   a.   How is knowledge/knowing and not-knowing expressed in
        these interviews?
   b.   What is (said to be) known and what is not known?
   c.   How is the difference between what could have been known
        (then) and what is known (now) constructed and dealt with?
        To which extent are people "locked in the (or their) past"?
        Where do people position themselves today? How do they
        position themselves with respect to the exhibit?
   d.   Is the exhibit addressed in the interview? How is its content
        presented?
   e.   How do following generations construct "knowing" and
        "not knowing"? What/how do they know, and how do they
        construct a "not knowing" other?
   f.   In dealing with the (not) knowing other or self – how are the

(discourse) participants of the war constructed? "Where" are they to be located in view of (knowing about) war crimes? If one does not know – who did what and was thus implicitly knowledgeable?

2. We approach the question of guilt and responsibility by analyzing patterns of argumentation when confronted with war crimes. As suggested above, justification and legitimation play a large role in these arguments, and typical topoi (like "doing one's duty") are frequent. In interviews, we are thus concerned with the following questions:
   a.   What are the macro- and micro topoi in the interviews?
   b.   Which topoi are the same, which are different for different generations?
   c.   What are the main topics of the interviews?

Finally, in our analysis we must consider that the interviews were conducted by Ruth Beckerman, a Jewish film producer and second-generation Holocaust survivor. Expected differences among interviewees across generations depend, as well, on her style of interviewing. That style, on the one hand, assumes an accusatory tone while also adheres to the norm of maintaining "distance" while interviewing. Answers and narratives are thus co-constructed in the interview and context-dependent on the questions and flow of arguments. While we do not explore recontextualization of the interviews into the film "East of War" in this chapter, we will do so at a later stage of the project.

4. Context and discourse model

The theoretical framework within which we discuss our material is the discourse-historical approach, developed to investigate historical, organizational, and political topics and texts (Wodak et al. 1990). This approach attempts to integrate available knowledge about the historical sources and the socio-political background in which discursive "events" are embedded. Further, it analyzes the historical dimension of discursive actions by exploring the ways in which particular genres of discourse are subject to diachronic change (Wodak et al., 1994; Wodak 1996; Benke 2000; Benke and Wodak 1999, 2001). In doing this, non-linguistic fields are not only needed as "information", but are necessary to do justice to the complex phenomena under discussion. Only an integrated picture allows us to understand context and its co- and interdependence with the discourses in which we are interested.

Methodologically, a guiding principle of the discourse-historical method is triangulation. Depending on the respective object of investigation, this approach attempts to transcend the pure linguistic dimension and to include more or less systematically the historical, political, sociological and/or psychological dimensions in the analysis, theory and interpretation of a specific discursive occasion. To grasp the interplay of the different theories/disciplines, Wodak (2000a) developed a model of the way in which context is conceived in a methodological perspective.

This model of the context takes into account four levels; the first one is linguistic, based on the choice of a specific grammar, while the other three levels are part of our social theories on context. At each of these four levels, analysts make choices about particular theories by which to explore phenomena located at this interpretative level (see examples in brackets).

1. The immediate language or text internal co-text (e.g. linguistic theories on intensification, predication, and semantic verb classifications);
2. The intertextual and interdiscursive relationship between utterances, texts, genres and discourses (discourse representation and allusions or evocations, e.g. speech act theory and argumentation theory);
3. The extra-linguistic social/sociological variables and institutional frames of a specific "context of situation" (middle range theories, e.g. psychology of trauma);
4. And, the broader sociopolitical and historical context in which the discursive practices are embedded – that is to say, the fields of action and the history of the discursive event as well as the history to which the discursive topics are related (grand theories) (see also Cicourel 1992).

In brief, this model locates different theories as they are applied in the analysis.

In accordance with the discourse model presented in Reisigl and Wodak (2000) and its further elaboration of the notion of discourse in Benke (2000), we see taking part in an interview as constituting a particular activity (a social practice), with an affiliated "genre" – the interview. This activity has a number of linguistically relevant properties: An interview is usually a two-party conversation in which one person asks/is in control, the other answers/responds. Both participants are co-present and, frequently, are strangers. These features determine the properties of the genre. Because the interview was taped, we were able to analyze the text of the interview. The discourse of interest to us, is "memories of the Nazi past" or, more specifically, "memories of the Wehrmacht" in Austria.

This discourse occurs in a number of different fields of action (e.g. public addresses on days of commemoration, private stories, literature, radio and TV documentaries, etc.). Here, we analyze how this discourse manifests itself in interviews with participants of different generations. These interviews during and inside the exhibition make explicit reference to other manifestations of this discourse (which are used or discounted as sources of information): the exhibition, books, war movies and plays, letters, private photos, conversations. Throughout the interviews we find a number of topics brought up by the interviewees. In our conclusion, we will come back to these topics and the associated discourses and discuss how the interviewees negotiated their discussion of the past through their choice of discourses.

5. Analysis

Our analysis of the selected interviews was performed on four "levels": (a) an analysis of the topics mentioned during interviews, (b) an analysis of the expression of knowledge and knowing, (c) an analysis of the topoi used (see Kienpointner 1992, 1996), and (d) an actor's analysis, i.e. an analysis of who was said to do what (see van Leeuwen 1995).

We are unable to present each of these analyses here. Instead, we briefly describe the interviewees, present our analysis of the topics examined in each interview, and discuss comprehensively each man's analysis. One male interviewee from each generation was selected as a case study to examine different modes of coping with the Nazi past.

The interviewee representative of the "Wehrmacht" generation is a former Wehrmacht officer. In the course of the interview, it turns out that his whole family has a long tradition of males who became professional soldiers. Asked about his military experiences, he tells a number of stories and provides long arguments why the Wehrmacht acted this or that way, completely identifying with the Wehrmacht's planning staff indicated through a frequent use of "we" and what "we had to do", while describing how different events "forced" the Wehrmacht to attack Serbia.

A second interview conducted with a member of the "children's generation" is comparatively short, and we do not learn much about the person himself. The interview can be divided into two parts – a first part in which the interviewee provides his evaluation of the exhibition, and the second part, in which he tells a story about his father (what his father did – or better – did not do). After that, he leaves.

The third interview with a student – a member of the grand-children's generation – starts with a lengthy evaluation of the exhibition, also through a number of arguments. The student further reflects on war crimes – what is it that shocks the most. Next, we find a short section of family history, followed by a lengthy argument that disputes the crimes, i.e. did everybody know/carry out the criminal orders? Are killings of partisans really a crime?

In analyzing the content or topics of each interview, we began with a classification of each utterance, determining whether it belonged to one of the following four "situations" (the classification was gained bottom-up: there were no consistently occurring situations that warranted another category):

- talking about the "past", about what happened in the "Wehrmacht"
- negotiating the relation to the interviewer

- talking about the exhibition
- bringing in other (known) beliefs, assumptions, knowledge.

In addition to these categories, we also marked the appearance of negations (negation of content), asking ourselves what function their frequent use would serve in each interview.

Assessing the three interviews along such lines, we find a remarkable difference between the first and the other two generations. The officer himself addresses almost exclusively only two situations – he talks about his experiences, and he negotiates the relation to the interviewer. All references to the exhibition are brought in by the interviewer, but never taken up by the old officer. This is all the more notable because the other two generations, with no direct experience, comment on the exhibition and call it into question. In both other interviews, the exhibition is itself an important topic covered in the interview. While they problematize the exhibition, the officer seems to see the exhibition as a statement about "his" past, and he is making a statement about (t)his past, to counter this statement. In all of this, the exhibition can be seen as a mere vehicle to transport some content. Whether it is right and good to present this to the public is not asked. Instead, the principal issue seems to be whether claims are true or not.

In looking at the sections we classified as negotiation, we find only a few instances of prolonged interaction. In these instances, the officer is usually rejecting something said by the interviewer. Since the interviewer was either asking for more information or calling something into question, these answers are not only a rejection of a topical proposal, but also an evasion; he seeks to avoid addressing the topic or to talk about that time. The other instances classified as "negotiation" are self-references made during an exposition, thus personalizing and relativizing the story being told.

The interview with the person of the second generation (henceforth M2) is quite different. In contrast to the officer, who talks a lot of "the past", telling his version of the story, M2 evades going into *medias res*, and opts for interpersonal statements as well as very general, positive and unproblematic remarks about the exhibition. This is also initially supported by the interviewer, who begins by asking what he thinks about the exhibit. When the interviewer later presses him to talk about his family history, he provides a short story, interspersed with negations and belittlements. After that he abruptly states that he would like to end the interview.

In this interview, we find long sections in which M2 interacts with the interviewer, telling her in very general terms that "he knows more now", as well as debating whether he is the appropriately chosen visitor to be interviewed. Interspersed we find a number of positive evaluations of the exhibition, and at the end a short narrative of the "past" about his father, which is full of devaluing elements.

An interview with an individual from the third generation (M3) is, again, completely different. Even more than with M2, we find only short passages of one or two sequential utterances that refer to the past. The bulk of the interview is comprised of discourse about the exhibition, the personal interaction with the interviewer, and an additional category when another context is brought into the exchange.

The personal interaction with the interviewer is also of a different type than in the other two interviews. Whereas we see tension between the officer and the partly aggressive interviewer in the first interview, the second interview evinced the subject's desire to be liked and accepted by the interviewer. In the third interviewee, however, one sees an almost presupposed mutual acceptance between the interviewer and interviewee. This can be seen by frequent use of solidarity strategies; i.e., he shows concern that people less educated about this past (than he and the interviewer) might be misled by the exhibition. At another point, the interviewee comments that a particular attitude would not be just towards the Nazi-victims (Jews). In other words, he constructs an implicit "we" of the interviewer and himself by pointing to third parties about whom both of them would supposedly be concerned.

Interpersonal differences are also reflected in the use of negation in the three interviews. Whereas the officer (M1) openly contradicts the interviewer, saying "I am skeptical" when she tries to confront him with historical facts, M2 repeatedly negates himself, what he has known, and the importance of his statements. M3, finally, strongly criticizes the exhibitions using a number of negations. At the same time he also says (like M2) what he has not seen or known. Like the officer, he at times contradicts the interviewer – never in a direct confrontation, but by deflecting it to more general statements about what is right and true. The refrain "I did not know that" also occurs in the officers interview, yet again with a different function, i.e., to dispel any possibility of implied responsibility.

6. Three types of trivializing and relativizing the past

Other recent studies on "coming to terms with the past" in Austria and Germany have illustrated that many people experience a strong need to justify and legitimize their actions (or the actions of others) during the Nazi era. Yet, the situation in Germany and Austria is not identical. Germans never had the opportunity to claim innocence. Nevertheless, as the focus-group study by Adorno (1975) demonstrated, many Germans shortly after the war used multiple justification and legitimation strategies, as well as denial and explicit anti-Semitism, to cope with actual or perceived accusations and their feelings of guilt. Later, Stern (1991) theorized that a strong philosemitism hid these justification strategies in the official discourse behind a proliferation of apologies.

In Austria, coming to terms with the Nazi past developed differently due to the important myths of "being the first Nazi victim" and the *"Stunde Null"* ("zero hour") in 1945. A discontinuity within Austrian history from 1934–1945 was officially created (Mitten 1999, 2000), and the memory of war crimes and the Holocaust was tabooed or others were declared guilty (e.g. the Germans, a group around Hitler or Hitler himself). These narratives were transported through numerous school books, official documentaries, scholarly works and the elites.

A distinct rupture in these discourses occurred in 1986; the so-called Waldheim Affair made it impossible to evade questions of guilt and responsibility as well as agency (Wodak et al. 1990). A justification discourse evolved that was directed against explicit or alleged accusations, and numerous strategies (very similar to those described by Adorno) evolved in the public sphere as well as in various discourse genres. The "commemoration" year 1988 (50 years after the "*Anschluß*") marked another important date in this Austrian narrative (Wodak et al. 1994); the same discourses could be heard throughout. With the Wehrmacht exhibition in 1995 the debate on Austria(n)'s agency continued, and many felt provoked to justify or legitimize a whole generation of men (the Wehrmacht soldiers), seen as accused by such a public display.

We will discuss, below, different ways of relativizing and – legitimizing[4] Austrian participation in and culpability for war crimes or trying to diminish evidence presented in the exhibition.

6.1. "I never saw anything!"

This topos ("I never saw anything") is the most important one used by former Wehrmacht soldiers (see also Heer 1999). This argument means that there might have been crimes, but that the person himself was never present when they happened. They were innocent because they had neither participated in nor witnessed any such events.

The war, such former soldiers claim, was so exhausting and strenuous that they had other things to do to survive, and could never have occupied themselves with deportations or extermination of Jews, Russian civilians or other groups of victims. Further, they had only heard about such atrocities after the war or by rumors. Never had soldiers been involved in war crimes as were the SS or SD.

One interview segment is illustrative:

(1) Officer: I don't consider the Wehrmacht as criminals. They behaved like all other soldiers. Usually better than the others. As for the Jews… if you ask me, I didn't see any. The only time when I saw Jews, it was a labor column, and they came from the concentration camp and unloaded wood at the station.

Interviewer: Where was that?

Officer: That was near Gomel? Gomel, Bobrisk, somewhere in the central section. So that was the only time. Yes, God, no, Pinsk?–that was almost a completely Jewish town. We went there because we were to break through the Priebitz? And there my people had… there were so many watchmakers working there. Some had their watches repaired. (Laughter) They were able to finish it more or less in a single night. And then we moved on the next day.

Interviewer: So, the Jews were still there?

Officer: Yes. They were there, when we arrived and while we were there and when we left there. But admittedly we were only in the place for about twelve hours.

Interviewer: But you were an officer, didn't you also... you can read here how many orders there were. That the Wehrmacht should have transport available, that the Wehrmacht was given the job of taking part in the shooting of Jews.

Officer: No.

Interviewer: The Lassmann (?), Reichenau order behind you...

Officer: Look, I mean, I didn't see any order from Reichenau. That is... Besides that was not the business that we were concerned with. I mean, we were concerned with carrying out the deployment order, and we did carry it out. We were not interested in anything else, because we didn't have time for it. That's a task that....

The interviewer states that the exhibition shows many crimes committed by the Wehrmacht. The immediate response by the officer is to reject this statement although he is standing in front of the photographs. He uses a mental verb "(I) regard" which stresses his own point of view and continues stating that the Wehrmacht was not criminal. Thus, he denies the main claim of the exhibition as such. He goes on comparing the Wehrmacht with other armies: the Wehrmacht was the same as all other armies, even better. He touches on the sensitive topic of "Jews", and the topos "I never saw any" follows immediately, embedded in the justificatory strategy of the non-criminal army and the comparisons which serve as macro strategies. He then relates a short story about the only time he actually *did* see Jews which contradicts his general statement and the topos but which (as always individual positive stories do) serves as an exception. Jews had brought wood, they came from a concentration camp, and he even remembers the name of the village. He continues by painting a peaceful picture of Jews who worked as watchmakers and who lived in another village.

The interviewer tries to confront him with the war crimes, asking him about the known commands in the Wehrmacht to shoot or exterminate Jews. The officer repeats the topos of "not knowing" again; he had never seen or heard of these commands and orders. Moreover – and that is the second important topos – they were much too involved in fighting, had no time, and were not interested in anything else except fighting.

The whole justification discourse of this war veteran is marked by the two topoi of not knowing and not having had time for anything else except fighting. He concedes that he saw Jews, but this unique story serves as positive self-presentation and as exception. Otherwise, he had not seen any Jews (except for the second story, where he was not involved). The true soldier thus performed his duty, and his duty consisted of fighting.

6.2. "I am not guilty (do not feel guilty) because XXX was on the other side"

The son of a Nazi victim, a member of the Christian Socialist Party, uses another justification device – his father's two-year imprisonment by the Nazi regime provides legitimation (using the topos of authority); because of his father, he is not affiliated with the perpetrators, and belongs to the side who suffered. Although he avoids speaking explicitly about any victims of war crimes, this reference to authority (his father) exculpates him and his family from any responsibility. The interviewer tries to get some opinions or impressions from him. Apart from saying that he is "*betroffen*"(moved) and that all this is "*erschütternd*"(disturbing), however, he does not talk about the exhibition's details and switches to his legitimation device.

However, the story about his father is not a story about a hero. He obviously experiences ambivalences and remarks that one did not have to do much to be put into prison, as well as that he was not a hero, which implies that he was not a member of the resistance. The man leaves the interview quite abruptly and rejects any further questions.

6.3. "And afterwards everything was... a bit different"

The member of the young generation (M3), a student, uses metadiscourse, argumentations and topoi which are typical of academic discourse. Two macro strategies are involved: the relativization of the exhibition by claiming that it is one-sided, that it contains mistakes, and that it is biased by referring to authorities (scholars, books). Second, the interviewee uses the German language particle "*halt*", described by Musil (2000) as the typical Austrian mitigating particle that evokes the image that the event being described was destined to come about this way and was fated (see examples below). Nothing could have been done to prevent such events. The young student himself was spared this fate because he was born after the war. Both strategies can be seen as trivializing the exhibition's claims.

Consider the following exchange with M3:

(2)   Interviewer: Did you discover anything new or did you know it all already?

M3:   No, that is to say...
Certainly I didn't particularly [get] the picture through this exhibition... But through this discussion about the Wehrmacht I can say, I always had the picture of the untarnished Wehrmacht, and of course I've had to revise that, yeah, but I would have liked a little more objectivity, and particularly, this doesn't fit in at all, I think, this thing at the end about the Austrian daily newspapers, where simply this – the cultural discussion with Scholten and so on is brought into it, actually that's got nothing to do with it, I think. The issue is the crimes of the Wehrmacht – whether they happened or not – and what happened and so on and it's incredibly important, but to use this subject for the clear party-political preference of the director of the exhibition is simply – for the victims too – I think – out of order.

In this sequence, following the question if he had learned something new, M3 claimed that the picture of the "*saubere* Wehrmacht" was already known to him, but that the exhibition had led to a reconsideration. Still, he wished there had been more objectivity. He then refers to an example from the exhibition that has nothing to do with the photographs and videos but with newspaper clips about the debate in Austria about the exhibition. He thus rejects some of the claims by invoking other evidence that does not touch on this point.

The next question by the interviewer – "What impressed you most?", "What was new?" – then triggers a longer response where M3 draws an analogy to young men of his age during the war and then uses the strategy of "fate". The implication – if one continues the analogy – is that he himself might have done similar things.[5] By using "*halt*", the interviewee suggests that the young generation in the war might have been a victim – a victim of this time and fate. His generation was lucky ("we are doing fine, but then, things were *halt* a little bit different").

The interview continues and after a question about his grandfather, the young man replies with a long sequence:

(3) Interviewer: Where was he?
    M3: He was in France and in Russia too. But they've all got critical captions, the photos... but it's very difficult, I think, because there are, there are so many sections and it doesn't – exactly, I wanted to say that too – that doesn't come out here at all. It was such a big machine, the Wehrmacht, with so many sections and armies and God knows what else, and it was not the case that every order was passed on. A commissar's order, for example, that has really been proved historically that it was not passed on to every group – shall we say – by every officer. That happened too... and if you say they were all like that, that's always wrong, that can't be true. Of course, previously the only truth was the whole of the Wehrmacht is untarnished – that can't be true either – big, big sections of them were very involved in all the crimes, that's certainly true, yeah, but if just the opposite is claimed, you become unbelievable, I think.

Here, he rejects a generalization never made by the exhibition. Nowhere was it claimed that all soldiers were criminals; rather, evidence claimed that the *institution* of the Wehrmacht was criminal. Thus, this young man uses a strawman, again typical for justification discourse. He implies that the exhibition had stated that all soldiers were perpetrators, and this would be "*unglaubwürdig*" (not believable).

This sequence illustrates the young generation's problem in both distinguishing themselves from the old generation and from accusations of the exhibition. The topos of fate serves to exculpate the

Wehrmacht; even if visitors to the exhibition had been alive at that time, it may have been impossible for them to act any differently. In addition, such a young visitor to the exhibit debates about details and emphasizes the topos of authority, thereby demonstrating his knowledge and attempting to deconstruct the exhibition's claims by trivializing them in different ways.

In all three interviews, multiple justification strategies are apparent. However, significant differences emerge that are certainly related to specific experiences of the men interviewed, to their generation and to their own biography and family history. All of them employ avoidance strategies of various kinds. In the first case, the concept of "normal war" predominates and serves as argument to trivialize any war crimes except for those concerning the Jews. In the second case, that M2's father was imprisoned is argument enough to spare the interviewee any further questions or thoughts. In the third case, the scholarly debate is used to restrict war crimes to certain actions only. The different quality of relativizing and trivializing strategies is also related to different forms of involvement in the whole subject. The officer personally has been present, the "son" experienced his father's fate first hand, while the young man is very distanced, has heard stories but is already far away from the emotional upheavals of the other two men.

7. Conclusion

In the previous sections, we have examined the linguistic particulars of each interviewee's contribution. In this final section, we return to the theoretical considerations and discuss the interviews and our analytical findings within their larger discursive framing.

The interviews are all part of the larger discourse of coming to terms with Austria's Nazi past. In the interviews, we find a number of topics that are touched upon in the engagement in this discourse, some of which are similar among all three subjects, while others differ.

7.1. The officer

Topical structure of the officer's interview
  Main topic: Coming to terms with Austria's Nazi past
        a. Subtopic 1: Family tradition
        b. Subtopic 2: "Normal war" (including partisans)
            i. Survival
        c. Subtopic 3: "The Jews"

When talking about the past, the officer distinguishes clearly between two topics[6] – "engaging in a 'normal' war" (this concerns the Wehrmacht), and "the Jews". The topic of the war is further elaborated – "Partisans" is an intrinsic part of this topic, and a particular subtopic of war is "Survival". The second major topic (introduced by the interviewer) is not developed in itself, thus the rather undifferentiated label "the Jews" (instead of "crimes against Jews" etc.) A third topic of this interview is family (and its tradition of men going to the army).

7.2. Man of the second generation

Topical structure of the interview
  Main topic 1: The Exhibition
  Main topic 2: Coming to terms with Austria's Nazi past
        a. Subtopic 1: Family
        b. Subtopic 2: "Being a victim"
        c. Subtopic 3: "Resistance"

Our next interviewee touches upon two major interrelated topics – the exhibition and Austria's past. While the exhibition is itself making a statement about this past, he intends to make no statement about this past in his contribution. The topic of "Austria's past" is further broken down into three interrelated subtopics: the "family", "resistance" and "being a victim". His story about his father brings in all three of these elements.

7.3. The student

Topical structure of the interview
    Main topic 1: Coming to terms with Austria's Nazi past
        a. Subtopic 1: The Wehrmacht
            i. Young People
            ii.   Partisans
        b. Subtopic 2: The Exhibition
        c. Subtopic 3: "The Jews"
        d. Subtopic 4: Family

The interview of the young man shows the most topics. All of them can be subsumed under the heading "Austria's Nazi past": he comments on the exhibition (questioning whether it truthfully presented the past), tells a story of his family, and talks about the Wehrmacht. In the latter, he develops two sub-topics – what did it mean for young people (like himself) to be in the Wehrmacht, and the topic of the "Partisans". Like in the officer's interview, he portrays the Jews as being something different.

Thus, in a topical analysis, we find a number of interesting commonalities: each interviewee – as different as they are – starts talking about their families. In the case of M2 this is initiated by the interviewer, but nevertheless M2 could have rejected or evaded the question. In two of the interviews (the officer and the young man), the crimes against so-called partisans are treated as intrinsic phenomena of "how wars are", ignoring and denying evidence presented in the exhibition, that the so-called partisans were not resistance fighters but civilians – including women, children and also Jews. In both cases, Jews are clearly distinguished as either not being killed by the Wehrmacht or, more implicitly, as being a "different issue" (contrasting them with the partisans), something which should not be brought up in this context (of the exhibition).

The one interview in which neither Jews nor partisans appear at all is, at the same time, the only interview of the three in which we find interdiscursivity to the well documented discourse of victimhood. In this interview, the father, who was an Austrian fascist party member – the party that led the fascist Austrian dictatorship before the *Anschluss* – turns up as a victim because he was put into prison by the Nazis after the *Anschluss*.

In the end, then, none of our three interviewees told "victim stories" (or mentioned victims), in which victims of Wehrmacht crimes are clearly acknowledged as such. A sign of a discourse which *would* come to terms with the past is certain to be an acknowledgment of victims, and a linkage between victims and perpetrators. For these interviewees, Jews are something separate, while partisans and their "handling" are the product of a "normal war".

In the words of each of these visitors to the Wehrmacht exhibition, family stories turn up as implicit sub-text; fifty years did not make this a remote past about which we cannot, or should not, think anymore. Instead, this past is as close to home as it can be, and conjures up family-related stories on every occasion. Not surprisingly then, justifications and legitimations remain present in texts of this discourse. Two particular strategies were employed in these interviews: problematizing knowledge (one's own, or other people's knowledge), and disputing the concept of crime (i.e. killing of partisans is not a crime but part of war). Sometimes both strategies are brought together, bringing the difficulty of coming to terms with this past for every generation into light.

Perhaps most evocative is the voice of a young man of the third generation, with which we close this essay. In the following segment, the young man talks more openly about his beliefs, difficult questions are allowed to surface, and differences are expressed. The "discourse of the past" is leaving the closet. It remains to be seen, where it is headed.

(4)   M: [..] it was often reported quite correctly that the soldiers were often standing around making sure that no one escaped the execution, and the military police actually shot the people. I mean, knowing about it is a completely different issue, but crimes – if one is to view being an accessory as a crime, then one is clearly right.

Interviewer: Well, the question is whether "making sure that no one escapes" is only being an accessory or is also a form of participation?

M: Yeah, that's the question, yeah.

Notes

1. This paper is part of the research project "History in the Making: Confrontation of a Taboo" of the Wittgenstein Research Centre: Discourse, Politics, Identity, at the Austrian Academy of Science (principal investigators: Ruth Wodak and Walter Manoschek, see www.oeaw.ac.at/wittgenstein). This research was made possible by the Wittgenstein Prize granted to Ruth Wodak by the "*Fonds zur Förderung der wissenschaftlichen Forschung*" (FWF), which is hereby gratefully acknowledged.
2. In this paper, we only analyze interviews with men. We will present an analysis of interviews with women, as well as an analysis of other forms of interactional engagement taking place in the exhibition (e.g. spontaneous discussions) at a later time.
3. We concede that on a pragmatic level stories usually do not require such a rich contextualization. However, we believe that in the face of the Shoa, any story of victimhood by soldiers, German civilian and other agents of the Nazi regime, who still had a measure of agency, implicitly relativizes the past and the victimization of other people who were denied their humanity. Stories about this past are, in most situational contexts, read within the wider context, and understood as relativization.
4. We refer to Reisigl and Wodak (2000) for the specific taxonomy of strategies and arguments used for positive self-presentation and negative other presentation, and to van Leeuwen and Wodak (1999) for a taxonomy of legitimation devices used to justify exclusionary or derogatory actions.
5. For example: "it is young soldiers, who are '*halt*' committing the horrible crimes, right?"
6. In this, we take a participant's perspective on topics – topics are differentiated or lumped together depending on whether the interlocutors show them to be different or not.

References

Adorno, Theodor W.
   1975   Schuld und Abwehr. In: Adorno, Theodor W. (ed.), *Soziologische Schriften II*. Frankfurt am Main: Suhrkamp, 121–324.

Beckermann, Ruth
   1998   *Jenseits des Krieges: ehemalige Wehrmachtssoldaten erinnern sich.* Wien: Döcker.

Benke, Gertraud
   2000   Diskursanalyse als sozialwissenschaftliche Untersuchungsmethode. *SWS Rundschau* 2, 140–162.

Benke, Gertraud, and Ruth Wodak
    1999   *"We are no longer the sick child of Europe"*: An investigation of the usage (and change) of the term "neutrality" in the presidential speeches on the National Holiday (October 26) from 1974 to 1993. In: Wodak, Ruth and Christoph Ludwig (eds.), *Challenges in a Changing World – Issues in Critical Discourse Analysis*. Wien: Passagen Verlag, 101–126.

    2001   Neutrality versus NATO: The analysis of a TV-discussion on the contemporary function of Austria's neutrality. *Contemporary Austrian Studies* 9, 37–68.

Billig, Michael, Susan Condor, Derek Edwards, Mike Gane, David Middleton, and Alan Radley
    1988   *Ideological Dilemmas: A Social Psychology of Everyday Thinking.* London: Sage.

Binder, Gerhard
    1966   *Epoche der Entscheidungen. Deutsche Geschichte des 20. Jahrhunderts mit Dokumenten in Text und Bild.* Stuttgart: Seewald.

Botz, Gerhard, and Gerald Sprengnagel (eds.)
    1994   *Kontroversen um Österreichs Zeitgeschichte. Verdrängte Vergangenheit, Österreich-Identität, Waldheim und die Historiker.* Frankfurt am Main: Campus Verlag.

Brainin, Elisabeth, Vera Ligeti, and Samy Teicher
    1993   *Vom Gedanken zur Tat. Zur Psychoanalyse des Antisemitismus.* Frankfurt am Main: Brandes und Apsel.

Cicourel, Aaron
    1992   The interpretation of communicative contexts: examples from medical encounters. In: Duranti, Alessandro and Charles Goodwin (eds.), *Rethinking Context: Language as an Interactive Phenomenon.* Cambridge: Cambridge University Press, 291–310.

Ehlich, Konrad
    1980   *Erzählen im Alltag.* Frankfurt am Main: Suhrkamp.

Erdheim, Mario
    1992   *Die gesellschaftliche Produktion von Unbewußtheit: eine Einführung in den ethnopsychoanalytischen Prozeß.* Frankfurt am Main: Suhrkamp.

Fairclough, Norman
  1995   *Critical Discourse Analysis: The Critical Study of Language.*
          London/New York: Longman.

Gruber, Helmut
  1991   *Antisemitismus im Mediendiskurs. Die Affäre "Waldheim" in der
          Tagespresse.* Wiesbaden: DUV.

Heer, Hannes
  1999   *Tote Zonen: Die deutsche Wehrmacht an der Ostfront.* Hamburg:
          Hamburger Edition HIS.

Jaspers, Karl
  1979   *Die Schuldfrage: Für Völkermord gibt es keine Verjährung.*
          München: Piper.

Kienpointer, Manfred
  1992   *Alltagslogik: Struktur und Funktion von Argumentationsmustern.*
          Stuttgart-Bad Cannstatt: Frommann-Holzboog.

  1996   *Vernünftig argumentieren: Regeln und Techniken der Diskussion.*
          Hamburg: Rowohlt.

Lendl, Barbara
  1999   *Verständlichkeit von juristischen Texten: eine Untersuchung anhand
          zivilgerichtlicher Urteile.* Unpublished masters thesis, University of
          Wien.

Leodolter, Ruth
  1975   *Das Sprachverhalten von Angeklagten bei Gericht.* Kronberg:
          Scriptor.

Manoschek, Walter
  1993   *"Serbien ist judenfrei": militärische Besatzungspolitik und
          Judenvernichtung in Serbien 1941–1942.* München: Oldenbourg.

Mitten, Richard H.
  1992   *The Politics of Antisemitic Prejudice: The Waldheim Phenomenon in
          Austria.* Boulder, Colorado: Westview Press.

  1999   *"Jews and other Victims": The "Jewish Question" and Discourses
          of Victimhood in post-war Austria.* Paper presented at the conference
          The Dynamics of Antisemitism in the Second Half of the Twentieth
          Century, SICSA, Jerusalem, June 1999.

2000   *Guilt and Responsibility in Germany and Austria.* Paper presented at the "Dilemmas of East Central Europe: Nationalism, Totalitarianism, and the Search for Identity." A Symposium Honoring István Déak, Columbia University, March 24–25.

Musil, Robert
2000   *Der Mann ohne Eigenschaften I.* Reinbek bei Hamburg: Rowohlt.

Naumann, Klaus
1998   *Der Krieg als Text: Das Jahr 1945 im kulturellen Gedächtnis der Presse.* Hamburg: Hamburger Edition HIS.

Neidhardt, Irit, and Willi Bischof (eds.)
2000   *Wir sind die Guten: Antisemitismus in der radikalen Linken.* Münster: Unrast.

Quasthoff, Uta M.
1989   Social prejudice as a resource of power: towards the functional ambivalence of stereotypes. In: Wodak, Ruth (ed.), *Language, Power and Ideology: Studies in Political Discourse.* Amsterdam, Philadelphia: Benjamins, 181–196.

Reisigl, Martin, and Ruth Wodak
2000   *Discourse and Discrimination.* London: Routledge.

Rosenthal, Gabriele (ed.)
1999   *Der Holocaust im Leben von drei Generationen. Familien von Überlebenden der Shoa und von Nazi-Tätern.* Giessen: Psychosozial Verlag.

Sacks, Harvey
1995   *Lectures on Conversation, Vols. I and II.* Cambridge, MA: Blackwell.

Schiffrin, Deborah
2000   Mother/daughter discourse in a Holocaust oral history: "Because then you admit that you're guilty". *Narrative Inquiry* 10(1), 1–44.

Siegler, Heinrech
1959   *Österreichs Weg zur Souveränität, Neutralität, Prosperität. 1945–1959.* Bonn: Verlag für Zeitarchive.

Stern, Frank
1991   *Im Anfang war Auschwitz: Antisemitismus und Philosemitismus im deutschen Nachkrieg.* Gerlingen: Bleicher Verlag. (The book has been published in English under the title *The White Washing of the Yellow Badge*).

van Dijk, Teun A.
1984   *Prejudice in Discourse.* Amsterdam: Benjamins.

van Leeuwen, Theo
1995   Representing social action. *Discourse and Society 6*(1), 81–106.

van Leeuwen, Theo, and Ruth Wodak
1999   Legitimizing immigration control: A discourse-historical analysis. *Discourse Studies 1*(1), 77–122.

Wodak, Ruth
1996   *Disorders of Discourse.* London: Longman.

2000a   *Does Sociolinguistics need Social Theory? New Perspectives in Critical Discourse Analysis. Keynote Address.* Paper presented at Sociolinguistic Symposium 11, Bristol, 27–29 April.

2000b   The rise of racism – an Austrian or a European phenomenon? *Discourse and Society 11*(1), 5–6.

Wodak, Ruth, Rudolf de Cillia, Martin Reisigl, and Karin Liebhart
1999   *The Discursive Construction of National Identity.* Edinburgh: Edinburgh University Press.

Wodak, Ruth, Florian Menz, Richard Mitten, and Frank Stern
1994   *Die Sprachen der Vergangenheiten. Öffentliches Gedenken in österreichischen und deutschen Medien.* Frankfurt am Main: Suhrkamp.

Wodak, Ruth, Peter Novak, Johanna Pelikan, Helmut Gruber, Rudolf De Cillia, and Richard Mitten
1990   *"Wir sind alle unschuldige Täter". Diskurs-historische Studie zum Nachkriegsantisemitismus.* Frankfurt am Main: Suhrkamp.

Wodak, Ruth, and Teun A. van Dijk (eds.)
2000   *Racism at the Top. Parliamentary Discourses on Ethnic Issues in Six European States.* Klagenfurt: Drava.

II. Language wars

Attitudes towards linguistic purism in Croatia: Evaluating efforts at language reform

Keith Langston and Anita Peti-Stantić

1. Introduction

The political and military conflicts associated with the disintegration of the Socialist Federal Republic of Yugoslavia (SFRY) have been accompanied by correspondingly fierce battles on the linguistic front. As is typically the case in such situations, words have often been used as weapons or tools for propaganda, to reinforce stereotypical negative images of the opposing side or to promote a biased version of events.[1] Words have themselves also been a source of conflict within the Yugoslav successor states. Language is a primary marker of identity, and the use of individual words often acquires a symbolic value. The collapse of the SFRY brought with it the demise of the concept of a unified Serbo-Croatian language and the (re)birth of three separate standard languages in its place: Bosnian, Croatian and Serbian.[2] Questions of linguistic identity and standards of usage, which had already been debated to some extent before the Yugoslav breakup, gained much wider attention as a result.

These struggles over linguistic issues continue today. In the case of Croatia, the focus on language as a symbol of national identity is seen in efforts to eliminate Serbian or other foreign words from the language and to replace them with purely Croatian equivalents. But attempts to change established patterns of usage in order to purify the language have not gone unopposed. Language purism, particularly in its more rigid or extreme manifestations, tends to be associated with particular political views. As a result, the use of specific words can reflect identification with, or opposition to, a particular group within Croatia.

This chapter examines attitudes towards linguistic purism in Croatia and attempts to gauge the extent to which certain proposed changes are being adopted.[3] In order to situate the current linguistic debates in their historical context, we will first give a brief overview of the development of the Croatian and Serbian languages, focusing on the standardization processes in the 19th century and language politics in the Yugoslav states before and after World War II. We will then consider efforts to promote language purism in Croatia in the 1990s and some of the motivations that underlie these attempts at language reform. The main body of the article is devoted to an analysis of the results of a questionnaire which was designed to investigate native speaker evaluations of individual lexical items and the degree of acceptance for specific forms. We consider several factors that may influence the acceptance of proposed changes in the standard language. Opinions about language purism were also solicited through interviews with some of the respondents to the questionnaire.

2. The Croatian language question in historical perspective

The existence of an autonomous Croatian language is seen as a hallmark of Croatian national identity; as one scholar put it: "The Croatian language, along with the Croatian army, is the guarantee of Croatian existence and independence."[4] Croatian's linguistic identity was for many years subordinated to that of Serbo-Croatian and was generally not recognized anywhere outside of Croatia itself. Yet, while the question of whether Croatian is an independent language or merely a variant or dialect of Serbo-Croatian gained international attention only after the collapse of the SFRY, the status of Croatian had long been a contentious issue within Yugoslavia in the context of the unitaristic language policies of the government.

There are few significant differences between Croatian and Serbian in purely structural terms. In fact, local dialects within Serbia and Croatia diverge much more from the respective standard varieties than the standard varieties differ from each other. The most immediately apparent distinctions between standard Croatian and Serbian are on the lexical level; e.g. Cr. *kruh* vs. S. *hleb* "bread"; Cr. *vlak*, S. *voz* "train"; Cr. *kazalište*, S. *pozorište* "theater", etc. There are also a number of phonological, morphological and syntactic differences, but none of these are great enough to impede mutual intelligibility.[5]

However, structural similarity and mutual intelligibility alone are not sufficient to determine whether Croatian and Serbian are one or two languages.[6] It is not possible to define what constitutes a language as opposed to a variant or dialect in terms of the inherent features of the language variety itself. Status as a separate language is primarily the result of social and political factors (Milroy and Milroy 1997). With respect to Croatian and Serbian, their high degree of similarity is due not only to their shared dialectal base, but also because they reflect processes of standardization which (from the 19th century on) were ultimately directed towards the creation of a unified Serbo-Croatian norm. At the same time, it must also be recognized that this unification was never completely successful. Contemporary Croatian and Serbian reflect two distinct literary and cultural traditions; on the basis of both their historical development and the current political realities, there can be no doubt that they should be treated as separate languages. The development of standard Croatian and Serbian is too complex to be discussed in any detail here, and there have already been a large number of publications devoted to this topic. However, a brief outline of some of the major points will be useful for an understanding of the current debates over the status and norms of the Croatian language.[7]

Much of the history of Croatian literature is characterized by the coexistence of regional written traditions that were relatively independent of one another. As the result of a gradual process of consolidation or decline of local written practices, by the beginning of the 19th century the written language variants had been reduced to two more or less cohesive types: one based on the štokavian dialect and another based on the kajkavian dialect of the Zagreb region.[8] While less homogeneous than the kajkavian literary dialect, the štokavian written tradition possessed a number of advantages that made it more suitable as a base for the formation of a standard language for the Croatian lands: the majority of the population of Croatia are štokavian speakers; štokavian was the dialect used in the enormously prestigious Baroque literature of Dubrovnik; and the literary activity of the Bosnian Franciscans in the 17th century provided the što-kavian written language with a broad popular base. Since štokavian dialects are also spoken in Bosnia-Herzegovina, Montenegro and Serbia, this dialect group had the potential of serving as a more wide-spread medium of communication.

The ultimate establishment of štokavian as the basis for a unified Croatian standard was achieved through the efforts of the members of the Illyrian movement (1835–1848), led by Ljudevit Gaj. The Illyrians espoused a Romantic, pan-Slavic ideology, and believed that the South Slavic peoples could gain political power only by joining together in a unified culture based on a common language. The ideal of national unity with the Serbs and possibly the other South Slavs continued to occupy a prominent place in Croatian pub-lic opinion for some time and played an important role in the further development of the Croatian language.

In the Serbian lands, the written tradition was historically based to a large extent on Church Slavonic. However, with the emergence of the middle class and the expansion of literacy, a new written standard began to develop at the end of the 18th century. Known as Slavo-Serbian (*slavenosrpski*), this language combined elements of the spoken vernacular with numerous borrowings from Church Slavonic, Russian, and other languages. Although it represented a step toward the development of a standard language suited to the requirements of a modern society, Slavo-Serbian did not possess the necessary degree of coherence and stability and furthermore was confined primarily to the more culturally advanced northern region of Serbia. There was an immediate need for a workable and easily learnable standard lan-guage that could unite all the Serbian people, a fact that was recog-nized by the great Serbian language reformer Vuk Stefanović Karadžić. Karadžić's solution to this problem was the creation of a new standard based on the štokavian koine of the oral folk literature and the spoken vernacular, and he began working toward this goal in the first decades of the 19th century.

Although Karadžić was interested in a purely national language for the Serbs (which in his view included all štokavian speakers), the

Illyrians were sympathetic to his linguistic reforms. In 1850, several members of this movement met with Karadžić, his follower Đuro Daničić and the Slovene linguist Franz Miklosich in Vienna. The participants of this meeting signed a document known as the Vienna Agreement (*Bečki dogovor*), which outlined the principles to be applied in the development of a single standard language for both the Serbs and Croats. Although this has traditionally been viewed as a landmark event in the creation of a unified Serbo-Croatian language, Croatian scholars emphasize that the agreement made little difference for Croatia in practical terms (Katičić 1984: 278). The štokavian norm that was already solidifying there was very close to Karadžić's model, since it had essentially the same neoštokavian dialect base and, like Karadžić, the Illyrians had also chosen the ijekavian pronunciation of the Common Slavic vowel *ě (see note 8). The main differences between the two norms were a preference for a morphologically based orthography and the maintenance of older distinct forms for plural case endings on the part of the Illyrians, as opposed to Karadžić's phonetically based orthography and innovative syncretic neoštokavian case forms in the plural.

The second half of the 19th century in Croatia was marked by polemics between various linguistic schools about the exact shape the standard language would take. Eventually, the norm established by Karadžić won out, for a number of reasons. The new štokavian standard was officially accepted in Serbia in 1868, when it was introduced into the schools, and by the end of the 19th century linguistic standardization was being completed in Dalmatia and Bosnia-Herzegovina along the same lines. These areas were the home of a sizeable Croat population, but were outside the political sphere and educational system of Croatia and Slavonia.

While Serbia had already achieved partial autonomy within the Ottoman Empire in the early part of the 19th century and gained full international recognition as an independent state in 1878, Croatia remained under Habsburg rule. An influential Croatian nationalist opposition movement opposed linguistic or any other assimilation with the Serbs on the grounds that this would hinder their struggle against Hungarian power, but more moderate Croats continued to be influenced by the idea of national unity with the Serbian people. A new wave of Hungarian oppression of the nationalist opposition in Croatia began in 1883, and ultimately it seemed that the only viable option was for the Croats to cast their linguistic lot with the Serbs and adopt Karadžić's štokavian norm. The publication and official acceptance of Broz's *Hrvatski pravopis* [Croatian orthography] in 1892 marked the establishment of Karadžić's orthographical principles for Croatian, and Maretić's grammar in 1899 resolved most of the remaining differences, although some purely Croatian lexical elements and other minor differences were still retained in usage. But while the Croatian standard ultimately incorporated many of Karadžić's proposals, the Serbs had departed by this time from some of the principles of Karadžić's norm, adopting the ekavian dialect pronunciation together with other elements of Belgrade usage. Thus, a complete unification of the Serbian and Croatian norms was not achieved and the end result was a polycentric standard language, with eastern and western variants centered on Belgrade and Zagreb, respectively.

The creation of a unified Yugoslav state in 1918 brought increased pressure to effect a further unification of Serbian and Croatian, but tensions between unitaristic tendencies and independent national traditions led to conflicts over linguistic issues that continued throughout the rest of the century. In the period before World War II attempts were made to impose Serbian ekavian forms throughout the Kingdom of Serbs, Croats and Slovenes. In reaction to this, during the war years the government of the Independent State of Croatia (*Nezavisna Država Hrvatska or NDH*) imposed an exaggerated linguistic purism and a radically revised orthography similar to that used in the 19th century before the adoption of Karadžić's phonetically-based spelling system.

The establishment of the SFRY after WWII led to a return to policies promoting linguistic unification, and in 1954 Serbian and Croatian linguists signed the Novi Sad Agreement (*Novosadski dogovor*), which declared the national language of Serbs, Croats and Montenegrins to be a single language with two pronunciations, ijekavian and ekavian (Moguš 1995: 218). This document further stated that in official use both components must always be included in the name of the language (i.e., *srpskohrvatski, hrvatskosrpski, hrvatski ili srpski*).

Although guarantees of linguistic equality for the different language varieties were included in the constitution of the SFRY, many Croats eventually came to feel that the Serbian variant of the official Serbo-Croatian language was gaining *de facto* status as the standard language. Belgrade was the center of political power, the majority of federal officials were Serbs, and Serbian predominated in the military and the media as well, with the inevitable result that Serbian linguistic features tended to filter into Croatian usage. From the Croatian point of view, their language was being treated as a provincial and less prestigious variant of the language spoken in Belgrade. Various scholars complained that traditional Croatian words were being branded as dialectal or archaic and were being forced out of usage since they were officially considered to be non-standard. As a result of this situation, any governmental attempts to promote further linguistic unification were suspect and tended to be interpreted as the forced imposition of Serbian norms.

On the Serbian side, Croatian efforts to maintain their linguistic individuality and resist Serbian influences were seen as the expression of nationalist, separatist tendencies which were anathema to the socialist regime, and these efforts were compared with the linguistic excesses of the pro-fascist Croatian government during WWII. Croatian's status as an independent language was asserted in the "Declaration on the Name and Status of the Croatian Literary Language" in 1967,[9] as well as in the new Croatian constitution in 1974, but some statements in these documents were interpreted by the Serbs as threatening the linguistic rights of the Serbian minority living within the Croatian Republic. These linguistic conflicts remained unresolved until the collapse of the Yugoslav state.

3. Linguistic purism and the promotion of language reform

Croatian already existed as a distinct standardized language in everything but name even before Croatia gained its independence: it was codified in dictionaries, orthographical handbooks and grammars as the ijekavian variant of Serbo-Croatian, and there was already an extensive corpus of literature written using the Croatian neoštokavian norm. Thus the changes in the language that have been proposed or are already occurring now represent a process of language reform which attempts to "redo" some elements of the corpus planning that had already taken place since the mid 19th century. These attempts at language reform focus primarily on the Croatian lexicon, although questions of orthography and grammar have also been discussed.[10]

The desire to purify the language and remove elements that are perceived as foreign can be motivated by a number of different factors which overlap to a certain extent. The use of "purely Croatian" words is an assertion of national identity, and linguistic purism is seen by some people as a badge of patriotism. For example, Stanka Pavuna in the preface to her language handbook *Do we speak Croatian correctly?* states that she compiled this work to assist Croats who "are striving to speak good Croatian and to demonstrate their national consciousness in everyday life also by means of language" (Pavuna 1993: i–ii). The intrinsic purity of the linguistic system is also a common motivation for this type of language planning activity. In the case of Croatian, there is a desire to remove elements that entered the language during the Yugoslav period and to return Croatian to some sort of idealized "natural" state before it was influenced by Serbian. This attitude can be illustrated by the following passage from the introduction to a language handbook written by Franjo Tanocki:

> The forced unification of the Croatian and Serbian languages did not succeed. The Croatian language managed to resist all attacks, but nonetheless the period of unification left deep traces upon it. The Croatian language suffered the imposition of many non-Croatian features which are not in harmony with the Croatian linguistic system and the Croatian linguistic tradition. The situation was such that many old Croatian words were forced out of use and these words must now be brought back into linguistic practice. (Tanocki 1994: 11)

Words that are perceived as non-Croatian are viewed by some as a threat to the very character of the language. Marijan Krmpotić, who advocates a radical degree of purism in his columns about language for the ultra right-wing newspaper *NDH*, has warned of the danger that "Balkan" elements from Serbian pose for the Croatian language.

Croatian is portrayed as a refined language belonging to mainstream European culture, in contrast to Serbian:

> The fundamental characteristic of native words in the authentic Croatian language is that they are for the most part semantically stable and unambiguous, i.e. they have a precisely defined meaning, just like words in other systematically organized languages that have influenced Croatian (Latin, German). On the other hand, Serbian, like the majority of Balkan languages, is relativistic and undefined, so that Serbian words for the most part are easily changeable and polysemous; i.e. they more or less vary their meaning depending on the context and time at which they are used [...]. However, when such polysemous unstable words from Serbian penetrate into Croatian, then they in turn create general confusion and the destruction of a whole range of native Croatian words. As a result Croatian indeed becomes impoverished and is spoiled and destroyed; it degenerates and degrades to the Balkan level. (Krmpotić 1999)

One of the most important factors driving the movement for language reform in Croatia is the desire to further differentiate Croatian from Serbian in order to establish more firmly Croatian's independent linguistic status and consequently Croatia's status as an independent nation following the war. In his regular column "Notes about the Croatian Language" that appeared for some time in the weekly paper *Hrvatsko slovo*, Stjepan Babić gave the following quote from a letter from one of his readers in reference to a previous article in the series: "Who needs your note that *hiljada* (thousand) is a Croatian word? *Tisuća* prevailed precisely because "they" use [*hiljada*]. Why do you introduce confusion into the completely understandable aspiration [...] that we should in no way be the same as "them" or similar to "them"?" (Babić 1996). Babić himself states in this same article that he views the further differentiation of Croatian and Serbian to be a national duty, although only to the extent that this is possible without unduly disrupting the existing Croatian linguistic system. Extreme advocates of purism, on the other hand, believe that radical changes are necessary. This may again be illustrated in the writings of Krmpotić, who is of the opinion that "everything that can be different than it is in Serbian should be adopted as Croatian" (Krmpotić 1997).

The desire to further differentiate Croatian from Serbian is manifested in many of the language handbooks and dictionaries that have
appeared in recent years. Particularly notable is the publication of a
number of so-called "differential dictionaries" (*razlikovni rječnici*) of
Croatian and Serbian, which list Serbian or international forms as the
alphabetized entries and suggest Croatian equivalents for these expressions. The handbooks on usage are very similar to these in their
organization, since for the most part they consist of short articles that
discuss pairs of words and give detailed advice and explanations
about which forms are recommended and which are considered Serbian or foreign and should be avoided.[11] It should also be noted that
common "international" words are often considered more characteristic of Serbian than Croatian usage by the authors of these works,
since Serbian has historically been more open to foreign borrowings,
while calquing or the creation of neologisms is viewed as more typical of the Croatian linguistic system (Samardžija 1993: 7–23; Ivić
1971: 194–195). Following are two brief excerpts from one of these
language handbooks that illustrate these types of attitudes towards
foreign or "Serbian" words:

> *GLAZBA* and *MUZIKA* ("music")
> The word *glazba* is a Croatian word, but rather than being a native expres-
> sion it is a neologism which was created by the great 19th c. Croatian lin-
> guist Bogoslav Šulek from the noun *glas* ("voice, sound") and the suffix -
> *ba*. [...] The word *muzika* is an international word of Greek origin which to-
> day is used in many European and other languages. This word, as well as its
> derivatives *muzičar, muzikant* ("musician"), *muzički, muzikalan* ("musical")
> and others, is characteristic of Serbian, but was also used in Croatian, where
> it was imposed as the exclusive form during the time of the forced linguistic
> leveling of Croatian and Serbian. In the contemporary Croatian language we
> will use these words only for specific expressive and stylistic purposes.
> (Tanocki 1994: 41)

> *ZEMLJOPIS* or *GEOGRAFIJA* ("geography")
> [*Geografija* and its derivatives] are of Greek origin, and like many other
> Greek and Latin words [...] became international words as a result of the
> prestige of these languages in the past. In such circumstances it was difficult
> for words based on native Croatian roots to become established in the
> Croatian language. [...] In the Croatian language we shall use words with
> native Croatian roots, and the use of borrowings for the same concepts may

be only for special expressive reasons, especially if these words are at the same time characteristic Serbian words. We must be especially careful with borrowings of Greek origin because of the close ties between Greek and Serbian. (Tanocki 1994: 42)

Although the need to further differentiate Croatian from Serbian has been cited by some proponents of language reform to justify proposed changes, we should emphasize here that many professional linguists in Croatia do not share this view. Linguists typically argue that the separate historical tradition of Croatian usage is sufficient to establish its identity as a separate language. Adherents of this position may also believe that the Croatian language suffered from the imposition of Serbian linguistic norms throughout this century and that a certain degree of linguistic purism may be desirable, but they assert that it is not necessary to take any steps specifically to decrease the similarities between Croatian and Serbian (Kačić 1995: 60).

In Croatian linguistic circles a distinction is often made between a natural degree of purism that is seen as being inherent to every language versus the type of aggressive and unselective linguistic purism promoted by some marginal elements in Croatian society (Katičić 1992: 55–62). Prominent linguists have repeatedly condemned excessive purism in various articles and interviews. For example, Brozović has referred to such efforts as "irrational linguistic aversions which damage the languages in which they take hold"; he states that "for the protagonists of such an approach, linguistic culture has no importance and stylistic values are insignificant; they are not interested in the richness of the expressive potential of the Croatian language nor the Croatian linguistic tradition itself, but rather are monomaniacally interested only in the superficial authenticity of the Croatian language at any cost" (Brozović 1998: 166).

Language planning typically implies some kind of governmental involvement, and the Croatian government was closely identified with language purism throughout the Tudjman-HDZ government of the 1990s. Purism was reflected in changes in official administrative usage (e.g. the use of *veleposlanik* "ambassador" instead of *ambasador*, *gospodarstvo* "economy" instead of *ekonomija*, etc.), but these terms did not automatically gain wider acceptance, and some proposed changes were eventually rejected at the official level. For example, in 1990 the government announced its intentions to replace the term *policija* "police" with *redarstvo*, but this met with such resistance that the idea was soon dropped (Lučić and Dikić 1999).[12] On the whole, little has been done in the way of establishing explicit official linguistic policies. The HDZ political party, which controlled the federal government throughout the last decade of the twentieth century, had as part of its platform from its Second General Congress in 1993 a statement about promoting "respect for the norms of the Croatian language" (Brozović 1994: 83). But it was not until 1998 that an official governmental advisory organization was established to deal with questions of the Croatian norm, the Council for the Norms of the Croatian Language *(Vijeće za normu hrvatskoga jezika)*, within the Ministry for Science and Technology) (Babić 1998: 160). Some relatively limited legislation regulating language usage was passed (for example, article 20 of the 1995 Law on Commercial Organizations *(Zakon o trgovačkim društvima)*, which mandated the use of Croatian for the names of businesses), but proposals for more wide-reaching laws against the use of foreign words were not adopted (Kramarić 1996).

Attempts at language reform must necessarily involve the educational system, but here too we find a fairly cautious attitude with respect to any explicit regulation of language. A new school curriculum was introduced in 1991, and one of the important changes had to do with the language used in instruction. New textbooks were introduced that avoid unnecessary use of foreign words, and teachers are expected to pay attention to proper usage on both the lexical and grammatical levels. It should be noted that this applies to teachers of all subjects, not only those who specialize in Croatian language and literature. Nonetheless, in response to direct inquiries to the Ministry of Education and Sports, we were informed that no official instructions had been issued to the schools with respect to linguistic purism or standards of usage. Rather, teachers are expected to refer to articles in the journals *Školske novine* and *Jezik* for guidance in this area.

In addition to the educational system, the media constitute another primary arena for the promotion of language reform. Language advice columns or broadcasts are a regular feature in the Croatian media; while this is not a new phenomenon and is certainly not unique to Croatia, the sheer volume of these relative to the small population of the country and the limited number of media outlets indicates a high level of attention to questions of usage. The major daily newspaper *Vjesnik* published for several years a column entitled *"Vjesnikov jezični savjetnik"* ("Vjesnik's language advisor") to which various linguists contributed articles. At the time of this writing *Večernji list*, the daily paper with the largest circulation in Croatia, is running a regular column *"Riječ o riječima"* ("A word about words") written by the linguist Alemko Gluhak, and many more examples could be cited from other Croatian papers and magazines. Croatian Radio has been broadcasting a segment on language advice called *"Govorimo hrvatski"* ("We speak Croatian") twice a day since September of 1992 and Radio Sljeme has a weekly broadcast *"Hrvatski naš svagdašnji"* ("Our everyday Croatian") which has been on the air since January of 1994. Croatian Television has two regular broadcasts devoted to language, *"Hrvatski u zrcalu"* ("Croatian in the mirror") and *"Riječi, riječi"* ("Words, words"), as well as a language advice segment on the daily news magazine program *"Dobar dan"*. One should also note that a large segment of the media was wholly or partly controlled by the government and therefore was available to propagate the linguistic views and policies of the ruling HDZ party throughout the 1990s.

In addition to providing linguistic advice, the media has a great potential to influence change simply by serving as a model for correct usage. Previous research has shown that some recommended changes in the language are being adopted in the press and in television news broadcasts (Langston 1999).[13] A comparison of text samples from the newspaper *Vjesnik* from 1985 and 1996–1997 (several years before and after the establishment of an independent Croatian state in 1991) revealed a small reduction in the overall frequency of loan words, as well as noticeable differences in the use of individual words and expressions. Certain official titles and terminology changed over this period of time; in the 1996–1997 sample *veleposlanik* "ambassador", *veleposlanstvo* "embassy", *izaslanik* "delegate", *izaslanstvo* "delegation", *tajnik* "secretary", *odvjetnik* "lawyer" are used exclusively, in place of *ambasador, ambasada, delegat, delegacija, sekretar, advokat*, which were the norm in the 1985 sample. The terms *ekonomija* "economy", *ekonomski* "economic" were standard in the earlier sample, but in the later one are almost always avoided in favor of the native Croatian terms *gospodarstvo* and *gospodarski*; the same is true of *sistem* and *sustav* "system". Other prominent changes involve words typical of journalistic style that are commonly found in news reports. For example, *priopćiti* "announce, inform" and *priopćenje* "announcement, report" have completely replaced *saopćiti* and *saopćenje*, which were the exclusive terms used in the 1985 sample. Similarly, *izvješće* "report, statement" is used in place of *izvještaj*, which was formerly the standard expression.

In all cases, the changes in usage reflected in *Vjesnik* are in favor of the forms currently recommended as being authentically Croatian. Although *Vjesnik* is state-controlled and would be expected to reflect the implicit language policies of the government, there is evidence that the independent press have also adopted at least some of the recommended changes in Croatian usage. The same research project also compared representative samples from other state-controlled or more nationalistic media with samples from the independent/liberal press and concluded that the usage of the former conforms essentially to that of *Vjesnik,* while the independent press continue to use some foreign or "Serbian" words that have been replaced by Croatian forms in the other media. Nonetheless, the samples from the independent press indicate that on the whole they are also following the trend towards the use of purely Croatian forms, albeit more slowly than the state-controlled media.

4. Reactions to language purism

In order to investigate the reactions of individual speakers towards changes in the standard language, we devised a questionnaire based on pairs of words that have been cited in recent language handbooks and dictionaries and that appear to have exhibited changes in their relative frequency in the media and in official usage (see the Appendix for a complete list of words and sources). One member of each pair is of foreign origin or is considered to be more typical of Serbian usage, according to these sources, and the other member is the recommended Croatian equivalent. For each of these pairs the respondents were asked to select the word that they considered "better" or "more correct"; the instructions also stated that both words could be marked if the respondent felt that they were equally acceptable.

In this section of the questionnaire, the pairs of words were presented in context. In almost all cases these were sentences from newspaper articles that originally contained one of the words in question, but for a few of the pairs for which we were unable to find examples in the press, we constructed sentences in a similar style. In a separate section of the questionnaire, respondents were asked to report for the same pairs of words which of the two variants they normally use; here the pairs of words were simply listed, but in a different order than in the first section. The questionnaire was completed by a total of 208 individuals in October 1998. The distribution of speakers according to age and sex is given in Table 1.[14]

Table 1. Distribution of speakers by age and sex

Ages	Female	Male	Total
14–20	67	54	121
21–30	21	6	27
31–40	14	7	21
41–50	19	8	27
51–65	7	5	12
Total	128	80	208

On the whole, respondents to the questionnaire judged the recommended Croatian forms as being correct more often than the foreign loan words and forms that are considered to be more typical of Serbian (52.5% vs. 37.3%; see Table 2). When it comes to their reported usage, however, the figures are reversed: they indicate that they use the Serbian or foreign forms more often than the ones that are considered to be purely Croatian (54.1% vs. 40.7%; see Table 3). It is interesting to note that the percentage of responses indicating that both forms are equally acceptable is quite small on the whole; it appears that speakers have definite opinions about these words, despite the

Table 2. Forms chosen as "more correct": male vs. female

		Female	Male	Total
Serbian/foreign	n	2205	1674	3879
	%	34.5	41.9	37.3
Croatian	n	3635	1822	5457
	%	56.8	45.6	52.5
Both	n	472	437	909
	%	7.4	10.9	8.7
No answer	n	88	67	155
	%	1.4	1.7	1.5
Total		6400	4000	10400

fact that the terms in question are nearly or completely synonymous. At the same time, there is a greater degree of mismatch than might be expected between the forms the respondents consider to be correct and their reported usage (almost 25%). In many cases individual respondents would actually identify the foreign/Serbian variant as correct while reporting that they normally use the Croatian variant; this indicates a certain level of confusion about the status of individual words.

The data in Tables 2 and 3 reveal some differences in the responses according to gender. The men judge the Serbian/foreign forms as correct or consider both forms to be acceptable more often than the women, and male respondents are also more likely to say that they use both forms. Although these differences are not particularly large in absolute terms, given the size of the sample they are statistically significant ($p < .001$). These figures may reflect what are often considered typical gender differences. Other sociolinguistic research has shown that, in most cases, women tend to use a higher proportion of prestige or standard forms than men and that women are especially sensitive to the new prestige variants in situations where changes are taking place in certain linguistic variables, and they tend to initiate change in this direction (Coates 1993: 67–68).

Table 3. Forms used more often: male vs. female

		Female	Male	Total
Serbian/foreign	n	3515	2113	5628
	%	54.9	52.8	54.1
Croatian	n	2633	1598	4231
	%	41.1	40.0	40.7
Both	n	186	267	453
	%	2.9	6.7	4.4
No answer	n	66	22	88
	%	1.0	0.6	0.8
Total		6400	4000	10400
Reported usage different from form considered "more correct"	n	1724	810	2534
	%	26.9	20.3	24.4

This interpretation should be viewed with caution, however, since explanations for such patterns of usage are dependent on many factors specific to the individual situation. In our data, women's reported usage of the Serbian/foreign forms is actually slightly higher than men's, although their judgments about the correctness of questionnaire items conform more closely to the new recommended standards. It is not necessarily clear what is prestigious or what actually represents the norm for the standard language at this point in time. As will be seen in some of the comments from respondents reported below, the use of "new" words may have positive or negative political connotations, depending on the speaker's viewpoint, and some people do not see any need for changes in the standard language.

The changes that are being investigated here apply to the learned set of norms that constitute the standard language. Thus, we assumed that a person's general educational background would likely affect the awareness of proposed reforms and the acceptance or rejection of various changes. In addition, the youngest respondents completed a significant portion of their education under the new curriculum introduced after Croatian independence, which should have an impact on their judgments and reported usage for the forms in the questionnaire. To test whether educational levels or the implementation of new standards in the educational system affected respondents' answers, we compared groups with a secondary versus a post-secondary degree among older respondents, and then compared those older respondents with people enrolled in an educational institution at the time of the survey. The distribution of respondents by education is given in Table 4.

Table 4. Distribution by educational background

Those enrolled in an educational institution at the time of the survey	
Secondary	88
Post-secondary	50

Other respondents: highest level of education achieved	
Primary (8 years)	1
Secondary	25
Post-secondary	40
Not indicated	4

As seen in Tables 5 and 6, the results of this comparison did not correspond to our expectations. Among older respondents, the effects of different educational levels are most evident in that a post-secondary degree is associated with a greater likelihood to accept both forms as correct (versus those with only a secondary education, 11.9% vs. 5.1%, respectively). Further, those with a higher education actually report that they use the Serbian/foreign forms *more* often (57.6% vs. 47.1%). Similar results obtain within the student group: those enrolled in a post-secondary institution are slightly more likely to accept both forms as correct (11.3% vs. 7.1%), and are also somewhat more likely to report that they use the Serbian/foreign variants (58.2% vs. 52.3%), but on the whole the differences within this group are smaller. It appears that the more highly educated respondents adhere more to the previous norm and are more reluctant to adapt their usage to changes in the standard language.

One could speculate that the greater (reported) usage of the "new" forms among less highly educated respondents may represent a type of hypercorrectness that reflects some degree of linguistic insecurity.[15] It is also possible that political factors play a role here. Purism is the prototypical expression of nationalism on the linguistic level, and more nationalist or right-wing political groups in Croatia are the leading proponents of linguistic reform. Language purism was strongly associated with the HDZ, the governing political party throughout the 1990s. The respondents with a higher level of education are perhaps less likely to accept linguistic purism in unquestioning terms as a kind of patriotic duty, and resistance to changes in the language may serve as an expression of more liberal and oppositionist political views. Precisely this opinion was expressed by one of the respondents in an interview (see below).

Table 5. Forms chosen as "more correct": level of education

		Education completed			Student at time of survey		
		Secondary	Post-secondary	Totals	Secondary	Post-secondary	Totals
Serbian/foreign	n	426	691	1117	1793	880	2673
	%	34.1	34.6	34.4	40.8	35.2	38.7
Croatian	n	732	1047	1779	2216	1320	3536
	%	58.6	52.4	54.7	50.4	52.8	51.2
Both	n	64	238	302	314	282	596
	%	5.1	11.9	9.3	7.1	11.3	8.6
No answer	n	28	24	52	77	18	95
	%	2.2	1.2	1.6	1.8	0.7	1.4
Total		1250	2000	3250	4400	2500	6900

More surprising is that very little difference exists between students and older respondents. The student group, indeed, exhibits a slightly higher percentage of Serbian/foreign forms chosen as correct. No obvious explanation for this latter observation suggests itself. A comparison of the responses to the questionnaire solely on the basis of age also fails to reveal any consistent patterns of correlation. The 14–20 and 51–65 age groups have the highest percentage of Serbian/foreign forms chosen as correct (39.8%, n = 2405 and 38.5%, n = 231, respectively), while the remaining groups range from 32.3% to 34.3%. With respect to usage, on the other hand, the 21–30 age group reports the highest percentage for Serbian/foreign forms: 60.1%, n = 811; compare this with the lowest percentage, which was reported by the 41–50 age group: 48.8%, n = 659.

Table 6. Forms used more often: level of education

		Education completed			Student at time of survey		
		Secondary	Post-secondary	Totals	Secondary	Post-secondary	Totals
Serbian/foreign	n	589	1152	1741	2302	1456	3758
	%	47.1	57.6	53.6	52.3	58.2	54.5
Croatian	n	583	771	1354	1858	905	2763
	%	46.6	38.6	41.7	42.2	36.2	40.0
Both	n	57	72	129	185	135	320
	%	4.6	3.6	4.0	4.2	5.4	4.6
No answer	n	21	5	26	55	4	59
	%	1.7	0.3	0.8	1.3	0.2	0.9
Total		1250	2000	3250	4400	2500	6900

Since we considered exposure to the language of the media as another possible factor influencing speakers' attitudes and usage, respondents were asked how often they read newspapers or watch tele-

vision news broadcasts. However, the results do not show any striking correlations with this factor. Almost no difference can be seen in
the respondents' judgments regarding which form is more correct
based on the level of media exposure. While there is a difference in
the reported usage of Serbian/foreign forms, it is not very great:
58.2% for those who only infrequently or rarely read newspapers or
watch news broadcasts vs. 51.9% for those with a higher level of
media exposure (see Table 7).

Table 7. Forms used more often: respondents with greater vs. lesser media
exposure

		More media exposure	Less media exposure
Serbian/foreign	n	3532	2096
	%	51.9	58.2
Croatian	n	2865	1366
	%	42.1	37.9
Both	n	329	124
	%	4.8	3.4
No answer	n	74	14
	%	1.1	0.4
Total		6800	3600

The most striking patterns in the questionnaire data are related to
the nature of the lexical pairs themselves. The pairs of words that are
studied here fall into two broad groups: those which consist of an
"international" word and its native Croatian equivalent (e.g. *kom-
pjutor* and *računalo*, "computer"), and those which consist of two
words that are both Slavic in origin but are based on different roots
or different word-formation processes. According to advocates of
language reform, one of these is more typical of Serbian usage and
should be avoided (e.g. *pažnja* vs. *pozornost* "attention, care", or *gla-*

sanje vs. *glasovanje,* "voting"). With respect to the first group, the respondents clearly judge the Croatian forms as better than the foreign borrowings in most cases, while for the second group, in which both forms are Slavic in origin, their judgments are more or less evenly split (see Table 8).

Table 8. Forms chosen as "more correct": pairs including a foreign borrowing vs. pairs of Slavic origin

		International vs. Slavic form	Slavic origin pairs
Serbian/Foreign	n	1455	2424
	%	29.1	44.8
Croatian	n	2936	2521
	%	58.8	46.6
Both	n	533	376
	%	10.7	7.0
No answer	n	68	87
	%	1.4	1.6
Total		4992	5408

This disparity has an obvious explanation in that these internationalisms are more easily recognizable as foreign, despite their adoption to Croatian phonology and morphology and long history of usage in the language. The Slavic forms that are considered Serbian do not stand out in the same fashion, and speakers may not perceive these as non-Croatian unless they have been instructed (in school or elsewhere) that these forms are no longer considered standard Croatian usage. The different treatment of these two groups is also reflected in the figures for usage. While respondents report that they use recommended Croatian forms equally often as the foreign borrowings, for the pairs of words that are both Slavic in origin their reported usage is significantly skewed in favor of forms that are supposedly more typical of Serbian (see Table 9). The exclusion of these words from standard Croatian clearly represents a change from previous patterns of usage that has not yet been adopted by many speakers.

Since the questionnaire was designed to investigate whether public promotion of language purism has any significant effect on the usage of individual speakers, it was necessary to include a reasonably large number of lexical pairs. Obviously, it is not possible for all pairs to have precisely the same status in the Croatian linguistic system, and we cannot assume that any two pairs will be evaluated in exactly the same manner by native speakers. Each lexical item has its own history and prior patterns of usage that affect its current acceptability and frequency of use. Many of the recommended Croatian forms in the questionnaire were used widely prior to 1991, although corresponding foreign or "Serbian" variants were more common and were generally not treated as stylistically marked. Now, however, Croatian variants are being promoted as the only "correct" forms by language purists.

Table 9. Forms used more often: pairs including a foreign borrowing vs. Slavic origin pairs

		International vs. Slavic form	Slavic origin pairs
Serbian/Foreign	n	2309	3319
	%	46.3	61.4
Croatian	n	2342	1889
	%	46.9	34.9
Both	n	294	159
	%	5.9	2.9
No answer	n	47	41
	%	0.9	0.8
Total		4992	5408

For certain of these words, the survey indicates high acceptance of the native Croatian variant, while there is still significant competition among other forms. For example, the form *tajnik* "secretary" was selected as correct by 186 out of 208 respondents, and was reported to be used more often than the corresponding form *sekretar* by 187. Similar figures obtain for *odvjetnik* "lawyer" (correct: 165/208, usage: 157/208). Yet, *djelatnost* "activity" was selected by less than half (correct: 82/208, usage: 77/208); the majority preferred the corresponding form *aktivnost*. Other words which were previously less familiar or had almost entirely fallen out of use before the 1990s also fared quite well in our survey. For example, the word *glede* "concerning, regarding", which had been considered archaic and was only rarely used, appears to have gained significant acceptance; it was selected as correct by 103 of the respondents, and 99 reported that they use it.[16]

Still, a number of forms now promoted as correct Croatian usage are recognized by very few of the people surveyed as the recommended form, and a small number claim to use these particular words themselves. For example, less than 10% of the speakers report that they use the forms *raščlamba* "analysis" (16/208), *preslika* "photocopy" (20/208), *nadnevak* "date" (18/208), and only about 10% chose as correct the forms *potvrdnica* "confirmation, certificate" (20/208) or *zapriječen* "prohibited" (25/208). To a certain extent, this may reflect a simple lack of familiarity with the Croatian word; but, in some cases, it seems due to the perceived strangeness or semantic opacity of the forms in question. One male in his early 20s reported to one of the researchers that, when he was filling out some official documents, he had to ask his father to help him because he was completely unable to guess what *nadnevak* meant. Some of the respondents wrote similar comments about individual words on their questionnaires; for example, one female student, age 21, wrote the following about *uljudbeni* "civilizational": "It's a 'good' Croatian word, but it will never be accepted into use."

In order to supplement information obtained in the questionnaire, we also conducted brief interviews with 25 respondents, giving them an opportunity to comment on their answers and asking their opinions about the current linguistic situation and the ongoing process of language reform.[17] A number of them made remarks about "politicians forcing new words" on the population, and one complained that some people consider themselves to be "better Croatians because they use more Croatian words." There is a definite perception that certain choices in language usage are representative of political views – particularly during the Tudjman–HDZ government until early 2000. A female journalist, age 34, said: "I consciously choose words precisely because I think that by means of this I make my political opinion apparent... I think that the HDZ is promoting something wrong in connection with language, which is an exaggerated type of purism and the discarding of all words that smell of the east" (i.e. Serbia). Several people emphasized, however, that they are not opposed to all change and that they have adopted certain expressions while rejecting others. This can be illustrated by the following statement from a college student:

> I use some new words which intuitively sound like good Croatian to me (for example *proračun* [budget], *tajnik* [secretary], *oporba* [opposition]), but some, which I feel are being forced on us, I don't use (for example *pozornost* [attention, care], *glede* [concerning], *potvrdnica* [confirmation, certificate], *preslika* [photocopy]). However, I think that on the whole these are also not used by other normal people outside of politics.

Some of those interviewed also pointed out that they had already been using some of the so-called "new" words well before the breakup of Yugoslavia because they had always paid attention to proper usage, and that they were guided more by what they heard in school, church or from cultured people in general than by any current attempts to promote language purism.

Although the questionnaire results did not show that the educational system exerted any strong purist influence, students in our sample clearly indicated that language changes are indeed being promoted actively within the schools. A number of students stated that certain teachers, although not necessarily teachers of Croatian language and literature, are very attentive to proper usage and correct students when they use foreign or Serbian words. Others commented that the teachers themselves are often very careful about the language they use in class, and that this is noticeable because they use different words when speaking more informally with individual students. The emphasis on using "pure" Croatian appears to have been fairly consistent from the beginning of Croatian statehood in 1991; a college student mentioned that she had no problem avoiding Serbian words in her own usage because "we already didn't use them in school. The teachers at that time (6 or 7 years ago) paid a lot of attention to this, because that was during the war. They pay attention today as well, but now we all speak only Croatian." And, despite the apparent absence of official educational guidelines for proper usage, changes in linguistic standards in the schools are understood to be officially prescribed, as seen in one high-school teacher's characterization of them as "the new purified curriculum."

It is clear that, for most speakers, the use of these "new" words is limited to situations when they feel they are expected or required. One student said: "Among us young people there are some who try to be very careful how they speak in school because they know that the teachers will correct them, but outside [of school] they speak normally." A private businessman stated that when he is addressing people who expect "*pravogovor*" ("correct speech"), e.g. those in certain administrative agencies, he adapts his speech and employs certain new words that he otherwise would never use. A certain amount of resentment exists among speakers at being told that the words they have always used are now considered non-Croatian; a female shopkeeper, age 40, stated:

> I don't pay much attention to words, only sometimes when the children come home from school with some unusual word that surprises me. I think that on TV they're exaggerating the use of words that are now claimed to be better than all those that we used before, as if we're all of a sudden illiterate, and that's just not true. We went to school too, and we also have some feeling for the language.

5. Conclusion

Like any type of linguistic purism, language reform in Croatia is "value-laden" and tends to evoke strong reactions from the speech community involved. Reactions to purism may be largely positive, negative or sharply divided, but they are almost never neutral (Thomas 1991: 1–2). We have examined the means used to promote linguistic purism and some of the attitudes that underlie these efforts among those actively involved in language planning. Reactions of individual speakers are more difficult to assess, and the lack of concrete data, both for earlier linguistic attitudes and patterns of usage as well as for the current state of affairs, poses a real problem in evaluating attitudes towards purism.

Accounts of the language reform process frequently have reported negative reactions to purism and a reluctance to accept changes on the part of Croatian speakers; sometimes, anecdotal evidence is cited to support such statements, but more often they are presented as a generally known fact. On the other hand, some linguists have claimed that such negative views are held by only a minority of Croatians, and that support for language reform is in fact "overwhelmingly high" (Katičić 1997: 188–189; Brozović 1998: 172–173). Our survey should only be considered preliminary, but it does indicate a significant level of resistance to change. Respondents actually judge the foreign/Serbian variants to be better than the recommended Croatian forms in many instances (37.3%), and they report that they themselves use the proscribed Serbian or foreign forms for over half of the lexical pairs in the questionnaire. Since individuals in formal survey or interview situations often give the answers that they feel to be "correct" or desirable rather than responding completely truthfully, their actual use of these forms is likely to be even greater. Negative opinions towards purism and language reform were also expressed freely in the interviews. A common thread underlying many of the comments was that changes were being imposed by authority figures (during the late Tudjman era), and people contrasted the use of "new" or "purely Croatian" words with what they described as "normal" speech. Attempts to change the language clearly are viewed by some people as unnatural and forced. Additional research using a larger, randomly constructed sample would be desirable in order to test the validity of our results and to further investigate factors that influence the acceptance or rejection of language reform.

Despite this resistance, it seems inevitable that more and more changes will be adopted if language purism continues to be promoted (either covertly or openly) by the new social democrat government, the educational system and the media. The teacher quoted above remarked that his students easily accept the majority of new words, since they had been taught according to the new curriculum since elementary school. Although several people in the interviews mentioned certain new words that they find completely unacceptable, these words differed from person to person and some of them were actually chosen by a significant number of people on the questionnaire. As the journalist that we interviewed pointed out "...there are words that were a thorn in the side to most people seven or eight years ago, but now they've become generally accepted – and this has been forgotten." Croatian language reform is still a work in progress, and it will be some time before we see what will truly become part of the standard language and what will be rejected.

Notes

1. For example, in the Croatian and Serbian media the emotionally charged terms *četnici* and *ustaše* were used regularly to refer to the opposing side; these were the respective names for the royalist Serbian forces in World War II and the followers of a nationalist Croatian movement who came to power at that time and established the Independent State of Croatia (Nezavisna Država Hrvatska), a Nazi puppet regime. For discussions of the use of biased language in the media in the former Yugoslavia, see Bugarski (1995) and Thompson (1994).
2. See Greenberg (1999). The potential exists for the development of a fourth national language, Montenegrin. Indeed, a separate Montenegrin orthographical handbook has already been published (Nikčević 1997). However, this has not yet been officially adopted anywhere other than by the PEN Centar, which published this work (Wayles Browne, personal communication, July 26, 1999).
3. Language attitudes can be assessed in several different ways; see Ryan, Giles and Sebastian (1982: 7–8), and Ryan, Giles and Hewstone (1988). One means of gauging language attitudes is through content analysis of societal treatment, which may include the examination of governmental and educational policies, prescriptive language books or other publications, and the language used in the media, among other techniques. Another approach is direct measurement through written questionnaires or interviews. Here we use a combination of these methods. A third common means of assessing language attitudes, indirect measurement through a speaker evaluation paradigm, was not used in the present study.

4. Kačić (former director of the Institute for the Croatian Language and Linguistics, 1996). This and all following translations are our own.
5. Lexical distinctions are not always clear-cut; for example, hljeb occurs in older Croatian literature and may still be used as an expressively marked variant and in the meaning "(round) loaf". Likewise, voz is used in Croatian in the meaning "wagon(load)". For a concise overview of phonological and grammatical differences between Croatian and Serbian, see Brozović (1997).
6. Although mutual intelligibility intuitively would seem to offer an unambiguous criterion for determining whether two speech varieties represent the same or different languages, intelligibility is actually a relative and to some extent subjective feature; studies have shown that speakers' evaluations of intelligibility may be subject to social and political pressures. See Edwards (1985: 20–21).
7. For a more complete discussion, the reader may refer to Banac (1984); Brozović (1978); Ivić (1971); and Katičić (1984). The summary given here is based on these works.
8. The Serbian and Croatian dialect area is divided into four main groups: štokavian, kajkavian, čakavian and Torlak. The first three of these are named for the different forms of the interrogative pronoun "what": što, kaj and ča. The štokavian group itself is divided into ijekavian, ekavian and ikavian dialects on the basis of the different reflexes of the Common Slavic vowel *ě.
9. This document was prepared by the *Matica hrvatska* and formally adopted by it and 17 other cultural and scholarly organizations. It was first published in *Telegram* (Zagreb), March 17, 1967, and has been reprinted by the *Matica hrvatska*, together with commentary by several linguists: *Deklaracija* (1991).
10. A number of writers have advocated a return to a morphologically based orthographic system similar to that used in the 19th c. (the so-called "korijenski pravopis"); e.g. Mate Šimundić in the preface to his *Rječnik suvišnih tuđica u hrvatskomu jeziku*, and László (1993). Certain grammatical features have also been identified as typically Croatian; see Langston (1999: 189–193).
11. For some examples of these recent handbooks and dictionaries, see the references cited in the Appendix.
12. The term *redarstvo* was particularly controversial since this was the official term for the police used by the NDH.
13. All the data cited here are from this article.
14. The questionnaire was administered to several groups of high school and college students in Zagreb (from a trade school, from the Archbishop's *Gymnasium*, and from classes at the Teacher's Academy and the University of Zagreb), so the youngest group makes up somewhat more than half of the total sample, but the older age groups are also well-represented. These latter respondents were contacted through networks of co-workers and acquaintances of one of the researchers.
15. Examples of hypercorrection by speakers belonging to lower socioeconomic groups have been reported in the sociolinguistic literature; e.g. Labov (1966: 88–101).

16. Sources such as Drvodelić (1989), and Anić (1991) mark this word as archaic, but in the 1998 edition of Anić's dictionary this qualification no longer appears.
17. The interviewees were not selected in any systematic fashion, but every attempt was made to include members of the various age groups and educational backgrounds represented in the survey.

Appendix: Lexical pairs included in the questionnaire

The first member of each pair is of foreign origin or is considered to be more typical of Serbian usage. Some of the forms that are considered typically Serbian have been adapted to Croatian patterns of phonology or word-formation, but are still seen by some people as being the direct result of Serbian influence on the language; e.g. *saopćiti* (Serbian *saopštiti*) "inform", which language handbooks and dictionaries recommend should be replaced by the "purely Croatian" form *priopćiti*. In all cases the first member of each pair is a form that has been in wide use in Croatian and was previously treated as stylistically unmarked. The recommended Croatian equivalents listed here are not recent neologisms, but are all words that previously existed in the language, although some of them had to a greater or lesser extent fallen out of use. Note also that in some cases the pairs of words do not share the exact same range of possible meanings.

The questionnaire originally contained 59 pairs of words, but 9 of these were omitted from the analysis here because of a potential ambiguity about the correct choice in the given context or because the pairs were later deemed to be problematic in some other respect. However, the elimination of these forms did not affect the overall results to any significant degree; the totals reported here for the 50 remaining pairs differ from the totals for the entire group of 59 pairs by only a fraction of a percent in most cases, and never more than 1.5%

1. advokat : odvjetnik	"lawyer"
2. aerodrom : zračna luka	"airport"
3. aktivnost : djelatnost	"activity"
4. aktualnost : suvremenost	"contemporaneity, currency"
5. ambasador : veleposlanik	"ambassador"
6. analiza : raščlamba	"analysis"
7. avion : zrakoplov	"airplane"
8. budžet : proračun	"budget"
9. centar : središte	"center"
10. civilizacijski : uljudbeni	"civilizational"
11. datum : nadnevak	"date"
12. delegacija : izaslanstvo	"delegation"
13. demonstrant : prosvjednik	"demonstrator"
14. desiti se : dogoditi se	"to happen, take place"
15. ekonomija : gospodarstvo	"economy"

16. Evropa : Europa	"Europe"
17. faktor : čimbenik	"factor"
18. fotokopija : preslika	"photocopy"
19. glasanje : glasovanje	"voting"
20. greška : pogreška	"mistake"
21. grupa : skupina	"group"
22. izuzetak : iznimka	"exception"
23. izvještaj : izvješće	"report"
24. izvod : izvadak	"certificate, transcript"
25. kompjutor : računalo	"computer"
26. kontrola : nadzor	"control, inspection"
27. molba : zamolba	"request"
28. obaveza : obveza	"obligation"
29. opozicija : oporba	"opposition"
30. osnivanje : osnutak	"founding, establishing"
31. pažnja : pozornost	"attention"
32. pomirenje : pomirba	"conciliation, reconcilement"
33. postepeno : postupno	"gradually"
34. potvrda : potvrdnica	"confirmation, certificate"
35. prilika : prigoda	"opportunity"
36. princip : načelo	"principle"
37. prisutan : nazočan	"[to be] present"
38. raskršće : raskrižje	"crossroads, intersection"
39. realizirati : ostvariti	"to realize"
40. rukovodstvo : vodstvo	"management, guidance"
41. u vezi : u svezi (s)	"in connection (with)"
42. štampa : tisak	"printing, the press, newspapers"
43. saopćiti : priopćiti	"to inform"
44. sekretar : tajnik	"secretary"
45. sistem : sustav	"system"
46. sport : šport	"sports"
47. stanica : postaja	"station, stop"
48. u pogledu : glede	"regarding"
49. uhapsiti : uhititi	"to arrest"
50. zabranjen : zapriječen	"prohibited"

Works consulted in the compilation of the questionnaire:

Brodnjak, Vladimir
    1991   *Razlikovni rječnik srpskog i hrvatskog jezika* [Differential dictionary of the Serbian and Croatian Languages]. Zagreb: Školske novine.

Dulčić, Mihovil (ed.)
1997   *Govorimo hrvatski: jezični savjeti* [We speak Croatian: Language advice]. Zagreb: Naprijed.

Mamić, Mile
1996   *Jezični savjeti* [Language Advice]. Zadar: Hrvatsko filološko društvo.

Pavuna, Stanka
1993   *Govorimo li ispravno hrvatski? Mali razlikovni rječnik* [Do we speak Croatian correctly? A small differential dictionary]. Zagreb: Integra.

Šimundić, Mate
1994   *Rječnik suvišnih tuđica u hrvatskomu jeziku jeziku* [Dictionary of unnecessary foreign borrowings in the Croatian language]. Zagreb: Barka.

Tanocki, Franjo
1994   *Hrvatska riječ: Jezični priručnik* [Croatian speech: A language handbook]. Osijek: Matica hrvatska.

Težak, Stjepko
1995   *Hrvatski naš osebujni* [Our distinctive Croatian]. Zagreb: Školske novine.

References

Anić, Vladimir
1998   *Rječnik hrvatskoga jezika* [Dictionary of the Croatian language]. Zagreb: Novi Liber, 3rd ed. Original edition, 1991.

Babić, Stjepan
1996   Osporavanje (Bilješke o hrvatskome jeziku 18) [Dispute (Notes about the Croatian language 18)]. *Hrvatsko slovo* (Zagreb), 19 July 1996.

1998   Osnovano Vijeće za normu hrvatskoga jezika jezika [The Council for the Croatian linguistic norm is established]. *Jezik* 45, 160.

Banac, Ivo
1984   Main trends in the Croat language question. In: Picchio, Riccardo and
          Harvey Goldblatt (eds.), *Aspects of the Slavic Language Question* 1.
          New Haven, CT: Yale University Press, 189–259.

Brozović, Dalibor
1978   Hrvatski jezik, njegovo mjesto unutar južnoslavenskih i drugih sla-
          venskih jezika, njegove povijesne mijene kao jezika hrvatske knji-
          ževnosti [The Croatian language, its place within the South Slavic
          and other Slavic languages, and its historical changes as the language
          of Croatian literature]. In: Flaker, Aleksandar, and Krunoslav Pranjić
          (eds.), *Hrvatska književnost u evropskom kontekstu* [Croatian litera-
          ture in the European context]. Zagreb: Liber, 9–83.

1994   Programska stajališta HDZ-a o hrvatskome jeziku [The HDZ plat-
          form on the Croatian language]. *Jezik* 41, 83–85.
1997   Gramatičke značajke hrvatskoga jezika [Grammatical characteristics
          of the Croatian language]. *Jezik* 44, 127–135.

1998   Aktualna kolebanja hrvatske jezične norme u slavenskome i europ-
          skome svjetlu [Current fluctuations in the Croatian linguistic norm in
          the Slavic and European context]. *Jezik* 45, 161–176.

Bugarski, Ranko
1995   *Jezik od mira do rata* [Language from peace to war]. Belgrade: Slo-
          vograf.

Coates, Jennifer
1993   *Women, Men and Language.* London/New York: Longman.

Deklaracija
1991   *Deklaracija o hrvatskome jeziku s prilozima i Deset teza* [The
          Declaration on the Croatian language, with supplements and the Ten
          theses]. Zagreb: Matica hrvatska.

Drvodelić, Milan
1989   *Hrvatskosrpski-engleski rječnik* [Croatoserbian-English dictionary].
          Zagreb: Školska knjiga.

Edwards, John
1985   *Language, Society and Identity.* Oxford: Blackwell.

Greenberg, Robert
1999   In the aftermath of Yugoslavia's collapse: The politics of language death and language birth. *International Politics* 36(2), 141–158.

Ivić, Pavle
1971   *Srpski narod i njegov jezik* [The Serbian people and its language]. Belgrade: Srpska književna zadruga.

Kačić, Miro
1995   *Hrvatski i srpski: Zablude i krivotvorine* [Croatian and Serbian: Misconceptions and fabrications]. Zagreb: Zavod za lingvistiku.

1996   Interview: Je li upitan Institut za hrvatski jezik? [Is the Institute for the Croatian language in question?] *Hrvatsko slovo* (Zagreb), July 12, 1996.

Katičić, Radoslav
1984   The Making of Standard Serbo-Croat. In: Picchio, Riccardo and Harvey Goldblatt (eds.), *Aspects of the Slavic Language Question* 1. New Haven, CT: Yale University Press, 261–295.

1992   *Novi jezikoslovni ogledi* [New linguistic essays]. Zagreb: Školska knjiga.

1997   Undoing a "unified language": Bosnian, Serbian, Croatian. In: Clyne, Michael (ed.), *Undoing and Redoing Corpus Planning*. Berlin/New York: Mouton de Gruyter, 166–191.

Kramarić, Ivica
1996   Kazne za nasrtaje na hrvatski jezik [Penalties for attacks on the Croatian language]. *Hrvatsko slovo* (Zagreb), March 15, 1996.

Krmpotić, Marijan
1997   Interview: Na pitanje – Za koga je još uvijek jezik Hrvata i Srba "jedan i jedinstven"– odgovara prof. Marijan Krmpotić [Prof. Marijan Krmpotić answers the question: For whom is the language of the Croats and Serbs still a "single and unified" language?]. *NDH* (Zagreb), June 1997. The online edition, http://www.hop.hr/.

1999   Sustavna gušitba hrvatske rieči [The systematic suppression of Croatian words]. *NDH* (Zagreb), May–June 1999. The online edition http://www.hop.hr/.

Labov, William
1966   Hypercorrection by the lower middle class as a factor in sound change. In: Bright, William (ed.), *Sociolinguistics*. The Hague: Mouton, 88–101.

Langston, Keith
1999   Linguistic cleansing: Language purism in Croatia after the Yugoslav breakup. *International Politics* 36(2), 179–201.

László, Bulcsú
1993   Vukovski je pravopis bezočna prijevara [The Vukovian orthography is an impudent fraud]. *Globus* (Zagreb), 15 October 1993.

Lučić, Predrag, and Ivica Dikić
1999   Tuđmanovo desetljeće [The Tudjman decade]. *Feral Tribune* (Split), 11 December 1999. The online edition http://www.feral-hr.com/.

Milroy, James, and Lesley Milroy
1997   Varieties and variation. In: Coulmas, Florian (ed.), *The Handbook of Sociolinguistics*. Oxford: Blackwell, 47–64.

Moguš, Milan
1995   *A History of the Croatian Language: Toward a Common Standard*. Zagreb: Globus.

Nikčević, Vojislav
1997   *Pravopis crnogorskog jezika* [Orthographical handbook of the Montenegrin language]. Cetinje: Crnogorski PEN Centar.

Pavuna, Stanka
1993   *Govorimo li ispravno hrvatski? Mali razlikovni rječnik* [Do we speak Croatian correctly? A small differential dictionary]. Zagreb: Barka.

Ryan, Ellen, Howard Giles, and Richard Sebastian
1982   An integrative perspective for the study of attitudes towards language variation. In: Ryan, Ellen, and Howard Giles (eds.), *Attitudes Towards Language Variation: Social and Applied Contexts*. London: Edward Arnold, 1–19.

Ryan, Ellen, Howard Giles, and Miles Hewstone
   1988   The measurement of language attitudes. In: Ammon, Ulrich, Norbert
            Dittmar and Klaus Mattheier (eds.), *Sociolinguistics: An Interna-
            tional Handbook of the Science of Language and Society* 2. Ber-
            lin/New York: Mouton de Gruyter, 1068–1081.

Samardžija, Marko
   1993   *Jezični purizam u NDH* [Language purism in the NDH]. Zagreb:
            Hrvatska sveučilišna naklada.

Šimundić, Mate
   1994   *Rječnik suvišnih tuđica u hrvatskomu jeziku* [A dictionary of unnece-
            ssary foreign borrowings in the Croatian language]. Zagreb: Barka.
Tanocki, Franjo
   1994   *Hrvatska riječ: Jezični priručnik* [Croatian speech: A language
            handbook]. Osijek: Matica hrvatska.

Thomas, George
   1991   *Linguistic Purism*. London/New York: Longman.

Thompson, Mark
   1994   *Forging War: The Media in Serbia, Croatia and Bosnia-Hercego-
            vina*. Avon: International Centre Against Censorship.

Wars, politics, and language: A case study of the Okinawan language[1]

Rumiko Shinzato

1. Introduction

A language which has enjoyed stable monolingualism over several centuries may experience "a sudden 'tip' after which the demographic tide flows strongly in favor of some other language" (Dorian 1981: 51). This sudden "tip" may be triggered by external forces such as wars, sharp economic expansion or contraction, compulsory military service, or education in the dominant language (Dorian 1989: 9).

Of these external forces, domestic and international wars and accompanying changes in hegemony have been the most crucial and influential factors causing such a "tip" in Okinawan. Okinawan is the indigenous language of the islands of Okinawa, the southern-most province of Japan. It is genealogically related to Japanese (see Chamberlain 1895; Tôjô 1927), but the two languages are mutually unintelligible. Okinawan was in contact with, in conflict with, and eventually replaced by standard Japanese within just over a century. As a result, Okinawan unavoidably seemed to be following a path to extinction. However, based on the recent linguistic picture, it appears that the trend to extinction has been reversed, or at least halted.

How can we reconstruct a sociolinguistic history of Okinawan? In this chapter, I pay close attention to such factors as politics, socio-economics, education, ethnicity, and mass media, and then examine the Okinawan case in light of current sociolinguistic theories of language maintenance and language shift.

2. Sociolinguistic history of Okinawan

The sociolinguistic history of the Okinawan language in Okinawa can be divided into six distinct periods from the perspective of language maintenance and language shift:[2]

First period: Before 1879 (End of domestic conflicts)
    Independent Ryûkyû kingdom[3]   Okinawan monolingualism

Second period: 1879 (End of domestic conflicts) –1895 (Sino-Japanese War)
    Japanese sovereignty   Breakdown of monolingualism
                                (Top-down standardization)[4]

Third period: 1895 (Sino-Japanese War) –1937 (Beginning of WWII)
    Japanese sovereignty   Bilingualism
                                (Bottom-up standardization)

Fourth period: 1937 (Beginning of WWII) –1945 (End of WWII)
    Japanese sovereignty   Language shift
                                (Accelerated standardization)

Fifth period: 1945 (End of WWII) –1972 (Reversion to Japan)
    U.S. occupation   Decline of Okinawan

Sixth period: 1972 (Reversion to Japan) – present
    Japanese sovereignty   Revival of Okinawan

As seen in this chronology, major wars and subsequent occupation changes serve to define each block, representing distinct levels of language maintenance and language shift in the case of Okinawan.

2.1. First period: Okinawan monolingualism (before 1879)

Before its absorption into the Japanese polity in 1879 as a province of Japan, Okinawa existed as an independent kingdom. Although Okinawa kept a formal tributary relationship with China, whereby a Chinese king granted a Ryûkyûan king his title and investiture, Okinawa was able to keep its political autonomy from China, since China had very little interest in interfering with Okinawa's internal political affairs. The ruler was the Ryûkyûan king, to whom the Okinawan populace pledged loyalty, and Okinawan ethnicity was the one with which they identified.

Because China granted special trade rights only to Okinawa, in return for this tributary relationship, Okinawa enjoyed political independence and benefited from trade with China and other Southeast Asian countries (Kerr 1958; Kinjô 1974).[5] Such international contacts undoubtedly influenced the creation of a unique blend of Okinawan culture (e.g., karate, dance, music, textiles, ceramics, etc.).

During this period, the majority of Okinawans were monolingual Okinawan speakers. Only elite officials and aristocrats in the capital learned to read and compose poetry in classical Chinese and Japanese. However, these classics were neither translated into Okinawan, nor was Okinawan used for higher level philological, philosophical and scientific endeavors. Thus, there was a tremendous difference of language use between the spoken and written domains (Karimata 1999). Okinawan exclusively occupied the spoken domain, whereas Chinese and Japanese were the languages of the written domain.

2.2. Second period: Breakdown of monolingualism (1879–1895)

Following its victory in domestic wars against the feudal Tokugawa government and its constituency of 300 years in Japan, the modern Meiji government abolished old feudal divisions and established new political divisions. In accordance with this move, Okinawa came to be absorbed into the Japanese body politic as Okinawa prefecture in 1879, and thereby was placed under the control of the Meiji government.[6]

To build national unity and to raise national consciousness, the Meiji government saw it necessary to transform Okinawans into loyal subjects of the Emperor. The government's efforts were met with both fervent support and persistent resistance. The Okinawan elite was divided into two factions: *Ganko-tô* [The Conservative Party], the pro-Chinese faction, which carried strong sentiment towards the previous glory of the Ryûkyû kingdom; and *Kaika-tô* [The Progressive Party], those willingly aligned with Japan to modernize

Okinawa. Faced with such "divided loyalty", the Meiji government took a conservative *do nothing* approach in Okinawa by withholding modernization programs such as land and tax reforms so as not to further antagonize the pro-Chinese faction (Kerr 1958: 445).

The government did, however, take the radical step of replacing old village schools, where the language medium was Okinawan, with new schools where Japanese was to be spoken. That is, the government attempted "linguistic conquest" to achieve political conquest (Trudgill 1974). As an initial step, the nation's first conversation training center was established in 1880 where monolingual Okinawan teachers were trained to become fluent in Japanese using a textbook called *Okinawa Taiwa* [Okinawan Conversations]. In 1884, Japanese language teachers started being recruited from the mainland Japan. In 1890, the *Imperial Rescript of Education* was incorporated into the school system to indoctrinate a new generation of Okinawans who would be obedient subjects of the Japanese Emperor (Okinawa-ken Kyôiku Înkai 1976). The educational goals of the Education Minister in 1890, Mori, "lay neither in mastering piecemeal the crust of western civilization, nor regulating educational system and provisions, but in pointing the direction toward which the whole nation should march" (Pittau 1965).

The late nineteenth century top-down attempt at linguistic Japanization of Okinawa had very little effect on peoples' lives and the Okinawan language. Japanese was slow to spread and the general public's command of Japanese in this period was still very low (see Iha 1975; Nakamoto 1896). This dismal effect was explained by strong Okinawan ethnicity (Shinzato 1970), and the low school enrollment (Okinawa-ken Kyôiku Înkai 1976).[7]

2.3. Third period: Bilingualism (1895–1937)

Japan's victory in the Sino-Japanese War in 1895 both incapacitated the pro-Chinese faction, and strengthened the Okinawan's ethnic identity as Japanese. This change is reflected in the story of ten voluntary military trainees from Okinawa who fought for Japan in the Sino-Japanese War:[8] Before the war, they were openly criticized by the Okinawan public; after the war, they were received as heroes by the same people. Similarly, a survey conducted among elementary school students in 1898 clearly indicates the shift of loyalty to the Japanese Emperor (Okinawa-ken Kyôiku Înkai 1976).

Okinawan's Japanese consciousness was further stimulated as increasing contacts with Japanese people through military service and emigration brought to light prejudices that some Japanese people harbored against Okinawans. Okinawan soldiers were mistaken for enemies because of their incomprehensible language; Okinawan immigrants in Hawaii and Micronesia suffered from discrimination by Japanese there.[9] Given such hardships, many Okinawans came to believe that the survival of Okinawa was only possible by full assimilation with Japan.[10] It is in this context that Okinawan people themselves saw the standardization movement and the acquisition of the Japanese language as a goal.

Through the joint efforts of scholars, teachers, and students, the standardization movements began at the grass-roots level. With Basil Hall Chamberlain's book (1895), which linguistically proved the genealogical relationship between Japanese and Okinawan, as a breakthrough,[11] several textbooks and disquisition were compiled by Okinawan scholars to facilitate acquiring of standard Japanese. While teachers made special efforts to improve pedagogy to effectively promote standard Japanese, students voluntarily implemented a punishment system using a *hôgen futa* or *batsu fuda* [placards that penalize dialect speakers], signs that hang from the necks of dialect users, thereby humiliating them (cf. *maid-chrochaidh* in Scotland, Dorian 1981: 24; wooden shoe in Occitan, Paulston 1987: 46).

Rapidly rising school attendance (see Table 1) and the use of government-authorized textbooks beginning in 1905 also facilitated the acquisition of Japanese.

In addition, the use of Japanese in new journalistic activities,[12] and the start of Japan's broadcasting organization, NHK (*Nippon Hôsô Kyôkai*) in 1925 accelerated the dissemination of Japanese in this period (Carroll 1995). By the end of this period, Japanese had secured its place in the school domain, while Okinawan still kept its status as the language of communication at home.

Table 1. School attendance in Okinawa

Years	Number of public schools	Number of students	Attendance rates
1880	14	n/a	n/a
1897	82	28,000	37%
1907	n/a	62,000	93%
1927	152	92,000	98%

Source: Kinjô (1974: 366–367)

2.4. Fourth period: Language shift (1937–1945)

Soon after the second major war with China began in 1937, which itself became part of World War II, the Education Council was formed to ensure militaristic education that would instill loyalty to the Japanese Empire. Schools packed with a whole new generation of Okinawans, for whom the notion of "divided loyalty" between China (Ryûkyû kingdom) and Japan was nothing but a memory of their grandparents, were ideal places to practice militaristic social psychology. In 1939, a prefecture-wide promotion of standard Japanese proceeded hand in hand with the *National General Mobilization Law*. A military decree was issued which declared that users of Okinawan should be regarded as spies (Miyawaki 1992). As this Japanese promotional campaign accelerated, its goal soon evolved from acquiring of Japanese to eradicating Okinawan. Radical measures such as *hôgen fuda*, corporal punishment, and emotional harassment were taken by school officials in order to exclude Okinawan from schools. In addition, the negative campaign invaded even into private domains by giving a special label of honor only to Japanese-speaking households.[13] Naturally, this humiliated and pressured Okinawan-speaking households to use Japanese.

As controversial as these measures may be, they were effective enough to bring about language shift in this period. The linguist Shuzen Hokama states that, as an elementary school student in 1933 (i.e., third period), he led a diglossic life, speaking Japanese at school and Okinawan at home. In contrast, his siblings, who were enrolled in elementary school in the early 1940s (i.e., this period), spoke only Japanese in both domains (Hokama 1981).[14]

2.5. Fifth period: Demise of Okinawan (1945–1972)

After World War II ended with Japan's surrender, the *San Francisco Peace Treaty* in 1951 placed Okinawa under the control of the USCAR (United States Civil Administration of Ryûkyû Islands). Okinawa's "residual sovereignty" remained with Japan, but Okinawa had no direct voice in the Japanese Diet (Parliament). Further, although Okinawa was allowed to have its own government, ultimate power rested with the USCAR, which could override and nullify any decisions and election results that were unfavorable to the U.S. Army (Kôdansha 1993). In addition, any accidents and casualties caused by the U.S. Army to the Okinawan people fell under U.S. jurisdiction, wherein decisions could not be reversed and to which Okinawans had no power to appeal.

Such infringement on Okinawans' basic human rights naturally triggered their grievance, rage, and distrust of the USCAR. To ease such anti-U.S. sentiment, the United States military assisted in establishing a university in Okinawa, and offered scholarships to Okinawan youths for study in U.S. colleges. At the same time, to suppress the increasing pro-Japanese sentiment, the U.S. military implemented a strategy to weaken Japanese-Okinawan ties. Travel between Okinawa and Japan was highly restricted for those who were ideological threats to the USCAR. The exclusion of the Japanese language was attempted by the USCAR, by requesting the implementation of English-medium education as well as the compilation of textbooks in Okinawan (cf. linguistic Japanization of Okinawa by the Meiji government in the second period). However, in the end, the persistence of the Okinawan officials won, and Japanese-medium education resumed with the arrival of textbooks from Japan in 1948 (Karimata 1998).

Despite the USCAR's efforts to divorce Okinawa from Japan, the Okinawan people's enthusiasm for reunification with Japan intensified during the Occupation. The fear of the U.S. bases and rage over perceived USCAR injustices made Okinawans resolute supporters of reversion to Japan on their own terms (e.g., immediate unconditional return of Okinawa to Japan without nuclear weapons and bases). As the prefecture-wide reversion movement gained momentum, interestingly enough, Okinawan came to be labeled as a dialect of Japanese, not as a separate language (Karimata 1998). As the reversion movement accelerated, the acquisition of standard Japanese was stressed increasingly at school even at the expense of stigmatizing the Okinawan language and ethnicity. In the minds of Okinawans, this left an inferiority complex towards Japanese people, and in return accelerated the decline of the Okinawan language.[15]

2.6. Sixth period: Revival of Okinawan (1972–present)

Reversion to Japan was realized in 1972. After this, travels between Okinawa and Japan no longer required passports and visas. Tourism promoting the subtropical climate, the beautiful ocean, and the exotic city scene became a major industry. A large influx of mainland Japanese tourists arrived, and Okinawans freely traveled to mainland Japan for schools and work. Marriages between Okinawans and Japanese increased. After the first troublesome decade of getting reacquainted, the distinct Okinawan cultural heritage came to be accepted and appreciated by Japanese people. In the 1970s to early 1980s, strong support came from Nobel Laureate Ôe Kenzaburô and a well-known Tokyo University professor and critic, Nakano Yoshio, who empathized with Okinawan people and wrote their books from the perspectives of Okinawans. Okinawan people came to view their differences from Japanese as a strength. In literature, prestigious Akutagawa-prize winning Okinawan writers expanded the initial experimental use of Okinawan from simple dialogues to the narrative itself (Hokama 1981).

In the mid-1980s and 1990s, a so-called *Okinawa boom*, instigated by the young generation of Okinawans often referred to as *new wave* spread to Japan. In music, distinguished artists composed music using traditional Okinawan tunes, and performed their original pieces on national and even on international stages. In theater, young actors in their twenties excited younger audiences with comical parodies using *Uchinâ Yamatuguchi* (Japanese built on Okinawan syntactic or lexical structures), while experienced Okinawan actors entertained older Okinawans using the traditional Okinawan language. TV and radio stations deliberately incorporated Okinawan programs, including the nation's only daily news in Okinawan. Comics filled with Okinawan phrases with Japanese translations in footnotes came to be widely read by both mainland and Okinawan youngsters (Makuta 1992).

The Okinawan boom stirred Japanese people's interest in Okinawan culture. Responding to a publication of an Okinawan key word book by young Okinawans in 1989, self-acclaimed Okinawan-fanatic Japanese also published a collection of essays about Okinawa in 1992.[16] NHK's nationwide broadcast of a year-long drama staged in the days of the glorious Ryûkyû kingdom run in 1993 was also an epoch-making event.

Rising Okinawan ethnicity during this period is undeniable, but its influence on the maintenance of Okinawan language is less clear. According to Motonaga's 1979 research (quoted in Machi 1992), only 21% of students used Okinawan at home. In contrast, Nakamatsu (1986) expressed his surprise to find that traditional Okinawan was still actively used in his 1986 recording of college students' conversations. Karimata (1999) predicts that Okinawan will continue to decline or change linguistically; however, Okinawan is likely to survive in traditional performing arts.

3. Sociolinguistic perspective

Following the delineation of the sociolinguistic history of Okinawan, this section examines its fall and rise in the recent theoretical framework of language maintenance and shift in comparative contexts vis-à-vis other endangered languages in the world.

3.1. Fall of Okinawan

When Okinawa was incorporated into the Japanese polity, Okinawan lost its status as a national language to its ruler's language, Japanese. As Japanese spread, the absolute dominance of Okinawan started breaking down (second period), language shift took place (fourth period), and then the maintenance of Okinawan was threatened (fifth period). This change in the maintenance and shift of Okinawan can be illuminated if seen in the framework of western sociolinguistic perspectives such as language planning, ethnicity, role of education, and mass media.

Adegbija (1997: 15) summarizes attitudes towards minority languages reflected in language policies with the evocative phrases in a continuum below, ranging from the most to least benevolent:

Rescue them
   Tolerate them
      Neglect them
         Assimilate them
            Kill them

Adegbija maintains that "killing tends to begin with assimilation into a bigger language or lingua franca, the ultimate intention being the annihilation or eradication of the language and the cultures they represent" (Adegbija 1997: 15). This seems to be the swaying attitudes which caused "language death", or "decline" in many languages such as Nubian in Egypt (Rouchdy 1989), Breton in France (Kuter 1989), Gaelic in Scotland (Dorian 1981), and American Indian languages in the United States. Expectedly, this annihilation policy was exactly the one pursued by the Meiji government. K. Satô quotes excerpts from Aota (1888), who described dialects of Japanese in such pejorative terms as "unsophisticated," "no merit, only harm," and "to be eradicated urgently" (K. Satô 1992: 101).

Language attitude translates into language policies. Speaking of desirable language policies, Kelman states that they "ought to be designed to meet the needs and interests of all segments of the population effectively and equitably, thus fostering instrumental attachments out of which sentimental ones can then gradually emerge" (Kelman 1971: 25). Sentimental attachment is observed when the subgroups see "the system as representing themselves," whereas instrumental attachment is evident when the system is seen as "a vehicle for achieving his own and the ends of members of other systems" (Kelman 1971: 25). Eastman echoes Kelman in that "most linguistic conflicts are rooted in grievances that are related to instrumental rather than sentimental attachment" (Eastman 1983: 35).[17] Or, to put it another way, tension resulting from the government's intervention can be minimized if "the government employs incentives that attempt to influence individual actions rather than directives that specify them" (Grin 1996: 32).

Meiji policies enhanced sentimental attachment with a new education system that advocated loyalty to the Emperor, but neglected instrumental attachment. The modernization programs such as land and tax reforms implemented elsewhere in Japan were withheld in Okinawa. As a result, the tax burden for the Okinawan people was increased. In addition, large Japanese companies gained monopolies over the principal Okinawan industry – sugar cane – and the Imperial Household thus realized "economic colonization" (Kerr 1958). Further, important posts in the Okinawan government were filled by Japanese, thereby blocking full legal and political participation by Okinawans in their own affairs. If full participation is denied, and socioeconomic mobility is stymied, then an imposed language functions as a divisive rather than as a unifying force. This was exactly the case with the factionalism of the second period. Seen in this light, it is not surprising that the government's policy aimed at annihilating Okinawan was met with powerful resistance.

The failure of top-down implementation as compared with the success of bottom-up promotion of Japanese finds parallels in linguistic histories of other languages. Paulston (1987) compares two languages, Catalan and Occitan, which are linguistically related, geographically congruous, and historically similar in both having a glorious past. Both languages were oppressed equally in the 18th century by their respective national languages (Spanish for Catalan, and French for Occitan). Later, however, their paths diverged. Catalan survives, while Occitan is facing extinction. Catalan people were economically well-off, proud of their ethnicity, and attached to their language, while Occitan people were poor, ashamed of their language, and ready to give it up. The Occitan parents were convinced that French was the key for upward mobility, and thus did not transmit Occitan to their children. That is to say, the Occitan people themselves propelled the spread of French in a bottom-up manner. The Catalan and Occitan cases parallel Okinawan in the top-down and the bottom-up periods of the standardization movement, respectively. Catalan resisted language shift just as Okinawan did in the top-down period, while Occitan was replaced by French, just as Okinawan shifted to Japanese in the bottom-up standardization period.

From the point of view of ethnicity, the contrast exhibited in the standardization movement in the second and the third periods reveals the close link between language and ethnicity (Fishman 1977; Giles, Bourhis and Taylor 1977). Before the Sino-Japanese War, Okinawans were dubious about their ethnic identity as Japanese and, as a result, their Okinawan language loyalty was so powerful that the central government's attempt at Japanizing Okinawa did not succeed. In contrast, when Okinawans started identifying themselves with Japanese ethnicity following Japan's victory in the Sino-Japanese War, their language loyalty to Japanese escalated. The genetic relationship proven by Chamberlain (1895) to exist between the Japanese and the Okinawan language added impetus to strengthen Japanese ethnicity. The newly evolving sense of Japanese ethnicity both on political and linguistic grounds led the standardization movement to evolve from top-down to bottom-up mobilization.

The significant roles that schools play in the annihilation of minority languages have been widely noted in the literature. In many cases, school policies contradict the following list of the primary factors necessary for language maintenance, which Rouchdy (1989: 94) extracted from the studies of Greenberg, Fishman, and Giles:

1. A situation of "stable bilingualism";
2. The maintenance/rise of ethnic identity;
3. The language being used for primary socialization and its frequency of usage and function.

In discussing the language shift of Breton to French, Kuter points out that "the school was an especially important institution in terms of its role in the formation of a negative Breton identity" (Kuter 1989: 80). The negative Breton identity was fostered further through the army and emigration. Since social advancement was linked to the mastery of French, Bretons worked towards de-Bretonization in language, costume and music. "With a firm belief that French is the language of the future, and Breton the language of the past, older generations of Bretons have taught their children to look to a French future" (Kuter 1989: 82). Thus, the unsuccessful maintenance of Breton was due to the lack of Rouchdy's primary factors, especially maintenance of ethnic identity (i.e., factor number two). When the third factor is absent, a condition exists that Mertz (1989: 111) calls "bilingual deficit" folk theory. In her fieldwork investigating the "tip" of Gaelic in Cape Breton, she came across the following testimonies from her informants:

> Parents thought teaching Gaelic "would sort of confuse the two languages in their minds" [M-14]. If the goal was to learn perfect, unmarked English with the accompanying cognitive benefits and increased possibilities for assimilation, parents must limit their children's exposure to Gaelic from the very beginning "because when you start out and use Gaelic... [learning English] is really hard" [M-6].

In the case of Okinawan, schools played a very significant role in the eradication of Okinawan in the fourth period. Two important factors contributed to schools' influence in this process: the increase in enrollment (which tripled compared to the second period) and the prevailing wartime nationalistic propaganda (cf. Kuter 1989). Almost all school-age children (98%) were given Japanese-medium education, instilled in loyalty to the Emperor, and trained to march obediently not to stop and think. National unity was the key to win the war, and any deviation from it meant disloyalty. Okinawan ethnicity was stifled, stigmatized, even effaced. From Tanaka (1940), the following specifics were extracted to show the extent of efforts paid by the teachers in this regard:

A *hôgen fuda*, or corporal punishment was implemented;
An essay question in a high school entrance examination asks "why is it wrong to speak the Okinawan language?" instead of "why is it also good to speak Japanese";
An overly motivated teacher would correct students' mistakes at the expense of hurting their dignity;
Students who were joyfully conversing in Okinawan turned silent as soon as a teacher approached;
Households using Japanese as a means of communication were given high recognition as *Kokugo no ie* "Household of the National Language".

The radical punishment system, the pejorative attitude towards Okinawan, and overt humiliation of Okinawan language speakers moved many Okinawans to deny their Okinawan ethnicity. The intrusion and interference of the teachers and school officials in students' private lives precluded a healthy primary socialization and consequently, stable bilingualism.

Dorian (1978: 653) warns, however, that the power of schools and official school policies should not be overemphasized. She contrasts Somali and Swiss German with East Sutherland Gaelic and Pennsylvania Dutch. The former languages are well-maintained in bilingualism without receiving any threat from non-indigenous languages routinely and universally used in schools. The latter languages, on the other hand, are dying, having been explicitly rejected by the schools. Dorian attributes this difference to the status of the ethnic identities. To be Somali and German Swiss is fully acceptable and desirable in each community, but to be Gaelic in Scotland or Pennsylvania Dutch in Pennsylvania is associated with stigmatization. She argues that, in the latter settings, the policy of schools takes on a symbolic force greater than its face value.

The same contrast could be applied to the difference in language maintenance between Japanese dialects of historic or commercial centers (e.g. Kyoto and Osaka), versus the Okinawan language. Neither is used officially at school; yet the former survives whereas the latter declines. Similarly, Bai (1994) reports that standard Chinese, Putonghua is difficult to spread to Shanghainese and Cantonese dia-

lect areas. The implication is that what made the Okinawan standardization movement successful was not so much the school's implementation of the Japanese-based curriculum, but rather its negative campaign against the Okinawan language and an Okinawan ethnic identity.

The role played by mass media, especially the public broadcasting
station NHK, should not be overlooked. Carroll (1995) states that
standard Japanese in its written form was promoted "by the national
education system, specifically via the school textbooks approved by
the Ministry of Education... national broadcasting provided the first
real opportunity for this to be extended to the spoken language" (Carroll 1995: 277).[18] Hiner (1975: 23, quoted in Carroll 1995: 278) summarizes NHK's role during World War II as follows: "By 1934 the
situation was worse, and for the next eleven years NHK was no more
than a propaganda conduit to promote nationalism and convincing
the people of the rightness of 'the new order in East Asia'". From the
above, it is easy to see that NHK served two roles – to disseminate
the spoken language and to promote nationalism. In the Okinawan
context, both roles were equated with the eradication of the indigenous language and the effacement of Okinawan ethnicity.

3.2. Rise of Okinawan

In the fifth period, Okinawan seemed to be approaching its final
stage of survival. In contrast, in the sixth period, especially from the
1980s to the early 1990s, it revived as part of a cultural renaissance
instigated by the *new wave* generation of young Okinawans. This
"Okinawan boom", as coined by the mass media, is reminiscent of
Fishman's remark: "...and yet the roots revive at times, even after
the trees have been burnt seemingly beyond recognition or recovery"
(Fishman 1984: 66–67).

Okinawan language and culture revival should be understood,
first, in a larger context of ethnic revival and self-determination that
occurred throughout the world as World War II drew to a close.
Multinational states in Africa and Eurasia dissolved or were sub-
jected to wars of separation. Europe saw the political assertion of

ethnic minorities (cf. Wickerkiewicz 1996; Tollefson 1997) and the United States moved towards protecting the human rights of ethnic minorities such as American Indians and immigrants (cf. Hornberger 1998). In this context, pluralism, or multilingualism came to be regarded as resources, rather than problems (Adegbija 1997; Hornberger 1998). Japan, too, broadened its focus from only the national "center" to include the periphery. The same agents (e.g., government officials, educators, mass media) that once acted to eradicate Okinawan and other peripheral dialects, transformed themselves into saviors who wished to protect, preserve, and promote these same dialects. Okinawan tourism, pop culture, and exported Okinawan products to the mainland Japan started to produce commercial profits. Thus, power, commerce and culture united to set the stage for the cultural renaissance in Okinawa (cf. Lingala in Zaire as discussed in Goyvaerts 1997).

In addition to power, commerce, and culture, another element is considered indispensable for the rise of Okinawan. That is what Omar (1998) calls "image building". Generally, language planning involves three areas: status, corpus and acquisition planning (Cooper 1989; Eastman 1990). Omar (1998) proposes to add "image building" as the fourth component. Having a good image (e.g., scientific image, professional image, image of high culture, etc.), she argues, is "a necessary ingredient in the building of confidence of its users" (Omar 1998: 49). In her analysis of Malay, she is convinced that although it has achieved the status of a national language, and has offered an identity for the people who use it, Malay lacks the image "that gives its users confidence and pride in using it. This is because it does not have the high-level prestige that should be accorded to it in various domains of use" (Omar 1998: 63). Thus, in Malaysia where there is a strong second language, English, Malay ranks below English in its economic value and in its contribution to the users' social advancement.

Omar's argument for image building also can be applied to the context of language revitalization during the past two decades if we broaden her definition. By "image", Omar meant a wider repertoire of language functions such as scientific and professional images, and images of high culture and refined social interaction. In the current context, "image" can be defined as the users' departure from a stigmatized negative image into one of pride and confidence in using it. With this definition, image building proves to be a significant factor in the revitalization of Okinawan. Several factors contributed to the creation of a positive image for Okinawan.

First, the linguistic prestige of the Okinawan language came to be recognized and widely propagated through various linguistic journals, magazines, and books, targeted to a wide range of audiences. The National Language Research Institute, the function of which is to plan a corpus of Japanese, compiled a dictionary entitled *The Okinawan Language Dictionary* (Note the title; it is not the Okinawan *dialect*). Many dialectologists and traditional Japanese linguists expressed their opinions on the linguistic value of Okinawan, since it preserves historically old structures and vocabularies, which are extremely valuable for research on classical Japanese grammar. A well-known magazine for general audiences, *Gekkan Gengo* [*Language Monthly*], ran several series to introduce Okinawan literature and language.[19]

Second, government-associated agencies made an effort to refine the image of Okinawan culture and language. NHK's 1993 drama, *Ryûkyû no kaze* [*Dragon Spirit*], was monumental in various respects: the entire discourse was carried out in Okinawan with Japanese subtitles, it disseminated historical information to which the general Japanese public had never been exposed, and it gave a refined and positive image of Okinawan culture. NHK's 1999 resolution rendering support to programs featured in local dialects was a significant change in the same direction (Shioda 1999). In 1992, the Ministry of Education, the authority that controls and approves textbooks for public schools, included an addendum to the existing curricula, expressing policies that acknowledge equally the values of both standard Japanese and Japanese dialects (K. Satô 1992). In 1998, the Ministry of Education allocated special funds for research and preservation of endangered languages in Japan and the Pacific rims.

Third, the present Emperor's strong interest in Okinawan culture, especially Okinawan literature, elevated Okinawan's image. The Emperor is known to have received lectures from the Okinawan scholar Hokama on a regular basis, and composed several Ryûkyûan poems himself. Receiving such a superior endorsement from the nation's most prestigious household was perceived in Japan as an extraordinary honor. The positive and strong influence of royal support for minor languages has been noted in other places in the world. For instance, Ennaji (1997: 4) states: "His majesty King Hassan II declared that Berber is an intrinsic part of the linguistic and cultural heritage of Morocco... This Royal decision will undoubtedly enhance the position of Berber and ensure its codification, standardization, and promotion as a language in its own right in the future." In discussion of the ethnic revival of the German minority in Poland, Wicherkiewicz (1996: 28) comments: "What brought the most fundamental changes to the life of the German minority in Poland was the official visit of Bundeskansler Kohl in November 1989. This event resulted in a number of Polish-German agreements, which also touched upon the situations of ethnic Germans in the country."

The last factor of "image building" originated in Okinawa, and was prompted by distinguished and popular Okinawan personalities. In sports, several Okinawan athletes, especially in boxing and baseball, climbed to the top in national and international matches. In the performing arts, young Okinawans created songs, plays, and movies reflecting Okinawan cultural heritage for both national and international stages. These young artists are idolized by even younger generations with their charismatic powers (cf. "ethnic movement" in next section).

As discussed above, the tide has clearly shifted in favor of preserving and promoting Okinawan language and culture. The crucial elements for revitalization such as power, commerce, culture, and image seem to all exist to a certain degree. But, are they strong enough to halt the decline of Okinawan and restore it to the level of stable bilingualism?

3.3. Future of Okinawan

Paulston (1992, 1987) offers a typological formulation of social mobilization of an ethnic group in a nation-state to explain and predict
language maintenance and shift. The four types she recognizes are
"ethnicity", "ethnic movement", "ethnic nationalism", and "geographic nationalism". "Ethnicity" is simply an unconscious source of
identity, which is not used purposely for power struggle; thus a typical course is assimilation and concomitant language shift. "Ethnic
movement" is "a conscious, cognitive ethnicity in a power-struggle
with the dominant group for social and economic advantage" led by
charismatic leaders (Paulston 1992: 71), but it does not maintain a
language, though it may slow the attrition rate. In "ethnic nationalism", the ethnic group is isomorphic with the nation-state, and language is a prime symbol of the nation. "Geographic nationalism" is
territorially based, consisting of citizens of (several) ethnic de-
scent(s).

Lewis (1993) studied change of identity of Quiché people in
Guatemala, Central America. Lewis claims that, in accordance with
the change in orthographic symbols (from assimilational alphabets to
dissimilational alphabets and finally to unificationist alphabets),
Quiché ethnic organization moved from "ethnicity" to "ethnic
movement" and finally to "ethnic nationalism" in Paulston's typology. According to Lewis, "one of the goals of those promoting this
K'iche' (and Mayan) ethnic nationalism is that the trends towards
assimilation and language shift be reversed" (Lewis 1993: 49). In
opposition to the perceived common enemy, Spanish, it was necessary to achieve a solidarity among Mayan people. Thus, a new
Quiché identity was created to unify Mayan subgroups vis-à-vis
Spanish, and the Mayan Language Academy was established to deal
with dialect variations within the Mayan languages and to invent unificationist alphabets to represent each of the Mayan languages (also
see Goyvaerts 1997).

The present state of Okinawan society seems to belong to what
Paulston calls "ethnicity", with some features of "ethnic movement".
According to an NHK's nation-wide survey, Okinawans always rank
ahead of other prefectures in their strength of consciousness of local

ethnicity (Sanada and Long 1992).[20] In this sense, it is a *conscious* source of identity as the one in "ethnic movement". Unlike an "ethnic movement", however, it is not aimed towards another political battle for independence from Japan, although some political activists are willing to fight for that goal.[21]

If the above assessment is correct, will Okinawa move to "ethnic nationalism" so that Okinawan will survive, or is it more likely that Okinawa will stay in the current situation, and the language will die? Or, will Okinawa remain at its current level of social mobilization, and yet the language will survive? This third option is not addressed in Paulston's framework, but it is worthwhile considering.

To answer this question, several facts have to be reviewed. First, unlike minority languages facing extinction, Okinawan may have already seen the worst. This is because the social mobilization patterns in Okinawa moved from "negative ethnicity" (i.e., the denial of Okinawan identity) to "positive ethnicity", and is moving towards "ethnic movement". That is, the probability of the maintenance of Okinawan is increasing. Second, the current linguistic and cultural revival were started by a younger generation in their twenties. Younger generations are confident and comfortable with their Japanese language ability, and have never experienced the linguistic inferiority complex their parents did decades ago. They are, in fact, *proud* of their cultural heritage.

Third, there are some economic incentives today for speaking Okinawan. In some business interactions, it is said that speaking Okinawan wins more trust, and thus more business. This recalls Villancourt's observation stated in Grin (1996: 24), that the Francophone shoppers are preferred in Quebec. Fourth, teens are learning new expressions in Okinawan through theater and pop songs. Discussing the similar rise of Lingala in Bukavu, Goyvaerts (1997: 26) reports about "a song culture with songs in Lingala that became extremely popular and turned out to be instrumental in the further propagation of Lingala among the younger generation throughout the Republic of Zaire". Fifth, Okinawan radio and TV stations offer Okinawan language instruction as well as local news in Okinawan. Sixth, at least some research reports the maintenance and acquisition of Okinawan by the younger generation (Nakamatsu 1986), and successful code-switching between a dialect and standard Japanese as a general trend in Japan (R. Satô 1992). Seventh, it is unlikely that Okinawa has developed into the state of "ethnic nationalism", a necessary state for the survival of an oppressed language in Paulston's model. The majority of Okinawan people do not wish for an internal war with Japan to win independence, nor is Okinawa strong enough economically to warrant independence (Endo 1996; Megumi 1996). This is reminiscent of the current Catalan attitude: "I'm a Catalan, but I'm not fanatic" (O'Donnell 1996: 44), or "let's not make a war of it" (O'Donnell 1996: 49).

To evaluate future prospects of Okinawan, one should consider factors that played key roles in revitalizing other minority languages. Some studies which discuss the revitalization of minority languages include Nahir (1998) for the revival of Hebrew; Adegbija (1997) for the survival of minority languages in Nigeria; Niedzielski (1992) for the Hawaiian model; Hornberger (1998) for the revitalizing efforts of indigenous and immigrant languages. The factors prevailing in the above success stories can be summarized as language policy, language education, and the commitment of the communities themselves. Seeing the Okinawan case in this light, the future of Okinawan in its traditional form as a medium of communication seems rather bleak.

It is true that there are some cultural revitalization initiatives seen in recent years as described above. Several language textbooks were published, and an Okinawan language center was established. However, there is no language policy at the state level. Thus, corpus planning, codification and elaboration have not begun. The design and development of orthography could certainly be a step towards the preservation of the language. However, there are no organized efforts for it. Consequently, there is no implementation of the Okinawan language in the public school curriculum as a second language. The Okinawan people's commitment to the preservation and promotion of language does not seem to be powerful enough to truly reverse the language shift. Okinawan monoglots and bilinguals are not committed to transmitting Okinawan to their offspring. A man in his fifties admitted that he speaks to his children only in Japanese out of desire for their academic excellence, although he himself had struggled with *hôgen fuda* as a child (Nagamoto 1992). A woman in her late thirties deplored the situation of her childhood when her grandparents spoke less and less Okinawan to her and her siblings (Machi 1992). Without intergenerational language transmission, reversing language shift is impossible (Fishman 1991).

Paulston's model predicts that "ethnicity", and "ethnic movement" cannot maintain the language, while "ethnic nationalism" will. According to Miyawaki (1992: 361), the Japanese government applied its domestic experience of linguistic colonization of Okinawa to other colonized areas including Taiwan (1895–1945), Korea (1910–1945), and Micronesia (1914–1945). After the war, as they became independent nations and reaching the stage of the "nationalism" in Paulston's framework, their native languages replaced Japanese as the medium of education, and survived. In contrast, Okinawan will probably not reach the stage of "ethnic nationalism". If so, will Okinawan eventually die out? Similar to that of Karimata's (1998), Okinawan in its traditional form will probably end as a medium of communication, but will probably survive as a language of classical performing arts. The form most likely to survive as a medium of communication will be a hybrid of Okinawan and Japanese.

However, as Williamson (1990: 120, quoted in Adegbija 1997: 24) eloquently states, the final answer rests with Okinawan people themselves:

> When all is said and done, however, the fate of a minority language rests with the speakers. If they care enough about it to develop it as a written language, they will find the means to do so. If they do not, it will remain a spoken medium only, or even die out in favor of a larger language.

4. Conclusion

The sociolinguistic history of Okinawan provides a good illustration of the intricate relationship between wars, politics and language maintenance. Domestic or international wars that generate change in sovereign authority, serve to define six stages of language maintenance, from absolute monolingualism, to bilingualism, language shift, decline, and finally to revitalization of Okinawan. By examining the reconstructed history comparatively with other minority languages in recent sociolinguistic research, this chapter touched upon such issues as language planning, ethnicity, role of education, mass media, and orthography, which bear significant relevance to language maintenance and shift.

Language shift, language obsolescence, and language revival now occupy a substantial and growing body in linguistic research. However, very few reports on Japan have been introduced to Western linguistics, with important exceptions by Miyawaki (1992) and Refsing (1986). But, as demonstrated here, ample insight can be gained and applied from comparative analysis. The Okinawan case, far from being esoteric or unique, falls well within a pattern of minority, small or regional language life cycles affected by the vicissitudes of war, politics and power.

The fate of "small" languages tells us much about the cultural hegemony of large powers, and can be regarded as a litmus test for war that is historically proximate. Symbolic violence is sure to precede, accompany and follow physical violence leaves telltale signs as indigenous languages wane under the influence of education, media and business domination from outside.

What a hegemon does to the weakest and most exposed within its grasp is highly indicative of intentions of the powerful. Unconstrained by countervailing capacities, the control exerted over the helpless through, for example, a monopoly over the power of naming (Bourdieu 1991: 239–243) will be subtle and non-intimidating, but dominance nonetheless. And, as in the case of Japanese in Okinawa before World War II, it conveyed the arrogant exceptionalism of racism that supported a wider and savage war. After World War II, the heavy footprint of American occupation and military presence led to both a political movement and a linguistic consequence.

Symbolic violence, inseparable from an exertion of hegemonic power, foretells physical violence. By examining the condition and health of regional languages and minority cultures, we can identify policies and behaviors of the powerful within their own countries that, if extended elsewhere, are sure to damage peace and build momentum towards war.

Notes

1. This research was supported in part by two research travel grants from the North East Asian Council of the Association for Asian Studies. I am grateful to the late Dr. Masato Matsui for granting me access to rare Ryûkyûan materials. Thanks are also due to Professors George DeVos, Nancy C. Dorian, George Grace, and Leon A. Serafim for their guidance and comments on the earlier versions of this paper.
2. Hokama (1971) offers a sociolinguistic history of the Okinawan language from 1879 to 1971, in which he divides the period into four subparts according to the names by which the Japanese language was referred to by the Okinawan people. They are:
    1. Tôkyô no kotoba – The Tokyo-speech Period (1879–1897)
    2. Futsûgo – The General-language Period (1897–1935)
    3. Hyôjungo – The Standard-language Period (1935–1955)
    4. Kyôtsûgo – The Common-language Period (1955–1971)
    For each period, he offers his assessment of the maintenance of the Okinawan language together with the changes in education, and socio-political contexts. The present study covers a wider period, and focuses on the nature and effect of the standardization movement, socio-political, or ethnicity issues relevant to language maintenance and shift.
3. Ryûkyû is another name given to Okinawa by China when it had a tributary relationship with them (see 2.1.) In this chapter, I intend to use the term Okinawan, instead of Ryûkyûan.
4. "Standardization" of language normally refers to corpus planning, which deals with orthography, grammar, dictionaries, etc. of a language (see Eastman 1990). However, diverting from the norm, in this chapter, the "standardization movement" refers to the process whereby standard Japanese replaced peripheral dialects (languages) as the language of the nation. This is because "standardization movement" has a lexically closer image to its Japanese counterpart, *Hyôjungo Reikô Undô*.
5. This statement may be misleading. Ryûkyû kingdom lost its absolute independence when the neighboring state, Satsuma, invaded Okinawa in 1609, unbeknownst to the then central government, the Tokugawa Shogunate, as well as to China. Since Satsuma's motives were to exploit secretly Okinawa's trade benefits, they prohibited Okinawans from speaking Japanese in order to diminish an atmosphere which might divulge to China Okinawa's ties with Japan. Since China only granted trade rights to Okinawa, not to Japan which refused the tributary relationship, revealing Okinawa's true political position would mean the end of trade benefits for Okinawa, and subsequently, the end of the exploitation for Satsuma.
6. This political move was delayed for eight years in Okinawa because of persistent resistance by top officials of the Ryûkyû kingdom and the pro-Chinese faction.

7. The low attendance rates are linked to several reasons discussed in Okinawa-ken Kyôiku Înkai (1976).
8. The conscription law was implemented in 1873 elsewhere in Japan, but was withheld in Okinawa until 1898. Therefore, these soldiers were volunteers.
9. It was in this period that emigration started to resolve the population pressure and chronic poverty.
10. The inaugural issue of the *Ryûkyû Shimpô* newspaper in 1893 eloquently expresses this position,
11. Given the close link between language and ethnicity (Giles, Bourhis and Taylor 1977: 325 and Fishman 1977: 25), it is not surprising to see how mutual unintelligibility of Okinawan and Japanese spawned the idea among both Japanese and Okinawans that the two groups were totally unrelated ethnically. In this sense, Chamberlain's book served as a basis to warrant assimilation with Japan.
12. Following *Ryûkyû Shimpô* newspaper, two other newspapers, *Okinawa Shimbun* (1905), and *Okinawa Mainichi Shimbun* (1908) started their publication (cf. Okinawa-ken Kyôiku Înkai 1976).
13. These aberrantly negative campaigns caught the attention of a visiting anthropologist from the mainland Japan in 1940. His casual comments that such measures are highly deplorable and self-destructive of a rich cultural heritage ignited a year-long controversy, not only involving the prefectural department of education, but also mainland intellectuals.
14. One of Baku Yamanoguchi's poems underscores the same scene. In the poem, Yamanoguchi greets a fellow Okinawan in the Okinawan language. To his surprise, the fellow replied in Japanese. When he protested saying "Did you also lose your language to the war?", the fellow leered and yet commented what a good command of Okinawan he has.
15. A similar linguistic inferiority complex, which affected speakers of Northern Japanese dialects, has been reported in R. Satô (1992).
16. They refer to the following two books: Mabui-gumi. *Okinawa Kîwâdo Koramu Bukku*. Naha: Okinawa Shuppan, 1989; Naichâzu. *Okinawa Iroiro Jiten*. Tokyo: Shinchôsha, 1992.
17. Shinzato (1970) states that the Meiji government's abolition of the kingdom was top-down unification in spite of the fact that there was a historically-grounded possibility of bottom-up unification.
18. Similarly, K. Satô (1992) reports that the majority of high school students in the northern or southern states of Japan agreed that the language used on TV is a model of standard Japanese.
19. See "Nihon Sogo ni Tsuite [On the Proto-Japanese]" by Japan's leading linguist at the time, the late Shirô Hattori, and an introduction of 16th century Okinawan literature, *Omoro Sôshi* with explanation, interpretation and translation by three Okinawan specialists, Chris Drake, Minoru Higa, and Masachie Nakamoto.

20. They also pointed out that in the same surveys, Okinawa topped the other prefectures for their shame and embarrassment of the interference of their local accents in standard Japanese. Thus, they argued that love for local culture only does not preserve the language, unless it is used widely in everyday life.
21. Endô (1996) calls ex-governor Ôta an agitator, promoting the idea of Okinawan independence from Japan

References

Adegbija, Efurosibina
    1997   The identity, survival, and promotion of minority languages in Nige-
            ria. *International Journal of the Sociology of Language* 125, 5–27.

Bai, Jianhua
    1994   Language attitude and the spread of standard Chinese in China. *Lan-
            guage Problems and Language Planning* 18(2), 128–138.

Carroll, Tessa
    1995   NHK and Japanese language policy. *Language Problems and Lan-
            guage Planning* 19(3), 271–293.

Chamberlain, Basil H.
    1895   *Essay in Aid of a Grammar and Dictionary of the Luchuan Lan-
            guage.* Tokyo: Transactions of the Asiatic Society of Japan.

Cooper, Robert L.
    1989   *Language Planning and Social Change.* Cambridge: Cambridge
            University Press.

Dorian, Nancy C.
    1978   The dying dialect and the role of the schools: East Sutherland Gaelic
            and Pennsylvania Dutch. In: Alatis, James E. (ed.), *International
            Dimensions of Bilingual Education.* Washington, D. C.: Georgetown
            University Press, 646–656.

    1981   *Language Death: The Life Cycle of a Scottish Gaelic Dialect.*
            Philadelphia: University of Pennsylvania Press.

    1989   *Investigating Obsolescence: Studies in Language Contraction and
            Death.* Cambridge: Cambridge University Press.

Eastman, Carol M.
1983   *Language Planning: An Introduction.* Navato, CA: Chandler & Sharp Publishers, Inc.

1990   *Aspects of Language and Culture.* San Francisco: Chandler & Sharp.

Endô, Kôichi
1996   Sendôsuru Chiji ni Tou [Questioning the governor, the agitator]. *Shokun* 10, 36–44.

Ennaji, Moha
1997   Introduction. *International Journal of the Sociology of Language* 123, 3–6.

Fishman, Joshua A.
1977   Language and ethnicity. In: Giles, Howard (ed.), *Language, Ethnicity and Intergroup Relations.* New York: Academic Press, 15–57.

1984   *The Rise and Fall of the Ethnic Revival: Perspectives on Language and Ethnicity.* Berlin: Mouton.

1991   *Reversing Language Shift: Theoretical and Empirical Foundations of Assistance to Threatened Languages.* Philadelphia: Multilingual Matters.

Giles, Howard, Richard Y. Bourhis, and Donald M. Taylor
1977   Towards a theory of language in ethnic relations. In: Giles, Howard (ed.), *Language, Ethnicity and Intergroup Relations.* New York: Academic Press, 307–348.

Goyvaerts, Didier L.
1997   Power, ethnicity, and the remarkable rise of Lingala in Bukavu, Eastern Zaire. *International Journal of the Sociology of Language* 128, 25–43.

Greenberg, Joseph H.
1965   Urbanization and migration in West Africa. In: Kuper, Hilda (ed.), *Urbanization, Migration, and Language.* Berkeley: University of California Press.

Grin, François
1996   The economics of language: Survey, assessment, and prospects. *International Journal of the Sociology of Language* 121, 17–44.

Hokama, Shuzen
1981   *Nihongo no Sekai 9, Okinawa no Kotoba* [The world of Japanese 9, the Okinawan languages]. Tokyo: Chûô Kôronsha.

Hornberger, Nancy H.
1998   Language policy, language education, language rights: Indigenous, immigrant, and international perspective. *Language in Society* 27, 439–458.

Iha, Fuyû
1975   *Iha Fuyû Zenshû* 7 [Collected papers of Iha Fuyû]. Tokyo: Heibonsha.

Karimata, Shigehisa
1998   Ryûkyuu Ôkoku no Kotoba [The languages of the Ryukyu Kingdom]. *Gekkan Gengo,* 26(7), 110–115.

1999   Kiki ni Hinsuru Ryûkyû Shohôgen [Endangered Ryukyuan dialects]. *Gekkan Gengo,* 27(11), 110–118.

Kelman, Herbert C.
1971   Language as an aid and barrier to involvement in the national system. In: Rubin, Joan and Bjorn H. Jernudd (eds.), *Can Language Be Planned?: Sociolinguistic Theory and Practice for Developing Nations.* Honolulu: East-West Center Press, 21–55.

Kerr, George H.
1958   *Okinawa: The History of an Island People.* Tokyo: Charles E. Tuttle Company.

Kinjô, Chôei
1974   *Kinjô Chôei Zenshû* [Collected papers of Kinjô Chôei] Vol. 1 & 2. Naha: Okinawa Taimususha.

Kôdansha, Ltd.
1993   *Japan: An Illustrated Encyclopedia.* Ottawa: Kôdansha.

Kuter, Lois
1989   Breton vs. French: Language and the opposition of political, economic, social, and cultural values. In: Dorian, Nancy C. (ed.), *Investigating Obsolescence.* Cambridge: Cambridge University Press, 75–89.

Lewis, M. Paul
 1993   Real men don't speak Quiché: Quiché ethnicity, Ki-che ethnic move-
          ment, K'iche' nationalism. *Language Problems and Language Plan-
          ning* 17(1), 37–54.

Machi, Hiromitsu
 1992   Ryûkyû Hôgen no Genzai [The present status of Ryukyuan dialects].
          Nihongogaku 11(9), 117–126.

Makuta, Satoshi
 1992   Uchigawa kara Okinawa o Mitsumenaosu Wakamonotachi [The in-
          side perspective of Okinawa as seen by the young generation]. *Shin
          Okinawa Bungaku* 93, 46–53.

Megumi, Ryûnosuke
 1996   Bôsôsuru Ôta Ryûkyû Kokuô ni Hanransu [Stopping Ryukyuan
          King Ôta, who is running out of control]. *Shokun*, 10, 26–34.

Mertz, Elizabeth
 1989   Sociolinguistic creativity; Cape Breton Gaelic's linguistic "tip". In:
          Dorian, Nancy C. (ed.), *Investigating Obsolescence*. Cambridge:
          Cambridge University Press, 103–116.

Miyawaki, Hiroyuki
 1992   Some problems of linguistic minorities in Japan. In: Willem, Fase,
          Koen Jaspaert and Sjaak Kroon (eds.), *Maintenance and Loss of Mi-
          nority Languages*. Amsterdam: John Benjamins, 357–367.

Nagamoto, Tomohiro
 1992   Hatachi no Kansei [The sensitivity of twenty-year olds]. *Shin Oki-
          nawa Bungaku* 93, 2–44.

Nahir, Moshe
 1998   Micro language planning and the revival of Hebrew: A schematic
          framework. *Language in Society* 27, 335–357.

Nakamatsu, Takeo
 1986   Daigaku no Kyanpasu de [On a college campus]. *Gengo Seikatsu*
          420, 80–84.

Nakamoto Masayo
 1896   *Okinawa Goten* [Dictionary of Okinawan]. Naha: Eishôdô.

Niedzielski, Henry Z.
    1992   The Hawaiian model for the revitalization of native minority culture
            and languages. In: Willem, Fase, Koen Jaspaert, and Sjaak Kroon
            (eds.), *Maintenance and Loss of Minority Languages*. Amsterdam:
            John Benjamins, 369–384.

O'Donnell, Paul E.
    1996   "I'm Catalan but I'm not a fanatic": Shifting tides in Catalan public
            opinion. *Language Problems and Language Planning* 20(1), 44–52.

Okinawa-ken Kyôikyu Înkai (ed.)
    1976   *Okinawa Kenshi* 1 [A prefectural history of Okinawa]. Haebaru:
            Sentoraru Insatsusho.

Omar, Asmah H.
    1998   Language planning and image building: The case of Malay in
            Malaysia. *International Journal of the Sociology of Language* 130,
            49–65.

Paulston, Christina B.
    1987   Catalan and Occitan: Comparative test cases for a theory of language
            maintenance and shift. *International Journal of the Sociology of
            Language* 63, 31–62.

    1992   Linguistic minorities and language policies: Four case studies. In:
            Willem, Fase, Koen Japaert, and Sjaak Kroon (eds.), *Maintenance
            and Loss of Minority Languages*. Amsterdam: John Benjamins, 55–
            79.

Pittau, Joseph
    1965   Inoue Kowashi (1843–1895) and the Meiji educational system.
            Monumenta Nipponica 20, 270–282.

Refsing, Kristen
    1986   *The Ainu Language: The Morphology and Syntax of the Shizunai
            Dialect.* Aarhus University Press.

Rouchdy, Aleya
    1989   "Persistence" or "tip" in Egyptian Nubian. In: Dorian, Nancy C.
            (ed.), *Investigaating Obsolescence*. Cambridge: Cambridge Univer-
            sity Press, 91–102.

Sanada, Shinji, and Daniel Long
1992   Hôgen to Aidentitî [Dialects and identities]. *Gekkan Gengo* 9, 72–
          79.

Satô, Kazuyuki
1992   Gendaijin no Hôgen Ishiki – Katte Hôgen wa Sutiguma Datta [Mod-
          ern-day Japanese perspectives on dialects – dialects were once stig-
          matized]. *Nihongogaku* 11(12), 98–110.
Satô, Ryôichi
1992   Hôgen no Shôrai [Future of dialects]. *Nihongogaku* 11(13), 117–
          129.

Shinzato, Keiji
1970   *Okinawashi o Kangaeru* [Thoughts on the history of Okinawa]. To-
          kyo: Keisô Shobô.

Shioda, Takehiro
1999   Terebi to Hôgen – Shichôsha ga Kanjiteiru Koto – [TV and dialects
          – viewers' thoughts]. *The NHK Monthly Report on Broadcast Re-
          search* 12, 68–79.

Tanaka, Toshio
1940   Okinawa-ken no Hyôjungo Reikô no Genkyô [The present status of
          standard Japanese use in Okinawa]. *Gekkan Mingei*, November/
          December 1940. Reprinted in *Waga Okinawa: Hôgen Ronsô*, edited
          by Tanigawa Ken'ichi. Tokyo: Bokujisha, 144–146.

Tôjô, Misao
1927   *Kokugo no Hôgen Kukaku* [Japanese Dialectal Divisions]. Tokyo:
          Ikuei Shoin.

Tollefson, James W.
1997   Language policy in independent Slovenia. *International Journal of
          the Sociology of Language* 124, 29–49.

Trudgill, Peter
1974   *Sociolinguistics: An Introduction.* Harmandsworth: Penguin Books.

Wicherkiewicz, Tomasz S.
1996   Ethnic revival of the German minority in Poland. *International Jour-
          nal of the Sociology of Language* 120, 25–38.

Language choice and cultural hegemony: Linguistic symbols of domination and resistance in Palau[1]

Kazuko Matsumoto and David Britain

1. Introduction

As contemporary research in linguistic ideology,[2] sociolinguistics,[3] critical discourse analysis[4] and the symbolic domination of language[5] has amply demonstrated, language can be a prime vehicle for *violence douce*, a hegemonic form of "'mild violence' which transform[s]… people's perceptions and change[s] the day-to-day reproduction of life… in the name of civilization and reason" (Engels and Marks 1994: 1). Because language forms the cornerstone of social relations and social change, and because it is often so taken-for-granted and so intimate, it provides a powerful and coercive conduit for the exercise of domination and cultural hegemony.

While acts of *violence directe* are more evident, attract greater attention and publicity, and are more symptomatic of conflict and resistance, the "success" of cultural hegemony, and in particular linguistic hegemony, by powerful groups can be measured by acquiescence to and participation in the domination by the dominated. "Hegemony", writes Bocock (1986: 76), "when successfully achieved, is unnoticeable in everyday political, cultural and economic life".

The colonial history of the Palauan Islands of the Western Pacific has been characterised by such *violence douce*. Here, we discuss how cultural hegemony and symbolic domination[6] have constituted and shaped language use in this trilingual nation state. Further, we consider how changing foreign political administrations (especially the Japanese and U.S.) and local social and clan structures have interacted to legitimate, habitualise, and "make-for-granted" the sociolinguistic order which both serves the economic, geopolitical, and personal purposes of the colonial powers and the local elites, and which has, apparently, engendered local compliance. The hegemony that reigned during the Japanese colonial period, however, was in many ways more "successful", more "complete" than under the subsequent American administration, and many linguistic "traces" survived into that era which today serve as paradoxical counter-hegemonic linguistic practices.

We begin with a brief synopsis of Palau's colonial and post-colonial history (Section 2). This overview is essential to portray the changing political climate of the country both at a local level, in terms of the evolution of local elite groups and clans, and at an (inter)national level, in terms of colonial intervention and economic, social and military development. Section 3 briefly details the field-work methods employed to investigate language use in the islands, and highlights the dramatic language shift in this trilingual nation during the past century. Section 4 discusses, in the local Palauan context, the development and legitimisation of a sociolinguistic profile common in many post-colonial speech communities – diglossia. We demonstrate the hegemonic nature of diglossia, how it is reified not just in the institutions of education, the media and the economy, but also how it is reinforced by contradictory and hypocritical behaviours of the local elite – the high clan members. Section 5 looks at the paradoxical Japanese "traces" in contemporary language use in Palau where previous deeply hegemonic practices have evolved into counter-dominant reminders of an apparently shallow and unconvincing English-language hegemony.

2. Palau's colonial histories

The Palau Islands are an archipelago located in the Western Caroline region of the Pacific, with a population of 17,000 (The Office of Planning and Statistics 1997: Table 1). The Austronesian indigenous language, Palauan, has, as the result of a century of colonial domination by Spain, Germany, Japan and the U.S., come into prolonged contact with other non-local languages. Table 1 summarises, in chronological order, the relation between the colonial contact languages and the factors that engendered language contact.

Although Palau finally became an independent nation in 1994, the effects of Japan and the U.S. still appear significant for three reasons. First, Palau was colonised recently. Second, Palau has received prolonged financial support from both countries, and still relies heavily on such help. Aside from war compensation, Japan has provided Palau with free financial and technical aid through the Overseas Development Administration (ODA) and the Japan International Cooperation Agency since 1981 when constitutional government began in Palau (Kobayashi 1994: 221–223; Shuster 1998: 188–191, 2000: 217–220).[7] The U.S., on the other hand, has supplied financial aid to Palau, first as the trustee of the U.S. Trust Territories of Pacific Islands (hereafter TTPI) and, second, $480 million in return for U.S. military access to Palau, that involves testing, storage and disposal of nuclear weapons, on the basis of the Compact Free Association since 1994 (Wilson 1995: 30–36; Shuster 1995: 126–129).

Table 1. Language contact history in Palau

Period	Language in contact	Factors engendering contact	Administration
1885–1899 (14 years)	Spanish	Christianity	Spanish administration
1899–1914 (15 years)	German	Commercialism Christianity Militarism	German administration
1914–1945 (30 years)	Japanese	Imperialism Militarism Commercialism	Japanese administration as Japan's Mandatory authorised until 1933 by the League of Nations
1945–1994 (49 years)	(American) English	Politics Militarism Territories of Pacific Islands	American administration as the U.S. Trust
1994 to Present Day	English and Japanese	Militarism Politics Cultural hegemony	The Republic of Palau

Third, Japan and the U.S. have had a strong effect on Palau because of strategic social and educational reforms that Japan and
America inaugurated in Palau during their administrations. Since
both countries identified Palau as a key strategic site for military
purposes, they implemented administrative policies designed to
maintain permanent access to Palau. More specifically, both countries introduced their own law and school systems using textbooks
and teachers from their homelands. Not only were their languages
imposed as classroom languages, but also the patriotic rituals of
Japan and the United States were instituted in Palau through
education, such as 修身 *shūshin* (moral education or ethics curriculum)[8] and 勅語 *chokugo* (Imperial Rescript);[9] and the U.S.-
oriented curricula (Imaizumi 1994a: 34; Wilson 1995: 27).[10] Moreover, programmes to bring Palauans on tours to Japan (called
内地観光 *naichi kankō*) and to provide grants for an increasing number of Palauans to travel and study in the U.S. were organised, with a
clear aim of making the Palauans pro-Japan and pro-U.S.,
respectively (Imaizumi 1994a: 29, 1994b: 568; U.S. Solomon Report
1963: 22, 47 and 52 in Anglim 1988).

In terms of reform of the political economy, however, the Japanese and American governments (i.e. 南洋庁 *Nan'yō-chō*; and the
TTPI government, respectively) each took different approaches. This
seems to reflect each government's different goals. The Japanese
government sought to achieve maximum profits from commercial
industry by integrating the Palauan economy into the Great East Asia
Co-Prosperity Sphere (i.e. 大東亜帝国圏 [*daitōateikokuken*]), in
addition to the establishment of a military base (Vidich 1952: 158).
Therefore, large government subsidiary companies were established
which recruited an enormous number of labourers from Japan as well
as smaller numbers from Palau and other Micronesian islands. The
only target of the American government, on the other hand, was to
legitimate their permanent use of land for the military purposes.
Therefore, they had no interest either in developing the local
economy or in international commercial trade (Vidich 1952: 269).
On the contrary, in order to ensure the retention of their permanent
relationship with Palau, the U.S. plan was to make the Palauans

totally economically dependent on the U.S. (U.S. Solomon Report 1963 in Anglim 1988: 10).

Such active participation by the Japanese government, and the lack of American involvement in the development of the *local economy*, led to differing effects on the formation of native "elites" in the *local political economy*. Traditionally in Palau, caste and kinship have had a complex relationship that underpins Palauan social hierarchy and economic and political organisation.[11] A hereditary caste hierarchy exists (i.e. *meteet; bukul a blai; olues blu;* and *ebuul*; from "top" to "bottom"), each of whose members' activities and behaviour are accordingly prescribed and limited (Vidich 1952: 58). For example, each clan group hereditarily has a different degree of involvement in political and economic affairs, in decision-making and in the possession of land and the traditional symbol of prestige, Palauan money (Vidich 1952: 58).

Further, individuals belong to two *kebliil* (i.e. the basic unit of the extended family); one has patrilineal linkage, the other matrilineal, although it is the *latter* that generally provides more privileges in Palau (Vidich 1952: 34–36). Each *kebliil* has, at least, three titleholders,[12] who have power over its members, and such power is exercised through a series of intensive obligations and rights of *kebliil* members to titleholders (Vidich 1952: 41–55).[13] There are a number of *kebliil* in each district, each of which is ranked according to traditional success in warfare, the possession of Palauan money and so forth. In particular, the top titleholders in Koror (*Ibedul*) and Melekeok Districts (*Reklai*) are the two high chiefs who hold the strongest power over the western and eastern parts of Palau, respectively. Therefore, traditional Palauan society is organised as a large neat pyramid. Roughly speaking, the two high chiefs are located at the top; the titleholders in each district are at the next stratum; and finally, all the *kebliil* members (i.e. the ordinary people) dominate the bottom. Thus, the stratification of traditional Palauan society is characterised by monopolisations of power by the high chiefs, the titleholders and the matrilineal kin of the *meteet*. Inevitably, this has brought about inter-group hostilities, competition and anxiety between those who, through ancestry, enjoy privileges, and those who do not (Vidich 1952; Shuster 1982).

During the Japanese era, the Japanese government introduced a capitalist ideology, providing rewards for skilled performance, regardless of the traditional social division (Vidich 1952: 194). This Japanese policy particularly appealed to individuals who felt disadvantaged by the stratification system based on lineage (Vidich 1952: 193, 205). Such individuals comprised two groups. One group was ordinary *kebliil* members who belong to the low-ranking clan (i.e. *olues blu* and *ebuul*) in the indigenous caste system. Another group was the partrilineal kin of high-ranking clan (i.e. *meteet* and *bukul a blai)*, who did not have the same rights to inherit title, lands and money as those of the matrilineal kin. Consequently, many Palauans accepted the capitalist ideology and eagerly participated in training offered by Japanese schools in new skills. In turn, this assured their upward mobility in the newly formed social hierarchy. In other words, they took advantage of its possibility for new prestige (i.e. educational and occupational) and for new income (i.e. Japanese yen) that would have been denied to them under the indigenous system. Many of them became retailers, brokers, real estate agents, accountants, clerks in department stores, hotel managers, and restaurant owners (Vidich 1952: 199). Further, some became police officers, court clerks and bureaucratic officials in the headquarters of the *Nan'yō-chō* (Vidich 1952: 199, 203, 205). The latter group not only co-operated with, but also manipulated the Japanese government, in order to enhance and stabilise their position within the native Palau society (Vidich 1952: 220–221). For example, a new regulation, which allowed them to buy traditional symbols of prestige (i.e. Palauan money) with yen, was legitimated (Vidich 1952: 214–215).[14] These groups formed a new local elite group of entrepreneurs and collaborators who enjoyed a new prestige and legitimacy under the Japanese regime. However, at the same time, the Japanese administration reduced and challenged the prestige, power and authority of the traditional elite, such as the high chiefs, the titleholders and the matrilineal kin of the *meteet*.

Thus, two opposing forces existed within indigenous Palauan society during the Japanese period: the new local elite (including entrepreneurs and collaborators who generally belonged either to the lower-ranking clan or to the patrilineal kin of high-ranking clan) became the dominant group, while the traditional elite (i.e. high chiefs, titleholders and matrilineal kin of high-ranking clan) became an opposition force, having seen their power and influence diminished.

On the other hand, wishing only to legitimate their use of land for military purposes. the American administration introduced "American-style consumerism" and encouraged "growth of the public sector and stagnation of the private sector" (U.S. Solomon Report 1963 in Anglim 1988: 10). This effectively made Palauans completely dependent economically on the U.S., leaving no operative industry. In particular, the U.S. planned to produce a local elite loyal to the U.S. by manipulating official appointments and by providing American funds "through the local elite whose interests would thereby become linked with those of the U.S." (U.S. Solomon Report 1963 in Anglim 1988: 10). For this purpose, the American government targeted the traditional elite, such as the two high chiefs, titleholders and matrilineal kin of the *meteet*, who were in opposition to the Japanese colonial administration (Vidich 1952: 272). Consequently, those traditional elite resumed their position of control and governed Palau, according to the traditional leadership and "native customary law" (Vidich 1952: 298). However, a superficial division of executive, legislative and judicial functions allowed the traditional elite to determine what constituted "native custom", one consequence of which was a regular abuse of power (Vidich 1952: 297–298).[15] Backed by slogans such as "Palau for the Palauans" and "Democracy for Palau", the U.S. government thus turned the traditional elite into the new local political leaders, who made up the "puppet" government (Vidich 1952: 344).

At the same time, this new power structure created a situation where the intellectuals who had acquired qualifications, skills and knowledge through education and jobs, and thereby achieved high income and prestige during the Japanese era, found it difficult to adapt to the relegitimised "traditional" native authorities (Vidich 1952: 323). The former local elite groups that had once belonged to suppressed lower-ranking clans were excluded from the new power structure, which was again monopolised by the traditional elite (Vidich 1952: 327–330). Conflict and resistance prevailed. The intellectuals denied the legitimacy of traditional leaders and the puppet government the power of which was granted only by virtue of the support of American administration (Vidich 1952: 273, 289, 293, 327–330, 344). Thus, the American regime reproduced the two (original) clearly opposing forces within indigenous Palauan society; the traditional elite became the dominant power, while the elite of the Japanese period became the opposition. Thus, both of the colonial administrations promoted different local elite groups, who tactically use the authority, prestige and resources of the colonial power to bolster their position and secure their own ends within the native society.

However, during the time (from the 1970s to 1994) when Palau was struggling to achieve independence from the U.S., the structure of such dominant and oppositional positions of the different elite groups changed. Occasionally violent conflict intensified between those who favoured and those who opposed the Compact of Free Association Agreement with the U.S. intensified, involving bombings and the death under suspicious circumstances of two Presidents of Palau. The traditional elite group generally supported the Agreement for its own sake, while the majority persistently opposed it in eight referenda over 10 years. However, through a manipulation of the Palauan constitution, and because the only realistic choice was between the Agreement and continued U.S. colonial rule, it was finally implemented in 1994.

How did such political complexity and fluidity of both the dominant and oppositional positions of the former colonial powers, and the constructions of local elite authority in Palauan society, facilitate hegemonic and counter-hegemonic linguistic practices in the islands?

3. Investigating language use

This research forms part of a broader investigation into multilingualism, language maintenance and shift, language obsolescence, and language (including dialect) contact in Palau. A variety of data were gathered in the capital, Koror, in 1997 and 1998. Six months of participant observation included 121 ethnographic interviews, 233 ethnographic questionnaires, 64 hours of recorded spontaneous conversation, and many hours of informal discussions with Palauans of all ranks (Matsumoto 1998, 1999, 2001a, 2001b, 2001c). Both the qualitative data based on ethnographic observations and interviews, and the quantitative data from the ethnographic questionnaire survey, highlighted how external hegemonic forces had instituted, developed and maintained diglossic linguistic practice, how that hegemony had radically altered parallel to changes in the colonial administration, and how paradoxical linguistic traces from an earlier diglossic relationship acted as a counter to what appeared to be an evolving English language dominance. Before discussing linguistic hegemony in Palau, a brief overview of language behaviour in *contemporary Palau* is necessary. An initial result of our questionnaire illustrates how the historical and political turmoil affected the language ability in the three languages (see Figure 1).

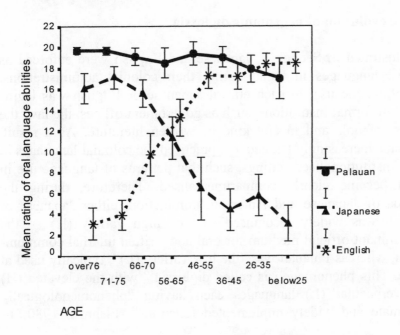

Figure 1. The relationship between oral language ability in the three languages and age (Rating of language ability: 0=lowest; 20=highest)

The older the speaker, the higher their Japanese oral language ability (i.e. speaking and understanding); younger speakers are prone to have higher English oral language ability. The crossing point of Japanese and English oral language ability among those aged between 56–65 neatly corresponds to the end of WWII.

Since independence in 1994, English has remained Palau's official language along with the indigenous language, Palauan, while the teaching of Japanese as a foreign language has been set up in Palauan schools. As a result, most older Palauans are Palauan-Japanese bilinguals. After 1945, however, competence in Japanese diminished rapidly, leaving many middle-aged Palauans as "semi-speakers", and younger islanders, who are bilingual in Palauan and English, as L2 learners. The legacy of the Japanese language period, however, has been both dramatic and powerful (as we will see in Section 5).

4. The evolution of hegemonic diglossia

As illustrated in Section 2, Japanese and English were enforced as official languages in Palau during their colonial administrations. Therefore, the use, in each era, of Japanese or English was legitimised in formal institutions, such as government offices, the law, the courts, schools and in any kind of written literature. As a result, Palauans increasingly learned and practised the colonial languages in those institutionalised settings, such that patterns of language use in Palau became clearly compartmentalised. Therefore, during the periods of Japanese and American domination, either Japanese or English was widely recognised as "the high variety (H)" – the predominant official medium for oral and written internal communication, whereas Palauan was "the low variety (L)", typically used at home. This phenomenon is called diglossia[16] with the elevated (H) and vernacular (L) languages each having "phenomenologically legitimate and widely implemented functions" (Fishman 1980: 1–15).[17]

Previous research on diglossia and hegemony[18] has suggested that five domains – namely, the economy (i.e. work); education (i.e. school); the mass media; literacy; and daily interaction (e.g. at home, neighbourhood, peers) – appear to be the key spheres where linguistic compartmentalisation is habitualised. In this section, therefore, examining the five key domains, we will address a number of research questions concerning diglossia and linguistic hegemony:

- To what extent did diglossic language practice, in effect, pene-trate Palau during the Japanese and American colonial govern-ments?
- Through which domains was diglossic language use developed and legitimised during each administration?
- Has political independence changed diglossic practice?
- Is diglossia the natural outcome of the course of history or a form of cultural and linguistic hegemony?
- Which dominant group benefits from diglossia in contemporary Palau?
- To what extent can the linguistic compartmentalisation implant the hierarchical status of the two languages in the speakers' consciousness?

Investigating the five key domains, we will begin by addressing *the first and second research questions*: i.e. to what extent linguistic compartmentalisation, in effect, penetrated Palau and through which domains diglossic language practice was developed and legitimised during the Japanese and American domination.

With regard to the educational domains, both the formal Japanese schools and organised out-of-school activities[19] provided institutions in which Palauan students not only learned Japanese but also used it in everyday contexts. The ethnographic questionnaire survey (Matsumoto 2001a, 2001c) suggests high attendance by Palauans of Japanese schools. Almost all elderly Palauans went to both elementary and secondary schools: more than 97% of those aged over 66 in 1998 had attended Japanese elementary school, while more than 83% had been in Japanese secondary schools. Moreover, 40% over 76, 37.1% of those aged 71–75, and 27% of those aged 70–66 in 1998 had received Japanese higher education. In ethnographic interviews with those who attended Japanese schools, all reported that they had to speak Japanese; in cases where they used

Palauan, they were punished. This suggests that Japanese as the high variety dominated the educational domain during the Japanese era, so that all of the participants used Japanese as a superposed variety.

As is common in many diglossic communities, Palau has an oral tradition; the language had no orthography until recently. Japanese textbooks in schools introduced Japanese writing systems to Palauan pupils; *katakana* (1st to 2nd grade), *hiragana* (2nd to 3rd grade) and *kanji* (3rd to 5th grade). Throughout the Japanese school education as well as in the subsequent labour market, therefore, Palauans were encouraged to write and read Japanese. However, *katakana* syllables have, consequently, come to be used as phonograms in *Palauan*. It appears that *katakana* was adopted as the Palauan orthography because Palauans learned *katakana* in the first and second grades and acquired it relatively more easily than *hiragana* and *kanji*[20]. Since then, *katakana* has started to function as an important medium for informal written communication between Palauans. For instance, Palauan in *katakana* was used for personal correspondence and short notes to exchange information in the market and so forth, as reported by Sakiyama (1990: 16) and as observed during our fieldwork.

Thus, during the Japanese era, the literacy domain demonstrates typical diglossic divisions of language use. Formal literature, such as school textbooks, major newspapers and official reports were written and read in Japanese, while informal materials, such as personal letters and short notes in the market were written and read in Palauan, using *katakana* as phonograms. In other words, a clear division between the high status of Japanese as a superposed variety, and the lower status of Palauan as a vernacular, was strictly maintained, with the H model shaping the newly developing orthography of the L.

Concerning work domains, dramatic economic progress in Palau during the Japanese period provoked intensive language contact with Japanese. First, Palau was the business and administrative centre of Micronesia[21] with an extensive employment market. Second, because Palauan students were the most academically successful in Micronesia, Palauans were more likely to be employed in higher status jobs. During the field research, many elderly Palauans proudly recounted how they used to work in the *Nan'yō-chō* or in large

Japanese enterprises, where the medium of communication was solely Japanese. Many Palauans therefore came into contact with Japanese in H domains. Further, in order to exploit Palau's natural resources, Japanese enterprises mostly brought manual workers from Japan, due to their expertise, rather than from Palau (南洋庁 *Nan'yō-chō* 1939: 59–61, 71).[22] This suggests that even the Palauans employed as *manual labourers* had face-to-face L-domain interaction with Japanese speakers at work.

Third, mass media are one of the domains in which the use of Japanese was dominant. However, whether the Palauans were actually an audience depends on the type of media. Japanese radio programmes were very popular among Palauans as well as the Japanese residents,[23] while the Japanese written media, such as magazines, newspapers and novels were less likely to have been popular in Palau and Micronesia as a whole. As mentioned above, this

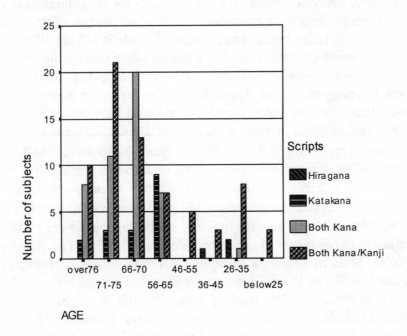

Figure 2. Japanese reading ability according to age

was partly due to the islands' oral tradition. The main reason for the low uptake of Japanese written media, however, is that they were printed in all three scripts i.e. *hiragana, katakana* and *kanji*; those who had acquired only *katakana* and/or *hiragana* would find comprehension of such texts problematic. Based on our ethnographic questionnaire survey, Figure 2 presents the self-reported ability in reading Japanese according to resident's age.

Nonetheless, there was one exception to this, namely "島民新聞" ([*tōmin shin'bun*] "Islanders Newspaper"), which was issued and distributed in Palau and written in Japanese, but using *katakana* only (Higuchi 1995: 188–197). It provided Palauans with war propaganda as well as reviews of *shushin* (morals and ethics) (Higuchi 1995: 195). No Palauan mass media existed at all during the Japanese period; hence, although written media may have had a restricted distribution among Palauans, the domain was clearly diglossic, with formal literacy in the H language predominant.

Finally, everyday interactions at home, in the neighbourhood and among peers should be considered. The chief means of communication in a Palauan home was Palauan,[24] while it is very likely that Japanese was frequently used when the islanders communicated with neighbouring Japanese residents. A massive influx of Japanese *civilian* immigrants into Palau during the Japanese administration meant that Japanese immigrants outnumbered Palauans in a ratio of four to one in 1941; in other words, about 24,000 Japanese and 6,000 Palauans were living in Palau (南洋庁 *Nan'yō-chō* 1942: 36–37). As noted earlier, importantly, most of these Japanese immigrants were farmers and fishermen who worked as a major labour force alongside Palauans in Japanese enterprises (南洋庁 *Nan'yō-chō* 1934, 1937, 1939, 1940, 1942). Thus, the majority of the Japanese were civilians, "rather than colonists" (Francis and Berg 1980: 471). The American scholar, Shuster, reports a personal interview with a Palauan; "The Japanese officials looked down on us Palauans but the ordinary Japanese was friendly...they tried to maintain good friendship" (Shuster 1982: 156). Such friendly past neighbourhood relationships have brought about a regular stream of visitors and a constant supply of retired Japanese from Japan, who were born and brought up in Palau, but who were expatriated to Japan with their Japanese immigrant parents after war. Reunions for those who used to study in elementary schools in Palau are still organised; in 1990, more than 100 Japanese and some Palauan graduates gathered in Hokkaido, Japan (*Hokkaidō Nan'yō-kai* 北海道南洋会 [Hokkaidō Nan'yō Association] 1990).

Second, the settlement pattern of these Japanese civilian immigrants in Palau was different from that which took place in other former Japanese colonies in Asia, such as in Korea and China, in that they generally lived alongside indigenous Palauan residents in the same community rather than in an exclusive Japanese community.[25] In Koror and Angaur, where Japanese residents outnumbered the locals, the Palauans and Japanese lived in mixed residential areas, and engaged in regular and "equal" interactions. These conditions correspond to the stories told by many elderly Palauans during ethnographic interviews conducted by Matsumoto in 1997–1998. When young, they used to play with their neighbouring Japanese children; thereby, even before going to school, many had already acquired Japanese, Japanese songs and fairy tales and special songs to memorise multiplication. Thus, although this depended on the residential area, in the main commercial centre of Koror and the industrial island of Angaur, at least, it is very likely that the Palauan children came into intensive contact with, and used, Japanese while playing. It should be noted, however, that even in this informal, friendly and intimate setting, the Japanese did not learn Palauan – not untypical, of course, of colonial diglossic speech communities.

On the other hand, during the American domination and since independence, linguistic compartmentalisation in the five diagnostic diglossic domains differs from the Japanese period. With regard to the educational domains, American textbooks are still predominantly used. American history and geography are taught. In particular, most Palauans attend higher education in English, not only in the U.S., but also in Palau or other Micronesian islands. According to the results of the ethnographic questionnaire survey (Matsumoto 2001a, 2001c), 41.7% of those aged 46–55; 70% of those aged 36–45; 60% of those aged 26–35 and 50% of those aged below 25 received higher education solely in English.

In the late 1980s, bilingual education (i.e. the use of both Palauan and English) was introduced to some elementary and high schools in Palau (Spencer 1994). However, the remainder still teach subjects in English only (Matsumoto 2001a, 2001c). Not until fairly recently was emphasis placed on the importance of the indigenous language by editing Palauan textbooks[26] and teaching school subjects in Palauan. As a result, at a few elementary schools, subjects have begun to be taught in Palauan only or, in most cases, both in Palauan and English (Matsumoto 2001a, 2001c). However, it should be noted that the remaining Palauan schools still teach solely in English, according to our questionnaire survey (Matsumoto 2001a, 2001c). Thus, although it depends on the educational level, overall the predominant use of English is still observed in education.

In terms of literacy, the Roman alphabet became used as another Palauan orthography. However, the development of a Palauan orthographic system has been controversial, and no system has yet been fully agreed upon and stabilised. As a result, use of both the Japanese *kana* (i.e. *hiragana* and *katakana*) and the Roman alphabet for Palauan reading and writing appears to be common practice (see Figure 3) (Matsumoto 2001b, 2001c).

The official ballot papers for the 1992 and 1997 general elections in Koror, Melekeok and Angaur States, for example, adopted dual orthographies in Palauan. They used a duel writing system for names of Palauan candidates (i.e. the Roman alphabet and Japanese *katakana*), with Palauan-English bilingual instructions both in the Roman alphabet.

In reality, however, Palauan reading materials are very limited in number and type (e.g. the Constitution of the Republic of Palau), while almost all reading materials are written in English and from America. The Palauan Constitutional Law of 1979 also indicates that, in judicial and administrative matters, English ought to prevail over Palauan, although the *national* language is Palauan and the *official* languages are currently both Palauan and English (Article XIII, General Provisions, Section 1). Therefore, all official documents and reports have to be written in English. Thus, it seems that the Palauan orthography, at this moment, has merely "decorative" or "symbolic"

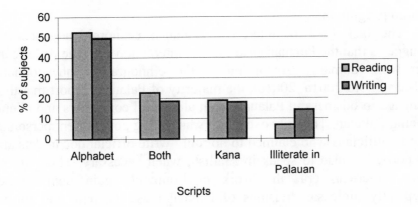

Figure 3. Self-reported ability in reading and writing Palauan in different scripts

functions, rather than practical and functional ones,[27] while English is still used for almost all literature in contemporary Palau. This demonstrates that literacy in Palau is still in the stage of classic diglossia, in that "the L form would generally seem odd in writing" (Holmes 1992: 33).

Third, mass media are a domain where English has dominated. For example, the only local Palauan newspaper (i.e. *Tia Belau*) is written solely in English, with the exception of Palauan words used in the cartoons and greetings in the personal news. Among television outlets, one Palauan channel (Channel 6), one Japanese channel (NHK) and several American satellite channels (i.e., Discovery Channel, CNN, Cartoon Network and a film channel) are available. However, it should be noted that Channel 6 is on the air for restricted hours, providing a rather narrow range of programmes, e.g. coverage of debates in the Palauan Congress, Micronesian and Polynesian shows, dances and cultural meetings and videotaped traditional Palauan ceremonies in private houses and it repeatedly broadcasts the same programmes. The radio programmes, however, are predominantly in Palauan, with considerable English-Palauan code-switching and Japanese borrowing. Thus, the mass media represents neatly exclusive linguistic compartmentalisation, where English as H is used in more formal contexts, such as newspapers and Congress, while Palauan as L is used in less formal contexts, such as the local radio programmes.

The lack of U.S. interest in Palauan economic advancement suggests that the Palauans had far less interaction with the Americans in work domains. According to the ethnographic questionnaire (Matsumoto 2001a, 2001c), the majority of Palauans report that they engage in business in Palauan, with almost all consumers and clients being Palauan. The only exception was among government personnel and politicians who claimed to not only write official documents and reports, but also to speak in English, when necessary. Thus, during the American era, the work environment again demonstrates typically diglossic divisions of language use. Official and formal institutions, such as government offices, the congress and court, oblige Palauans to use English, while in private spheres or local workplaces Palauan is the major means of communication. In other words, a clear division between the high status of English as a superposed variety and the lower status of Palauan as a vernacular was strictly maintained.

Finally, informal interactional domains should be examined. At home, Palauans speak in Palauan, as they did during the Japanese period, while the lack of American immigrants into Palau indicates that there were not many neighbourhood or peer-group domains where English was used. In contrast to the Japanese era, the small number of Americans temporarily stationed in Palau were military and administrative personnel, missionaries and school teachers.[28] Thus, the degree and frequency of everyday interaction between Americans and Palauans appear to have been far lower than between the locals and the Japanese.

So, throughout the colonial history of Palau, formal domains, such as education, literacy and the mass media have consistently been dominated by either Japanese or English. These formal social institutions appear to help reproduce a diglossic situation that is typical to post-colonial nations, where the former colonial language is an official high language, while the indigenous oral language is an informal low language.

An interesting point in the case of Palau is, however, the complete replacement of the high language, from Japanese to English, in a range of formal social institutions. Nevertheless, the disposition not to appropriate the Palauan language for formal social institutions still remains, despite the fact that Palauans have finally won their independence. Thus, the answer to *the third research question* as to whether the political independence has resulted in any change in diglossic practice seems to be "no".

We turn now to address *the fourth and fifth research questions*. Is diglossia the natural outcome of the course of history or a form of cultural and linguistic hegemony, in which a certain dominant group coerces others into accepting these practices as the norm, in order to take control and advance their interests? If the latter is the case, then, who benefits from the English imperialism in independent Palau?

A re-examination of the practices in formal social institutions, with some reference to the results of the ethnographic questionnaire survey (Matsumoto 2001a, 2001c), spotlights the establishment and maintenance of the symbolic authority of "status" in Palau. Concerning the mass media, for example, it seems that the Palauan channel on TV intentionally emphasises "localness", by broadcasting videotaped Polynesian dancing shows and Palauan traditional ceremonies, such as *bu'ul dil* (the birth ceremony) and *oheraol* (the house-building ceremony) in private houses. The obvious audience demand to watch the news, drama and films is fulfilled by the American or Japanese television programmes. Coverage of debates in the Congress is mainly in English, although the majority of the Palauan audience would be more likely to understand if it was in Palauan, rather than in English. This is because of their higher oral language ability in Palauan, as Figure 1 shows (in Section 3). The Palauan newspaper is written in English, even though it is known that it is incomprehensible to elderly Palauans, who are only literate in Japanese and Palauan, as Figure 4 illustrates.

Concerning language used in education, although Palauan teachers have started to deliver classes in Palauan, their students are still told to take notes in English. Higher education in Palau is open only to those who have a good command of English.

A most revealing example is that many elderly Palauans, who have no command of English at all, still watch American cartoons with their grandchildren everyday, without understanding them.

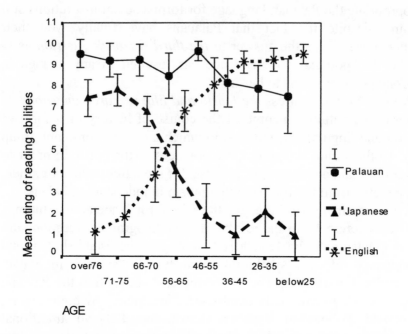

Figure 4. Reading abilities in three languages according to age. (Rating of language ability: 0=lowest; 10=highest).

Figure 5 illustrates the overall trend that the older the Palauan resident is, the more often they watch Japanese programmes and the less often the Palauan and American channels. However, those aged over 76 appear to show an anomaly in the frequency of watching Japanese and American satellite programmes. As opposed to the overall trend, their frequency of television watching in Japanese is lower than those aged between 71–75 and between 66–70, while that for English is much higher than those aged 71–75. Comparing this to Figure 1 in Section 3, it demonstrates that those elderly Palauans have no oral ability in English, but frequently watch English programmes.

As Woolard points out, "the test of legitimacy is the extent to which the population that does not control that variety acknowledges and endorses its authority, its correctness, its power to convince, and its right to be obeyed" (Woolard 1985: 741). Similarly, Holmes maintains that "people generally admire the H variety even when they can't understand it", exemplifying that "people generally respect and admire those that have mastered classical Arabic. But most of them couldn't understand what he was saying" (Holmes 1992: 34–35).

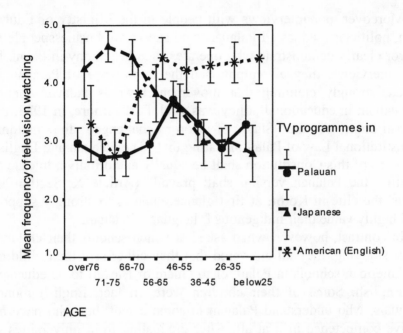

Figure 5. The frequency of television watching in the three languages according to age. (Frequency: 1=not at all; 2=rarely; 3=sometimes; 4=often; 5=everyday).

Thus, it appears that the conventional use of English in formal social institutions is not a natural outcome. Rather it serves to maintain the unassailability of the symbolic domination in Palauan society, by establishing the norms that accord legitimacy to English in public. At the same time, it restricts access to valued knowledge only to those who control English. Eckert (1980: 1056) rightly claims:

Diglossia does not arise; it is imposed from above in the form of an administrative, ritual or standard language. By virtue of its political and economic status, this language becomes requisite for access to power and mobility within the society. Therefore, diglossia cannot be socially or politically neutral... It is the availability of the high language to the masses (through free public education) that renders a language standard and thus democratic; but this does not render diglossia neutral.

Moreover, our interviews with people in the Ministry of Education, politicians, educated Palauans and successful businesspeople in Koror clearly demonstrate who operates such hegemony in Palau. In the interviews, they all emphasised the importance of Palauan in Palau, strongly claiming that movement towards Palauan monolingualism in educational policy was vital. Furthermore, in 1983, the Constitution of the State of Koror challenged the national Constitutional Law of Palau in stating that "The Palauan and English versions of this Constitution shall be equally authoritative; in case of conflict the Palauan version shall prevail" (Article X, Section 1). Thus, the elite in Koror, at first glance, appears to strongly support and highly value their indigenous L language, Palauan.

In contrast, however, when asked at which schools their children were studying, they all answered that they either sent their children to American schools in Palau, or to Guam or Hawaii to be educated in English. Some of their children were, in fact, English monolinguals, who understand Palauan to some extent, but who have no active competence in it at all. After graduating from universities in the U.S., these children of the elite will come back to Palau as the promised few who will automatically climb to the top of the socio-political hierarchy of Palauan democracy.

Thus, it becomes clear that the Palauan elite tactically manipulate language ideology through formal social institutions, in order to wield power and advance their interests. On the one hand, the elite continues to reproduce the normative hierarchical language ideologies, where English is dominant and Palauan is the oppositional language, through a range of formal social institutions. However, in public, they encourage others to promote the indigenous language while educating their own children in American schools. Such hypocrisy is not unusual. Engels, for example, discusses how upwardly mobile middle class Indians rejected local education systems and qualifications when universities on the British model were set up in colonial India (Engels 1994: 87–109). And Hill provides another interesting parallel to the Palauan case. In her research on language ideologies in a Mexicano (Nahuatl) speech community, she contrasts the nostalgic views of the high-status men who yearn for the good-old-days of *legitimo mexicano* (Mexicano with no Spanish borrowings) with those of women and low-status men who argue for bilingualism and reject the myth of the glory days past. Ironically, Hill finds that it is the upper status men who speak Mexicano in a very hispanized way, and the others use many fewer borrowings and are often able to speak only poor or even no Spanish at all (Hill 1998: 68–86).

Such a form of hegemony is quite common in many post-colonial communities. The local elite tends to strive towards the standardisation of their indigenous L language and the development of local orthographies. Yet they and/or their children are most educated in the former colonial H language, which stabilises "their" social position as the elite, while reinforcing the powerless position of the "others" they pretend to support. From this perspective, diglossia can be seen as "a force of stability" and "a structured means of reserving the vernacular for in-group use while speakers use the standard language for entrance into the wider society" (Eckert 1980: 113). The existence of such a "structure" or such "social mechanisms" that facilitate social hegemony has been pointed out both by Kaviraj (1994: 19),

> Hegemony refers to the conventional modes of arranging compliance to constituted authority, and this authority's search for a *langue* which makes such compliance assured and habitual,

and Bourdieu (1991: 113):

> [...] the language of authority never governs without the collaboration of those it governs, without the help of the *social mechanisms* capable of producing this complicity.

The *langue* and *social mechanisms,* in the case of Palau, are diglossia, that it is a "structure" that facilitates hegemony – the colonial power can govern with the H, and the people comply because they can continue to live their routines in their L1 L language. Both sides can then be portrayed as hegemonically satisfied.

Further, an examination of the status of the indigenous language that has evolved in contemporary Palau provides a number of differing perspectives. As highlighted in Figures 6 and 7, the results of the ethnographic questionnaire survey (Matsumoto 2001a, 2001c) clearly show that Palauan is recognised as the most important language in Palau, and that there is strong agreement to preserve it in Palau, rather than English and/or Japanese. These results indicate that Palauan is regarded not as the oppositional, but as the dominant language ideology amongst the Palauans. This is at odds with expectations based on previous diglossic studies in other communities in the world, where the indigenous oral language often has low status and is rated poorly by its own native speakers.

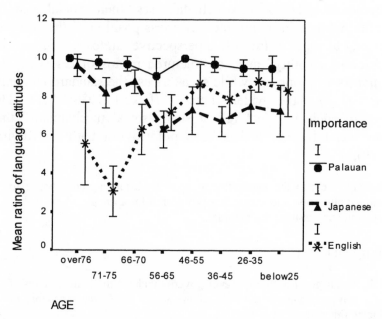

Figure 6. Assessment of language importance by Palauans. (Rating of language attitudes: 0=extremely unimportant; 10=extremely important).

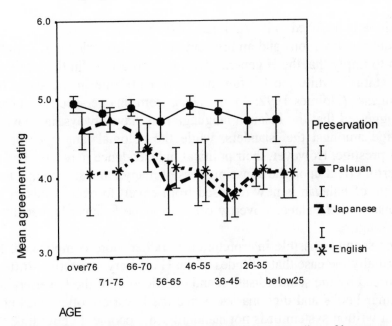

Figure 7. Desire to preserve language among Palauans. (Scaling of language attitudes: 1=strongly disagree; 2=disagree; 3=neither; 4=agree; 5=strongly agree to the proposition "In Palau, Palauan, Japanese and/or English should be preserved").

There are two possible ways to account for these unusual findings, in relation to *the sixth research question*: the extent to which the linguistic compartmentalisation implants the hierarchical status of the H and L languages in speakers' consciousness. First, symbolic domination in social institutions may not necessarily create authentic linguistic hegemony in the collective consciousness of Palauans. In other words, in spite of a century of coercive institutional domination, Palauans not only maintain the ability to use, but also value their language higher than other tongues. The attitudes to the H and L in a diglossic situation should be considered. As Holmes claims, "attitudes to the L variety are varied and often ambivalent" (Holmes 1992: 35). For instance, in the case of diglossic Paraguay, where Spanish (the language of colonisers) is the H, while Guaraní, the American Indian indigenous language is the L, of which most Paraguayans are proud (Rubin 1968). However, in Tahiti, some people deny the existence of L, while others are often more emotionally attached to it (Valdman 1988: 67–80).

Thus, such various and ambivalent attitudes towards the L variety seem to imply that the H generally has *overt* prestige "in the sense of high status", while the L often has *covert* prestige in the sense of "fondness" (Holmes 1992: 35–6). Thus, from this perspective, it can be suggested that the Palauan language may have always had covert prestige amongst the islanders, while the colonial languages have overt prestige. However, their political independence may have had a powerful effect upon the consciousness of many Palauans, so that the prestige of Palauan is now reversed from covert to overt. Thus, it is reasonable that Palauans overtly came to value Palauan higher than other tongues.

The second possible interpretation is rather more complicated. It is normally the case that attitudes to the H are very respectful – often reinforced by the standardisation and codification of the H variety in grammar books and dictionaries. Since the L variety often does not have a written system or is not standardised, "people do not think of the L variety as worth describing" (Holmes 1992: 35). In Haiti, for instance, although the Constitution declares that both French and the Creole are national languages, many Haitians still consider French, the H variety, to be the "only" "real" language of the country (Valdman 1988).

However, when the L language starts to gain status, its speakers start to use it in writing too (Holmes 1992: 36). As mentioned above, although not yet successful, the local elite has been attempting to establish and standardise Palauan grammars and an orthographic system, and to edit Palauan textbooks. Moreover, it was appealing to ordinary Palauans that the Constitution of the State of Koror promoted Palauan higher than English. Therefore, Palauans may value their language more highly than English and Japanese because, witnessing efforts by the elite, ordinary Palauans have "bought" the idea that Palauan is good, useful, multifunctional, an international language, supported and promoted by the nation's leaders. At the same time, however, this means that the ordinary people deny themselves access to languages which will bring them greater wealth. In other words, by encouraging the ordinary islanders to value Palauan, the elite Palauans may be succeeding in keeping the population acquiescent and making them feel that their culture is in control and dominant, even though the powers in the country, in fact, deny status to Palauan and have little confidence in Palauan education. As Gaitskell (1994: 110-130) explains, "the exercise of hegemony is the result of a kind of bargaining in which some account is taken of the interests and tendencies of the dominated group". Thus, the elite Palauans reproduce hegemony, tactically playing with the fluid dominant and oppositional ideologies of the former colonial and indigenous languages. From this perspective, the speakers' consciousness is moulded by the *langue* or social mechanism that is operated by elite Palauans.

5. Sweet bean paste and pickled radish: Japanese "traces" as counter-hegemonic resistance

According to our participant observation and recordings of naturally occurring conversations among Palauans at home, in communal gathering places and pubs, Palauan is the dominant language in the islands (Matsumoto 2001a, 2001b). However, linguistic borrowings, food-culture, lifestyles and music exceptionally and persistently provide examples of the paradoxical practice of Japanese linguistic resources. In diglossic situations, there is a tendency that "the H vocabulary includes many more formal and technical terms such as *conservation* and *psychometric*, while the L variety has words for everyday objects such as *saucepan* and *shoe*" (Holmes 1992: 33). However, in the case of the Japanese borrowings in Palauan, not only formal and technical words, such as *cheisei* (Jp. *eisei* "sanitation"); and names for modern products, such as *dengki* (Jp. *den'ki* "electricity") are adopted, but also those for everyday objects, such as *ben'jio* ("toilets"), the names of gardening equipment (e.g. *kumade* "bamboo rake"), kitchen utensils (e.g. *zaru* "colander"; *manaita* "chopping board") and clothes (e.g. *stangi*, Jp. *shitagi*, "underwear"). Also striking are numerous core Japanese adjectives that have been borrowed. For example, *uresi* (Jp. *ureshī*) "happy", "glad"; *omosiroi* (Jp. *omoshiroi*) "interesting", "funny"; *sabisi* (Jp. *sabishī*) "lonely"; *daiziob* (Jp. *daijōbu*) "all right", "OK"; *sukareter* (Jp. *tsukarete-iru*) "be tired", "exhausted"; *komeng* (Jp. *gomen*) "sorry"; *choisi* (Jp. *oi-shī*) "tasty"; *kantang (Jp. kan'tan)* "simple", "easy"; *kichigai* "crazy", "crazily". Furthermore, many other commonplace lexical items have come from Japanese: e.g. *chimi* (Jp. *imi*) "meaning"; *zikan* (Jp. *jikan*) "time"; *basio* (Jp. *basho*) "place"; *mongdai* (Jp. *mon'dai*) "problem"; *iakusoku* (Jp. *yakusoku*) "promise" (both n. and v.t.); *mongk* (Jp. *mon'ku*) "complaint", "complain"; *iotei* (Jp. *yotei*) "plan", "schedule"; *choto* (Jp. *oto*) "sound", "noise"; *kata* "shape"; *chazi* (Jp. *aji*) "taste"; *tsios* (Jp. *chōshi*) "condition", "state". An increasing number of English loan-words have also been adopted into Palauan. However, the categories of English loan words tend to represent a typically H lexicon, such as formal and technical jargons (e.g. *saing* "sign"; *kasinoma* "cancer"), but crucially *not* items of core vocabulary.

In addition, there are no McDonalds, big steaks with heaps of French fries or baked potatoes, nor Americanised local pop music in Palau. At home, Palauans eat rice, grilled or raw fish with soy sauce, using chopsticks. Japanese seasonings (e.g., soy sauce, *miso* and *ajinomoto*) and rice are something with which all kitchens in Palau are equipped. Japanese specialities, such as: *katsu-dong, oyako-dong, buta no shooga yaki*, which is stir-fried pork with ginger and soy sauce; and a variety of noodles, namely *yakisoba, udong, soba, raameng*, dominate the menus in restaurants. For lunch at work or on an *engsoku*, (a Japanese borrowing for "picnic"), Palauans prepare or buy *bengto* – the Japanese borrowing meaning "lunch box", filled with typical Japanese food, such as rice balls covered by seaweed paper, with *umeboshi* ("pickled plum") or *takuwang* ("pickled Japanese radish") inside; *tori no karaage* (referring to "deep-fried chicken with ginger"); *tempura*; and other kinds of Japanese pickled vegetables. The New-Year celebrations provide further examples. Palauans cook Japanese New-Year specialities, such as *osiruko* ("sweet bean paste") with rice cakes, and visit neighbours and relatives, saying *"omedeto"*, which is a Japanese borrowing, meaning "Happy New Year!". In addition, some Palauan socio-cultural practices derive from the Japanese era; *mizumaki*;[29] gardening using *kumade* (bamboo rake); and building *kakine* (fence). *Kinrōhōshi* (a Japanese borrowing, meaning volunteer work activities) is still practised; every Sunday, volunteers clean streets and gathering places, by picking up rubbish. At barbecues, *katorisengko* (Jp. *katorisen'kō*, "mosquito coil") are set up around the table. Thus, as Francis and Berg point out, it appears that the Palauan norms of living, eating and drinking vigorously incorporated Japanese practices (Francis and Berg 1980: 474).[30]

Thus, this suggests that something as culturally intimate as eating practices have been "invaded" by a Japanese culture. The extent to which McDonalds, Coca Cola and jeans have penetrated a country's way of life is often taken as a symbolic measure of the extent to which Americanisation has progressed. By the same token, the extent to which Japanese food and life style traditions have been assimilated into Palau may show the extent to which their hegemony was successful.

Finally, concerning music, on radio and during Palauan *traditional* ceremonies, pure Japanese *en'ka,* a kind of folk music, is played, as well as songs using a mixture of Palauan and Japanese words to Japanese melodies. For instance, the Japanese song, *kitaguni no haru*, called *shirakaba* in Palau, and *naniwabushi dayo jin'sei wa*, called *tetengkoteng*, were still ranked in the "top ten" (based on the number of requests by listeners) in 1998. Importantly, these Japanese songs are not the songs that were popular during the Japanese colonisation, but were chart successes in Japan during the 1980s when Palauans were fighting for their independence from the U.S. and when the Japanese government began to supply financial and technical aid to Palau (see Section 2). In other words, Palauans are trying to keep up with contemporary Japanese music: in particular, songs from the 1980s continued to attract Palauan ears in the late 1990s.

These paradoxical practices in informal social institutions may be due to different forms of domination and contact which occurred in Palau during each colonial era. As discussed in the previous section, common to the development of diglossia during both Japanese and American periods is their emphasis on literacy and education. However, what made their rule different was the use of Japanese which permeated daily informal interaction (e.g. in the neighbourhood and peer-group) and the work domain. It was relatively easy for the numerous Japanese civilian residents to transmit Japanese food-culture, lifestyles and music to their neighbouring Palauans in everyday life, while the lack of face-to-face interaction between Americans and Palauans did not lead to the same outcome in the informal social institutions. However, the key is its continuation. Therefore, the question that can now be addressed is what makes the Palauans continue to appropriate Japanese linguistic resources for these informal social institutions, after half a century of American domination in Palau?

There are three possible ways to account for this counterintuitive finding. First, such a finding may derive from a strong impact of *imperialism*, through which the Japanese colonial government attempted to transform Palauan values. Through their proactive stance in infiltrating Palauan social life and mores, the Japanese were successful in exerting power over the routine activities and common-sense meanings of everyday life for Palauans, which, as Giddens (1984) reminds us, represents a much more intimate and local stranglehold on behaviours and values, particularly since the routine and the local are so important for our socio-psychological well-being. Engels and Marks (1994: 3) noted a similar tactic in their investigations of hegemony in Africa and India: "Imperial hegemony had to come to terms with, incorporate and transform values".

Another possible interpretation is that this may be due to the effects of *intermarriage* – there are many half and quarter Japanese-Palauans in Palau. One of the Japanese government strategies was to encourage and reward intermarriage into Palauan families, particularly high-ranking clan and the titleholder families. Moreover, the influx of male civilian immigrants, the pattern of their settlement and the friendly relationship between the islanders and Japanese civilian immigrants seem to have all encouraged intermarriage.

As Figure 8 illustrates, the results of the ethnographic question-naire survey regarding the self-ascription of their own multiple ethnic identities (Matsumoto 2001a, 2001c) reveals that the Palauans feel most strongly that they are "Palauan". However, importantly, notice that Japanese identity never reaches the minimum score of zero and stays higher than American identity across all age groups. Thus, a sentimental attachment to "Japaneseness" amongst Palauans, particularly Japanese-Palauans, is likely to result in the use of Japanese resources in informal social institutions.

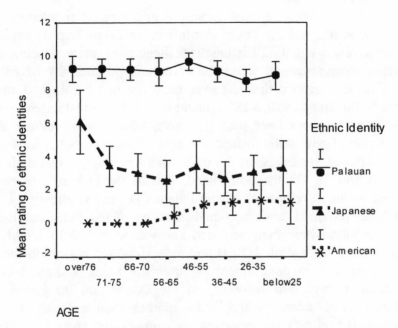

Figure 8. Multiple ethnic identities according to age. (Score: 0=not at all; 10=extremely to the question "do you feel that you are Palauan, Japanese and American? If so how strongly?").

The third interpretation goes beyond the first and second accounts. A combination of a sentimental attachment to "Japaneseness" and that Japanese used to serve as the high language in Palau, leads to Palauans using Japanese resources in informal social institutions, in an attempt to challenge the English dominant ideology in current Palauan society. In other words, this is a contest by the ordinary Palauans, who have barely any access to the newly created English-dominant social institutions. And this is a contest by the former local elites during the Japanese period (i.e. the entrepreneurs and collaborators who belong to the low-ranking clan, the patrilineal kin of the high-ranking clan, and the Japanese-Palauans), whose authority was reduced during the American regime. In other words, the adoption of Japanese resources in informal social institutions appears to serve as a symbolic resistance against the English dominant mainstream.

The contrast between the Japanese and American attempts to permeate social and economic institutions in Palau help us explain the relatively weak English language hegemony there. During the Japanese administration when the economic productivity of Palau soared to the greatest that has ever been reached before and since (Francis and Berg 1980: 438), education did, to a great extent, control access to the labour market. The academic achievement and acquisition of new skills in Japanese schools ensured better jobs and higher salaries, regardless of the traditional hereditary social division (see Section 2). On the other hand, due to the lack of American interest in the development of the Palauan economy, although U.S. education provided academic qualifications to the Palauans, there were no jobs where their acquired knowledge and skills could be fully applied or rewarded. In Bourdieu's view, the education factor alone cannot be a determinant of linguistic value without taking economic factors into account: "to the extent that the education system controls access to the labour market, then and only then it [education] becomes an important determinant and purveyor of this [linguistic] value" (Bourdieu 1982: 33–34, cited in Woolard 1985: 740). The weak relationship between the education system and the labour market during the U.S. domination thus brought serious drawbacks for English linguistic hegemony.

Therefore, if we consider the degree to which Japanese and American hegemony in Palau was successful, it seems that even after 50 years of American domination, the paradoxical Japanese traces have evolved into counter-dominant reminders of an apparently shallow and unconvincing English-language hegemony. The extent to which the Japanese hegemony is successful may be estimated by the extent to which the Japanese traces are immersed into everyday cultural life in the Palauan islands.

6. Conclusions

Nearly a century of coercive institutional domination by colonisers instilled the colonial languages, English and Japanese, into Palauan's high culture. The Japanese hegemony was more "successful" in that it penetrated the local and the everyday in a way which led to the diffusion of Japanese cultural (and therefore linguistic) norms and values to the general Palauan populace.

With the arrival of the Americans in 1945, English was established as the dominant language ideological force in formal social institutions. Given that the U.S. saw Palau as little more than a strategic aircraft carrier during the Cold War, however, it did little to advance the interests of Palauans, while attempting to make them dependent economically on American aid and support. Diglossia replaced diglossia, but was established, promoted and maintained in rather different ways. While the Japanese era saw a rather interventionist and integrationalist approach at engendering consent, the U.S. period was characterised by an aloof and hands-off stance.

Two paradoxes have emerged from our investigations of hegemony in this Western pacific context. Firstly, the role of the (different) local elites in promoting the cause of the overseas power, to the detriment of sections of their own populations. Engels and Marks have noted a similar process elsewhere:

> In India... the middle class developed such a dominant position especially in nationalist politics, but also in the new and crucial professions of law, education and medicine, that the powerless... were often subjected to two sets of related but at times competing hegemonic ideologies of the colonial state and of the indigenous elite. (Engels and Marks 1994: 4)

Such words closely mirror developments in Palau over the past 80 years.

Secondly, there is the role of Japanese *after* WWII. The success of their hegemony was such that core cultural and linguistic practices had been adopted and adapted to such an extent that they survived beyond the disintegration of the Japanese empire, and beyond the rule of the local meritocratic political system they had installed in Palau. Japanese words, phrases and expressions today form a substantial part of core Palauan vocabulary through the assimilation of borrowings.

And, these linguistic traces have served as counter-hegemonic displays against the domination both of the distant foreign rulers and the hypocritical traditional elites. The existence of such traces provides substantial evidence of the important role of *"L-domain" face-to-face contact* both in linguistic borrowing and diffusion,[31] and in the manufacture of consent and hegemony in colonial settings.

Our ethnographic questionnaire survey reveals that during the U.S. era, without intimate contact with Americans and with English, authentic linguistic hegemony has *not* been created in the collective consciousness of Palauans. To provide a language to a community without a cultural framework in which to practice it is hardly likely to be immediately successful. The vast majority of Palauans consider that Palauan is their first language, the most important language in Palau, and strongly agree that Palauan should be preserved there, rather than English and/or Japanese. Thus, in spite of a century of diglossic symbolic domination, the Palauans maintain the ability to use and value their indigenous language, while they tactically play with the fluid dominant and oppositional ideologies of the former colonial languages.

Notes

1. We would like to thank: all those in Palau who kindly extended their warm hospitality during fieldwork trips in 1997 and 1998; the audience at the 6th International Conference on World Englishes: World Englishes and Asian Identities, 27–30 July 1999, in Tsukuba, Japan for useful comments on a previous version of this paper; as well as Hiro Kurashina, David Shimizu, Donald Shuster, William Wuerch, Mary Spencer and Wakako Higuchi at Guam University, and Yoji Yamaguchi at the Asia-Pacific Institute at the Asia Centre of Japan in Tokyo.
2. See, for example, Blommaert (1999); Jaffe (1999); Woolard (1985) and the papers in Schieffelin, Woolard and Kroskrity (1998).
3. See, for example, Milroy and Milroy (1999); Lippi-Green (1997).
4. Most well known is the work of Norman Fairclough (1992, 1995, 2000).
5. See Gal (1987, 1989, 1993, 1995), and Heller (1992, 1995).
6. We use the terms interchangeably here, following Woolard (1985: 740).

7. Particularly since the Japanese-Palauan, Kunio Nakamura, became President of the Republic of Palau (1994–2000), a closer relationship between Palau and Japan has been reported. Shuster (2000: 217) reports that "President Nakamura"s courtesy visit to Emperor Akihito in early 1996 and the special status Mr. Nakamura, as a son of Japan, has for the Emperor" brought about enormous support for Palau. For example, $36 million was donated in order to rebuild a concrete bridge connecting the capital, Koror, to Babeldaob island which had been built by the U.S. in 1977 but which collapsed in 1996.

8. This involves diligence, benevolence, gratitude, honest and loyalty to the Emperor of Japan (*Kojien Dictionary* 1998: 1260).

9. This refers to the divinity of the Emperor and national pride (*Kojien Dictionary* 1998: 1752). Both *shushin* and *chokugo* were abolished in Japan in the end of WWII.

10. This was specifically designed to make the islanders become loyal to the U.S. (see the U.S. confidential document called the "Solomon Report" (1963) and Kobayashi (1994)).

11. See Vidich (1952), Palau Community Action Agency (1976) and the four volumes of anthropological studies by Hijikata (1993) for more details. The literature shows some discrepancies in detail which we do not attempt to address here. See Matsumoto (2001a) for further details.

12. They are (1) male headship; (2) assistant male headship; (3) female headship (Vidich 1952: 41–43).

13. When the *kebliil* head makes demands for food and Palauan money, a meeting called *aldaldu* is held for the collection of the money (Vidich 1952: 55).

14. Both sides benefited from this regulation. It was good for the Japanese government officials, since by fixing the exchange rate between the Palauan money and Japanese yen, they could stabilise the value of Palauan money (Vidich 1952: 254). It was also good for the Palauan manipulators, since in doing so, they were able to obtain both the new (i.e. education, occupation and income) and traditional (the Palauan money) prestige.

15. For instance, Heine (1970: 197) reports that the "elected" magistrates were almost always the hereditary chiefs.

16. For comprehensive views of diglossia, see Hudson (1992: 611–674, 1994: 926–930).

17. Ferguson (1959: 336–337) initially introduced the notion of diglossia, which deals with "distinct varieties of the same language", excluding "two distinct languages", although one of his examples was French and Haitian Creole. Therefore, this study applies the definition of diglossia proposed by Joshua Fishman (1967, 1980), that includes genetically unrelated varieties.

18. For example, Rubin (1968); Greenfield (1972); Fishman (1968: 21–49, 1972: 15–32); Woolard (1985).

19. For example, adult education (*seinen-dan*), old boy (*dōsō-kai*), and house-boy (*renshūsei*) systems were organised (see Matsumoto 2001a).

20. Due to the oral tradition in Micronesia and the irregular notation of the three

Japanese scripts, many *Micronesians* acquired only *katakana* script (Shuster 1982: 165–166; Sakiyama 1990: 16). Because of the phonological complexity of Palauan, *katakana*, however, is not a satisfactory phonogram to fully notate the Palauan language (Interviews 1998 January–April).

21. The Headquarters of the *Nan'yō-chō* was established in Koror in 1921.

22. For example, 8,148 Okinawan fishermen and farmers from Tohoku and Kanto Districts (1,133 and 1,782 respectively) were sent to Palau in 1938, while the total population of indigenous Palauans was 6,509 in 1937 (*Nan'yō-chō* 1939: 59–61, 71).

23. In the ethnographic interviews with elderly Palauans, for example, they commented that they used to listen to Japanese pop songs everyday through Japanese radio programmes, and they even proudly sung them.

24. Japanese colonial policy in Micronesia differed from that of Korea, China and Taiwan in that the imposition of Japanese language use at home was not enforced in the former, but was in the latter.

25. Each area of the Japanese Empire was governed by a different colonial government, each with its own policies.

26. The first textbook on Palauan history was published and began being used in schools in 1999 (Shuster 2000: 220).

27. In an ethnographic questionnaire survey, literate people could choose either a Palauan, Japanese or English version of the questionnaire depending on their language ability and preference. However, nobody in fact asked for the Palauan version of the questionnaire.

28. For example, Shuster (1982: 200) reports that there were only 20 children of American employed in Palau in 1952.

29. The practice, on very hot and dry days, of scattering water on the ground, in order to reduce the temperature and to avoid soil or dust being blown in the air.

30. During field research, many Palauans described certain rural islanders in other parts of Micronesia as "savage", simply because they eat *sashimi* (i.e. raw fish) *without soy sauce and chopsticks*. These comments exemplify how strongly that they believe that this way of eating fish is "Palauan".

31. As highlighted, for example, by Thomason and Kaufman (1988), and Trudgill (1986). See also Lippi-Green (1989: 213–234).

References

Anglim, John
    1988   Palau's strategic position places Palauan democracy at risk. *Working Paper* 40, 1–42. Peace Research Centre, Research School of Pacific Studies, Australian National University.

Blommaert, Jan (ed.)
    1999   *Language Ideological Debates*. Berlin: Mouton de Gruyter.

Bocock, Robert
1986   *Hegemony*. Chichester: Ellis Horwood.

Bourdieu, Pierre
1982   *Ce que parler veut dire*. Paris: Fayard.

1991   *Language and Symbolic Power*. Cambridge: Harvard University Press.

Eckert, Penelope
1980   Diglossia: Separate and unequal. *Linguistics* 18, 1053–1064.

Engels, Dagmar
1994   Modes of knowledge, modes of power: universities in 19th-century India. In: Engels, Dagmar and Shula Marks (eds.), *Contesting Colonial Hegemony: State and Society in Africa and India*. London: British Academic Press, 87–109.

Engels, Dagmar, and Shula Marks
1994   Introduction: Hegemony in a colonial context. In: Engels, Dagmar, and Shula Marks (eds.), *Contesting Colonial Hegemony: State and Society in Africa and India*. London: British Academic Press, 1–18.

Fairclough, Norman
1992   *Critical Language Awareness*. Harlow: Longman.

1995   *Critical Discourse Analysis: The Critical Study of Language*. London: Longman.

2000   *New Labour, New Language*. London: Routledge.

Ferguson, Charles
1959   Diglossia. *Word* 15, 325–340.

Fishman, Joshua A.
1967   Bilingualism with and without diglossia: Diglossia with and without bilingualism. *Journal of Social Issues* 23(2), 29–38.

1968   Sociolinguistic perspective on the study of bilingualism. *Linguistics* 39, 21–49.

1972   The relationship between micro- and macro-sociolinguistics in the
           study of who speaks what language to whom and when. In: Pride,
           John and Janet Holmes (Eds.), *Sociolinguistics: Selected Readings*.
           Harmondsworth: Penguin, 15–32.

1980   Bilingualism and biculturism as individual and as societal phenom-
           ena. *Journal of Multilingual & Multicultural Development* 1, 1–15.

Francis, Hezel, and M. L. Berg
1980   *Micronesia: Winds of Change*. Saipan: Trust Territory of the Pacific
           Islands.

Gaitskell, Deborah
1994   At home with hegemony? Coercion and consent in the education of
           African girls for domesticity in South Africa before 1910. In Engels,
           Dagmar, and Shula Marks (eds.), *Contesting Colonial Hegemony:
           State and Society in Africa and India*. London: British Academic
           Press, 110–130.

Gal, Susan
1987   Codeswitching and consciousness in the European periphery. *Ameri-
           can Ethnologist* 14, 637–653.

1989   Language and political economy. *Annual Review of Anthropology*
           18, 345–367.

1993   Diversity and contestation in linguistic ideologies: German speakers
           in Hungary. *Language in Society* 22(3), 337–360.

1995   Cultural bases of language-use among German-speakers in Hungary.
           International Journal of the Sociology of Language 111, 93–102.

Giddens, Anthony
1984   *The Constitution of Society*. Cambridge: Polity Press.

Greenfield, Lawrence
1972   Situational measures of normative language views in relation to per-
           son, place and topic among Puerto Rican bilinguals. In: Fishman,
           Joshua A. (ed.), *Advances in the Sociology of Language Vol. II*. The
           Hague: Mouton de Gruyter, 17–35.

Heine, Carl
  1970   Micronesia: Unification and the coming of self-government. In:
            Ward, Marian (ed.), *The Politics of Melanesia: Fourth Waigani
            Seminar at Australia National University.* Canberra: Australia Na-
            tional University, 193–206.

Heller, Monica
  1992   The Politics of codeswitching and language choice. *Journal of Multi-
            lingual and Multicultural Development* 13(1&2), 123–142.

  1995   Language choice, social institutions and symbolic domination. *Lan-
            guage in Society* 24(3), 373–405.

Higuchi, Wakako
  1995   パラオに残る日本語伝説 [Japanese legends in Palau]. 文藝春秋
            Bungeishuju 27(4), 188–197.

Hijikata, Hisakatsu
  1993   *Society and Life in Palau.* Tokyo: The Sasakawa Peace Foundation.

Hill, Jane
  1998   "Today there is no respect": Nostalgia, "respect" and oppositional
            discourse in Mexicano (Nahuatl) language ideology. In: Schieffelin,
            Bambi B., Kathryn Woolard, and Paul V. Kroskrity (eds.), *Language
            Ideologies: Practice and Theory.* Oxford: Oxford University Press,
            68–86.

Hokkaidō Nan'yō-kai 北海道南洋会 [Hokkaidō Nan'yō Association]
  1990   *第5回全パラオ小学校連合同窓会北海道大会 [5ᵗʰ Reunion for
            the Palau Elementary Schools, Hokkaido, 8–9 July 1990].*

Holmes, Janet
  1992   *An Introduction to Sociolinguistics.* Longman: London.

Hudson, Alan
  1992   Diglossia: A bibliographic review. *Language in Society* 21, 611–674.

  1994   Diglossia. In: Asher, R. E. (ed.), *The Encyclopedia of Language and
            Linguistics.* Oxford: Pergamon Press, 926–930.

Imaizumi, Yumiko
   1994a   南洋庁の公学校教育方針と教育実態：１９３０
            年代初頭を中心に [Polices and practice in Japanese public schools
            in Micronesia: During the early 1930s], *沖縄文化研究 [A Study of
            Okinawan Culture]*. Tokyo: 法政大学沖縄文化研究所 [Institute of
            Okinawan Culture at Hosei University], 567–617.

   1994b   国際連盟での審査にみる南洋群島現地政策：１９３０
            年代初頭までを中心に [How the League of Nations examined the
            Japanese policies in Micronesia: Until the early 1930s], *歴史学研究
            Rekishigaku Kenkyu [A Study of History]* 665, 26–80.

Jaffe, Alexandra
   1999   *Ideologies in Action: Language Politics on Corsica*. Berlin: Mouton
            de Gruyter.

Kaviraj, Sudipta
   1994   On the construction of colonial power: structure, discourse, hegem-
            ony. In: Engels, Dagmar and Shula Marks (eds.), *Contesting
            Colonial Hegemony: State and Society in Africa and India*. London:
            British Academic Press, 19–54.

Kobayashi, Izumi
   1994
            *アメリカ極秘文書と信託統治の終焉－ソロモン報告・ミクロ
            ネシアの独立 [U.S. Confidential Paper and Termination of the UN
            Trusteeship: Solomon Report, Independence of Micronesia]*. Tokyo:
            Toshindo Publishing.

Kojien Dictionary
   1998   (5th ed.) Tokyo: Iwanami Shoten.

Lippi-Green, Rosina
   1989   Social network integration and language contact in progress in a
            rural alpine village. *Language in Society* 18, 213–234.

   1997   *English with an Accent*. London: Routledge.

Matsumoto, Kazuko
   1998   A discussion of methodology and data in ethnographic research: A
            case of field research in the Republic of Palau, Micronesia. Paper
            presented at 3rd Annual Graduate Sociolinguistics Conference, June
            1998, Essex.

1999   The politics of language choice amongst Palauan, English and Japanese: Symbolic domination in the Republic of Palau, Micronesia. In: *World Englishes and Asian Identities: IAWE-VI at Tsukuba, Japan. Proceedings of the Sixth International Conference on World Englishes 27–30 July 1999.* Nagoya: IAWE-Japan, 91–95.

2001a   Language Contact and Change in Multilingual Palau, Micronesia. Unpublished Ph.D. Thesis. Colchester: University of Essex.

2001b   A social network study of language shift and maintenance in a multilingual Micronesian society. *Essex Graduate Student Papers in Language and Linguistics,* Vol. 3. Department of Language and Linguistics, University of Essex, 105–132.

2001c   Multilingualism in Palau: Language contact with Japanese and English. In: McAuley, Thomas E. (ed.), *Language Change in East Asia.* London: Curzon Press, 87–142.

Milroy, James, and Lesley Milroy
1999   *Authority in Language: Investigating Standard English* (third edition). London: Routledge.

Nanyō-chō [South Seas Government]
1934   南洋群島要覧 *[Annual Report on Micronesia].* Tokyo.

1937   南洋群島要覧 *[Annual Report on Micronesia].* Tokyo.

1939   南洋群島要覧 *[Annual Report on Micronesia].* Tokyo.

1940   南洋群島要覧 *[Annual Report on Micronesia].* Tokyo.

1942   南洋群島要覧 *[Annual Report on Micronesia].* Tokyo

The Office of Planning and Statistics
1997   *1995 Census of Population and Housing: Palau.* Koror, Palau.

The Republic of Palau
1979   *Constitution of the Republic of Palau.* Koror, Palau.

Rubin, Joan
1968   *National Bilingualism in Paraguay.* The Hague: Mouton.

Sakiyama, Osamu
  1990   日本語のもうひとつの歩み [A development of overseas Japa-
            nese]. みんぱく *Minpaku,* 15–17, Tokyo.

Schieffelin, Bambi, Kathryn Woolard, and Paul Kroskrity (eds.)
  1998   *Language Ideologies: Practice and Theory.* Oxford: Oxford Univer-
            sity Press.

Shuster, Donald
  1982   Islands of change in Palau: Church, school, and elected government,
            1891–1981. Unpublished Ph.D. Thesis. Honolulu: University of
            Hawaii.

  1995   Micronesia in review: Issues and events, 1 July 1993 to 1 July 1994:
            Palau. *The Contemporary Pacific: A Journal of Island
            Affairs.* 7(1), 126–129.

  1998   Micronesia in review: Issues and events, 1 July 1996 to 1 July 1997:
            Palau. *The Contemporary Pacific: A Journal of Island Affairs* 10(1),
            188–191.

  2000   Micronesia in review: Issues and events, 1 July 1998 to 1 July 1999:
            Palau. *The Contemporary Pacific: A Journal of Island Affairs.* 12(1),
            217–220.

Solomon, Anthony
  1963   *A Report by the U.S. Government Survey Mission to the Trust Terri-
            tory of the Pacific Islands.* (Excerpts from this report: reprinted in
            McHenry, Donald F. (1975), *Micronesia: Trust Betrayed: Altruism
            vs. Self-interest in American Foreign Policy.* New York: Carnegie
            Endowment for International Peace; reprinted in Kobayashi, Izumi
            (1994), *U.S. Confidential Paper & Termination of the UN
            Trusteeship: Solomon Report, Independence of Micronesia.* Tokyo:
            Toshindo).

Spencer, Mary
  1994   The dream of balanced bilingualism in Micronesia: Evidence from
            Palau. Paper presented at National Association for Asian and Pacific
            American Education Conference, 28 April 1994, Honolulu, Hawaii.

The State of Koror
  1983   *Constitution of the State of Koror.* Koror, Palau.

Thomason, Sarah Grey, and Terrence Kaufman
1988 *Language Contact, Creolization, and Genetic Linguistics.* Berkeley: University of California Press.

Trudgill, Peter
1986 *Dialects in Contact.* Oxford: Blackwell.

Valdman, Albert
1988 Diglossia and language conflict in Haiti. *International Journal of Sociology of Language* 71, 67–80.

Vidich, A.
1952 The political impact of colonial administration. Unpublished PhD Thesis. Cambridge: Harvard University.

Wilson, Lynn
1995 *Speaking to Power: Gender and Politics in the Western Pacific.* London: Routledge.

Woolard, Kathryn
1985 Language variation and cultural hegemony: Toward an integration of sociolinguistic and social theory. *American Ethnologist* 12 (4), 738–748.

"Keep your language and I'll keep mine": Politics, language and the construction of identities in Cyprus

Marilena Karyolemou

1. Introduction

In July 1989, the House of Representatives in Cyprus decided that the languages of instruction at the University of Cyprus, which was to open its doors in 1992, would be Greek and Turkish.[1] The decision put an end to an issue that was widely discussed in parliament[2] at the end of 1980 and the beginning of 1981, again at the end of 1986, and in several inter-ministerial and experts' committees since the early seventies.

This decision could seem odd to those familiar with the political problem known as the "Cyprus question" who are aware that Greek Cypriots and Turkish Cypriots have been living apart since the Turkish invasion of 1974. What was the purpose of such a decision? Apart from the few Turkish Cypriots who have chosen to stay in the southern part of Cyprus, it is obvious that no Turkish Cypriot can, for now, join the University of Cyprus. Further questions are raised by coalitions formed during subsequent House of Representatives discussions of the issue as some political parties switched positions between different sessions. During the 1986 discussions, both the communists of ΑΚΕΛ[3] and the rightists of ΔΗΣΥ[4], parties presumably with opposite ideological and political credos, defended the position that Greek and Turkish should be the languages of instruction. This seemingly odd alliance was opposed by the centrist party (ΔΗΚΟ[5]), then in power, which was pushing for a Greek-only solution. Equally paradoxical were 1989 discussions in the House, when an English-only option received support from only one party –

the Communists – despite many inter-ministerial committees, several reports of the UNESCO experts and the 1981 unanimous vote of the House of Representatives suggesting that English be one of the official languages of the University.

Realistic language planning cannot ignore that the two communities are separated by war, invasion, an occupation. That the island's two principal ethnicities were distinguished by their language and faith did not, until 1974, mean separation and division. Thereafter, however, speaking about each other in ways that preclude moving beyond stalemate has been part of the Cypriot "cold war" for almost three decades (Neack and Knudson 1999). Another important non-linguistic factor, however, had to be considered. Whatever decision was made, the interpretation of it was certain to be highly political, with political implications for the Cypriot society as a whole and for the Turkish Cypriot community in particular. For instance, what message would the Cypriot government send if the final decision leaned towards a Greek-only solution? Would not such a decision violate the constitutional provisions of the Cyprus Republic that recognized both Greek and Turkish as official state languages? Could it not be considered that such a decision would exclude Turkish Cypriots were political problems ever solved since the university would be unable to serve as a higher education establishment for *all* Cypriots? By adopting Greek-only instruction, the university would become, de facto, a communal or a national/Greek University.[6]

The languages-of-instruction question at the University was closely related to issues far wider than the character of the university itself.[7] It was also inextricably linked to the political choices of the broader Cypriot society. Therefore, it is not at all surprising that divergences in opinion that usually characterize the political dialogue in Cyprus, especially in efforts to find a solution to the "Cyprus problem", were crystallized and sometimes even amplified, in this discussion.

2. Linguistic equality and language use

Since the fall of the wall of Berlin and the reunification of Germany, Cyprus has the sad privilege of being referred to as the only divided country in Europe. The island's division due to the 1974 Turkish invasion was the culmination of a lengthy polarization of the Turkish and the Greek communities, which together made up 98% of the island's population. It would not be an exaggeration to say that this polarization had been favored by the 1960 Constitution. Pursuing a tradition of separation, which had been inaugurated by the Ottoman Empire and remained strong during the entire British occupation, many of its provisions established a clear distinction between the two communities. This concerned not only power sharing, where a proportional representation was adopted in the executive, legislative and judicial domains, according to a 3 to 1 ratio, but also areas such as education, that remained under the control of the two Communal Chambers that handled issues regarding education and religion.[8]

From the first decades of the 20th century, while Cyprus was still under British occupation, the demographic distribution of the two communities showed a strong tendency towards concentration of the population in ethnically unmixed rural communities or conglomerates within cities. The tendency to create ethnically unmixed areas led to the reduction of mixed villages from the number of 300 in 1891 to 254 in 1930, then to 114 in 1960 and, finally, to 48 in 1963. The rate of this concentration was inversely proportional to rising nationalism in both communities (Loizos 1981; Asmussen 1996).

The island's linguistic scenery followed, as expected, the paths of the demographic and the political dissociation of the two communities (Péchaux 1976, 1988). The 1960 Constitution safeguarded the linguistic equality of the two ethnic languages by recognizing them as official languages of the Cyprus State, thus consolidating the right of all the citizens to use the language of their choice in order to address executive and judicial organs. Linguistic equality was applied everywhere: in the State's supreme legislative body, the House of Representatives, Greek and Turkish deputies were using their mother tongues; in public administration and in all State organizations documents were published in both languages; both languages were inscribed on coins and stamps; on road signs the names of places were written in both Greek and Turkish. On the State radio and television stations, the same regulation foresaw the transmission of programs in Greek and in Turkish (adhering to the 3 to 1 ratio).[9]

Such strict regulation regarding the representation of the two communities in all domains of public life, and that they used to share the same geographical space, raises practical questions. For instance, how were the communication problems solved between the members of the two communities who worked together or came into daily contact?

The principle of linguistic equality and the coexistence of Greek Cypriots and Turkish Cypriots in the same working places, and the need for many to be acquainted with the language of the other community for public service employment – in theory – should have favored the appearance of a broad, if not generalized, bilingualism.

Available evidence suggests that there was a limited degree of bilingualism that took the form Turkish L1-Greek L2, thus favoring the use of Greek as a second language. But bilingualism in the form of Greek L1-Turkish L2 was much less frequent. Since Turkish Cypriots received no formal instruction in standard Greek at all, bilingualism was developing in favor of the Greek vernacular of Cyprus, that is the Cypriot dialect. Turkish Cypriots used the dialect in their everyday contacts with the Greek Cypriots. Although people occasionally reported cases of language shift in favor of Greek, these were exceptional and depended upon individual choices.[10] Turkish was maintained as the mother tongue of the great majority of Turkish Cypriots. Likewise, Cypriot Greek remained the mother tongue of the large majority of Greek Cypriots. The low degree of intermarriage that characterized the period after independence[11] reinforces this conclusion. The rare cases of intermarriage primarily involved people from villages where Greek Cypriots and Turkish Cypriots lived together. As the number of mixed villages diminished and contacts between members of the two communities became rare, intermarriage also became uncommon and the degree of bilingualism diminished accordingly.

Bilingualism involving Greek and Turkish was observed mainly within the lower and middle classes, whose members had often little or no formal language instruction. It comes as no surprise that bilinguals in both communities, albeit few, were more often encountered among villagers rather than among city people. Unlike what used to happen in the lower and middle social strata, upper social classes were often using English as a lingua franca for inter-communal communication. The use of English had been facilitated because many members of the two communities were graduates of English-speaking secondary schools or had been educated in English-speaking universities abroad. Although teaching English had been banned from Greek Cypriot primary and secondary education for several years after independence (Persianis and Polyviou 1992), its presence remained quite notable: knowledge of English was compulsory for clerks, English was used in written administrative documents, in the bank sector, in the correspondence of several Ministries, on road signs, and in the judiciary.

The low degree of bilingualism may be puzzling. Being a Turkish or a Greek Cypriot did not just signify having Turkish or Greek as a mother tongue; characteristics other than language such as religious faith and cultural allegiance equally contributed to someone being identified as member of one or the other ethnic group. As a consequence, of course, language was not sufficient for someone to move from one ethnic group to another. Therefore, learning the ethnic language of the out-group did not entail a high cost; bilinguals were not to be considered neither as renegades by the in-group nor as intruders by the out-group.

That learning the ethnic language of the out-group was "low cost" in psychological terms might have had a positive effect on bilingualism. But such a potential effect was negated by the ephemeral coexistence of the two communities and their gradual geo-political separation. While such division culminated in 1974, separation began as early as 1963–64 making contacts between members of the two communities more difficult and less desirable (Mavratsas 1998).

Further, the conception and functioning of the educational systems had assumed an essentially divisive role. From the very creation of the Cyprus Republic, education was considered as a strictly communal matter, not a state affair. Until 1965, Cyprus had no Ministry of Education. Two Communal (ethnic) Chambers were given separate authority over religious and educational matters. This provision carried on a well-established Ottoman tradition, whereby each ethnic community was responsible for its educational affairs.[12] In the new state, the central government did not have any authority over curricula, the appointment of teachers or the choice of books.[13]

In reality, the two educational systems were running parallel, both reproducing in large part those of Greece and Turkey, from where they received substantial help in the form of books and sometimes even teaching staff. Reluctance to build a common educational system or, at least, to accept some coordination by a central authority was due to the role that education was committed to play in the process of ethnic awareness. The educational systems were assigned the task of inculcating each ethnic group's values and beliefs, i.e. of instilling ethnic loyalty and religious conformity. This meant that Greek Cypriot schools taught loyalty to the Hellenic world, the Greek language and Orthodoxy, while Turkish Cypriot schools were stressing loyalty to Turkey, to the Turkish language and to Islam. These loyalties, perceived not only as distinct but also as completely incompatible, created and widened the gap between members of the two communities, leading to the formation of a strong ethno-nationalistic feeling. This ethno-nationalistic feeling impeded loyalty to the newly born state (state-nationalism) (Haymes 1997), a loyalty necessary to enshrine the integrity of the new political entity.

3. Language in higher education

In the final decision regarding the languages of instruction at the Cyprus university, it was necessary to consider the future relationship between the university and a) the wider Greek speaking world, where the Greek Cypriot community belonged ethnically and culturally, b) the Turkish Cypriots, who in spite the actual separation many Greek Cypriots consider as co-citizens and partners in a future federal state and c) the broader region of the Middle and Near East, where Cyprus belongs due to its geographical position.

Each of these spaces urged the adoption of a different linguistic option: e.g. ethno-cultural allegiance operated in favor of the Greek language, political allegiance in favor of the Turkish and the Greek languages, whereas the prospect of the creation of a regional University, an intellectual center for the whole region, pointed towards adopting English, *lingua franca* in the entire Eastern Mediterranean and the Near East.

In tertiary education, there existed already the example of private institutions with English as the language of instruction. This choice was due to two main factors. First, many of the private colleges used to collaborate with universities abroad, providing a short curriculum to their students (two to three years) with the possibility for them to complete their education in English speaking universities in Great Britain and the USA. Second, private colleges tended to attract a large number of their student-customers from the Middle and the Near East, the Arab Emirates, India and Pakistan. The use of English for instruction was also effective, either partly or totally, in some public institutions of tertiary education such as the Higher Technological Institute, the Hotel and Catering Institute, the Nursing School, the College of Forestry, the Mediterranean Institute of Management, etc (Persianis 1994–95).

The main phases of the discussion that took place in the House of Representatives occurred in October 1986 and July 1989. During the first period, debate focused on two options – the only-Greek option, supported by the centrist party (then in power) and socialist left (EΔEK[14]) (to a smaller extent) and the two-languages option which was supported by the communists and the extreme right.[15]

As highlighted earlier, the 1986 discussions saw political parties that are ideologically situated at opposite ends of the political spectrum – the communist left and the extreme right – adopt identical positions on the issue in favor of both Greek and Turkish. This alliance is even more paradoxical given that the Cypriot communist party systematically adopts a non-nationalistic approach, emphasizing characteristics that unite Greek Cypriots and Turkish Cypriots while the rightists promote and emphasize ethnic-cultural and thus Hellenic values (Peristianis 1995). The main common arguments used to justify this option were: (1) the respect of the Constitutional provisions, which gave equal official status to both ethnic languages, and (2) the respect of both communities' right to be instructed in their respective mother tongue.

Putting aside the political reality of the last few decades, i.e. the separation of the two communities and the consequent linguistic isolation, the two parties supported a linguistic choice, according to which Greek Cypriots and Turkish Cypriots would be able to share one of the most important cultural and intellectual institutions on the island (the University).

The Communists and the rightists shared a common position that formed the basis for such a language preference. In spite of the severe grievance that the Greek population of the island had suffered from the Turkish invasion – nearly one third of them were displaced by force from their homes – both parties agreed that the only possible way to achieve an agreement on the basis of a federal state where both Greek and Turkish Cypriots would participate, was to create a climate of cooperation and mutual trust between members of the two communities. The will to establish mutual trust was expressed in the political doctrine of *rapprochement,* which aimed at bringing together the two communities. This doctrine was formulated by the communist party in the aftermath of the Turkish invasion. In an effort to avoid the errors of the past, the communists asserted that mutual trust, lost in the midst of continual hostilities, could be generated, in spite of the physical separation of the two communities, only through truthful cooperation and support.

In light of political developments a few years later, this position was also adopted by the right-wing party, which was recognizing how important it was to extend the hand of peace to Turkish Cypriots if a viable solution to the Cyprus problem was to be found. Turkish Cypriots were seen to be suffering equally under a regime that gave Turkish military forces and new settlers from Turkey overwhelming power. The Turkish military occupation thereby reduced Turkish Cypriots to misery, third class citizens on their native island. The languages-of-the-university issue was a good opportunity for Greek Cypriot politicians to show that they really cared about Turkish Cypriots, even if separated, and that they were prepared to make decisions on such crucial matters as education by taking into account the Turkish Cypriot point of view *in absentia.* They therefore believed that opting for a two-languages-of-instruction policy would give the message of their political determination to cooperate with the "other community".

This was not at all the position of the center party that argued in favor of Greek-only instruction, supported by the socialist party and encouraged by several officials of the Greek government in Athens. The position of the center party was dictated by its stand on the Cyprus question. It criticized the Greek Cypriot side as compromising with an occupation force (the Turks of Turkey) aided by the Turkish Cypriots in their efforts to abolish the Cypriot Republic. According to them, Turkish Cypriots had acted against the integrity of their own state and, therefore, voluntarily placed themselves outside the legally recognized state. Their position was also dictated by their role as the party in power and by their relation to the government in Athens. In spite of occasional disagreements, these relations are traditionally regulated on the principle that, regardless of their political orientations and choices about interior or exterior policy, Greek governments are Cyprus' principal ally in the quest for justice. It is not, therefore, unusual to find out that the best ally of a socialist government in Athens is a rightist government in Cyprus and vice versa.

It is apparent that positions taken by political parties, i.e. the two-language-position and the Greek-only position, were driven more by political and ideological motives than by linguistic or pedagogical concerns. As a consequence, practical aspects of proposed solutions were altogether dismissed from the discussions.

4. *"Keep your language and I'll keep mine"*

From discussions that took place during this first phase is evident that all those who supported the two-languages solution had in mind creating a university with two parallel monolingual academic curricula, i.e. where students would be enrolled on the basis of their mother tongue and ethnic background. In other words, the two-languages-of-instruction solution projected a *diglossic* rather than a *bilingual* university where Turkish Cypriots would be instructed in Turkish and Greek Cypriots in Greek.

Practical considerations about the economic burden and functional difficulties that would be encountered in a university where courses would have to be taught in two languages were absent from these discussions. No concern was expressed regarding financial consequences of a dual administrative and academic body; obviously, after a separation of two decades and a half, few bilingual teachers or administrators remain who could be employed at the University.

Despite their stated intentions, the deputies' decision reproduced the linguistic model that had prevailed in primary and secondary education since the creation of the Cyprus Republic and for as long as the two communities had lived together. This model kept each community "stuck" to its ethnic tongue. Any possibility for students to join the curriculum in the language of their choice, irrespective of their ethnic origin, or to create a bilingual curriculum in every discipline, with all students obliged to enroll regardless of their ethnic origin or mother tongue, with teaching carried out in both languages, were not at all considered.

That such practical matters of organization were ignored could be because politicians were well aware that such a decision – although implying that the Cypriot Republic would have to provide in Turkish the curricula that are now being provided in Greek – was unlikely to materialize in the foreseeable future because of the communities' separation. Even for the few Turkish Cypriots who continue to live in the Cyprus Republic after 1974 and can now enroll at the Cyprus University, this question was not raised; they are all now bilingual in both Greek and Turkish and thus able to attend university courses in Greek.[16]

A bilingual university would raise wider issues of educational organization that, given the primary role of education in the production and reproduction of cultural-ethnic identities, are often perilous to discuss. Such an institution would, for instance, have to deal with such questions as the possibility of a systematic teaching of the two languages in secondary and even primary education. Such an eventuality is very hard to consider, due both to the political reality of isolation and the ways in which Greek and Turkish have always functioned as strong ethnic markers. Even if a federal state were foreseeable, this adjustment would require some degree of coordination between the two educational systems to establish a partially bilingual curriculum. But, educational systems have always been kept apart and under the authority of communal/ethnic institutions. Unless a lot of good will prevailed, such an attempt would be doomed to fail.

5. The idea of a mediating neutral language in higher education

A different solution was offered during the second phase of discussions that led to the final vote of July 13, 1989. Meanwhile, the Greek-and-Turkish-languages-of-instruction solution had gained ground, since it was by then supported by all parties including the centrists which, during the previous phase, had supported the Greek-only solution. This time dissenting voices focused on the role of English within the university. The old alliance of the right and communists broke up and a new coalition was created between the right wing, the center and the socialist left, on the one hand – which altogether rejected the use of English – versus the communists, the only party to support the use of English as one of the languages of instruction.

There was a series of arguments put forward to defend the use of English as a language of instruction. The first one was *economic*: an English teaching Cypriot University would attract students from other countries of the Middle East with obvious financial advantages for the economy of the island. The second one was *academic*: the use of English would encourage foreign scholars to visit and teach at the University, a fact that could guarantee high academic standards, thus making the University of Cyprus a regional cultural and intellectual center. But the main arguments in favor of English were of linguistic and ideological nature. The communist party argued that since the long separation of the two communities had led to linguistic isolation, the members of each community having no contact with the language of the other community, the use of a third common language would be necessary for communication between them. This could be possible by using English since this had become the first foreign language for many individuals in both communities (see also Karyolemou 1996). Again, the idea of a bilingual university in a future federal state, where all the students would be instructed in both Greek and Turkish regardless of their ethnic origin, was not even considered.

The position in favor of English was systematically outlined by the communist party, which argued that the English language could be used, along with Greek and Turkish, for specific academic subjects like economics, physical sciences, mathematics etc. These subjects were considered as culturally "neutral" because they did not involve any reference to cultural elements such as religion, literature, philosophy, etc.

The idea of a neutral language that could play the role of a binding link between the two communities had already been evoked in the unanimous resolution adopted by the House of Representatives in January 1981.[17] In many inter-ministerial committee reports and in several memoranda issued by UNESCO experts, it was pointed out that English, a language that had managed to gain a place in the island's linguistic scenery despite the limited duration of the British occupation in Cyprus (1878–1960) – a language deprived of the emotional and symbolic charges of the two ethnic languages – could assume an essential role in inter-ethnic communication.

6. Language options in bi- or multi-ethnic states

In cases of coexistence between different ethnolinguistic groups, three possibilities exist for solving the communication problem created by the use of different mother tongues, especially when these tongues have been recognized as official languages of the State on an equal basis.

First, each language can be used exclusively and solely by its native speakers. This is a phenomenon of *linguistic exclusivity*, capable of leading to a situation of non-communication unless corrective measures are taken. This case is similar to the case of *diglossia without bilingualism*, described by Fishman (1999), the difference being that in cases of diglossia without bilingualism usually appears a class of bilingual speakers who serve as mediators between the two (or more) ethnolinguistic groups. In cases of linguistic exclusivity, however, each ethnolinguistic group remains strictly monolingual. We can easily understand why linguistic polarization is not substantiated at a state level: it can easily lead to chaos. However, we can witness it in international organizations or organs such as the European Parliament, where each Euro-deputy may use, in the course of his interventions, his mother tongue. In such cases, simultaneous translation reduces the communication gap created by language variety. This is exactly what used to happen in the Cyprus House of Representatives, where simultaneous translation disentangled the problem created by the application of the principle of linguistic equality. As Grin suggests, simultaneous translation and interpretation is an alternative solution to inter-group communication when there is no "broad distribution of second language skills in the population" (Grin 1999: 18).

Second, broad bilingualism can develop, where most speakers, regardless of their ethnic origin, use both languages. Bilingualism may vary quantitatively, as to the number of speakers, as well as qualitatively, regarding the domains of language use. Bilingualism can be extended quantitatively but limited qualitatively – that is, linguistic abilities in the second language may be limited only to certain domains or for specific communicative acts. Likewise, it can be limited quantitatively, i.e. a second language might be confined to a small number of speakers, an elite, but still be extended qualitatively if speakers can handle both languages equally well in all domains and for all acts of communication. Bilingualism can also be equilibrated, i.e. quantitatively and qualitatively extended or limited. Although usually bilingualism develops in favor of the majority language, especially when this majority is politically and/or economically strong, it is not rare to see a minority language strengthen when this language is empowered by a small but politically or economically dynamic community, or supported by the existence of a regionally or wider linguistic community. Social and psychological benefits for bilingual speakers play a particularly important role in developing bilingualism; absence of benefits such as social advancement or recognition will impede the learning of an ethnic language as a second language. Persistent conflict between different ethnolinguistic groups may create conditions in which speakers of one language espouse values contrary to those promoted by another language group, thus rendering any identification to the out-group impossible and hindering any desire to learn and use the other group's language. Further, if persistent conflict yields political and economic self-sufficiency and geo-demographic division, contact between communities may become unnecessary, superfluous or even impossible. Further, if restrictions are imposed by the in-group upon its members, then bilingualism will be unlikely to rise above zero.

Many researchers have found that, as contacts between different ethno-religious groups weaken and each group becomes politically and economically autonomous (autonomy may be partial since group A may be autonomous vis-à-vis group B, but not vis-à-vis group C), the need to communicate with other ethno-religious groups will diminish, especially when coming apart takes the form of a complete rupture due to armed conflict. Similarly, Grin (1999: 18) notes that economic relations can affect the development of bilingualism or the maintenance of minority/ethnic languages. He suggests, for instance, that prosperous "ethnic businesses" influence patterns of linguistic behavior because they make unnecessary the knowledge of any language other than the minority/ethnic language and tend to favor monolingualism.

Third, different ethnolinguistic groups can use a lingua franca for intercommunication. A lingua franca can be an endogenous language – a natural medium of communication for a specific group of speakers. Or, it can be an exogenous language that counts large numbers of non-native speakers who can use it to a satisfactory degree. Very often this lingua franca is a legacy of colonization and does not constitute a native language for any indigenous group within the country. Recourse to a third language as a lingua franca could be part of a broader language policy that recognizes an exogenous language as the official language of a state. This policy has been named elsewhere a "policy of third resort" (*politique du tiers-refuge*; Karyolemou 1994b), because it is used as an excuse by authorities and people in power who do not wish to chose an official language among the endogenous languages. In this sense, the "policy of the third resort" creates more problems than it solves, generating a cleavage between those who master the language – a minority of speakers who have received a formal instruction in that language and can therefore control power – and the majority who do not command the language and are, consequently, excluded from exercising power.

Such cases are often encountered in African countries where the languages of the former colonizers had become official languages of the independent states. This state of affairs, as Nguessan (1998) underlines, has been disastrous not only for communication but also for democratic processes, since it excludes masses not only from positions of power but, more importantly, from the exercise of their basic civic rights.

In conflicts between ethnic or cultural groups, an exogenous *lingua franca* appears sometimes as a neutral, mediating language – especially when endogenous languages are marked strongly as ethnic attributes, and bilingualism or multilingualism is blocked by: (a) separate primary and secondary educational systems for each ethnic group in which no provision exists to promote other ethnic languages, (b) persistent demographic and political cleavages between different ethno-linguistic groups which at times yield armed conflict, and (c) rival values conveyed by ethnic languages that indelibly mark in-group membership.

Of course, learning a language is rarely sufficient to acquire in-group identity because other elements such as religion and cultural background partake in defining such membership. But in many cases, learning the language of another ethnic group is inhibited by psychological reasons that involve negative perceptions of other ethnic languages and their speakers.[18] In such cases, inter-ethnic communication can be established either through simultaneous translation or through the use of a *lingua franca*. While these two solutions are not necessarily opposed to each other – simultaneous translation may be accomplished through a *lingua franca* – simultaneous translation is more often encountered in organized bodies and institutions while the use of a *lingua franca* is more often encountered in face to face interactions.

7. Inclusion and exclusion through language planning choices

Language planning choices made by authorities or states play an essential role not only in engineering bi- or multilingualism (by favoring one of the three alternatives discussed above) but also and more importantly, in sharing power. Through language policies, authorities can allow or forbid mass participation or participation of specific ethnic or cultural groups in the control of state mechanisms.

De jure or *de facto* language policies are dictated by the political and ideological orientations of specific political parties or polities. Recognizing only one official language out of a multitude of languages spoken within a multilingual state, for example, excludes from power those who lack sufficient knowledge of the official language, whereas it benefits native speakers or those who have learned it as a second language. In such cases, antagonism between native speakers of an official language and second language learners of the same language may occur as the latter may exert pressures for access to elite positions. It may also be that native speakers adopt coercive measures in order to halt growing demands for a redistribution of elite positions by setting and encouraging a new linguistic goal. This has been, for instance, the case with Dutch colonials in Indonesia, who regularly encouraged the learning and use of Dutch. During the early 20th century, they suddenly revised their position in favor of Malay, a minority language in the Indonesian archipelago but a widely used *lingua franca*. Fearing that an increased demand on behalf of Indonesians to learn Dutch would increase competition for access to leading posts led The Hague to take such a step (Bostock 1997).

Does linguistic equality mandated by official recognition alone establish cooperation and trust between different ethno-cultural groups? Incontestably, each ethnic group's right to use its mother tongue in all instances of social life, including education, is an essential human and community right. To recognize the equality of languages, however, does not automatically guarantee equal treatment of all languages in all instances of communication, if only because there are numerically superior (widely used) and numerically inferior (lesser used) languages. Even less does such official recognition guarantee bilingualism. Two main factors can prevent the expansion of bilingualism – first, the absence of a desire to learn a second language and, second, the lack of means to accomplish such a goal.

When political events lead to internal conflicts and a polarization of different ethnic groups, the desire to learn each other's language can be obliterated. This is true particularly when ethnic groups are economically, politically or otherwise independent from one another. In such cases, inter-group communication problems can be resolved by using a third common language.

Open conflict clearly is not a prerequisite for the emergence of a *lingua franca*. Yet, internal conflict and ethnic isolation heighten the need for a *lingua franca*. Besides its function as a *common* medium, a *lingua franca* is also *neutral*, since it is dissociated from any positive feelings speakers usually attach to their ethnic languages, or from negative feelings generated by using the other group's ethnic mother tongue.

Of course, one can contest the notion of "neutral language" especially when the language considered as neutral is that of a former colonial power. The term "neutral" does not imply absolute neutrality but, instead, a relative neutrality compared to the subjectivity that characterizes the ethnic languages involved. A *lingua franca* is neutral for those who use it as a second language in a specific context of conflict where ethnic languages are invested with strong ethnic values. In other words, a *lingua franca* is a common linguistic locus to which speakers of ethnic groups in conflict can adhere without fearing a loss of their own language and, thus, a part of their identity.

Further, can using a *lingua franca* override ethnic languages or, in the long run, contribute to a common supra-ethnic identity that prevails over existing ethnic identities? To ask such a question admits that language is the unique element, or at least the most important attribute, that defines ethnic identity. Language, however, is not the only element that carries identity functions, although it is often among the most important. It would be difficult to claim that using a third common language will lead automatically to a modification of ethnic identity patterns when other characteristics, such as religion, cultural background or even color, function as identity markers. We can say, however, that social and political conditions could amplify or diminish languages' salience as identity markers. If we admit that giving up an ethnic language can lead to, or is the result of, ethnocultural dislocation,[19] then we could predict that political conflicts will strengthen the ethnic groups' desires to maintain separate identities and thus preserve their distinct ethnic languages. At the opposite, peaceful coexistence and social prosperity would probably weaken ethnic barriers and would possibly divest ethnic languages of their identity values.[20]

Strangely, factors that create the need for a *lingua franca* are also those that play a negative role in its widespread development and that could inhibit a common linguistic identity altogether. Although strongly valued ethnic tongues that function as identity attributes in a context of conflict favor the use of a *lingua franca*, such value-laden languages also render their replacement difficult, if not impossible. Yet, the scarcity of inter-group contacts, although it reduces the degree of bilingualism and creates the need for members of different ethnic groups to use a *lingua franca* whenever they come in contact, also impedes its spread as a common mediating language since speakers rarely use it and tend to return to their ethnic languages to assure intra-ethnic communication. For a *lingua franca* to impose itself over highly valued ethnic languages, either a strong political will or a group who adhere to its use and could serve as a model population for the remaining speakers is necessary. Even then, politicians may not be able to persuade speakers to abandon their mother tongue for a third language.

Authorities can use language policy decisions to include or exclude ethnic groups from social processes. Whether political or ideological criteria inherent to language policy will favor social inclusion or exclusion for ethnic groups depends on many factors, such as political unity and positive/negative mutual perceptions. Further, although it may appear strange, language inclusion and language exclusion policies can evolve. As a consequence, a language policy that appears as an inclusion policy when compared to other options present at the same time may later appear to be exclusionary. Thus the two-languages option in Cyprus can be considered as an inclusion policy when compared to the Greek-only option in 1986, which was clearly a policy of exclusion since it did not allow Turkish Cypriots to attend courses at the University of Cyprus. But, this same option could be seen as exclusionary when compared to the third-language option of 1989, since it actually leaves each community attached to its own ethnic language.[21]

8. Conclusion

Discontinuities between language policies and *de facto* language treatment have led many scholars to question the validity of attitudes that take officially-formulated language policies at face value. These scholars thus dissociate *language policy* from *language planning*, two terms that define two distinct processes that pertain to the theory and practice/implementation of language management choices (Cooper 1989; Schiffman 1996).

However, despite scholars' reluctance to consider declared language policies as realities, their symbolic value ought not be discarded, particularly because such policies regulate relations between ethnic groups. Language policies can function as mechanisms of integration or exclusion across ethnic groups in public administration, economic sectors, and education. Education is highly sensitive because it is the main arena in which the production and reproduction of identities are articulated. Thus, in cases of bi-ethnic or multi-ethnic states, education can be used to keep ethnic groups further apart or create a common ground or reference between them. That all ethnicities can benefit from common educational institutions can have a positive effect on their mutual perceptions. Language can play an essential role as the primary factor used to include or exclude speakers from participating in the same educational establishments. Thus, inclusive or exclusive social strategies can be based primarily on language policies.

In cases of ethnic conflict and ethnic separation, such policies are more important because they tell us a lot about political and ideological choices of a given system. The idea of a *lingua franca* is not unusual, offering both a solution to inter-ethnic communication problems created by a lengthy separation between ethnic groups that share the same geography and a neutral means of communication for members of different ethnic groups. Two characteristics render the use of a third language as a *lingua franca* more appropriate than one or the other ethnic mother tongue. First, a third language is by definition a foreign language and its use requires an equal effort by all speakers regardless of their ethnic origin. Second, it has no strong identity functions for either community.

Whether a third neutral language can contribute to a common identity is still unanswerable. Recent developments in the Balkans, the Soviet Union and elsewhere suggest that ethnic differences can survive an apparent linguistic unity. In the majority of cases reported, a common third language does not eradicate ethnic awareness or the will to maintain separate ethnic identities. We could suppose that this also holds where ethnic groups have been in persistent conflict. Further, one could say that the ultimate acceptance of each other is the recognition of each other's language, which leads us straight to mutual bilingualism.

Notes

1. *Minutes of the House of Representatives,* 5th Parliamentary period, Session C, July 13, 1989, n° 43, pp. 2962–3036. See also *Gazette*, appendix 2430, July 28 1989, 3450.
2. For a detailed account of the discussions that took place in parliament see Karyolemou (1999) and (2001).
3. ΑΚΕΛ, Ανορθωτικό Κίνημα Εργαζομένου Λαού (Progressive Party of the Working People).
4. ΔΗΣΥ, Δημοκρατικός Συναγερμός (Democratic Rally).
5. ΔΗΚΟ, Δημοκρατικό Κόμμα (Democratic Party).
6. Many deputies supported this position during the discussions that took place in Parliament at the end of 1986. See for instance: *Minutes of the House of Representatives,* 5th Parliamentary period, Session A, October 30, 1986, n° 5, 298–303; *Minutes of the House of Representatives,* 5th Parliamentary period, Session A, November 6, 1986, n° 6, 344–374; *Minutes of the House of Representatives,* 5th Parliamentary period, Session A, November 13, 1986, n° 7, 451–502; *Minutes of the House of Representatives,* 5th Parliamentary period, Session A, November 20, 1986, n° 8, 577–611; *Minutes of the House of Representatives,* 5th Parliamentary period, Session A, November 27, 1986, n° 9, 638–649; *Minutes of the House of Representatives,* 5th Parliamentary period, Session A, December 11, 1986, n° 11, 785–840; *Minutes of the House of Repre-*

sentatives, 5th Parliamentary period, Session A, December 18, 1986, n° 12, 936–940. This discussion was also reflected in the Cypriot daily press (see Karyolemou 1994a, 1994b).

7. Several conferences were also organized on the subject during this period. See Karyolemou (1994b).

8. Article 20 of the Constitution states: " 2) Free primary education shall be made available by the Greek and Turkish Communal Chambers in the respective communal primary schools. [...] 4) Education other than primary education, shall be made available by the Greek and Turkish Communal Chambers, in deserving and appropriate cases, on such terms and conditions as may be determined by a relevant communal law".

9. For every three hours of Greek programming, there was one hour of broadcasts in Turkish.

10. I am referring to post independence conditions. During the Ottoman rule, there were many cases of shifts towards the Turkish language as a consequence of repeated conversions to Islam of autochthonous people who wished to escape from the heavy taxation and miserable conditions imposed on them by the Ottoman administration. It is also well established that, during the late years of British occupation and first years of independence, many Greek-speaking Muslim Cypriots shifted to Turkish as a result of extended education provided, and sometimes imposed, by Turkish Cypriot authorities.

11. Inter-marriage usually favors the development of bilingualism.

12. The Ministry of Education was created on March 1, 1965, after all Turkish Cypriots had withdrawn from their positions in the central government and public administration. Their withdrawal was a form of reaction to a proposal by the Greek presidency aiming at bringing about amendments in the Constitution of 1960. The new ministry took in charge only the educational affairs of the Greek Cypriot community until then handled by the Greek Communal Chamber. See *Minutes of the Communal Chamber,* June 25, 1964. See also *Gazette,* appendix 395, March 31, 1965, 325–334.

13. In fact, the central government was subsidizing the two Communal Chambers responsible for educational matters. Financial allocations, however, were not enough, thus creating a constant financial problem for both Chambers (Karagiorges 1986: 33; Drevet 1991: 158 onwards).

14. ΕΔΕΚ, Ενιαία Δημοκρατική Ένωση Κύπρου (United Democratic Party of Cyprus).

15. For a detailed account of the debates during this period see Karyolemou (1999).

16. Only three Turkish Cypriot students have joined the University of Cyprus since its creation in 1992; all of them studied in the Department of Turkish Studies.

17. The House of Representatives voted the unanimous resolution on August 1, 1981. *Minutes of the House of Representatives,* 3rd Parliamentary period, Session E, January 8, 1981, No. 13, 542–544.

18. Sciriha (1995, 1996) has shown that only 7.2% of the Greek Cypriot interviewees (30 persons on a sample of 500) expressed the wish to learn Turkish as a

foreign language. Further, in so doing most of them were motivated by negative reasons ("in order to know our enemies' language"). She concludes that: "According to the respondents, knowing the Turkish language meant having a close affinity with the Turks, and for the all too obvious reason, such an idea was anathema to a number of these respondents [...] By selecting one language over another, in this case Turkish, respondents would have displayed an act of identity with the Turks" (1996: 49).

19. "Giving up a traditionally associated ethnic mother tongue is both a result of and a cause of ethnocultural dislocation. Although some dislocated ethnic groups have been able to weather such dislocations with their identity intact, most have not been able to do so" (Fishman 1999: 154).

20. Although we have quite a few examples where language differences are sharpened in spite of social prosperity and political unity (Belgium, Canada and more recently Switzerland; see Tourret 1999), we must, nevertheless acknowledge that political strife and social rivalry do not contribute to de-ethnicize language.

21. For a detailed discussion of the evolution of language policies and of changes in language policy patterns in context see Karyolemou (1999).

References

Asmussen, Jan
    1996   Life and strife in mixed villages: Some aspects of interethnic relations in Cyprus under British rule. *The Cyprus Review* 8(1), 101–110.

Bostock, William
    1997   Language grief: A "raw material" of ethnic conflict. *Nationalism and Ethnic Politics* 3(4), 94–112.

Cooper, Robert
    1989   *Language Planning and Social Change*. Cambridge: Cambridge University Press.

Drevet, Jean-François
    1991   *Chypre, île extrême: Chronique d' une Europe oubliée*. Paris: Syros/Alternative.

Fishman, Joshua
    1999   Sociolinguistics. In: Fishman, Joshua (ed.), *Handbook of Language and Ethnic Identity*. Oxford: Oxford University Press, 152–163.

Grin, François
    1999   Economics. In: Fishman, Joshua (ed.), *Handbook of Language and Ethnic Identity*. Oxford: Oxford University Press, 9–24.

Haymes, Thomas
    1997   What is nationalism really? Understanding the limitations of rigid theories in dealing with the problems of nationalism and ethnonationalism. *Nations and Nationalism* 3(4), 541–557.

Karagiorges, Andreas
    1986   *Education Development in Cyprus*. Nicosia.

Karyolemou, Marilena
    1994a   *La communauté sociolinguistique chypriote grecque: Présentation et analyse des problématiques linguistiques à travers les discours métalinguistiques parus dans la presse écrite (1985–1992)*. Published in microfiches. University Paris V - Sorbonne.

    1994b   Linguistic attitudes and metalinguistic discourse: An investigation in the Cypriot press. In: Philippaki-Warburton, Irene, and Katherina Nikolaidou (eds.), *Themes in Greek Linguistics*. Amsterdam: John Benjamins, 253–259.

    1996   Ambiguïtés des choix linguistiques: une langue internationale partagée ou deux langues nationales, l'exemple de l'université de Chypre. In : Juillard, Caroline, and Louis-Jean Calvet (eds.), *Les politiques linguistiques, mythes et réalités*. Paris: AUPELF-UREF, 223–228.

    1999   One language or two for a new university: Language, politics and ideology in Cyprus. Paper presented at the *International Conference on Language Policy at the Millennium*. University of Bar-Ilan, 21–23 November 1999.

    2001   From linguistic liberalism to legal regulation: The Greek language in Cyprus. *Language Problems and Language Planning* 25(1), 25-50.

Loizos, Peter
    1981   *The Heart Grown Bitter. A Chronicle of Cypriot War Refugees*. Cambridge: Cambridge University Press.

Mavratsas, Kaisaras
    1998   Όψεις του ελληνικού εθνικισμού στην Κύπρο [*Aspects of the Greek nationalism in Cyprus*]. Nicosia: Katarti.

Neack, Laura, and Roger M. Knudson
1999   The multiple meanings and purposes of peacekeeping in Cyprus. *International Politics* 36(4), 465–502.

Nguessan, Michel
1998   Language and human rights in Africa. In: Kibbee, Douglas (ed.), *Language Legislation and Linguistic Rights.* Amsterdam: John Benjamins, 261–268.

Péchoux, Pierre-Yves
1976   Les dimensions géographiques d'une guerre localisée: Chypre 1974–1976. *Hérodote* 3, 11–44.

1988   Chypre, géopolitique d'une île fracturée. *Hérodote* 48(1), 127–146.

Peristianis, Nikos
1995   *Δεξιά-αριστερά, ελληνοκεντρισμός-κυπροκεντρισμός: Το εκκρεμές των συλλογικών ταυτίσεων* [Right-left, Greek-centeredness-Cypriot-centeredness: The pendulum of collective identifications after 1974]. In: Peristianis, Nikos, and Giorgos Tsaggaras (eds.), *Ανατομία μιας Μεταμόρφωσης: Η Κύπρος μετά το 1974* [Anatomy of a metamorphosis: Cyprus after 1974]. Nicosia: Intercollege Press, 123–156.

Persianis, Panayiotis
1994–95   The Greek-Cypriot educational policy in Cyprus as an expression of conflict at the political, cultural and socio-economic levels. *Modern Greek Studies Yearbook* 10(11), 89–116.

Persianis, Panayiotis, and Panayiotis Polyviou
1992   *History of Education in Cyprus: Texts and Sources.* Nicosia: Cyprus Pedagogical Institute.

Schiffman, Harold
1996   *Language Policy and Language Culture.* London/New York: Routledge.

Sciriha, Lydia
1995   The interplay of language and identity in Cyprus. *The Cyprus Review* 7(2), 7–34.

1996   *A Question of Identity: Language Use in Cyprus.* Nicosia: Intercollege Press.

Tourret, Paul
    1999   Fractures linguistiques et tensions politiques en Belgique et en Suisse. *Hérodote* 95(115), 63–76.

Advertising for peace as political communication

Renée Dickason

1. Introduction

Can the propensity for violence between religious, ethnic or other groups co-habiting one territory be mitigated via a mass media "advertising for peace" campaign? In 1988, the British Government, in the form of the Northern Ireland Office (NIO), decided to try a new communicational approach to abate terrorist violence in the Province.[1] The "Troubles", with different and necessarily contradictory interpretations of their origins had, after attempts at imposed political solutions and various failed initiatives, entered a further spiral of violence. The idea was born that the question of Northern Ireland might be less intractable if a solution were pursued that, at least partly, depended on a long-term and progressive communicational approach.

The technique adopted by the NIO and its advisers was, at first sight, both experimental and surprising: *Advertising for Peace*, a series of television advertisements, conceived by the Belfast agency of the American advertising multinational *McCann-Erickson*, was to be aired on *Ulster Television* and *Channel 4*, during normal commercial breaks, just like the promotion of mundane consumer products. Although the campaign was reinforced by a limited amount of outdoor, press and radio exposure, television remained far and away the dominant medium.

This chapter examines this novel communicational approach to Northern Ireland's political problems. It was actually to be the favoured method of the British Conservative governments of Margaret Thatcher and John Major, under whose auspices no fewer than 17 different commercials were transmitted during the period from 1988 to the eve of the Labour Party's election victory on May 1,

1997. The technique of television advertising for such a purpose certainly can be considered surprising, but perhaps also experimental.

It is, no doubt, exaggerated to postulate that the Ulster (i.e. the province of Northern Ireland) initiative was anything as grand as a research project for the investigation of new techniques of "managing" terrorism, political violence, civil unrest and community conflicts (to name but some of the more salient features of the troubled Northern Irish situation). It is equally undeniable that *Advertising for Peace* proposed potential new solutions to the problems of political communication. At another level, however, Ulster offered, by its precisely definable context and identity and by its varied links with Ireland, Great Britain and the wider world, a rich field for hypothesis and conjecture of information management.

The "Troubles" had their origins in the Civil Rights Movement of the late 1960s, which sought in vain to achieve equal status for the underprivileged Catholic community. Civil disobedience and sectarian violence followed and, in December 1969, the Provisional IRA was born, which led rapidly to a further deterioration in the security situation. In 1972, the British (Labour) government suspended the Province's parliament and imposed direct rule from London.

The following year came the political initiative of the Sunningdale Agreement, which attempted to address grievances of the Catholic minority in matters of civil rights and to set up a power-sharing executive. The reaction to Sunningdale from sections of the unionist majority was both predictable and uncompromising: the Ulster Workers' Council strike of 1974 effectively barred the implementation of the Agreement and brought the downfall of this particular proposal.

The continued stationing of British troops, whose initial posting in 1969 had been welcomed in nationalist areas of the Province, came to be seen not as a valuable part of the defence of the beleaguered minority community, but rather as the presence of an army of occupation. Hunger strikes in 1981, which led to the death of Bobby Sands and other activists, gave rise to the IRA's celebrated strategy of the armalite and the ballot box, by which republicans excluded no possibility in their attempts to free the Province of British rule.

A further political initiative had occurred with the Anglo-Irish Agreement, signed by Taoiseach Garret Fitzgerald and Prime Mini-

ster Margaret Thatcher in 1985. The Agreement was highly significant in that it added an official all-Ireland dimension to the
problems of Ulster for the first time: the Irish government was to
have some say in events north of the border, and, as a kind of quid
pro quo, also became more actively and directly involved in cross-
border security questions. The immediate effects of this accord were
not auspicious, however, not least because articles 2 and 3 of the
Republic's 1937 Constitution remained in place, maintaining the
territorial claim to all the 32 counties of the island. The British
government resisted the anticipated unionist backlash, in a way,
which had not happened after the Sunningdale Agreement, but the
situation on the ground was far from favourable.

Unemployment was a major problem throughout the 1980s and
the years 1987 and 1988 were marked by an increase in terrorist
violence and by a regular and horrific series of "tit for tat" killings in
which Catholics and Protestants were murdered for no other reason
than their presumed religious allegiances. Within this worsening security context (from 237 in 1985, the number of shootings rose to
674 in 1987 and 537 in 1988, with in each year 93 people being
killed)[2], the need was felt for a new kind of initiative which would
try to find a longer-term solution to the problems, which could build
on slow advances and which, perhaps above all, would bypass both
local politicians and paramilitary groups and directly involve the
"people" in the fight against violence.[3] No doubt it was also hoped
that some sort of bandwagon effect might be achieved: the belief that
progress could be made and was being made might act as a catalyst
encouraging and furthering actual progress.

In an attempt to explain and to analyse the remarkable experiment
which *Advertising for Peace* represents, we are faced with a situation
in which imponderables and dichotomies abound: the mixture of
apparent transparency and real opacity in the approach of the British
government, a world of mistrust, manipulation and double-speak on
all sides, a constantly changing political and security situation and,
last but not least, the issue of the effectiveness and legitimacy of such
methods. This effort to suggest, if not to explain, the complexities
surrounding *Advertising for Peace* will be conducted in three parts:
the external parameters to the campaign, the different messages and

the techniques of their transmission and finally, and most tentatively of all, the consequences.

2. External parameters

2.1. New methods of communication

Using advertising to ameliorate or alleviate the situation in Ulster had been tried in the 1970s at the time of the launch of the Confidential Telephone. The differences between the old and new methods of communication were clearly marked, however. The 1970s campaigns had been conceived directly by the Northern Ireland Office, while *Advertising for Peace* was a series which bore the imprint of a professional and highly respected advertising agency, which had already made its mark in the Province and was noted for its contribution to various government information campaigns, as well as holding a number of major commercial accounts such as Coca Cola, Del Monte, Esso and Nestlé. The potential advantage of this apparently indirect approach to creative questions, with the material at arm's length, as it were, from the commanding government authority, was obvious.[4] It was also clear that, unlike many advertising campaigns, *Advertising for Peace* could only adopt a long-term and gradualist approach. It was essential to avoid causing offence and adverse reactions in both the short and the long term, while ingrained attitudes and behaviour were unlikely to change overnight.

Informative governmental television advertising on questions of general and personal interest has been a long tradition in the United Kingdom.[5] Public attitudes to such material are critical, as viewers are keen to spot errors and to detect what they perceive as a waste of their money as taxpayers, but not necessarily negative. Many government campaigns are regular and long-running and some have achieved notable success, by giving regular advice on benefits and on welfare matters, by presenting health warnings about the risks of smoking and more recently of AIDS, as well as by helping to promote responsible behaviour on the roads and in the home. General lessons important for *Advertising for Peace* were drawn from the accumulated experience of government campaigns. The use of "realistic" detail is a recurrent and expected characteristic of such messages and accuracy is essential. It is also true that the need to respect sensibilities is of paramount importance as conspicuous failures rapidly attract adverse publicity. Within Ulster itself, the campaigns favouring tourism, encouraging investment in privatised industries and condemning drinking and driving[6] were well established, preparing the ground for further initiatives from government sources.

2.2. Media background

The relationship between advertising and television, or more theoretically between the medium and the message, needs to be considered. *Advertising for Peace* was transmitted on Northern Ireland's commercial television channel, Ulster Television (UTV) and, to a minor extent, on the other national independent channel, Channel 4. At first sight, this is natural enough, since advertisements were screened in slots purchased through normal channels of media buying and since the BBC does not carry commercial advertising. This simple comment is, however, an over-simplification.

The BBC does, in fact, advertise its own products, give air time for certain kinds of charity work and has long carried governmental information messages. Ed Moloney (1998) states that BBC Northern Ireland's refusal to screen *Advertising for Peace* was actually an editorial decision, although the Corporation was cajoled into accepting the transmission of a daily 15-second message advocating Confidential Telephone usage mentioned in the advertisements. Further, the advertisements were subject to the controls imposed on transmissions made by commercial television in the United Kingdom. Moloney further affirms that the body responsible for commercial television in the United Kingdom in 1988, the Independent Broadcasting Authority (IBA)[7], exercised its powers by insisting that certain changes be made to the first of the advertisements, *A Future*, in order to avoid the impression of sectarian bias. The same commercial was amended to conform to IBA rules on subliminal advertising and the campaign as a whole was subject to the normal screening restrictions, which do not allow the transmission of material unsuitable for children's viewing, including violence, before 9 p.m.

Channel 4 was initially a wholly-owned subsidiary of British independent television. Until 1992, advertising time on Channel 4 was sold by the regional ITV companies (Ulster Television, for Northern Ireland). Since then, it has been entirely independent and self-financing. It remains a company the statutory responsibilities of which include innovation and the encouragement of minority programming. Although based in London, Channel 4 had substantial editorial freedom, both before and after changes brought about by the 1990 Broadcasting Act.

UTV is a different case. It is a successful broadcasting enterprise whose shares are quoted on both the Dublin and London Stock Exchanges. Of all Britain's regional ITV companies, UTV is also the one with the strongest dedication to its local role. The annual performance reports on the ITV companies, published by the Independent Television Commission (ITC) for 1997 and 1998, emphasised that the company exceeded its minimum licence requirements for regional programmes "by a large margin" (1997) and "by a significant margin" (1998). The channel has, over the years, remained strongly locally focused, producing few programmes which have been scheduled nationally within the UK, but with increasing coverage of all-Ireland matters, sometimes in co-operation with the Republic's broadcaster RTE. Its profits and revenues continue to grow (with pre-tax profits for 1998 reaching £12.5m, on a turnover of £37.2m) and, most notably of all, it has preserved its identity. UTV is now one of only three fully independent television companies. The other companies, some of them with areas smaller than UTV's 2.3 percent of the national viewing population, have amalgamated into four major groupings, headed respectively by Carlton Television, Granada Television, Meridian Television and Scottish Television.

UTV was the medium of choice for the campaign for other reasons. BBC Northern Ireland is controlled from London while, more generally, objectivity within the Ulster media is a rare commodity. The written press tends to be sectarian in character. The

News Letter (the United Kingdom's oldest surviving newspaper, founded in 1737) and the *Irish News* are principally read, respectively, by the unionist and nationalist communities, and, although the *Belfast Telegraph*, a popular evening newspaper with a circulation of some 130,000, has managed to broaden its appeal from its original unionist base to attract readers from both traditions, the medium typifies the polarisation of the society as a whole. The situation is complicated by the availability of Northern and Southern Irish newspapers, radio and television on both sides of the border. Local Radio in the Province is sufficiently individualistic in its musical and programming styles to be considered free from sectarian arguments, but Ulster Television still holds a somewhat privileged place as being a medium which attracts a wide audience which it claims to be non-sectarian.[8] Moreover, it is generally the case in British broadcasting that ITV (represented locally by UTV) is the service which caters most for the lower socio-economic groups – precisely the less-privileged classes that are over-represented in Northern Ireland. Therefore, it is unsurprising that, as Table 1 reveals, UTV has a wider appeal in its region than other ITV companies in theirs.

Table 1. Northern Ireland and UK TV viewing by channel

Year	% viewing of channels N. Ireland				% viewing of channels UK			
	BBC1	BBC2	UTV	C4	BBC1	BBC2	ITV	C4
1991	33.2	8.66	44.6	9.51	35.4	10.46	42.5	9.82
1993	28.4	8.42	43.6	11.49	32.7	10.27	39.9	11.0
1996	27.2	9.00	41.5	10.87	32.4	11.56	35.0	10.80[a]

[a] Source: *The Media Pocket Book 1992, 1994* and *1997*.

These figures are significant, for, although *Advertising for Peace* was not directed as precisely as is often the case for commercial campaigns at certain sub-groups of the population, it was mainly the less favoured social classes who were represented in the advertisements and who constituted the main target audience.

The use and manipulation of media have been matters of concern for the British and Irish governments; media-government relations became worse in the lat 1980s. Matters came to a head when the Special Air Services (SAS) killed three IRA activists in Gibraltar in March 1988. At the sub-sequent funerals held in Belfast, a loyalist gunman attacked mourners and two British Army corporals in civil-ian dress were beaten up by the crowd and handed over to the IRA, who shot them. The British government insisted that the BBC and Independent Television News hand over footage of the incident to the police. Thames Television's programme *Death on the Rock*, which raised serious doubts about the official version of the SAS killing was broadcast despite government protests, on May 5th. Relations between the media and the govern-ment rapidly worsened and, in October, the British Home Secretary, Douglas Hurd imposed the so-called Broadcasting Ban (forbidding the appearance on the air-waves of members of certain proscribed organisations), in an attempt calculated in the phrase of the time *"to deprive terrorists of the oxygen of publicity"*. The words of such fi-gures could still be broadcast but had to be spoken by actors. The British ban was not substantially different from the Irish Republic's Broadcast Ban, which had been imposed in 1971, according to Sec-tion 31 of the 1960 Broadcasting Authority Act. Subsequently, both the BBC and the IBA (and its successor the ITC) issued instructions to journalists on the depiction of paramilitary activities. Pressure and restriction were imposed to prevent the screening of certain programmes or items (see Curtis 1998: 289–299).

Moreover, television is, in its reception areas, an imprecise medi-um. UTV transmits programmes which had the potential to reach two thirds of the population of the Irish Republic in the early 1990s and now cover some 80 percent, and indeed one of the selling points of the company's airtime is that the viewing figures south of the border substantially boost the actual audience for advertisements. Similarly, some two thirds of homes in Northern Ireland are capable of re-ceiving broadcasts from the Republic by RTE. Within this symbiotic relationship, the question may reasonably be asked how far

Advertising for Peace might have been intended for a more general Irish audience, at a time when the Republic's role in attempting to find a solution to the problems of Ulster, and its say in the Province's internal affairs were both increasing. One of the unresolved questions surrounding the campaign is precisely the indirect influence on the political process which might be achieved by advertisements primarily addressed to ordinary citizens or, indeed, how far the treatment of paramilitaries in advertisements prepared the ground for changes in governmental policies and conduct.

2.3. The political background

The campaign, furthermore, must be seen within the broader context of initiatives to promote Northern Ireland and to enlist support for an anti-terrorist movement, not just within Ulster but in a worldwide Irish community. The Northern Ireland Office, operating through the more anonymous-sounding Northern Ireland Information Service (NIIS), has long been engaged in a substantial promotional effort of the Province through a variety of more or less transparent means. The NIIS now publishes a quarterly magazine, *Omnibus*, the objective of which is principally to give a positive, up-beat view of the region to national and international readers. In an apparent effort at transparency, the NIO boasts its own website, producing regular news releases and comments on events in Northern Ireland (and so, incidentally does the Royal Ulster Constabulary).

At the time of *Advertising for Peace,* the general thrust of the NIO's promotional activities, according to Miller (1994), was inherently schizophrenic. The ministry simultaneously tried to emphasise the return of normality to Northern Ireland, an area notable for the friendliness and initiative of its people, while indicating very clearly that the activities of republican paramilitaries were the essential causes of abnormality and strife. This dichotomy is substantially represented in *Advertising for Peace.* The attempt to stress the growing normality of Ulster was very marked in the advertisements after the first paramilitary ceasefires began in 1994, while the picture of the terrorists as not just dangerous and violent, but

destructive and counterproductive was a recurrent motif of the
adverts. *Advertising for Peace* can thus be seen as both an extension
and a development of the modes of thinking which had long prevailed within the Northern Ireland political authorities.

If these background features of the advertisements are clear, other
aspects remain veiled in secrecy. The advertising campaign undoubtedly cost a substantial amount of money for production, creative
charges and booking necessary airtime slots for broadcast of the advertisements. McCann-Erickson have been generous in their assistance and have provided invaluable technical details, ranging from
scripts to intertextual material and indications of filming intentions.
They remain, however, anxious to preserve commercial confiden-
tiality. Precise costing figures are hard to come by, and neither the
agency nor UTV have found themselves able to supply a detailed list
of the number of advertising spots which were used, nor the exact
timings of particular advertisements, even if the names of the popular, mass-audience programmes in and around which they were screened are well enough known. Certain figures have been vouchsafed
by the NIO, and by Sir Patrick Mayhew, Secretary of State for
Northern Ireland in John Major's government, and a limited number
of sometimes contradictory details are available from other sources.[9]

In addition to the NIO itself and the less well-known NIIS, there
are other semi-official bodies which serve to represent the UK authorities within the Province such as the Central Community Relations
Unit and the Community Relations Council. This situation leads to
substantial anomalies. For example, although there were no talks at
official level between UK authorities and Sinn Féin, covert contacts
were maintained before the 1994 ceasefire. Public pronoun-cements
of the British government and its civil servants undoubtedly were
false and a change in republican strategies was anticipated and
reflected in certain aspects of the *Advertising for Peace* commercials.
Similarly, there was public reticence about the campaign. The first
official comment about the objectives of the enterprise came in 1993,
with a press release from the Northern Ireland Secretary, Sir Patrick
Mayhew. Only in March 1995, when the first ceasefire was under
way, did Andy Wood, the Director of the NIIS, consent to an interview on BBC2's *The Late Show*. Wood also presented the series of

advertisements broadcast thus far at the Venice Film Festival in November. Some of his comments made during these appearances are extremely revealing, and are cited below, although they undoubtedly had the benefit of hindsight.

Thus, *Advertising for Peace* was born in an atmosphere of uncertainty, secrecy and some confusion. Some of the reasons for this discretion can be easily imagined. A certain degree of secrecy was dictated by the absolute imperative to avoid any comment which might exacerbate a delicate and volatile situation. These parameters necessarily affected both the messages and the techniques of the advertisements themselves. The closeness of the advertising agency McCann-Erickson to the realities of the situation on the ground within the Province was a key factor in alleviating some of these difficulties.

Yet, it is also true that, in 1988, no firm long-term policy or plan had been determined. If one message of the first advertisements was evident – the promotion of the Confidential Telephone which could be used by any citizen to inform the police anonymously of events which s/he had witnessed – the future development of the campaign could not be known in advance. *Advertising for Peace* was particularly conditioned by external events. The general lines of the series are clearly recognisable, but they represent an ongoing approach adapting to the evolving needs of the political and security situation. Other variations included the relatively specific targeting of certain sections of the population at different stages.

It is difficult to sum up in a few words all the detailed messages and subtleties of *Advertising for Peace*. Classic theories of communication suggest that successful message transmission depends not only on the sender's intention with his skill at encoding the message, but also on the channel of transmission and the competence of the receiver to interpret (decode) the information. In this sense, *Advertising for Peace* had two senders – the NIO and McCann-Erickson – and a double channel of communication, television and advertising.

The greatest complexity, however, arose over the receivers. All messages can be understood and appreciated at different levels and particularly so in the Northern Irish situation where interference, unwillingness to co-operate and a propensity for misinterpretation may diminish the degree of communication. The difficulties facing McCann-Erickson were therefore manifold. The typology of the television advertisement as a (hybrid) genre and public reactions may play a role, and the changing sequences of real events surrounding the fictional campaign also had to be managed. The following analysis can therefore hope only to indicate the most salient, but hopefully the most important features of the enterprise.

3. *Advertising for Peace*: A study of campaign messages and techniques

3.1. Four principal phases

The campaign itself, over a period of some nine years, traversed four broad phases. The initial intention was to encourage the use of the Confidential Telephone, which had begun in 1972 but which, in 1988, became a more organised facility, allowing callers from anywhere in the Province to use the same telephone number, which replaced the local numbers hitherto available for the purpose. By 1993, although the number of telephone calls had increased and although a greater quantity of information was becoming available to the authorities, the level of violence within Northern Ireland showed little perceptible decrease and the campaign moved over to a more offensive stage. Commercials still appealed for public's help, pointing in brutal fashion to the horrors of paramilitary activity and accentuating the criminal nature of such actions, but also demonstrated the painful consequences, not just for victims, but for the terrorists themselves, and for the families of all concerned.

When the IRA and loyalist paramilitary ceasefires were announced in August and October 1994, the tone and tenor of the advertisements changed abruptly, away from the picture of destructive terrorism to highly optimistic normality. It is now well-known that this ceasefire was not a total cessation of violence. "Punishment beatings" (in reality kneecapping, elbowcapping and other forms of extreme brutality) continued as the paramilitary groups sought to maintain and even extend control over their own particular areas. Such doubts never, of course, appeared in the commercials.

The IRA bombing of Canary Wharf in February 1996, which signalled the end of the ceasefire, swept away the optimism and placed the NIO in a quandary over the advertisements it should broadcast. The authorities' initial reaction was relatively measured; the optimistic advertisement *Boys* was still screened, but with an amended final shot emphasising the compatibility of "different traditions", before the decision was reached to rebroadcast two of the most explicit violent advertisements *I wanna be like you* and *Lady* and to devise a new one, depicting the horror once again facing inhabitants of the Province. To reinforce its message, the NIO opted for a new advertisement featuring a child. The table below represents schematically each of these phases with the advertisements concerned:

I. Confidential Telephone : phase 1 (1988–1991)
   *A Future (*1988)
   Silence (1990)
   Jigsaw (1991)
   Bleak (1991)
   Eye Shutter (1991)

II. Confidential Telephone : phase 2 (1993)
   Lady
   I wanna be like you
   Car Wash
   Next
   Time to Stop

III. The Time for Reconstruction (1994)
   Time to Build

IV. Time for the Bright Side (1995)
   Citizens
   Boys
   Yours and Mine

Stars
Humour

V. Timebomb (1997)
   Lady
   I wanna be like you
   New Boys
   Timebomb

Andy Wood's retrospective account of the original instructions supplied to McCann-Erickson for the campaign reveals a great deal
about the commercials' messages and their mode of expression. On
The Late Show in 1995, he declared:

> The initial brief was "give us a product, a service which will enable people
> in Northern Ireland, the people who are suffering directly and indirectly as a
> result of paramilitary activity ... to report suspicious activity".

Wood's observation clearly expresses the desire to appeal directly to
the "people", i.e., to the viewing public. His terminology, however, is
of particular relevance. We should note the deliberate moderation of
tone in such terms as *"paramilitary"* and *"suspicious"*, as well as
the recourse to the language of commercial advertising, *"product"*
and *"service"*. This gives useful pointers to the way in which *Advertising for Peace* may best be considered. The campaign necessarily
exhibited developments in advertising techniques, in accordance with
what McCann-Erickson called their *"psychological creativity"*,
while avoiding pitfalls of careless language.

Advertising for Peace was notable for its consensual approach and
for the moderate terms employed, which is no surprise considering
the undertones which may be implicit in even the most "trivial"
words. Curtis (1998: 134) points out in meticulous detail that even
the name of the territory is contested; loyalists favour the historically
inaccurate *Ulster*, republicans prefer the designation the *Six
Counties*, and nationalists frequently adopt the equally imprecise
North of Ireland. She quotes the advice allegedly given by Northern
Ireland Secretary James Prior to his wife before their visit to Derry

(or Londonderry) in 1982, *"My dear, you just say how delighted you are to be in 'this wonderful city of yours'"*. The vocabulary employed to refer to the "Troubles" is indeed a serious and delicate matter. According to Curtis, a speaker's choice of place-names indicates nothing less than whether or not s/he considers the British presence in the North as legitimate.

Similarly, the BBC's guidance to producers proscribed terms such as *"guerrillas"*, *"commandos"*, *"volunteers"* and *"Provos"* to refer to republican paramilitaries, preferring the term *"terrorists"* for all such organisations. It was the latter term, which was adopted by *Advertising for Peace*, although the words *"terrorist"* and *"terrorism"* each occurred only once in the whole series. Such moderation is seen as a counterpoint to graphic and explicit scenes of violence in many of the advertisements. The greater neutrality of the spoken (and to an extent of the written) word suggests that language was only part of the message, and that it needed to be both illustrated and reinforced by sounds and images.

In a sense, the fundamental dichotomy of the whole campaign was that it sought consensus while condemning what was obviously unacceptable violence. The campaign criticised the behaviour of some, while striving to sidestep the major underlying question of the legitimacy of the British presence in Northern Ireland. The cautious and low-key language symbolised the underlying dilemma.

Beyond this, the written and spoken texts of the commercials must also be seen as elements of a deliberate advertising technique, many of which are familiar to most television viewers. One might quote such features as the appeal to both rational and emotional registers, the studied use of visual and verbal techniques, the use of repetition, suggestion and slogan, recourse to music and the imperative mood. Language was therefore part and parcel of the technique of influence, but also integral to the attempt to create a sense of identity and a mood of complicity. Linguistic register and accent, for instance, were sometimes used to strengthen identification with, and acceptance of, the authenticity of the characters portrayed. On other occasions, in order to appeal to particular socio-economic groups, aspects of popular and television culture, popular idiom and specific kinds of intertextual references were included.

Creating an impression of reality was vital were the advertisements to be "credible" and, therefore, to strike the viewer as immediate and accurate. Absent such traits, a viewer was unlikely to react favourably or with commitment to the message. "Reality" has long been standard practice in British governmental informative advertising. The volatility of the Northern Irish situation, however, was such that particular care was required particularly because the commercials were intended for multiple transmission and therefore liable to detailed critical assessment. These advertisements also appealed to basic emotions, home, well-being of family and friends, innocence of youth, human solidarity, and belonging to a specific and identifiable community in which the viewer might reasonably have a sense of pride.

3.2. Major characteristics

Advertising for Peace was marked by variety and thematic development, on the one hand, and by its verbal and visual repetition, on the other. Various techniques were interwoven to create an overall effect, the success of which depended partly on complexity and an ability simultaneously to suggest and appeal to different registers. The same advertisement is not always perceived in identical fashion; its reception depends on the context (real or televisual) in which it is viewed and, for example, on the familiarity and/or novelty of what is being screened.

The "realism" of the advertisements was achieved in a variety of ways. The settings were, for the most part, recognisably similar to those within the Province. In *A Future*, for instance, while the pictures of boarded-up houses and graffiti appeared authentic, the documentary character of the commercial was reinforced by the additional use of archive material shot on the streets of the Province. Many of the events depicted were, as Andy Wood was at pains to point out, true to life, *"...The one thing I have always insisted on in these ads,"* he stated in 1995, *"is that they should stand a journa-listic test. That any incident which is portrayed in them should actually have happened."*

This argument is inconclusive, however, for it should be borne in mind that what the commercials portrayed a representation of events, not news, current affairs or history. The incidents depicted might well, sadly, be true, but the advertisements were not simply a factual account; they were a carefully selected and situated narration of events. The characters themselves did not speak directly: their "thoughts" might be heard in voice over, their "ideas" might be translated into or transmitted by song, they might look directly at the camera in an apparent attempt to convince, and their accents might seem to be authentic. But, all this was no more than a portrayal of reality. The characters' words were not their own, but composed for them and spoken by actors unknown in Northern Ireland. On the other hand, the intention was to use this impression of identity and place not only to convince the viewer to react to what was going on but, more importantly, to reimagine and restructure the future.

Ultimately, *Advertising for Peace* was a highly ambitious and perhaps excessively hopeful project. In such a context, problematic questions were underplayed or simply omitted. The central but delicate question of religious allegiance, for instance, was handled with great discretion and only in such a way as to reinforce the community message.[10]

Several of the longer advertisements were based on the principle of dramatisation, using, in Wayne Booth's (1961) memorable distinction, both "showing and telling", i.e. not only portraying but explicitly stating the specific message (either by the written or the spoken word, or both). In this attempt at mediatisation of personal experiences, the situation faced by one individual shown as representative of that faced by others. More important, the individual's reaction to events would affect, so the message of the adverts ran, the fate of himself, his family, and indeed the whole community. Awareness and education were to become self-education, which would then promote adherence to common social values. A part of this feeling of community was attributable to a shared heritage, and this was where notions of place and cultural identity coincided.

Such joint experiences aided the advertiser's purpose. Television culture and awareness of the mechanisms (sound and vision) of advertising were part of this equation; knowledge of music and film

were others. Music almost always has a mnemonic effect (widely exploited in advertising jingles, of course). Further, music acts as an
emotional stimulus, with the additional advantage of being polysemic
and capable of arousing various emotions at once, through its ability
to evoke personal and collective memories. Nostalgia and childhood
recollections were abundantly exploited in *Advertising for Peace*.
Apart from the familiar tune *Danny Boy* (the Londonderry Air) and
extracts from the Byrds' *Turn, Turn, Turn*, based on verses from
Ecclesiastes, which was a major popular success in 1967, the series
also used the words and music of Diana Ross and of two artists closely associated with the movement for peace and reconciliation in
Northern Ireland. Harry Chapin, an American singer who performed
regularly in the Province until his death in 1981, was one of these
artists. Also featured was Ulster's own Van Morrison, whose own
recordings of *Brown-Eyed Girl* (1973), *Have I Told You Lately*
(1989) and *Days Like This* (1995) accompanied advertisements
screened during the paramilitary ceasefires.

Borrowings from other elements of popular culture helped to
reinforce the effect of the campaign: the melodramatic qualities of
Lady and *I wanna be like you* were deliberately close to those of such
highly successful mass audience movies as *The Godfather* or again
Flashdance, music from which accompanied *Lady*. Comparing of the
Provisional IRA to the Mafia had been attempted by British newspapers in the early 1980s, and substantially disproved by Sinn Féin's
electoral success during the same period. Still, the notion that
paramilitary activity in the 1990s was a kind of turf-warfare, with
different groups endeavouring to keep and extend control over their
areas, had some credence given the number of punishment beatings
and shootings.

Identity goes beyond cultural memories, of course. The language,
clothes and interests of characters depicted in *Advertising for Peace*
were both familiar to those living in the Province and typical of the
socio-economic groups to which the characters supposedly belonged.
Local accents of the voice-overs reinforced adherence to place
strengthened by the concept of a shared cultural experience. In this
way, the ads hinted clearly at the absurdity of prejudice and the
counter-productive nature of conflict. If the toddlers in *Citizens* were

able to coexist peacefully, if children in *Northern Irish Humour* could share common jokes (sometimes almost unintelligible without local knowledge) then why, so the viewer was expected to ask himself or herself, could adults not be more tolerant with their neighbours.

Within this manicheistic vision, two other general points can be observed – the contrast between past, present and future and an attempt to rehabilitate the police. The first of these arguments needs no explanation. Yet, the Royal Ulster Constabulary has long attracted contradictory reactions within the Province, arousing both the admiration of the unionist community and the deepest suspicion among nationalists. An overrepresentation of Protestants in its ranks has been the main cause of these partisan reactions.[11] Any campaign which advocated active cooperation with the police, therefore, had to avoid offending a major part of the population particularly because the idea of acting as an informer was both generally and specifically repugnant.[12] The anonymity of the Confidential Telephone was designed to avoid the dangers of paramilitary reprisals, but the freefone line was ultimately just another means of informing and the *Advertising for Peace* campaign had to be discreet and reserved in its approach. Caution was particularly evident in early commercials, first in the simple printing of the Confidential Telephone number at the end of the advertisements, absent any mention of the number by the narrator.

Second, information provided was to help save the innocent (*"to save a life"*) rather than to arrest the guilty. Police were sympathetically portrayed as going about their daily, inoffensive and routine activities. Only when ceasefires were announced did officers' faces (actors of course) become visible, suitably adorned with smiles which corresponded to the return to normality and the building of relations for the future. In the idealised and highly structured representation of Northern Irish society given in the advertisements, the movement from the past – the time of darkness, horror and violence to the stability of the present, which contained hope for a better future – was a regular feature. The message was not static, however; and the campaign developed through various phases.

3.3. Stages of advertising for peace

3.3.1. 1988–1991

The first of these advertisements rapidly set the tone and theme for the campaign's initial phase. In *A Future*, a narrative commercial lasting 60 seconds, emphasis was placed on a central character, a young married man, surrounded by the gloom, destruction and horror associated with violence. The young man resolved, in the interests of himself and his family, to take the decisive step of using the Confidential Telephone and tell what he had seen. For this action not to appear suspect, it was essential to establish that the man was not a sympathiser with the security forces. The opening sentence, *"all my life people have hated the Police and Army"* partly accomplished this task, his euphemistic references to acts of violence as *"having a go"* and *"something really rough"* completed it. The deliberate recourse to clichés such as *"reared in the streets"*, *"looked the other way"* and *"something better than this"* and the familiar language *"screwing it up"*, *"hoods"*, *"fed off our backs"* further consolidated his status as representative of a certain socio-economic group, confirmed by his clothes and the limited décor of his home. This linguistic authenticity gave added authority to scenes of paramilitary activity, bombings, a double kneecapping carried out by hooded and armed men, the abandoning of a dead body in a back alley, all further reinforced by realistic-looking slogans *SS RUC*, *ARMY OUT* and the depiction of a collection for prisoners in a pub. The depressing setting, with its dark alleys, narrow streets and boarded-up buildings, was completed by archive footage of real bombings and explosions.

The message created the link between terrorist activity and economic collapse, with, for example, the picture of a building site with the sign *"site closed"* carefully synchronised with the voice-over commentary, *"they've left me with no job"*. Andy Wood was to expound this argument in the clearest possible terms on the *Late Show*. The aim, he stated, was *"to help the police to bring to justice people who were having a bad effect on their environment, on their prospects, the area they lived in, and people who were affecting their quality of life ... as long as paramilitary activities continued they did*

more than blight lives, they blighted areas, they blighted environ-
ments, prospects for investment. " The advertisements did not go this
far. *A Future* did not refer directly to the police and none of the
commercials specifically evoked the motif of bringing criminals to
justice.

The linguistic techniques of this first commercial were particularly revealing. The adjectives used, "rough, hard, better,"
smacked rather of understatement than of emotion. The force of the
language was apparent only by the ironical intonation placed on
"heroes", and "their kind of justice", and by the accumulation of
accusations which answered the pertinent question *"What have these*
hard men done for me?" "They've left me with no job and no hope,
they've wrecked where I live, they've hi-jacked our cars, fed off our
backs." Such questions and answers were timed to coincide with
images of dilapidated houses, an exploding car bomb and the col-
lecting tin for prisoners being passed round in a bar. The testimony
of the young man, for that was what the advertisement ultimately
represented, was given in voice-over commentary dominated by the
first person pronoun *"I"*. The movement from *"I"* to *"we"*, contrasted with the mocking references to paramilitaries as *"hard men"*
or simply *"them"*, represented an attempt to associate the wider
community with the individual's symbolic decision. The flatness of
the delivery and the use of a virtually static camera (suggesting
objectivity) emphasised the appeal not to emotion but to logic. All of
these techniques contributed to the impression of the accuracy of this
initial advertisement in terms of tone and content – which was
essential for the acceptability of the series which was to follow.

The thematic link between *A Future* and other advertisements in
the first phase was undeniable. Attempts were made to dehumanise
the terrorists themselves, by their anonymity and by the emphasis on
the repeated nature of their brutality – *"kill again and again"* – and
by the progressive use of more openly critical vocabulary in written
texts (*"twisted murder"*, *"sneer with cruel contempt"*, *"kill*
Christmas", emphasis added). A consistent effort was made to distance the community from the *"killers"*, by the simple use of the pronouns *I/we and you,* compared with *they.*

Subsequently, the sense of unity was extended to the police whose role was depicted as that of the protectors of the whole community, a highly significant step considering that paramilitary groups consistently claimed to be the defenders of the interests of their supporters. From *Bleak* onwards, officers were visible, although anonymous in the exercise of their duty, and *"help the police to help us all"* became part of the exhortation made to viewers.

Gradually, the messages became more insistent. Silence (the title of the second advertisement) came to be represented as an act, not of solidarity but of betrayal, as the effort was made to emphasise the need above all to accept individual responsibility in the attempt to *"save a life, prevent a tragedy, stop the killing"* and *"beat the bombing"*.[13] *A Future* did not mention the actual number of the Confidential Telephone, *Silence* gave it, but only in a written text and the reinforcement of written text by the spoken word was added in *Jigsaw*. The use of imperatives and modality was an indication of the development. *A Future* contented itself with the almost optional *"you can help"*, *Silence* adopted the first person imperative *"let's (put life first)"*. Subsequently a series of instructions were given, *"use the Confidential Telephone, put life first, watch out, look out, help out"*, all the more powerful for being dynamically monosyllabic.

Needless to say, the methods employed in these first commercials varied. It was no accident that *Bleak*, an advertisement timed for Christmas, a time of potentially increased risk, was accompanied by the music of the carol *In the Bleak Midwinter*, while the printed text emphasised the repeated nature of atrocities. *Jigsaw* and *Eye Shutter* stressed that any piece of information, however trivial, might help in the fight against death, mayhem and destruction, reinforcing the point by a rapid series of brief shots. The thematic links between these early advertisements were reinforced by the number of repeated shots: *Bleak* reused scenes from *A Future* and *Jigsaw*, along with archive film, *Eye Shutter* consisted entirely of shots used in *Bleak*. With the exception of *A Future*, where a specific audience of young men between 25 and 35 seemed to be targeted, opening advertisements were intended progressively, to appeal to the whole community, for everyone had his or her part to play in the humanitarian effort of saving lives.

3.3.2. 1993 and early 1994

The second pre-ceasefire series of advertisements evoked, in a more graphic way than its predecessors, the horrors associated with terrorist violence. This series also represented a more nuanced view of paramilitaries, who were portrayed (in four of the five commercials) as victims of circumstance, just like those they attacked. The view persists that this different treatment was far from accidental: the belief was growing in official circles that a ceasefire on the part of paramilitary groups was a real possibility and that a less categorical portrayal might be productive. *Lady* and *I wanna be like you*, both repeated in early 1997, when a second ceasefire seemed remote, addressed specific audiences with specific messages. In the former advertisement, as the title suggests, the focus of attention was on women, the innocent victims of terrorist violence.

The commercial's message, depicting the broken lives of two women, was based heavily on parallelism in the film editing and in the language, which emphasised the similarity between these two characters: both briefly enjoyed the pleasure of marriage, and the lives of both were ruined by violence leading to the disappearance of the beloved. The detailed ritual of two different but similar wedding services in churches of different denominations further stressed the common tragic destiny awaiting the two couples. The repeated vow *"till death us do part"* rapidly became ironic as one of the husbands was brutally murdered by the other. The women's *"two tragedies"* were mirrored by a further thematic and verbal parallelism in the fate of their husbands, one *"a victim of violence,"* the other *"a prisoner of violence"*. Just as the young father in *A Future* was symbolic of the young men of Northern Ireland, the two women represented wives, mothers, sisters and girlfriends who had suffered through their loved ones' willing or unwilling involvement in terrorist violence and whose lives were diminished by it. The message of the advertisement was one of loss and grief, but it became more urgent than that. It was not enough, as the first female voice-over in the series put it, desperately to want the violence to cease, but it was vital to go beyond this passive stage to take the step of decisive action. *"Don't suffer it, change it"* was the slogan common to the advertisements in this phase, and improvement could of course be achieved thanks to the Confidential Telephone.

The second advertisement in the series used many of the same techniques. *I wanna be like you*, another narrative advertisement of exceptional, almost short-film length (150 seconds), backed by mnemonically and thematically relevant popular music,[14] made a deliberate attempt to equate paramilitary groups with criminal activity. The parallels with *The Godfather* are striking. The target audience, according to Andy Wood, was *"those who were in fringe paramilitary activity waiting to join the real killers"*, again from the less privileged socio-economic groups, and the motifs of lost innocence (hauntingly evoked by echoes of the nursery rhyme *Hey Diddle Diddle*), failed parental responsibility and the inevitable long-term fate of those who live by the gun were explicitly evoked. The father's neglect of his son was mirrored by the son's indifference to his father as he in turn slipped into the ways of violence which were to lead to his own untimely death. The sins of the fathers were truly visited upon the children, the vicious circle of violence was unbroken as the final scene in a cemetery made clear, ironically to the accompaniment of the sung words *"We'll have a good time then"*, while the steady rain replaced the tears which the father's past made him still unable to shed.

As with *Lady*, the realism of the advertisement was horrifying. In the former case, the killer shot his victim repeatedly at point blank range; in the latter, the use of slow motion filming stressed the gruesome effects of semi-automatic weapons. The focus was put on the terrorists themselves, who were no longer the anonymous perpetrators of violence, hooded or unseen. Instead, they were portrayed as human beings whose scandalous acts of criminality and brutality were carried out flagrantly and with malice, method and pleasure, but who were equally to finish up as victims of violence.

Car Wash (a brief advertisement of only 40 seconds) represented a break from this relentless series of extreme violence. Other differences lay in the chosen setting, an affluent private housing development, and in the reliance on image and sound effects alone to carry the message that the use of the Confidential Telephone could avert a tragedy, an argument proved to be true as a police Landrover arrived in the nick of time, to prevent yet another shooting. The polarisation between the would-be killers and their apparently innocent victim was carefully maintained while the suspense of the episode was achieved by parallel editing.

Next acted as a catalogue reinforcing the message of the previous advertisements. Apart from the shots giving the message (white letters on a black background), the visual part of the advertisement was made up of clips from the previous spots *Lady* and *I wanna be like you*, including the murders, accompanied by the tune of *Danny Boy*,[15] hummed like a lament by a female voice. *Next* acquired its force by repetitious litany of family members and friends who might be on the terrorists' list of future victims.

Arguably, *Time to Stop* was the most powerful of all these advertisements. The horrific scenes of the previous films were shown again, but with the difference that what the caption declared to be the *"true sound of terrorism"* was heard, with explosions, sirens, gunshots, screams and breaking glass punctuating the pictures. Most poignant of all were the silence and the sobs of the terrorist's mother as she looked down on her son in his open coffin, a scene taken direct from *I wanna be like you.*

Through its extreme brevity, *"The true sound of terrorism. Now is the time to stop. Don't suffer it, change it. Call the Confidential Telephone 0800 666 999"*, the written message took the argument to a stage of greater immediacy. The soundtrack stated unequivocally: *"It doesn't have to be like this"* and went on to reinforce the written message by repeating *"Now is the time to stop"*. With this advertisement, the patient and gradualist approach adopted so far seemed to have reached its ultimate stage. A variety of arguments advocating change and improvement had been deployed, but the moment for decisive action had at last been reached. The explicit statement that it really was *"time to"* change reflected the underlying hope at the moment of its transmission, and can be seen as quite deliberately preparing the ground not only for the anticipated ceasefires, but for the commercials which were to follow them.

3.3.3. 1994–1996

The transformations in the advertising parameters during the first ceasefire could hardly have been made more evident. *Time to Build* was based on a manicheistic opposition of past and present, contrasting the periods of despair and hope with the help of scenes of radical change; grey neglected streets and barbed wire gave way to a skipping rope with brightly dressed children at play, while the sinister symbol of a gun was metamorphosed into a starting pistol for a marathon and a cricket bat rediscovered its original innocent use in the hands of a child and a smiling (unarmed) policeman. The symbolism of reconstruction (a new motorway, *"open in 1995"*) and of common endeavour (the Belfast Marathon, a popular participatory sporting event) was strong, while the notion that peace was overdue is reinforced by the popular song *Turn, turn, turn* with its repeated motif of *"a time to"* and its use of the visual metaphor of the harvest. The Confidential Telephone number was still visible, but the emphasis on the role of the police was radically different; the police were no longer unidentifiable in their body armour, but accessible and friendly, their function transformed into that of *"keep[ing] the peace"*. The return to normality, typified by smiling female shoppers, was a strong motif in these commercials.

Other advertisements during this optimistic period were grouped under the heading *Time for the Bright Side*, which conveyed a happy message accompanied, in the best traditions of commercial advertising, by a logo (a rainbow) and the slogan, voiced by Van Morrison, the still not wholly convinced or convincing *"wouldn't it be great if it was like this all the time?"* Morrison's words and music brought to the series the popular appeal to optimism and shared experience, *"everything falls into place, there'll be days like this"* (Boys), *"fill my heart with gladness, take away my sadness, ease my troubles that's what you do"* (Yours and Mine).

Six themes capable of unifying the whole Northern Irish population were developed: friendship, solidarity, humour, heritage, childhood innocence and sport. The cosy and comforting atmosphere of *Citizens* displayed a number of toddlers (*Catholics and Prote-stants*, for the first time told by an English voice in an opening reminiscent of the demonstration technique of many commercials) happily displaying the absence of differences between them as they played. The narrative commercial *Boys* (June 1995) took the argument one stage further. The beauties of the coastal landscape were a feature of this advertisement, with the symbolic colours of green and orange being well to the fore, and indeed the depiction of "neutral" rural settings was a way of sidestepping the urban locations with their undertones of sectarianism. The key moment in the commercial came when the two teenagers discovered that they belonged to different traditions and silently exchanged what were to be regarded as tribal tokens (a Gaelic football badge and a King William badge) as a sign of lasting friendship. For the first time in the whole campaign, religious/political differences were openly shown, only for them to be demonstrated as no obstacle to lasting harmony. As the optimistic words of Van Morrison's accompanying song emphasised, such happy times should be no exception.

Yours and Mine, another 100-second advertisement had more in common with a tourist commercial, with its calm and beautiful vistas, historic and prehistoric sites and its emphasis on tradition and manual skills. The choice of detail and of music was not a matter of chance, of course. Two greyhounds were shown, the first wearing a green jacket, the other with an orange one, while the eternal elements of air, fire, earth and water were to the fore. Time-honoured crafts were presented, the overall impression being one of harmony and beauty, with more than a touch of sensuality.

The symbolism was also carefully calculated: the war memorial at Enniskillen, the scene of one of the worst terrorist outrages, was juxtaposed with a stained glass window depicting St. Patrick, while the fusion of femininity and nature was achieved with the final shot of a slim female figure walking along a beach at sunset. Serenity and harmony were the pervasive elements of what might almost have been an earthly paradise, as eternal values triumphed over mundane concerns.

The final two advertisements in this series, respectively entitled *Stars* and *Humour*, sought to reinforce the feel-good factor. Children were shown exchanging their favourite jokes, including one about a visiting American coming (predictably enough) to look at a new factory. In *Stars*, some of the Province's best known recent sporting and show-business personalities, from Alex Higgins to Kenneth Branagh, were briefly shown to indicate the abilities of the Northern Irish, images with which the whole province could identify and of which it might feel justly proud. This series of advertisements was unfailingly optimistic, the day-to-day problems of the ceasefire were forgotten and many conventional commercial advertising techniques were employed to produce an effect which the *Irish Times* referred to, with very little exaggeration, as *"sickly sweet"*. The IRA bomb at Canary Wharf was to change all that.

3.3.4. 1997

After transmitting the modified advertisement, *New Boys*, the NIO returned abruptly in January 1997 to the hard-hitting messages of three years before. *Lady* and *I wanna be like you* were rebroadcast, the latter also in an abbreviated 30 second form. At one point, plans were well advanced for the screening of a new advertisement showing Nazi mobs attacking churches and synagogues. In the event, this plan was shelved in favour of a more poignant, but equally disturbing new advertisement, *Timebomb*, which won awards at both the Montreux and London advertising festivals. The advertisement pulled no punches, the happy children's playground atmosphere of *Citizens* was briefly evoked, before the dream was transformed into a nightmare, with familiar objects being horrifically distorted, with details of radio news bulletins describing real terrorist and sectarian violence replacing music and with the children being reified and petrified in a world where nothing was as expected. Nothing, at the start of the advertisement, prepared the viewer for the ending, the featured child having lost his hopes, while Diana Ross's song posed the more general question, *"do you know where you're going to?"*; the inference was that the inhabitants of Northern Ireland, by accepting the return to violence, had lost their way. For this advertisement, a new slogan was developed, *"Heal the Hate, Free the Future"*, which nevertheless brought more repetition than novelty. Only the word *"hate"* had not already featured in slogans.

4. *Advertising for peace*: A tentative assessment

Evaluating the campaign's results is speculative. For government advertising, even more than for its commercial equivalent, there is no sure way of knowing whether the campaigns are having the desired effect. In this particular case, the subject needed to be handled with more than the usual discretion. As an example of quality advertising, the campaign had much to commend it and, from the point of view of McCann-Erickson, it was undoubtedly a success. It was a further opportunity for the agency to emphasise its efficiency, professionalism and ability to act successfully in various fields. From the technical point of view, the "psychological creativity" of the commercials was unquestionable.

This is only part of the question, of course. In their handsomely presented video tape of the advertisements, McCann-Erickson have attempted to prove the advertisements' efficacy by providing figures and details of the apparent reactions to the campaign, presenting it in a most favourable light. These data are presented in Table 2.

The reliability of these observations as scientific data is a matter of conjecture. Although the cassette contains no information on how findings were obtained, and McCann-Erickson have been unwilling to shed further light on the matter, at least some of these statistics seem to have been generally accepted, and were partially reprinted, for example, in *Scotmedia*, the *Irish News* and the *Belfast Telegraph*.[16] Taken at face value, these comments would seem to indicate that the advertisements remained faithful to the words of McCann-Erickson's own logo, representing a kind of *"truth well told"*. But, in fact, the comments do no more than raise the central dilemma of the effectiveness and legitimacy of the commercials.

Whatever reticence one may have concerning McCann-Erickson's data, there is little doubt that the commercials did strike a chord with a substantial part of the population and that the NIO did indeed manage to communicate with the citizens. The opposition at the time of the transmission of the commercials was relatively muted. Voices were raised over the cost of the advertisements and the Northern Ireland Tourist Board was consistently concerned about the effects of the depiction of violence on the number of potential visitors to the

Table 2. Campaign efficacy measured by public reaction

name of advertisement(s)	launch date	reaction
A Future	Jan 1988	51% increase in calls
Silence	1990	22.4% increase in calls
Jigsaw, Bleak, Eye-shutter	1991–1992	477% increase in calls, 81% of all adults favourable to the Police, 8% unfavourable
Lady, I wanna be like you, Car wash	July 1993	The all-time peak response, 729% higher than 1988; public approval at 71%, disapproval at 5%
Next	Nov 1993	64% all-adult favourability to the Confidential Telephone, only 3% unfavourable
Time to Stop	Spring 1994	88% of all adults view Confidential Telephone as important to Northern Ireland.
~~ First ceasefire declared August 31st, 1994 ~~~		
Time to Build	post ceasefires, October 1994	86% all-adult favourability, 3% of adults unfavourable
Citizens	April 1995	82% all-adult favourability, 6% of adults unfavourable
Boys, Yours and Mine, Stars, Humour	June 1995	82.5 % believe these ads will make a difference to Northern Ireland. Overall "Bright Side" research result: 86% favourability, 75% of adults believe they encourage people to accept each other's differences

Province from the Republic of Ireland. Yet it was not until the campaign was over that hostile reactions became more numerous. Only
the plans for the new advertisements after the breakdown of the
ceasefire attracted real controversy, as some held that the NIO had
committed a grave error of overreaction when considering plans for
scenes reminiscent of the 1938 Nazi "Kristallnacht", before ordering
production of *Timebomb*.[17]

If we accept that, in general terms, the government succeeded in
opening a direct channel of communication with the people, we may
nevertheless wonder what use was made of this opportunity. The task
of educating and transforming attitudes of the Northern Irish
population was always extremely difficult to achieve. The mutual
mistrust between the communities was a well-nigh insuperable
obstacle, while it was equally difficult to convince the nationalist
population of the good faith of any enterprise emanating from the
British government. The long history of prejudice, half truths and
manipulation had led to a long-established fear of *"dirty tricks"* and
"black propaganda",[18] which set more obstacles in the way of
mutual understanding. The rigorously consensual solution adopted
was both the strength and the weakness of the campaign. Few would
criticise the desire to stop shootings and bombings and the messages
of the post ceasefire commercials were couched in the positive terms
of construction and healing which corresponded to the optimistic
mood of the time, but the degree of active political communication
was limited. The commercials attempted some redefinition of the
role of the police and consciously conveyed the government's view
of events. Major controversial questions, however, were avoided and,
if the advertisements did indeed *tell the truth*, this was far from being
the whole truth. Both the NIO and McCann-Erickson can actually be
accused of having concentrated more on the communication (the
telling) than on the *truth* itself.

The arrival in power of the Labour Party under Tony Blair in May
1997 was to herald a radical change in approach. The new Prime
Minister had other plans in mind, which were more far-reaching than
those of his predecessor and which eventually took shape in the 1998
Good Friday Agreement. In this changed atmosphere, different
tactics were needed and Labour's new Secretary of State for

Northern Ireland, Mo Mowlam, was quick to stop the advertisements. By the October of 1997, Andy Wood found himself unexpectedly on leave and, although extracts from the commercials were used in 1998 to encourage a yes vote in the referendum on the Good Friday Agreement, the campaign itself was at an end. In any case, it may have already achieved all that might have been expected of it.

The process leading from awareness to action may take some considerable time and it is clear that, although *Advertising for Peace* was not based on commercial objectives, the campaign had lasted long enough for it to have attained all the results it could have realised. An optimistic verdict would be to regard it as a stage in the gradual process of transformation of attitudes within the Province which had a number of beneficial results in both the short and the long term and may well have contributed to the calling of both paramilitary ceasefires. A contrary opinion would be to consider the advertisements as a missed opportunity, as the government failed to profit fully from the window of communication which had been opened in order to address major political issues.

Another question nevertheless remains – namely the legitimacy of governmental use of the media in a democratic country to change the attitudes of the people. *Advertising for Peace* went further than ordinary public service advertising in its attempt to condition and manipulate the public, and further doubts were raised by the fact that the NIO's approach was not, as we have argued above, fully transparent. It is true that the advertisements did not attempt to denigrate contrary opinions, but the accusation of propaganda was sufficiently worrying for Andy Wood, on *The Late Show,* to take pains to refute the charge by stressing the "authenticity" of the scenes portrayed and by emphasising that the advertisements had passed what he called the *"journalistic test."* He nevertheless did not tackle the issue of unreasonable manipulation. Behind this reticence, of course, lies the whole status and legitimacy of the British presence in Ulster, which was left aside by the campaign. This central point is one which future negotiations, which may in part have been facilitated by *Advertising for Peace*, will one day have to address.

Notes

1. This article considers the terms Ulster, Northern Ireland and the Province as equivalents. The choice of the different expressions intends no sectarian or political nuances.
2. Figures from different sources are never completely compatible. The details on bombings and shootings are taken from Brennan and Deutsch (1993: annexe I), and seem to be based on RUC data. Barton (1996: 184) quotes similar figures. Marie-Therese Fay et al. (1999: 159) gives a total of 99 deaths in 1987 and 100 in 1988.
3. The use of such methods by the government was indeed a first: the idea of popular pressure was not new, however. The *Peace People* of 1976, led by a Catholic and a Protestant, Mairead Corrigan and Betty Williams, represented a spontaneous, and subsequently highly mediatised popular reaction to the effects of violence. The movement rapidly ran out of steam, but not before the two leaders had been awarded the Nobel Prize for Peace in 1977. It still exists in a much diminished form.
4. The actual degree of "distance" is open to conjecture. Since his resignation from the post of Director of the Northern Ireland Information Service, Andy Wood's public pronouncements have indicated with increasing clarity his and the Service's involvement in the campaign on a day-to-day basis.
5. Most commercials are organised through the Central Office of Information, a descendant of the wartime Ministry of Information, which handles worldwide promotion of the UK as well as domestic government advertising campaigns. The market is considerable; the COI's annual turnover, in 1990–1991 for example, was £167.6m.
6. McCann-Erickson's anti-drinking and driving commercial, entitled *Flowers*, produced for the Department of the Environment won two Hollywood Ollie trophies in the International Broadcasting Awards ceremony of 1997.
7. Commercial television in the UK has been successively regulated by the Independent Television Authority (ITA), the Independent Broadcasting Authority (IBA) and the Independent Television Commission (ITC). Despite the changes in name, the duties and responsibilities of these bodies have remained largely unaltered.
8. The bulk of the initial finance of Ulster Television came from the protestant community. It was only the insistence of the Independent Television Authority that raised catholic participation to 25 percent when the licence was granted in 1958. Speaking at the Royal Television Society dinner in December 1993, Desmond Smyth, the managing director of UTV claimed, "Regular research confirms that our news service is highly regarded by both main traditions in Northern Ireland. People of both traditions trust our service. That is something which we value, but needless to say it is accompanied by an onerous responsibility."

9. According to a NIIS press statement of 7th July 1993, *Lady* and *I Wanna Be Like You* cost £373,000 to produce and the price of *A Future* was £90,000. Miller (1994) gives total NIO advertising spending of some £35 million for 1987–1993, while Andy Wood, in private correspondence to the author, dated August 1996, quoted a total cost for *Advertising for Peace* of around £4 million, "split roughly 50-50 between production costs and airtime costs."

10. Of the adverts screened before the 1994 ceasefire, only *Lady* referred to religious allegiances, but emphasised what the traditions had in common. Only with *Boys,* were *differences* openly suggested and exploited.

11. In 1994, under 8 percent of RUC members were Catholics; during the ceasefire, on May 25th 1995, the *Irish Times* reported that the proportion of Catholics applying to join had risen from 12.2 percent to 21.5 percent.

12. The *tout* (informer) is a despised figure in Irish history. The use of *supergrasses* and the Diplock courts (which sat without a jury in the 1980s) did nothing to improve this perception.

13. In the same vein, Northern Ireland Secretary Sir Patrick Mayhew's press statement of 7th July 1993 observed, "If only one life is saved as a result of these films, they will have been worthwhile."

14. Harry Chapin's *The Cat's in the Cradle.*

15. Again the choice of music was deliberate. *Danny Boy* was composed in the village of Limavady, the nearest town to which, Greysteel, had witnessed, just before the broadcasting of *Next*, a particularly barbarous shooting incident.

16. On their cassette, McCann-Erickson further listed "typical research spontaneous responses", again without details of how they were obtained. They are quoted below, but some of them do seem almost to be too good to be true, in their closeness to what might be supposed to have been the desired reactions to the commercials in question:

Name of advertisement	"typical research spontaneous response"
Boys	"The two badges offered nice emphasis and both sides of the divide could relate to it"
Yours and Mine	"It made me think what a beautiful place we live in and what a shame it is to destroy it"
Stars	"It made me feel proud to be Northern Irish as you realized how many great people come from here"
Humour	"The kids get us to laugh at ourselves—wouldn't it be really great like this, instead of violence" (sic.)

17. The *Belfast Telegraph* of February 7th 1997 observed that "business leaders and some historians [have] slammed the project as inappropriate" while the

(London) *Daily Telegraph* of January 29th 1997 quoted historian Andrew Roberts as stating that "there [were] some things too horrific for PR men and agencies to play with." Andy Wood and Sir Patrick Mayhew both defended the analogy.

18. Documented, for example, in a series of articles published by the *Irish News* under the generic title of the *Dirty War*, in comments by London's Liberal *Guardian* newspaper and in the catalogue established by Miller (1994).

References

Barton, Brian
  1996   *A Pocket History of Ulster*. Dublin: O'Brien Press.

Booth, Wayne
  1961   *The Rhetoric of Fiction.* Chicago: University of Chicago Press.

Brennan, Paul, and Richard Deutsch
  1993   *L'Irlande du Nord–Chronologie 1968–1991*. Paris: Presses de la Sorbonne Nouvelle.

Curtis, Liz
  1998   *Ireland: The Propaganda War*. Belfast: Sasta.

Fay, Marie-Thérèse, Mike Morrissey, and Marie Smyth
  1999   *Northern Ireland's Troubles*. London: Pluto.

Media Pocket Book
  1992, 1994, and 1997 editions   Henley-on-Thames: NTC.

Miller, David
  1993   The Northern Ireland Information Service and the media. In: Eldridge, John (ed.), *Getting the Message*. London: Routledge.

  1994   *Don't Mention the War*. London: Pluto.

Moloney, Ed
  1998   Closing down the airwaves: The story of the broadcasting ban. In: Royston, Bill (ed.), *The Media in Northern Ireland*. Basingstoke: Macmillan. Also available on
            http://cain-ulst.ac.uk/othelem/media/moloney.

American warriors speaking American: The metapragmatics of performance in the nation state

Mark Allen Peterson

1. Introduction

On August 1, 1996, at 12:57 p.m., the U.S. House of Representatives began debating H.R. 123, a bill to declare English the official language of the U.S. government. H.R. 123, if passed, would have rolled back a 1992 law that required voting, tax and social security information in some communities to be published in more than one language.

Some two hours into the debate, a curious exchange took place. Democratic Congressman Patrick Kennedy of Rhode Island linked the official-English bill to recent welfare and immigrant reform legislation "when they knocked off all the legal residents who were tax-paying residents of my State who can go and fight in our wars and yet they are going to be denied the rights of their citizenship based upon the bill my Republican colleagues passed yesterday." California Republican Duke Cunningham responded by asking Kennedy whether "he ever volunteered for service? Has he ever volunteered to go fight those wars himself? I thought not." Kennedy's subsequent response was stricken from the record due to the congressman's failure to seek recognition from the chair before speaking. New York Democrat Jose Serrano, after failing to get Kennedy's response placed in the record, defended his colleague by saying, "I served, and I served with many Hispanics who did not speak English. Some of them never came back from the Vietnam War and died while speaking only Spanish."

This exchange, although brief, is rich with layers of cultural meaning. It is one of three points during the three-hour debate in which military service was raised as a trope. Although these utterances total only 108 of 8523 lines of transcript, the exchange between Kennedy and Cunningham was important enough to spin off into the mediascape through the efforts of military veterans seeking to bring the importance of the exchange to a larger forum. But important in what way? The answer lies in the nature of cultural values confounded by Kennedy's allegation and the nature of Cunningham's response.

Language is one of the primary vehicles through which many states, including the United States, attempt to define their national character. Participation in war is one of the key ways through which citizens demonstrate their belief in and commitment to the nation. This exchange raises the question of what happens when master narratives of military service and language come into conflict. What are "Americans" to make of persons who speak no English yet are willing to risk their lives in wars the state says are necessary for the nation's survival? What does such a case say about the relationships between language, nation, patriotism and war?

In this chapter[1] I examine the portions of the Congressional debate concerned with non-English speaking veterans as well as coverage in the newspaper *The Stars and Stripes*. Through both sources, an "expressive economy" (Briggs 1996a) is revealed in which ideas about what it means to be "an American" are articulated and contested but ultimately go unresolved. Such debate is important for several reasons. First, "it is in the context of confrontation, when persons negotiate their social universes and enter into discourse about it, that the character of the system is revealed" (Comaroff and Roberts 1981: 249). Second, the context in which the social universe is debated affects not only the rules of confrontation and negotiation but through this, the nature of the argument itself and the shape of the cultural representations under dispute. In this case, the performative contexts of the Congressional debate and the mass media debate, although intertextually related, create different narratives because different kinds of cultural objects are at stake.

I argue that while at the level of political performance speakers attempt to draw on cultural categories to achieve situation-specific objectives, the media's appropriation of their discourse shifts it to a metadiscursive level in which the primary discourse becomes the object of the second discourse. At this secondary level, it is the representational truth of assertions made at the primary level that are being contested. For these social actors, more than a vote is at stake; it is the *truth* of specific (and contradictory) narratives of national identity.[2]

2. Debating language

Congress constitutes a "discourse community" marked both by particular ways of speaking and by common values and topics. By "discourse community" I mean "a set of individuals who can be interpreted as constituting a community on the basis of the ways in which their oral or written discourse practices reveal common interests, goals and beliefs, i.e. on the degree of institutionalization that their discourse displays" (Watts 1999). The commonality of discourse is not only semantic but is also constituted through standardized metacommunicative practices. Thus, while members of Congress often appear to be polarized over particular issues, they are bound by a set of common discursive practices through which they construct a common ground within which debate can take place. It is through these shared metacommunicative practices that Congress can constitute itself and construct a common value orientation within which to debate.

Congressional debates take place within a formalized setting, employing a highly elaborated code of discursive conduct. Debates are presumed to break along party lines, distinctions between which are spatially and ideologically indexed by the term "sides." Each opposed side controls a certain number of minutes in the debate. The minutes are usually apportioned to each side according to a complex set of rules involving seniority and rotation.

In the debate on H.R. 123, minutes were primarily controlled by Cunningham, as the representative who introduced the bill, and by William Clay of Missouri. These minutes can be delegated to other members of the House at the will of the speaker controlling the time. Minutes are apportioned through specific metalinguistic utterances such as:

> Mr. CUNNINGHAM. Mr. Chairman, I yield 2 minutes to the gentleman
> from Pennsylvania [Mr. GOODLING], chairman of The Committee on
> Economic and Educational Opportunities. [H9738]

Members controlling time can not only yield (or refuse to yield) time to other debaters but can delegate the power to control and apportion time:

> Mr. CUNNINGHAM. Mr. Chairman, I yield 15 minutes to the gentleman
> from Florida [Mr. CANADY], and I ask unanimous consent that he be per-
> mitted to control that time.
> The CHAIRMAN. Is there objection to the request of the gentleman from
> California?
> There was no objection. [H9738]

These metacommunicative utterances serve not only to apportion the time that a speaker may contribute to the debate but also to mark the speaker's right to speak through his or her recognition by the chair. In Congressional debate, all proper utterances are addressed to the chair. Improper utterances – not addressed or not recognized by the chair – may be stricken from the record; more commonly, improper remarks are not noted at all. Once recognized, each debater offers a speech, prepared or improvisatory, setting out his or her understanding of what the bill would or would not do and why the speaker supports or opposes it. Members may petition the chair for the right to revise and extend their remarks, allowing them to correct mistakes or make points they failed to make in their actual discourse. Revised remarks are marked in the Congressional record by a different font and extensions and insertions into the record are printed in an appendix to each day's volume.[3]

To have a policy debate, the debaters must first establish a common ground from which to argue. It is largely through this elaborated metacommunicative code that congressmen are able to construct a common ground for their debates. Performing in Congress, therefore, involves mastery of a metalanguage through which a metadiscourse can be constructed. Debate in Congress is constituted by a two-tier discourse, occupying at the surface level an opposition between two political ideologies. Beneath these lies a body of myth and metaphor from which Congressmen construct a shared foundation for debate. Following Bourdieu, I refer to the surface level as marked by opposition between *orthodox* and *heterodox* discourses, while the unexamined – and perhaps unexaminable – discursive substrata I will refer to as *doxa*.[4]

3. Myths of state

This *"doxa,"* this discursive common ground, is constructed through speeches in which Congressmen describe what, in their opinions, the bill would or would not accomplish if passed, and why these results are or are not desirable. The common ground so constructed often takes the form of an American myth of origin. In the debate over H.R. 123, this common ground involved imagining America as a nation of immigrants possessing different languages and traditions who somehow forge a common identity as Americans.

This myth of the melting pot is an old one which has not yet lost its power to persuade. Sollors (1986) has examined the myth of the melting pot at length, looking at it as a discursive weapon against an alternative construction, *nativism*. Nativist traditions are those which attempt to define America in terms of some essential characteristic, that belongs only to those born and raised – "bred" – in the United States. Varenne (1998: 27–49) argues that as the "melting pot" metaphor loses its power, "the other images being proposed (rainbows, mosaics, etc) are to be used in the same manner: they are weapons against those who would close the frontiers in the name of some substantive quality that only native born people encultured near the ideological centers, that is, 'Americans,' would possess." This is so, he says, because "we, the people" is continually "reconstructed as a plurality of individuals, and not a community with particular properties" (Varenne 1998: 35).

Such myths of state exist as cultural resources which can be used by rhetoricians to construct accounts of the world. Yet such myths and metaphors are differently embedded in actual discourses according to the performative competence of the speaker and the particular ends toward which the discourse is aimed. An adequate paraphrase of the myth as abstracted from the three-hour debate over official English would go something like this:[5]

AMERICA IS A NATION OF IMMIGRANTS. The DIVERSITY provided by these IMMIGRANTS is A NATIONAL TREASURE, part of OUR COMMON HERITAGE. THE ENGLISH LANGUAGE is THE COMMON BOND that UNITES US AS A NATION.

IMMIGRANTS come to AMERICA to ACHIEVE THE AMERICAN DREAM. But one cannot ACHIEVE THE AMERICAN DREAM without a GOOD WORK ETHIC and a good UNDERSTANDING OF ENGLISH. Acquisition of ENGLISH and the SUCCESS and CITIZENSHIP that come with it bring IMMIGRANTS PRIDE.

We should first note that an isomorphic relationship is assumed between a place, the people who live in that place and the language spoken by those people. Acquisition of the language of a place therefore becomes central to the process by which those from outside a place become the kind of people who live in that place.[6] For example:

Yes, they knew that English proficiency was good for the overall well-being of society and for the tradition, the more than 100 years tradition of the melting pot that united all of us in our hopes and ideals as a nation. [H9739]

Second, the Congressional debate constructed language as a relatively simple and bounded form of knowledge. One knows English or one does not; one has "proficiency" or one does not. The logic expressed by the debate ties language to social action through a conduit metaphor,[7] i.e. language is a vehicle for the expression of thoughts and if we want access to the thoughts of another, or to express our own thoughts, we must use the same vehicle. The complications of what is meant by "knowing" or "learning" English, or what constitutes English "proficiency" are not raised. Particularly ignored is the possibility that many of those who "don't know English," are already Americans by virtue of being born in this country.

Third, immigration is constituted as a relatively uncomplicated social process, the first stage through which persons become Americans. "Immigrants" in these narratives are self-controlled agents in charge of their own destinies who have come to America in search of a better life. Such immigrants learn American ways of speaking, American values and in the process, become American. Those who do not or cannot become American will need assistance or require discipline. In the official and officiating discourse of the state, the question is not raised as to whether the U.S. is still a nation of immigrants (much less whether, given slavery and other forms of involuntary servitude, it ever was). Rather, the question as formulated by Congress is whether these are the same kinds of immigrants who will "melt" in the national crucible.

Both opponents and supporters of H.R. 123 publicly articulate this ideological construction of identity as a common ground through which the debate can proceed. Differences over the bill, in other words, do not usually take issue with the underlying mythos. Rather, disputes center on different understandings of the nature of the "problems" created by the evident failure of some non-English speaking people to undergo the process of becoming English-speaking Americans. The existence of persons within America who do not speak English, but may still benefit from federal programs, constitutes a breach of civil order; the debate is over what steps, if any, should be taken to restore the breach to the place-people-language isomorphism presupposed by this official discourse of nationhood.

Supporters of the bill argue that diversity is only a strength insofar as it can be shared through a common language. Without this common language, legislators argued that immigrant communities would fragment into myriad political and cultural groups, rather than combining into a holistic America. To prevent this, immigrants must be "empowered" to learn English through incentives, specifically, the "natural" desire of immigrants to better themselves through participation in the political process and in federal benefit programs (all the materials about which would be printed only in English if the bill passed). Multilingual programs provide a disincentive to learn English – and hence themselves constitute a danger to the cohesiveness of the nation – so they must be discontinued at least within the federal government.

Opponents of the bill argued that there were not enough English classes to meet the demands of immigrants and that the desire of immigrants to learn English is overpowering. What is lacking is empowerment of these immigrants to learn English through federally-funded programs. Toward this end, Mr. Serrano introduced an "English Plus" bill that would preserve current multilingual programs while increasing federal spending to teach non-English speakers the English language.

Clearly, English occupies a position in the U.S. as a "legitimate language," a language that has acquired pre-eminence through institutionalized discourses and hence offers a valuable form of cultural capital,[8] recognized as such by Congress. Congressional debaters on both sides express certainty that immigrants cannot "get ahead" without knowledge of English. The debate concerns how this knowledge is to be provided to citizens. What is the appropriate role for Congress to play in eliminating non-English speaking members of the body politic? How, in other words, can the state force people to learn what they need to know to become linguistically correct members of the society? This aspect of the debate turns on very different notions of how "learning" is constituted. Supporters of H.R. 123 claimed that "multilingualism" and "bilingualism" had been tried and proven ineffective as pedagogical tools and had to be discarded. Instead, people will learn what they "must" if there are proper incentives. An adequate paraphrase of the theory of learning put forward by the bill might be:

> PEOPLE DESIRE TO LEARN but will nonetheless ONLY do so if there are sufficient INCENTIVES to DRIVE them to do so. YOU DON'T DO THEM ANY FAVORS BY MAKING THINGS TOO EASY. If you do, they won't PUSH THEMSELVES as HARD as they NEED in order to be able to ACHIEVE THE AMERICAN DREAM.

The theory of learning supposed by supporters of Serrano's English Plus bill, on the other hand, can be paraphrased like this:

> PEOPLE WANT TO LEARN but are BLOCKED by obstacles, including FINANCIAL AND SOCIAL BARRIERS that HOLD PEOPLE BACK. The federal government must diminish or REMOVE THESE OBSTACLES by making available RESOURCES so that these AMERICANS CAN GET THE EDUCATIONS they both WANT and NEED in order to ACHIEVE THE AMERICAN DREAM.

Here again, there is common ground: both proponents and opponents of the Official English bill assume that non-English speakers are immigrants, that these immigrants "desire" to learn language in order to "get ahead." Getting ahead is never explored in terms of the possible range of ambitions and requisite literacies to meet those ambitions; rather, the phrase is only more thoroughly mythologized by speakers on either side through the ambiguous but rhetorically powerful phrase, "achieving the American dream." Myths of nation like "the American dream," "land of immigrants" and "melting pot," taken up as social and political charters, preclude more nuanced discourses which might recognize the flexibility and multiplicity of people's actual associations and self-identifications.

At the primary level, then, the debate offers a stage in which political actors can display their adherence to opposed political ideologies. The orthodox discourse, represented by the bill's supporters, offers the ideology Sarat and Berkowitz have called "civil republicanism," the pursuit of the common good through shared values, character and interests (Sarat and Berkowitz 1998: 81–102).[9] The pursuit of the common good can only be pursued through communication in a common language within a public sphere constituted by a fundamental set of shared values. The goal of legislation is to ensure some minimum level of assimilation. The solution proffered by H.R. 123 would have ensured the coherence of the civil society by excluding voices of those who do not meet its standards. This is cast as a teaching process: those who wish to participate will already have the desired values of self-reliance and discipline and will use these to educate themselves in order to be able to participate.

The discourse of civil republicanist orthodoxy is marked by tolerance: other languages are all right in their place, which is to say, in the home or the "grassroots" community. These languages are *not* all right in the public sphere, in the realm of civil society, where a common language is necessary to create a level playing field. This tolerance is built on notions of what kinds of behaviors (including linguistic behaviors) are publicly or privately appropriate.[10]

The speeches against the bill illustrate the principle Sarat and Berkowitz call "liberalism," in which free individuals pursue their own interests in their own ways, a disorderly process that can be made orderly only through appeals to the state as guarantor of order (Sarat and Berkowitz 1998: 86–88). Opponents of the H.R. 123 argued again and again that diversity is a national resource, not a source of civil disorder. On the contrary, these legislators insisted that immigrants need to learn English not to reduce civil disorder but to survive in an America in which English is the *de facto* language of public discourse and employment. Serrano's substitute bill offers a solution in which the government constructs the civil society not by excluding those who "refuse" to learn English but by providing resources for those "unable" to learn English to do so.

4. Metapragmatics in and of the nation

But the debate is more than just a polarity of ideologies. Most remarkable is the ability of the two sides to construct the common ground within which the debate takes place through the play of metapragmatic signs. Signs are metapragmatic insofar as they index the ways in which language carries socially powerful meanings through its contextual connections. Metapragmatic signs can be explicit or implicit. In legal discourse, for example, verbs such as "enacts" and "provides" are explicit metapragmatic signs that point to the powerful social functions of the language.[11]

Metapragmatic signs thus interpret what language does and what people do with language. In the former case, what Briggs calls "type-based" metapragmatic constructions interpret whole classes of utterances (Briggs 1996b). These classes can be genres of speaking ("a woman's gossip can drive a man mad") or defined languages ("English is what binds us together as a people"). Briggs (1996b) calls those metapragmatic constructions that interpret specific utterances ("her endless gossiping drove her husband mad") "token-based". Linking tokens to types is a powerful rhetorical trope. If a speaker establishes a type-based construction such as "English is what binds us together as a people," and then make a token-based construction such as "immigrants whose English is not adequate for participation in public action," s/he implies that some members of society are not bound to the whole.

At one level, the entire Congressional debate is a forward-looking metapragmatic speech event. The debate is part of – indeed, the generative phase of – the process by which legislation gets constructed. Whereas legal language uses metapragmatic verbs such as "enacts" and "provides" to index the socially constitutive power of the language (Mertz 1996), H.R.123 is a metapraxis that has not yet happened. Congressmen thus index the powerful social effects the bill *will* have, if passed, through phrases like:

> We are hearing a lot of nonsense, I believe, about all the terrible things this bill would affect. What does this bill really affect? Let me tell my colleagues, it really affects official business, and official business is defined. [H9763]]

> Instead of empowering people in the use of English by ensuring adequate funds for English as a second language classes, this bill attempts to protect the English language as though it were under some bizarre attack by other languages. This bill will obstruct such basic government functions as tax collection, disaster preparation, water and resource conservation, and execution of civil and criminal laws and regulations. [H9739]

Congressmen also use metapragmatic verbs to index their own authority and power to enact the bill. Individually, Congressmen "rise" to "support" or "oppose" the legislation. In a debate such as this, where the speeches are prepared in advance and the vote is clearly split down party lines, the function of such speeches is not so much to persuade one's colleagues but to provide an opportunity to explicate in advance one's vote on the legislation, not in the least as a basis for explanations to constituents.

In addition to these self-referential metapragmatic constructions, there is a significant second level of metapraxis in the debate over H.R. 123. Because the bill involves altering the legal status of English, legislators position themselves in support of or opposition to the bill by describing what the English language does, and hence why this bill is necessary or unnecessary. Thus, legislators use metapragmatic constructions such as:

> After all, it is the English language that unites us, a Nation of many differ-
> ent immigrants as one Nation. Over and over again we see that it is the
> English language that empowers each new generation of immigrants to ac-
> cess the American dream. [H9747]]

> English proficiency was good enough for the overall well-being of society
> and the tradition, the more than 100 years tradition of the melting pot that
> united all of us in our hopes and ideals as a nation. [H9739]

The two levels are related. Congressmen explain in their speeches
what English is and does, what this bill would do or does, and thus
why they support or oppose the bill. Through this they construct
common ground. Agreement on what English *is* allows them to disagree on what Bill *would do*. They agree on the metapragmatic type
and dispute only whether or not a particular instance is a token of
that type. In doing so, they constitute a two-tiered ground on which
to construct their debates.

This common language underlying both heterodox and orthodox
positions, grounds both in a common mythic tapestry woven of
deeply rooted cultural idioms. It is a common ground constructed
through a shared metalanguage, including complex rules of debate.
When debate becomes disorderly and threatens the overall coherence
of the frame, this metalanguage can be wielded as a tool to repair
breaches and restore equilibrium, as we will see in the next section.

5. Contingency and performance

If myths of the immigrant nation and of the role of education in
shaping successful citizens form the ground for debate, the exchange
on which I focus is noteworthy because it breaks through the pattern
of prepared speeches into the realm of unexpected and unplanned
discourse.[12]

Kennedy began the exchange with a long preamble:

> Today my colleagues are talking about the divisiveness of this issue. The
> reason they are talking about divisiveness is because this is a divisive issue.
> This bill plays directly to the politics of fear and prejudice for which this
> Congress has become so well-known. A politics of divide and conquer.

Mr. Chairman, this is reminiscent of the Patrick Buchanan campaign to define which people are more American than others. Or should I say which people are more white, are more white than other Americans? This is playing politics that the Republican party knows very well: Create an enemy to solve all our country's anxieties and fears. We saw it begin with the gay bashing. Then it proceeded to the welfare bashing. Then the last 2 days we have seen it with the welfare bashing and the immigrant bashing when they knocked off all the legal residents who were taxpaying residents of my State who can go and fight in our wars and yet they are going to be denied the rights of their citizenship based upon the bill my Republican colleagues passed yesterday. [H9763]

Unlike the majority of the speeches in the debate, Kennedy's performance is not specifically about the problem of drafting legislation to solve a problem of linguistic disorder. Rather, Kennedy used his time to construct a specifically motivated interpretation of the bill which shifted from the mythic ground to the immediate legislative context of the bill, that is, the previous day's legislative calendar. In doing so, Kennedy chose to index the immediate political and legislative – rather than abstract social, educational and historical – context of the bill. He concludes with a warning, again tying the bill not to imagined immigrants but to specific social situations covered by the media during the period of the debate:

If they do not like the way they look, if they do not like the way they sound, then they are not Americans. All I have to say to my colleagues is they should be careful with all these hot button issues that they are pushing because no one should wonder when the churches start burning in the South and the race riots start breaking out in Los Angeles where all these hot button issues have led us to, and that is fanning the flames of intolerance that this country cannot afford at this time. [H9763]

Liebowicz (1992) has noted that bilingualism becomes a particularly important issue in the United States at times of heavy immigration. The connection between immigration reform and the official English debate is made explicit by Kennedy.

Kennedy's rhetoric constitutes a dramatic shift from the general tenor of the debate. His construction of the bill's context cries out for a rebuttal from the opposition and he receives one from Cunningham. But Cunningham does not directly confront or contradict Kennedy's construction of the situation. Rather, he calls into question Kennedy's right to *make* this construction because Kennedy has never served his country through military service:

> Mr. Chairman, I yield myself 30 seconds to ask the gentleman from Rhode Island a question. Has he ever volunteered for service? Has he ever volunteered to go fight those wars himself? I thought not. [H9763]

Cunningham's response is thus not to repudiate Kennedy's indexical trope but rather to seize a piece of it and, in a metonymic shift, make the part stand for the whole. Seizing on Kennedy's claim that some of his constituents served the U.S. without speaking English – the only one of Kennedy's claims that specifically links language to citizenship – he challenges Kennedy's right to speak to this question. To do so, he invokes a powerful American mythology, that of the veteran's sacrifice.

Veterans are constructed in American popular mythology as persons who have made a sacrifice for the nation. At great personal cost, they have "answered their country's call." In doing so, they have put their lives and livelihoods at risk. Many have "paid the price of our freedom" in the form of physical and psychological disabilities; many have "made the ultimate sacrifice" by dying for their country. This discourse constructs a moral economy. Although a veteran serves not out of expectation of repayment but out of his or her own sense of duty, honor, responsibility and gratitude to country, the country owes the veteran "a debt we can never repay." Veterans thus occupy a sacred character, one ceremonially institutionalized in a series of federal holidays, particularly Veterans Day and Memorial Day.[13]

Particularly important for Cunningham's rhetorical move is the use of veterans – as persons who have "risked all" for their country – as a foil for civil servants. Civil servants like Kennedy may have chosen a career that demonstrates a commitment to their country but they do so without serious sacrifice. In political debates over benefits, veterans' advocates often imply a qualitative difference in risk taken by the veteran and the civil servant. This is made particularly clear where veterans point to discrepancies between the quality of their own health care and that offered by the Federal Employee

Health benefits Program, considered by many to be the best health benefits program in the U.S. Many veterans will claim that it is inappropriate that civil servants who "have never heard a shot fired in anger in their lives" may receive more comprehensive health benefits than "those who put their lives on the line." One of the consequences is that civil servants who are not themselves veterans are often presumed to be unable to speak of and for veterans.[14] In his response to Kennedy, then, Cunningham is changing the ground of the argument by calling into question Kennedy's right to speak to issues by simultaneously implying that Kennedy has no experiential knowledge of military service (as Cunningham, a Navy veteran, does) and that he lacks such knowledge because of his own choice not to serve his country in a way that requires personal sacrifice.

6. Repairing the breach

Kennedy responded, as did a number of other Congressmen, but their words were not taken down and are not part of the record since the speakers had not been recognized by the chair. The only reference in the Congressional Record to the brief acrimonious exchange is the chair's effort to call the house to order:

> The CHAIRMAN. The House will be in order. The gentleman from Rhode Island is not under recognition. No Member has been recognized. [H9763]

The chair then recognized a speaker, who in turn yielded his time to another. Just as the Congressman began his speech, however, he was interrupted by Serrano, who called for a point of order.

> Mr. SERRANO. Mr. Chairman, I have a point of order.
> The CHAIRMAN. The gentleman will state it.
> Mr. SERRANO. My impression was that Members had risen to deal with the issue of the gentleman's comments, and I want to know if those Members have been entertained at all, or if the gentleman from Rhode Island had any opportunity to speak about a very personal statement that was made upon his life and his commitment to this country.

> The CHAIRMAN. The chair perceived that the gentleman from Rhode Island was attempting to engage the gentleman from California in debate, and not asking that his words be taken down.
> Mr. SERRANO. In that case, Mr. Chairman, if that is the ruling of the Chair, is it still in order for this gentleman to ask that the gentleman's words be taken down?
> The CHAIRMAN. The gentleman should have made that demand at the time. Intervening business has gone on. It is too late at this particular point. [H9763]

Having failed to have the remarks read into the record, Serrano allowed the Congressman recognized by the chair to complete his speech. When he finished, Serrano intervened again:

> Mr. SERRANO: Mr. Chairman, I yield myself 30 seconds. Mr. Chairman, I am troubled by the comments by my friend from California, Mr. Cunningham, about the integrity and commitment of the young gentleman from Rhode Island, Mr. KENNEDY. I do not think anyone could question the commitment either of the gentleman or his family to this country. I would simply say that we have to watch our words. I served, and I served with many Hispanics who did not speak English. Some of them never came back from the Vietnam War and died while speaking only Spanish. [H9763]

Serrano here attempts to restore equilibrium in two ways. He first enters the metacommunicative frame in order to seek to get Kennedy's response on the record. The chair invokes House rules to refuse. Serrano then uses his own position, as a military veteran, to speak to the truth of the question Cunningham raised and thus attempt to restore Kennedy's credibility. Having finished, he yields time to another opponent of H.R. 123 who returns the debate to its normal routine of turn-taking.

Although the chair is complicit in using the rules to silence Kennedy and Serrano is seeking to use those same rules to allow his colleague to speak, both are employed in an effort to restore the discursive equilibrium that has been breached. This insistence on the maintenance of an equilibrium that allows for routinized speech-making is partly a function of the metapragmatics of Con-gressional performance. Congress is engaged in the first step of a complex perlocutionary act – production of a discourse that, if it survives the Senate and White House, will become law and change social realities for tens of thousands of persons. The pragmatic goals of the Congress make arguments about assertions a secondary, and often unproductive, exercise. As a body, Congress is largely uninterested in pursuing the specific truth claims made by individual members.

7. Into the mediascape

Coverage of the bill's debate by the news media was lukewarm. Most news outlets covered the passage, but did not focus on the debate itself. The most important reason was that the bill was of little importance to journalists or their sources within Congressional committees. My own sources, some of whom had written statements that Congressmen presented on the floor, characterized the bill in the following ways:

This is just a performance. The vote's sewn up.

This is a loyalty bill. Unless you have overriding concerns about your constituency you're supposed to vote with the party on this one.

It doesn't make any difference one way or the other. There's no way the Senate's going to let this one come to the floor.

Media reports that covered the issue in any detail spoke of "winners" and "losers" in the debate or looked outside Congress for experts who could talk about the potential impact of the bill were it passed in the Senate (whether, for example, it would receive a presidential veto). In doing so, these reports accepted and reproduced the metapragmatic goals of the House itself, goals concerning the passage of legislation. In this understanding, the specific rhetoric of the speeches is oriented toward clarifying one's vote, not toward establishing the truth or falsity of claims made as part of the discussion. Journalism, of course, is also a discursive community bounded by different discursive projects and practices than Congress. Journalism orders its discourse around the representation of "facts" and the passage of this bill constituted a coherent fact. Detailed analysis of the debate is thus less interesting to most journalists than the issue of the bill's potential relevance to law and regulation, and its impact on people.

This can make news coverage deeply dissatisfying for those citizens for whom such debates are about more than who won, but are instead concerned with the truth of the cultural categories on display. That is, insofar as official discourses draw on widely-shared myths and metaphors and on common sense, they are not exclusive prerogatives of the state. Citizens may seek to exercise their democratic franchise not only through resistance to the state but also through loyal efforts to shore up gaps created by official discourses. In the case I examine here, the failure of Congress to adequately address the central issue of the *truth* of the assertion made by Kennedy and reaffirmed by Serrano, created an interesting spillover of the debate into media.

The day after the debate, a small, conservative veterans organization, the Coalition of American Veterans, issued a statement by fax to a number of media outlets. The statement recapitulated the exchanges between Kennedy, Cunningham and Serrano and argued that Serrano's (and by extension Kennedy's) claim was an insult to the "real" American veterans who served their country in Vietnam. The press release quoted the organization's president, Gil Macklin, as saying:

> The remarks by Congressman Serrano stating that American servicemen went, fought and died in Vietnam without ever being able to speak English is [sic] rubbish. You can't get through basic training without the ability to speak and understand English.

One newspaper which did pick up the story was the U.S. edition of The Stars and Stripes, a weekly newspaper covering legislative and administrative issues concerning military veterans.[15] Editors at The Stars and Stripes were amused by the story, but not sure what to do with it.[16] It was assigned a story slot in a regular column, "On The Hill," in which legislative debates of interest to veterans routinely were followed.

This assignment had a number of consequences. First, this column was written by editorial staff rather than reporters and the stories that appeared in it were not usually bylined. The page usually featured three stories, none of which exceeded 500 words. An internal company memo (dated 1994) described the page:

> Our main competition are the monthly glossy magazines put out by the veterans service organizations. These have very long lead times, with the result that their legislative news is always out of date. The purpose of this page is to demonstrate that we can offer more legislative news, written in a more interesting and understandable style, in a more timely manner.

Initial efforts by the newspaper to confirm the truth of either Macklin's or Serrano's claims from the Pentagon proved fruitless. The Pentagon said that, under current conditions, it would be impossible for a recruit to get through basic training with out knowing English. In response to the specific question of whether the U.S. might have had servicemembers who could not function in English during the Vietnam or Korean wars, the agency asked for a few days to investigate its records.

In the meantime, an assistant editor called the American G.I. Forum, a national veterans service organization serving Hispanic and Latino veterans and asked the press representative whether she could locate any veterans who could speak to this issue. This organization also asked for time. The story was shelved for that week's issue.

Some time the following week the American G.I. Forum put staff members in touch with a retired Army combat medic, Sgt. Frank Perales. Perales' own story complicates the simplicity with which language communities are constructed by the political and popular imaginations: born and raised in Nebraska, Perales said he grew up an English monolingual. During WWII, he was assigned to Panama where he first learned Spanish. This stood him in good stead as a combat medic during the Korean and Vietnam Wars, where he was often assigned to work with Spanish-speaking veterans. The newspaper reported:

> "Some of these guys, they had a little English, but very little and they were in the army," he told *The Stars and Stripes*. "I used to wonder about that."[17]

Perales' rhetorical strategy is worth noting. He confirms Serrano's claim while at the same time remarking on how odd it seemed to him, thus positioning himself with Serrano's detractors, if only in order to confound them. His testimony says, in effect, "I wouldn't have believed it if I hadn't seen and heard it myself."

Perales went on to tell a number of interesting stories, only one of which made it into the published article. This was a humorous tale of a soldier who may have entered the military with some knowledge of English but lost it during more than a decade of service in a Spanish-speaking part of the American military system. The lengthy anecdote was reduced to three brief paragraphs in the final story:

> He said when he was assigned to Valley Forge medical center he met a sergeant who had served in Puerto Rico for "about 17 years" who knew no English but rose to the rank of E-7. The sergeant had no difficulties, Perales said, until he was unexpectedly transferred to Fort Benning, GA.
>
> "They thought he was crazy because they'd give him an order and he'd just stand there," Perales said. Perales saved him from being committed for psychiatric evaluation.
>
> "This was in the days of electroshock therapy, hydrotherapy, even insulin treatments to induce shock," Perales said. "I hate to think what would have happened to him."[18]

Even in its abbreviated form, this speaks to both the plurality of linguistic relations and to the dangers of officiating discourses. The story of the Puerto Rican sergeant serves to confirm Serrano's claim but it also has a number of other implications. The sergeant's story illustrates the kinds of fears that give rise to official English movements: the fear of a soldier who does not obey orders because he cannot understand them. At the same time, the sergeant's situation serves as a chilling cautionary tale for non-English speaking Americans: this is a country where the discourses of officialdom are capable of misconstruing non-English monolinguals and subjecting them to the segregation, surveillance and possible physical punishment American society reserves for the insane.

Perales' was chosen by the newspaper's editors from three potential sources interviewed by reporters as persons to speak for (and hence "stand for") Hispanic veterans in this news story. The American GI Forum turned up another Hispanic veteran, who spoke for and about non-English speaking veterans, but he was neither as engaging nor as articulate as Perales, nor had he served for so long a period. A third possible source was a retired lawyer from Washington, DC, who had served in Korea and had worked in an office handling arrivals of personnel after he was wounded. He told a reporter, "Hell, yeah, toward the end they were sending anybody they could get who could hold a rifle. They didn't care what language you spoke." Perales was chosen over the other vet because of his ability to speak standard English in an articulate and entertaining manner. He was chosen to speak over the lawyer in part because of his Hispanic surname.

The authority of news lies in deixis. News is indicated as true by virtue of its ability to refer to things in the world about which it reports. At the same time, news is a construction. It is put together through the negotiated efforts of journalists and their sources. Journalists therefore choose sources on the basis of their ability to indicate their authority to speak on behalf of the community, event or process they are purported to be part of (and hence metonymically stand for). Journalists tend to prefer official discourses as they speak with institutional authority. Thus, confirmation of accusations made by the CAV as to the falsity of Serrano's claim were first sought from the Pentagon. Bureaucracies like the Pentagon, in turn, have their own ways of authorizing speech, particularly the process Herzfeld (1997: 135) describes as "legalism – the bureaucrat's insistence on establishing facts by writing them down." This reliance on records can obscure on-the-ground realities and also, in the case of wars that ended more than 20 years earlier, leave the institution at a loss to find documents that could either confirm or deny Serrano's claim.

After the story ran, the editors got a telephone call from a spokesman for the CAV. He thanked them for doing a story based on the press release, but expressed his disappointment with the way the story had run. He suggested that the Pentagon was refusing to clarify the situation not because of inadequate records but because they did not wish to embarrass a Congressman. He added further his conviction that Perales had political agendas such that his testimony could not be trusted. He acknowledged that the newspaper could not have produced a different story than they had, given their discursive practices. At the same time, through the phone call he attempted to reestablish his own claim, that only speakers of English can serve their country, risking and perhaps sacrificing their lives for the nation. Perhaps more important, the phone call sought to address the failure of the press to establish the truthfulness of this claim by emphasizing that the truth *could* have been established if not for people willing to lie to further political goals. The call, in other words, was used to reassert the real possibility of knowing the truth, even while recognizing the difficulty, if not impossibility of representing it.

8. Metadiscourse and metapragmatics

In this article I've offered an example of American political discourse conceived as practice. Such a phrase is meant to encompass language simultaneously as a signifying practice and as a form of social action occurring in discrete historical moments and having observable effects and consequences. I have examined two sets of "metadiscursive practices," that is, discursive practices "that seek to shape, constrain, or appropriate other discourses" (Briggs 1996a: 19).

Both Congressional and journalistic discourses select, shape and order polyvocality into more-or-less coherent voices. Congress and journalism differ dramatically, however, in the play of metapragmatic signs through which these metadiscourses are constituted. The metapragmatic signs in both cases provide the means for "participants' coming-to-grips with the effectiveness and meaningfulness of the events in which they … take part" (Silverstein 1996). The primary function of Congressional metapragmatics in performance is to refer to categories supposedly existing in the real world – immigrants, non-English speaking monolinguals, foreigners assimilated as Americans – and to use these to construct a common mythic language that explains the two bills under discussion in terms that will lead to a vote. Breaches of this metapragmatic function by alternative indexical operations – such as Kennedy's references to the legislative and historical context of HR 123 and to its putative consequences – are rapidly and easily repaired through the metacommunicative practices that define Congress as a discourse community.

But the contingent nature of language in performance opens up possibilities for meaning to "leak" from one discursive context into others. The repair of the breach in discourse did not satisfy some members of the veterans community who found their own identities challenged by the statements of Kennedy and Serrano. Efforts to restore equilibrium are performed at the cost of pursuing the specific truths of such assertions. Citizens whose sense of identity as "American" through both service and language was challenged by the debate, sought the media as an alternative metadiscursive practice, one which could potentially valorize their assertion that English acquisition *is* a prerequisite of military service. By subsuming the status of veteran into that of English-speaking American, these veterans hoped to resolve the discursive dissonance posed by the possibility that two definitions of American could be found in contradistinction to one another. That the media failed to fulfill veterans' hopes stems from journalism's own metapragmatic practices, which involve defining and indexing institutionally recognized social actors who speak about and stand for the social categories being represented.

In the end, this is a debate about the purity of the symbols through which we make ourselves. It is a boundary dispute over the metonymic categories that define the inchoate "I" who claims to be American. It is about the failure of cultural categories to adequately map empirical realities and the struggles of various social actors, using a complex of interrelated and intertextually linked discourses, to stake out claims to that identity.

The official English bill passed in the House but never came to the Senate floor. The symbols and tropes were put away, to be dusted off and used again when the issue arises again, as it inevitably will. This battle for control over the symbolic definition of American was lost, but the war over who may or may not claim such an identity, goes on.

Notes

1. I would like to thank Richard Senghas, Cindy Dunn and the other members of the workshop on "anthropololitical linguistics" at the 1998 American Anthro-

pological Association meetings for inviting me to participate and think more deeply about issues I had earlier worked on as a journalist. I must also thank the staff at *The Stars and Stripes*, particularly the managing editor Fred Geiger and publisher Howard Haugerud, for allowing me access to the newspaper's resources after I left the newspaper to pursue other activities. I also owe a debt of gratitude to Shelley L. Wallace, who managed to dig the story in question out of the archives and send it to me in Cairo without any more to go on than a rough guess as to the date it ran. Analysis of the discourse on which this paper is based was partially supported by an American University in Cairo faculty research support grant.

2. For an account that puts this debate into an historical and comparative context, see Peterson (1999).
3. Interestingly, the metacommunicative utterances by which speakers request permission to revise and extend their remarks are not printed verbatim (as are requests for recognition or to yield time) but rather paraphrased thus:

(Mr. GOODLING asked and was given permission to revise and extend his remarks.) [H9738]

4. On these concepts, see Bourdieu (1977: 164–171, 1990: 66–68, 110–111). It is important to recognize that, in saying that doxa are unexaminable, it does not follow that they are necessarily "believed" by Congressmen who articulate different orthodox or heterodox positions in debate. Doxa are naturalized as "common sense"; they are taken for granted and, given the time constraints and objectives of Congressional debates, critical evaluation is unusual if not impossible. Indeed, one of the jobs of Congressional staffers is to take positions Congressmen have made on the basis of a complex variety of information, including political networks and evaluations of likely voter responses, and convert them into rhetorical forms that can be publicly articulated.
5. I am following here the conventions outlined by Polanyi (1989) in extracting "cultural constructs" from narrative texts and converting them into the form of "culturally significant propositions." Capital letters here denote culturally significant terms or phrases that recur many times throughout the text under analysis.
6. There are some ten exceptions to the Emerson bill, and they are revealing. For example, because the bill justifies itself by constructing a theory of the nation as a "land of immigrants," autocthons – speakers of Native American and Alaskan native languages – are exempt. They are not immigrants; therefore they cannot justly be compelled to "melt" into English under the immigrant myth around which this political rhetoric is constructed.
7. For explanation of metaphors as schemas that shape conceptualizations of the world, see Lakoff and Johnson (1980).
8. On "legitimate" (and legitimizing) language as cultural capital, see Bourdieu (1991).

9. In categorizing "civil republicanism" as the orthodox discourse, I am following Bourdieu in equating orthodoxy with political dominance. Those who espoused civil republicanist discourse controlled the bulk of resources in Congress at the time of this debate.

10. And, as Fairclough (1982: 33–56) has pointed out, standards of appropriateness are always ideological.

11. For discussion, see Mertz (1996: 135–157).

12. It is by no means the only such break, but it is the only one which invoked the military metaphor.

13. This is a simple paraphrase of a rather complex and multi-layered discourse. For a fuller explication of the moral economy of veterans, see Scott (1993). For an early account of ceremonializing veterans' symbolism, see Warner (1953).

14. This has a number of interesting ironies. One is that, in recent years, measured by the number of federal benefits offered to veterans, legislatures and administrations dominated by non-veterans consistently have done more for veterans than have legislatures and administrations dominated by veterans. The Clinton Administration did far more for veterans in terms of legislation and regulation in its first four years than did the Bush (1989–1993) Administration in spite of – or perhaps because of – Bush's unassailable credentials as a decorated combat veteran and Clinton's record as a "draft evader."

15. This newspaper should not be confused with the Pacific, European and Middle East newspapers, also named *The Stars and Stripes*, which are published by the U.S. Department of Defense. The weekly newspaper for veterans is the only remaining survivor of a chain of veterans journals published by the National Tribune Corporation since 1889. According to its publisher, the National Tribune Corp. purchased *The Stars and Stripes* in 1927 from the veterans who originated it during the First World War. The only connection between the Washington weekly and the Defense Department's daily was a 1942 agreement allowing the War Department to use the name for a newspaper to be published "for the troops" during World War II.

16. My reconstruction of the internal workings at *Stars and Stripes* is based on my own memories as well as interviews with one of the other two editorial staff members who worked on this story. We were unable to recall who wrote the lead of the story or performed several of the other tasks; I was the staff member who interviewed Frank Perales.

17. Floor debaters use battlefield English. *The Stars and Stripes*, August 28 – September 1, 1996: 5.

18. Floor debaters use battlefield English. *The Stars and Stripes*, August 28 – September 1, 1996: 5.

References

Bourdieu, Pierre
  1977   *Outline of a Theory of Practice.* Cambridge: Cambridge University Press.

  1990   *The Logic of Practice.* Stanford, CA: Stanford University Press.

  1991   *Language and Symbolic Power.* Oxford: Polity Press.

Briggs, Charles
  1996a   Introduction. In: Briggs, Charles L. (ed.), *Disorderly Discourse: Narrative, Conflict and Inequality.* Oxford: Oxford University Press, 3–40.

  1996b   Conflict, language ideologies and privileged arenas of discursive authority in Warao dispute mediations. In: Briggs. Charles L. (ed.), *Disorderly Discourse: Narrative, Conflict and Inequality.* London/New York: Oxford University Press, 204–242.

Comaroff, John, and Simon Roberts
  1981   *Rules and Processes: The Cultural Logic of Dispute in an African Context.* Chicago: University of Chicago Press.

Fairclough, Norman
  1982   The appropriacy of appropriateness. In: Fairclough, Norman (ed.), *Critical Language Awareness.* London: Longman, 33–56.

Herzfeld, Michael
  1997   *Cultural Intimacy: Social Poetics in the Nation State.* New York/London: Routledge.

Lakoff, George, and Mark Johnson
  1980   *Metaphors We Live By.* Berkeley: University of California Press.

Leibowicz, Joseph
  1992   Official English: Another Americanization campaign. In: Crawford, James (ed.), *Language Loyalties: A Sourcebook on the Official English Controversy.* Chicago: University of Chicago Press.

Mertz, Elizabeth
   1996   Consensus and dissent in U.S. legal opinions: Narrative structure and social voices. In: Briggs, Charles L. (ed.), *Disorderly Discourse: Narrative, Conflict and Inequality*. London/New York: Oxford University Press, 135–157.

Peterson, Mark Allen
   1999   Communication and cultural identity: Language policies in comparative perspective. In: Farag, Mahmoud (ed.), *Human Development for the 21ˢᵗ Century: Proceedings of the 6ᵗʰ AUC Research Conference*. American University in Cairo, 230–242.

Polanyi, Livia
   1989   *Telling the American Story*. Cambridge, MA: MIT University Press.

Sarat, Austin, and Roger Berkowitz
   1998   Disorderly differences: Recognition, accommodation and American law. In: Greenhouse, Carol J. (ed.), *Democracy and Ethnography: Constructing Identities in Multicultural Liberal States*. Albany, NY: State University of New York Press, 81–102.

Scott, Wilbur
   1993   *The Politics of Readjustment: Vietnam Veterans Since the War*. Aldine de Gruyter.

Silverstein, Michael
   1996   Monoglot "standard" in America: Standardization and metaphors of linguistic hegemony. In: Brenneis, Donald, and Ronald Macauley (eds.), *The Matrix of Language: Contemporary Linguistic Anthropology*. Boulder, CO: Westview.

Sollors, Werner
   1986   *Beyond Ethnicity: Consent and Descent in American Culture*. New York: Oxford University Press.

Varenne, Herve
   1998   Diversity as American cultural category. In: Greenhouse, Carol J. (ed.), *Democracy and Ethnography: Constructing Identities in Multicultural Liberal States*. Albany, NY: State University of New York Press, 27–49.

Warner, Alfred Lloyd
   1953   An American sacred ceremony. In: *American Life*. Chicago: University of Chicago Press, 1–26.

Watts, Richard J.
  1999   The social construction of Standard English: Grammar writers as a 'discourse community'. In: Bex, Tony, and Richard J. Watts (eds.), *Standard English: The Widening Debate*. London/New York: Routledge.

Conclusion: Word peace

Daniel N. Nelson

"...Let mortals beware of words, for with words we lie, can say peace when we mean war..." (Auden 1971: 40)

1. Of talk, text and conflict*

Human conflict begins and ends via talk and text. We generate, shape, implement, remember and forget violent behavior between individuals, communities or states through a specific discourse. It is discourse that prepares for sacrifice, justifies inhumanity, absolves from guilt, and demonizes the enemy.

Before, during and after war, revolutionaries indict and exhort, presidents inspire and motivate, generals rally and mobilize. Whether the audience consists of workers and peasants, voters or troops, or elite and foreign listeners (the national legislature or other countries' leaders and populations), we text and talk our way to and from human conflict.

Indeed, we talk our way into war and talk our way out of it. After war, the deftly wielded pen can rewrite history such that victory arises from defeat, and covenants are drafted so subtly that "peace itself is [but] war in masquerade." (Dryden 1961: 9)

Rhetoric, communications and images have been understood as essential to political life.[1] The art of oratory and skill of argumentation, understood by Ancient Greeks for their formative place in government, law and legitimate rule, held honored places in the requisite skills for early democrats. In American political development, the *Federalist Papers*, Lincoln's "Gettysburg Address", or Martin Luther King's "I Have A Dream" oratory hold iconic stature, evoking the capacity of words, speech or text to frame, mobilize, and motivate political thought and action.

But, somehow, the path to war, fighting war, and wars' aftermath, were seen as determined emotional, irrational or biological traits (Lorenz 1966; Wilson 1978) *or* by the reified state and its needs, about which there needed to be no convincing, cajoling, or persuasive.

The latter has been the predominant theme of international relations literature. The realm of armaments, strategy and war were imbued with its own higher and compelling logic separated from the environs of mere mortals. For nationalist historians, war was appealing – indeed, "elevating" – because it led to the disappearance of the individual "before the great conception of the state".[2]

The "State", compelled to defend "its" interests with "its" power were matters dictated by a cold, hard rationality, and not subject to debate, alternatives or opposition. Treitschke says that "the State has a personality...[and] a deliberate will"; as a "great collective personality" (1963: 9–10). Similarly, Colin Gray writes that "The United States has a permanent need to match *its* power and *its* purpose", employing the words statecraft and strategy as if their meanings were pre-determined and etched in stone. National security and strategy "matter more than any other subject for the well-being and occasionally even literal survival of societies"; further, "strategy is a pragmatic subject that has a practical outcome" (1990: 24–25). No ifs, ands or buts; when one is talking about "the State", such an approach seems to say, there are no nuances, no subtleties, and no questions of meaning. Take no prisoners.

The monarch, the president, the generalissimo – their actions, compelled by "reason of state" – create crises, initiate conflict, and prosecute wars at any cost and by any means to win. With *raison d'etat, Staatsrason* or national interests as an invisible hand, violent conflict had an unavoidable presence in politics among states and nations... the "natural" extension of politics, an omnipresent element of human experience, and inevitable "as long as there are sovereign nations possessing great power".[3]

Particularly by the time of the Cold War, but beginning long before, preparing for war was the leitmotif of "national security," on the assumption that such major conflict could not be avoided. Indeed, peace was thought as a product of ensuring preparation for violent conflict since the latter would deter potential aggressors – "peace through strength", as was the NATO and U.S. slogan during so many years of the Cold War.

U.S. President George W. Bush's advisors and speechwriters have managed to create for him an early 21st century version of such peace-through-preparing for war. Addressing a university audience on May 1, 2001, but aimed at listeners around the world, Bush spoke about missile defenses. On the one hand, the President said that, "This is an important opportunity for the world to rethink the unthinkable and to find new ways to keep the peace" by "seek[ing] security based on more than the grim premise that we can destroy those who seek to destroy us".[4] In the same breadth, however, the American leader spoke with Bush-like passion about threats around the world from "today's tyrants... gripped with an implacable hatred of the United States of America. They hate our friends. They hate our values. They hate democracy and freedom." Against such threats, he continued, the U.S. and its allies must "deter anyone who would contemplate... us[ing]" weapons of mass destruction and must develop "new concepts of deterrence that rely on both offensive and defensive forces".[5]

The language of peace has been, then, far less autonomous and much less expressive than the language of war. Indeed, the latter has even begun to supplant the former, making substantial inroads by insisting that raising capacities for war, not abating threats, is the route to peace. Strength, power, weapons – to defend, deter, and defeat if required by "vital national interests" – are conflated, intermingled, re-packaged and spun to equal, yes, the discourse of "peace".

Alice and Orwell would have understood.[6]

2. War, peace, democracy

The discipline of international relations traditionally has regarded violent conflict as a logical, persistent, and "normal" component of politics. Not an "act of God", but rather derived "directly out of things which individuals, statesmen and nations do or fail to do, war is a consequence of polities or lack of policies" (Earle 1941: vii). Human conflict on a mass scale waged between states thus happens in the "ordinary" course of existence, politics is inseparable from military power, and force lay at the foundation of states.[7]

States using *power* guided by, and in pursuit of, *national interests* resort to war because, in conditions of international anarchy, they can do nothing else. "They" do so regularly, after a rational calculus of the "strategy of conflict" and the probabilities of war's gain and loss, costs and benefits.[8] Some less-than-realist realists have allowed that growing interdependence among states, cemented through international institutions and regimes (e.g. multilateral arms control accords with implementation mechanisms such as those to ban chemical and biological weapons) can engender cooperation among states. While not denying national interests or the fungibility of power, such an "institutionalist" school moves away from seeing inter-state conflict as inevitable (Keohane 1984; Keohane and Nye 1989).

Neither of these approaches, however, suggests that a state's type of political system will materially affect a state's inclination to initiate war; a state's own (reified) logic marches to the drummer of only *its* interests.

In the last two decades, however, studies proliferated that were vaguely derived from the Kantian proposition that republics (and their characteristic distribution of socioeconomic power to merchants and the bourgeoisie) were less likely to make war against one another (Kant, quoted in Reiss 1970). The modern democratic peace literature has explored relationships between regime type and the war-proneness of states.[9] Taken as a whole, the body of work seems to challenge little of the realist or institutionalist schools – finding only that normative or structural traits intrinsic to democratic regimes mitigate their bellicosity vis-à-vis other democratic regimes.

Yet, sheer scope and empirical weight of democratic peace studies – a kind of cottage industry for some journals, publishers and many departments of politics and international relations – have caught the attention of policymakers. From the empirical work on the democratic peace hypothesis has been extracted, crudely, the "democracies don't fight democracies" mantra – and thereby translated into a policy of democratic "enlargement" by the US and other Western states (The White House 1995).

As the accouterments of democratic political systems such as "free and fair elections" have become more widespread in the last couple decades of the twentieth and beginning of the twenty-first centuries[10], one might infer from the democratic peace literature a probability of less war. Anyone so hopeful or naïve, however, is apt to be disappointed. Indeed, *realpolitik's* expectation of war as part of the usual course of political affairs receives superficial support from data about post-Cold War violent conflict around the world. Far from diminishing, the frequency of conflicts with over 1,000 casualties per year (a common threshold definition of "war") rose substantially from the mid 1990s into the new century, with over three dozen major active conflicts underway in early 2001.[11]

The democratic peace literature does not suggest more democracies equals less war. And, careful and repeated re-analysis of data have found that democratizing systems, perhaps because of their domestic uncertainties or unstable neighborhoods, are rather prone to engage in war. Further, the kind of crisis may be far more decisive in the kind and level of violent conflict; crises where democracies confront no reciprocal threat (i.e., where they can get away with acting bellicose) taking the path of war *more* often than non-democracies.[12]

Peace through democracy is, then, a dangerously oversimplified inference from complex scholarship – the logical and empirical foundations of which are being chipped away.[13] Peril arises to the extent that policymakers derive guidance from their partial understanding of such complex relationships. U.S. President Clinton observed in the preface to the *National Strategy of Engagement and Enlargement* in 1995 that "the larger the pool of democracies, the better off we, and the entire community of nations, will be. Democracies ...are far less likely to wage war on one another". To the extent that such a view promotes intervention to generate or protect democracy, war or near-war may follow from efforts on behalf of a type of governance rumored to do better at war-avoidance.

Waging war to make the world more democratic in order to have less war may strike more than a few as a grand paradox. Yet, within such a looking glass, we construct our discourses on peace and war.

Peace through war (preparedness for war or, simply, "strength") and peace through democracy are, together, the linguistic equivalent of a möbius strip – where both surfaces are the other, and no one side is itself alone.

In these mainstream discourses, we are denied a way to talk about peace as peace and are left to contemplate what peace is not (Nelson 1999).

3. Towards war, during war

The approach of war involves constructing an enemy – an "other" who is so foreign and distant that *who* becomes *it*. *It* can be tortured, maimed, slaughtered; *who* cannot.

In *At War With Words* we have seen ample evidence of such be-fore-war, pre-war, towards-war discourse. Talk-show hosts for whom each broadcast offers a chance to demonize political opponents contribute to accumulated malevolence. And, in small countries, immense cultural divides form and are cultivated; identities that could be said to have marginal differences are made to seem from another world, thereby ensuring the place and role of *it*, not *who*. We see a parallel "otherizing" of Ghanaian reformists who are denied legitimacy and portrayed as a threat. Threat, too, can be extracted from leaders' public statements even by journalists whose self-definition is one of liberal objectivity.

In war – cold or hot, between or within states – language is used ruthlessly. Terrible weapons can be sanitized, violent acts justified, acquiescence encouraged, and language hegemony asserted. Un-willing and unable to articulate the true destructive power of nuclear weapons, the entire concept of such arms was reduced to human and humanized scale. Political leaders addressing their population and voters prior to using military force (in 1999 against Serbia) engage in convoluted justification, while image manipulation played a major role in a government media campaign to dissuade Northern Irish populations from further violence, and the wars and competitions of major powers systematically obliterate native languages.

At the intersection of human conflict and language, when war is soon to begin or has already commenced, key facets of the struggle are about and through words. Ways to talk about our horrible weapons, to excuse our use of deadly force, to tell others to lay down their arms, and to "mark" our control of enemy territory by eradicating the "other" language and subjugating native tongues are all essential linguistic elements of war and near-war.

In such stages of human conflict, then, there is an unmistakable preparation by and through language of an enemy, an other, an "it" with whom there can be no reconciliation or compromise. From such an opponent emanates threat that, in turn, demands heightened capacities to include the most heinous weapons. These, however, will be humanized, the use of deadly force justified, stability promoted, and local identities that might challenge a dominant power are erased.

4. After war, forgetting war

When wars "end" and conflict subsides, however, do text and talk prompt healing and reconciliation, or weave "*dolchstoss*" conspiracies to rationalize preparations for the next war? Do we begin to speak about peace when wars stop, or begin preparing linguistically for the next war?

An end to war lies somewhere on the continuum of violent human conflict. Wars' terminations usually mean a substantial reduction in violent acts, particularly by one state against another, but it almost never ceases all violent acts; air attacks may stop, but the torture, rape and killing of prisoners may accelerate. Ceasefires, green lines, and demilitarized zones reduce or end artillery duels, but the destruction of property on both sides continues. Cold wars, too, may end with walls pulled down, but tensions that flare into conflict recur.

Language policy may determine whether or not peoples will find reason to live together peacefully again or, incrementally, distance themselves to the point of renewing conflictual encounters. The degree to which one state and one group insist on suzerainty means cultural hegemony – a hegemony that, in and of itself, seems to be a predictor of future conflict.

Cypriot choices of language of instruction on a divided island, Palauan resistance to cultural extermination, ethnic cleansing in Croatia, and the rhetoric by which American politicians intermingle warrior images with language policy–all are post-shooting war linguistics wars that forecast and foretell. Conflicts continue and causes extend well beyond the withdrawal of troops, weapons, and foxholes.

In some cases, purposeful choices can be made through which exclusionary, hegemonic language policies are avoided. Rejecting at every opportunity the dominance of one culture over another – at some cost maintaining indigenous languages spoken by few people, or selecting a "third" language as a means of instruction in higher education (or governance), are paths by which to dissipate conflict potential. In multi-national, multi-ethnic states, however, the rampant politicization of language means that linguistic nuances become the front lines of peace and war. Linguists can drawn into the discomfiting role as shock troops for linguistic cleansing, while politicians' rhetoric is armed with stilettos that imply others' lesser worth because of minority or non-standard language.

Linguistic peace, then, is hard to find even when guns are not drawn. And, absent word peace, conflict recurs.

That generations after war remember war selectively or not at all means that renewed conflict – for retribution or to redress defeat and humiliation – is not unimaginable (Harkavy 2000). Perhaps the lack of guilt and responsibility for atrocities of the past constitutes a collective effort to forget. Yet, it is clear that individuals who committed, facilitated *or* resisted the most heinous acts of twentieth century warfare tell us, via their written or oral record, about their deepest sentiments and motives. Even attempts to forget responsibility and eschew guilt are not silent. And, some of the loudest voices are those that resisted "silently".

5. Word peace

The struggle for identity lies at the nexus of war and peace. Individuals, groups or nations for whom recognition, self and agency are denied are those whose potential for violent behavior is pronounced. Stated differently, endangered identity is the hallmark of war-proneness and the prognosis for peace rises when identities are not at risk.

At the forefront of identity is language. It follows that conflict generation or avoidance may have strong ties to governments' language policies and to the socioeconomic conditions that enhance the health of one language vis-à-vis others.

Those most unsure of their identity are, at once, most hateful of "Others" identity – a visceral *identity envy*. Indeed, the concept of enemy may be linked most strongly to a threat to identity.

As identity challenges rise in immediacy and intensity, the response is natural – to eliminate others and the bases for their self. Armies destroy not merely or primarily the personnel and equipment of other armies, but (increasingly) the identity of the enemy (e.g., eliminating the enemy's sense as an advanced, civilized society). Identities can be outlawed by states, or obliterated by institutions as well – and both of these can be parts of warring strategies.

Identity wars are those that seek to enforce homogeneity not accept heterogeneity, insist on conformity and condemn uniqueness, and demand quiescence while suppressing free expression. Because globalization has fostered a sense that identities are threatened, such a ubiquitous process is coextensive with more war.

The twentieth century's most murderous regimes – Nazi Germany, Stalin's Soviet Union, Pol Pot's Kampuchea – earned that opprobrium less from their efforts to conquer other states than their attempts to exterminate people, groups, and entire populations. These regimes, condemned for their aggression, were to have added and even heavier guilt for their war on those whose *identities* differed – as Jews, Roma, landowners, or intellectuals.

And, in that regard, language that most affirms identities is that which best protects peace. To abate the perception of threat from those who differ requires identity-affirming language from people and institutions in public life. Such word peace is clearly not that which we find embedded in documents that end wars, but rather in the behavior and policies of those who occupy social, economic and political authority prior to the emergence of conflict. Those with political authority, public responsibility or cultural legitimacy will have to speak of peace and security in decidedly new ways. Peace and security are neither the automatic correlates of democracy, nor the products of larger capacities to deter, defeat and extinguish the *other* state, nation, group or person. Rather, these desiderata of every society follow from values, institutions, laws, and processes that build and protect identities – ensuring that what one *is* is not *otherized* by the state, its leaders or what they do.

In that effort, words – spoken and written – are both the architect and building blocks. To be at peace with words requires a different language…a language that focuses not on capacities but on threat abatement, not on defense and deterrence but on identity affirmation. Absent such a linguistic shift, we are condemned to be *At War With Words*.

* Portions of this conclusion first appeared in "Language, Identity and War", *Language and Politics* 1(1), 2002.

Notes

1. Many of Karl W. Deutsch's works, for example 1953, 1957, 1964, emphasized and developed the role of communication patterns among groups as a key determinant of friendship or hostility, and the relationship between communications and the integration of political communities.
2. German historians and philosophers such as Heinrich von Treitschke (1963) and others glorified power and the state.
3. Attributed to Albert Einstein as cited in Andrews (1990).
4. Speech of U.S. President George W. Bush at George Washington University, Washington, D.C., 1 May 2001. Available at http://www.crnd.org, last accessed on 31 May 2001.
5. Speech of U.S. President George W. Bush at George Washington University, Washington, D.C., 1 May 2001. Available at http://www.crnd.org, last accessed on 31 May 2001.
6. "War is Peace" was, of course, one of the Party slogans on the Ministry of Truth edifice in *Nineteen Eighty-Four* (Orwell 1949: 5).
7. This, of course, is substantively the argument of Thucydides (1934), especially

the Melian Dialogue, Book V., Machievelli (1990) and Clausewitz (1976) were succeeded, in the late twentieth century, by other "realists" who see the international system's anarchy as leading, inexorably, to interstate conflict and war. An evocative example of this recent view is Mearsheimer (1990).

8. Certainly one of the more mechanistic views of inter-state behavior, including war, was Schelling's (1960) view of conflict based on classic game theory. Brilliantly conceived, his work is nevertheless extraordinary in its reductionism, assuming that individuals play out their political roles rationally.

9. The liberal/democratic peace literature of contemporary international relations – not to mention its Kantian intellectual roots – is now vast, and incorporates many assumptions about the pacific effects of democratic processes, institutions or norms. Perhaps most indicative of this literature is Russett (1993), especially chapters 2 and 6. See also Owens (1994).

10. For ratings of political liberties and other concepts through judgmental surveys of experts, see Freedom House's freedom index, available at http://www,freedomhouse.org/ratings/index.htm, last accessed 1 June 2001. The mean rating (on a 1–7 scale) and the sheer number of countries receiving better scores improved during the 1980s and 1990s.

11. For summaries of such data, see SIPRI (2000), and the Center for Defense Information (CDI) website, www.cdi.org, "World at War".

12. Regarding the role of crisis types vis-à-vis regime types, and the failure of the democratic peace literature to account for such an effect, see Ben-Yahuda and Margulies (2001).

13. Just how oversimplified and misleading the democratic peace literature, and inferences from it, became are succinctly and convincingly discussed by Gowa (1999).

References

Auden, W.H.
    1971   Hymn to the United Nations. *The New York Times* (October 25).

Ben-Yahuda, Hemda, and Iris Margulies
    2001   Regime type and state behavior in threat and opportunity crises: A monadic study of the democratic peace theory, 1918–1994. *International Politics* 38(3).

Clausewitz, Carl von
    1976   *On War*. Edited by Michael Howard and Peter Paret. Princeton: Princeton University Press.

Clinton, William
    1995   Preface. In: The White House, *A National Security Strategy of Engagement and Enlargement*. Washington, D.C., February.

Deutsch, Karl W.
    1953   *Nationalism and Social Communication.* Cambridge, MA: MIT Press.

    1957   *Political Community and the North Atlantic Area.* Princeton: Princeton University Press.

    1964   *Nerves of Government.* New York: Free Press.

Dryden, John
    1961   *Absalom and Achitophel.* Edited by James and Helen Kinsley. London: Oxford University Press. Original edition, 1682.

Earle, Edward Mead
    1941   Introduction. In: Earle, Edward Mead (ed.), *Makers of Modern Strategy*. Princeton: Princeton University Press.

Gowa, Joanne
    1999   *Ballots and Bullets: The Elusive Democratic Peace.* Princeton: Princeton University Press.

Gray, Colin
    1990   *War, Peace, and Victory: Strategy and Statecraft for the Next Century.* New York: Simon and Shuster.

Harkavy, Robert
    2000   Defeat, national humiliation and the revenge motif. *International Politics* 37(3): 345–368.

Keohane, Robert O.
    1984   *After Hegemony: Cooperation and Discord in the World Economy.* Princeton: Princeton University Press.

Keohane, Robert O., and Joseph S. Nye
    1989   *Power and Independence.* Glenview, IL: Scott, Foresman and Company, second edition.

Lorenz, Konrad
    1966   *On Aggression.* New York: Harcourt, Brace and World.

Machiavelli, Niccolo
  1990   *Arte della Guerra* [The art of war]. (Translated by Neal Wood.) New York: Da Capo Press.

Mearsheimer, John J.
  1990   Why we will soon miss the Cold War. *The Atlantic Monthly* 266(2), 35–50.

Nelson, Daniel N.
  1999   Stable Peace or Secure Peace? *International: Die Zeitschrift fur internationale Politik* 5/6: 14–17.

Orwell, George.
  1949   *Nineteen Eighty-Four*. New York: Harcourt Brace Jovanovich.

Owens, John M.
  1994   How liberalism produces democratic peace. *International Security* 19(2): 87–125.

Reiss, Hans (ed.)
  1970   *Kant's Political Writings*. (Translated by H.B. Nisbet). Cambridge, U.K.: Cambridge University Press.

Russett, Bruce
  1993   *Grasping the Democratic Peace*. Princeton: Princeton University Press.

Schelling, Thomas
  1960   *Strategy of Conflict*. London/New York: Oxford University Press.

SIPRI
  2000   *SIPRI Yearbook 2000*. Oxford: Oxford University Press.

Thucydides
  1934   *Peloponnesian War*. Translated by Richard Crawley. New York: The Modern Library.

Treitschke, Heinrich von
  1963   *Politics*. (Translated by Hans Kohn.) New York: Harcourt, Brace and World. Original edition, 1916.

The White House
  1995   *A National Security Strategy of Engagement and Enlargement*. Washington, D.C., February 1995.

Wilson, Edwin O.
    1978   *On Human Nature*. Cambridge, Mass.: Harvard University Press.

Name index

Subject index